Myths and the Mythmaker

Scottish Cultural Review
of Language and Literature

Volume 16

Series Editors
Rhona Brown
University of Glasgow

John Corbett
University of Glasgow

Sarah Dunnigan
University of Edinburgh

James McGonigal
University of Glasgow

Production Editor
Ronnie Young
University of Glasgow

SCROLL

The Scottish Cultural Review of Language and Literature publishes new work in Scottish Studies, with a focus on analysis and reinterpretation of the literature and languages of Scotland, and the cultural contexts that have shaped them.

Further information on our editorial and production procedures can be found at www.rodopi.nl

Myths and the Mythmaker

A Literary Account
of J.M. Barrie's Formative Years

R.D.S. Jack

Amsterdam - New York, NY 2010

Cover Image: An early photograph of J.M. Barrie taken by J. Howie Junz at Edinburgh, c.1882.
Reproduced with the kind permission of Céline-Albin Faivre.

Cover Design: Pier Post

The paper on which this book is printed meets the requirements of "ISO 9706: 1994, Information and documentation - Paper for documents - Requirements for permanence".

ISBN: 978-90-420-3218-7
E-Book ISBN: 978-90-420-3219-4
©Editions Rodopi B.V., Amsterdam - New York, NY 2010
Printed in The Netherlands

To Isla

Contents

Acknowledgements

I must begin with an apology as well as an expression of gratitude to the librarians and trustees of the Beinecke Research Library at Yale. I have been grateful for their support and kindness during my recent visits to the library. Nonetheless, to complete the monograph supported by one of their scholarships eighteen years after holding it makes it unlikely they can have maintained hope of final fruition. In that spirit, I hope they may reconsider my current status as the academic equivalent of the "lost boys".

I should also like to express my indebtedness to the AHRC, to the British Academy and the Carnegie Trust for the Universities of Scotland for offering financial support for this project. The staff at the British Library, the National Library of Scotland, the University of Edinburgh Library and the manuscript division of Nottingham University Library have vied with their Beinecke colleagues in helpfulness.

In personal terms, I should also like to record my thanks to a large number of friends and colleagues starting with my wife, Kirsty, who has borne the brunt of my day to day concerns over its long and, at times, difficult birth. Sandra Atkins, Andrew Birkin, Sarah Dunnigan, Alastair Fowler, Isla Jack, Andrew Nash, Leonee Ormond and Murray Pittock have generously offered help and guidance. I am also deeply indebted to Ronnie Young for his constant support as copy editor.

Introduction

As my contribution to the celebrations associated with the 150th anniversary of Barrie's birth I had originally intended a sequel rather than a prequel to my earlier book, *The Return to the Never Land* (1991). After all, significant critical advances have been made since then by Barrie specialists, notably Andrew Nash, Herbert Sussman and Eve Kosovsky Sedgwick. It is, however, extremely difficult to disabuse scholars and non-specialists alike of the simple and superficially attractive account of Barrie as a childish man and populist writer which has dominated accounts of him in the media. I have therefore confined myself almost entirely to the early Victorian period of his life and therefore his self-imposed literary apprenticeship. The reasons for so doing and the aims contemplated are set out below.

Essentially, the book seeks to counter five difficulties which currently dominate the popular view of J.M. Barrie. Most obviously, he has come to be associated with his most famous character, *Peter Pan*. This kind of simplification is always a danger for an author. It is especially so when the character concerned is one whose definition is immaturity. Secondly, and as a consequence of this, the canonical base on which this vision is based has been simplified and reduced to those texts which present the "childish author" in the most convincing terms. Thirdly, the coincidence that Freud had recently produced Oedipal terminology in which to couch this attractively simple vision has made Barrie's life of more interest than his art. In the absence of any clear idea of the principles behind his art his own greatest fear has been realised. That is, the writer who wrote, "God blast anyone who writes a biography of me!" is now more often viewed as a psychological study than a literary genius. This is not because he has been ill-served by biographers from Mackail via Dunbar to Birkin and Chaney. The curse is more appropriately directed at those literary critics who have failed either to do the necessary background research or even to assess him on his own terms. The fourth aim, therefore, is to fill the gaps, critical and canonical, left by those who have proclaimed the Oedipal and escapist myth. The last aim is to use this re-assessment of Barrie's early life in art to anticipate his mature drama and argue the case for re-instating him as a genius in the canon.

To achieve these ends, five strands of argument are advanced. These aim

- to match the detailed biographical accounts of the period by replacing the narrow canonical focus on which he is popularly assessed and instead cover all of his major Victorian prose and drama.
- to counter the claim that he is only a light, sentimental writer by looking at his own advanced critical ideas as fostered at Edinburgh University by Professor David Masson and adapted in his early days as literary critic in Edinburgh and Nottingham.
- to counter the current belief that his brother David's early death lay behind an Oedipal trauma which doomed him to immaturity as a type of Peter Pan. Instead, his own consistent claim to a histrionic personality, which defies definition but encourages imaginative writing, is advanced and related to the account of personality presented in Professor Campbell Fraser's psychology course at Edinburgh.
- to explain, in these terms, why Barrie, at the end of his Victorian apprenticeship, decided to follow the dramatic rather than the narrative route as the means of achieving his highest literary aims.
- to assess whether the new evidence, and the critical principles suggested by it, offer as promising a means of re-considering his mature, Edwardian plays as they appear to do for his earlier work.

R.D.S. Jack   29 June 2010

Chapter One

The Critical Myth

A neat Freudian myth has for a long time defined and dismissed J.M. Barrie as a writer. Despite recent attempts to challenge it, he is still popularly viewed as a troubled man with Oedipal failings, whose only enduring work is, fittingly, the story of another little boy who would not grow up. Most literary historians still link him with his most famous creation. They therefore write him off as an immature populist. Additionally, in Scotland, he is condemned for ignoring that land's industrial present in favour of a form of sentimental parochialism which marks him out as a member of the so-called "Kailyard" or cabbage patch movement.

To confirm this, one need only think of the most recent expressions of interest in him. While Lisa Chaney's *Hide and Seek with the Angels* (2005) continues the biographical thoroughness of Mackail, Dunbar and Birkin, she also confirms that interest in his life rather than his art has increasingly characterised that tradition. Psychology too is the focus for film-makers and for broader academic studies. Johnny Depp's sympathetic portrayal of Barrie concentrates on his unhappy marriage to Mary Ansell and infatuation with Sylvia Llewelyn Davies in *Finding Never Land* (Paramount 2004) while Piers Dudgeon's study of Barrie and the Du Mauriers builds unquestioningly and imaginatively on Oedipal premises (Dudgeon 2008). Even the works favoured for modern re-editing reflect his early autobiographical prose rather than those mature dramas. The problem with Ian Campbell's recent edition of *A Window in Thrums* (2005) is not the quality of his contribution but why an early collection of articles in a mode Barrie rejected continues to warrant more attention than those mature dramas which are his sole claim to genius. A near obsession with the supposed Oedipal trauma of his brother David's death which is factually only addressed in two of the early Thrums narratives is the answer despite the fact that Barrie, in *The Greenwood Hat*, placed these tales among his *juvenilia* and would certainly have preferred to be immortalised in different terms (see Barrie 1930c).

This was, after all, the man who had a deep, enduring distrust of biographers. It may, indeed, have been this concern which finally led him to choose drama over prose. Certainly, when giving advice to Cynthia Asquith near the end of his life, he admitted that he had found it impossible to cut out "your own self" in novels and so had turned to the shorter, more impersonal dramatic form (BVS A3/5.9.35).

It does not do so in a vacuum. A counter-case of this sort originated with Jacqueline Rose's tightly argued work, *The Case of Peter Pan: Or The Impossibility of Children's Fiction*. Rose concludes her analysis by warning would-be biographers that Barrie's work is peculiarly difficult to analyse in "real" terms. "It is virtually impossible", she says, "to place Barrie in relation to his text" and this makes it "all the more striking that *Peter Pan* has come to be discussed in almost exclusively biographical terms" (Rose 1984: 76). Two short but perceptive literary studies of Barrie's writing also appeared – Allen Wright's *The Glamour of Twilight* and Leonee Ormond's *James Barrie* followed (Wright 1976; Ormond 1987). Ormond in particular makes serious claims for Barrie's thematic range and breadth which have not been adequately recognised but are wholly consistent with Barrie's own account of his youthful "craving to be the heaviest writer of his time" (Barrie 1930c: 6). My own contribution to the debate, *The Road to the Never Land*, appeared four years later (Jack 1991).

Subsequently there have been a series of literary analyses, all suggesting a more complex view of Barrie's work. In terms of literary production, the work of Andrew Nash and Isla Jack is particularly important (Nash 1998, 1999, 2006, 2007; I. Jack 2003), while in the area of gender studies, Eva Kosovsky Sedgwick and Herbert Sussman are among those who have sensitively re-interpreted Barrie's prose and drama (Sedgwick 1991; Sussman 1995).

All of these works present a starkly contrasted Barrie to the naïve, childish writer proposed by leading proponents of the Oedipal and Kailyard schools such as Harry M. Geduld and George Blake (Geduld 1971; Blake 1951). As Peter Hollindale notes in his excellent survey of modern criticism until 1995, this "other" Barrie is not at all simple but

an elusive writer, characteristically engaged in layered composition, offsetting mode against mode and genre against genre, and one authorial persona against another in a complex game which makes it very difficult for critics to confront either the dramatic corpus or the single work whole. (Hollindale 1959: xxx–xxxiv [xxx]; cf. Jack 1991: 3–24)

Literary histories are naturally slow to reflect ideas which radically challenge established attitudes. As a result most still share Phyllis Hartnell's view of Barrie. Hartnell follows a chapter entitled *Ibsen, Chekhov and the Theatre of Ideas* with a shorter one listing those who failed that challenge. Here Barrie finds his place. "In reaction against it are the romantic dramas of Rostand, the fantasies of Maeterlinck, and the whimsical plays of James Barrie" (Hartnell 1968: 214–39). Alastair Fowler was for a long time a lone voice in opposition. For him Barrie offers a "strong challenge to naturalistic realism", "proves hard to assess", writes "plays which call for robust emotional participation", and employs a method that entitles him to be considered an early modernist" (Fowler 1987: 358). More recently, however, the open-minded principles advocated in the recent *Edinburgh History of Scottish Literature* have allowed imaginative authors concerned with universal themes an equal right to be heard beside those who, more directly, express their Scottishness (Brown 2007: 1: 7–12).

But a problem does remain. Ask any group of people interested in the arts what they think of J.M. Barrie, and the result in 2009 will be much the same as in the 1990s. A personal anecdote may reinforce this point. When I was working on *The Road to the Never Land*, I clearly defined it as a literary study. Despite this, my colleagues would later ask how my "biography" was getting on, so embedded was their belief that Barrie's earlier claim to literary greatness had been thoroughly examined and found wanting. I encountered much the same reaction twenty years later. For most, the curiosity of Barrie's life retained some interest and *Peter Pan* remained his sole claim to fame.

The biographical-critical imbalance implied by this is noted by Hollindale: "The man has in fact been much better served than the writer" (Hollindale 1995: xxxi). This is not, after all, surprising. The academic works I cited as proof of a critical revival are read by a small minority. By contrast the oddities and contradictions of his life offer ready-made drama for wider media attention. Often, such works offer their own intelligent opposition to the simpler equations of the critical myth. Most notably, this is the case with Andrew Birkin's television series and the biography which resulted from it (Birkin 1978; 1979). On their own terms both series and book are excellent. Birkin's scholarship is thorough and his skills of popular transmission unquestionable. Only the *focus* – biographically and textually – causes concern. Birkin may question the simplistic conclusions reached in the early twentieth by Freudian critics but, to gain attention, he has to begin within the narrowly circumscribed world Barrie popularly inhabits.

Consequently, any serious attempt to challenge the prevalent, autobiographical view of Barrie must begin by re-assessing the popular view. In doing so, the would-be critic at once encounters two problems which the biographer does not have to face. The Victorian years are among the most interesting of Barrie's life but, by definition, the works he wrote at that time are not among his finest. Secondly, while the open-minded biographer moves into an already densely inhabited area of research, the critic makes the same move only to find one void after another. The generative evidence provided in his Notebooks, manuscripts and early drafts have been ignored. His academic training at Edinburgh University is seen to be irrelevant. His own critical articles and academic research projects are mentioned but not analysed. His journalistic roles as leader writer and literary critic are left unconsidered. Even his own, admittedly idiosyncratic, autobiography, *The Greenwood Hat*, is seldom referred to (Barrie 1930c).

To discover why the two visions of the Kirriemuir author's place in literary history as explained by Hollindale are so radically different, implies that these academic and canonical gaps be filled.

Reviewing Barrie's Reputation

In any age, it is to be expected that new writers will, in part, make their claim for recognition by challenging the leading authors of the previous generation. Barrie's swift descent from "genius to parenthesis" in literary histories is, nevertheless, unusual. After all, in his own day, he was held to be a genius, fit to rank with Hardy and Shaw. He succeeded the former as President of the Society of Authors and far outsold the latter on the London stage. One would, therefore, naturally assume that those who enthused about him in his own day would have constructed a large body of criticism justifying their high evaluation of him.

Instead three kinds of avoidance strategy can be detected. The leading dramatic critic, William Archer, exemplifies one kind of avoidance strategy. When analysing the great dramatists of his day in

The Old Drama and the New, Archer reaches Barrie only to bypass him, "I am content to treat him shortly because he raises no critical question [...] no rational being doubts that Sir James is a humourist of original and delightful genius" (Archer 1923: 331). If some avoid analysis on grounds of self-evident genius, others use his hyper-complexity as their excuse. This is the strategy of Hugh Walpole. When introducing the 1938 collection of Barrie's speeches, *McConnachie and J.M.B*, he remarks,

It has been [Barrie's] misfortune that so many people have taken him at his surface-word. The majority of us have no time, as regards other people, for more than surfaces – and so Barrie tricked nine-tenths of us, and knew well that he was tricking us. (Barrie 1938: 3)

He makes no attempt to account for this allegorical duplicity. The reader is left to do this on his own.

From this develops a third kind of dogmatic vagueness. This uses Barrie's uniqueness as a means of claiming his ultimate mysteriousness. Barrie's magic is brilliant but inimitable in its blend of fantasy and seriousness, romance and satire. A sophisticated statement of the position comes from G.K. Chesterton. What sets Barrie apart is the fact that he is "The most modest of men and the most impudent of artists". By that impudence, Chesterton argues,

I mean a sort of impossibility; a sudden steepness in the story as it winds its way through strange countries, to which I know no parallel, and which I find difficult to describe [...] in Barrie the imagination works in ways which nobody can expect, even if he is expecting the unexpected. (Chesterton 1920: 59, 206)

There is much to be said for this view. Indeed, as Barrie also straddles the Victorian, Edwardian and Modernist periods, the difficulty has a historical and categorical dimension as well. For anyone seeking a less rarefied account of individual texts, Chesterton's "transcending" technique offers no more practical aid than Archer's or Walpole's.

The danger of later assaults on an author whose case for genius is based on enthusiastic generalisations was anticipated in 1923 by Ashley Dukes. Barrie's fame, he argues, was now so firmly established that it had become heresy to suggest even minor weaknesses in his work. While agreeing that the Scottish author *was* "indubitably a genius" and going on to explain some of the ways in which he proves this, Dukes believes the longer a counter-case is suppressed the

greater the danger of "an ultimate revolt against him" will be (Dukes
1923: 10–12).

The full length studies of Barrie which appeared while he was
still alive mirror this situation. Eulogising largely replaces analysis in
H.M. Walbrook's *Barrie and the Theatre* (1922), Thomas Moult's
Barrie (1928), F.J. Harvey Darton's *J.M. Barrie* (1929) and J.A.
Hammerton's *Barrie: the Story of a Genius* (1929). Unlike to-day's
biographies, however, they begin from the logical assumption that his
life is only interesting because of the quality of his art. The studies,
which immediately followed his death, Patrick Chalmers' *The Barrie
Inspiration* (1938) and W.A. Darlington's *Barrie* (1938), also accept
this premise.

Of course, Barrie's long, unusual and dramatic life along with the
volume of the work he produced make it difficult to be at once critic
and biographer. So, when Denis Mackail's *The Story of J.M.B.* (1938)
appeared, he made no pretence at being a literary critic. Still, as both
he and his wife were among the author's circle of friends, he provides
by far the most reliable and detailed account of the life. There is a
subversive side to this. As his followers rightly valued his authority,
they were slow to notice when the great man "slept". The frequency
with which I shall cite Mackail only to question his conclusions
reflects this situation. They indirectly express my admiration for his
work by challenging its enduring influence when it misleads.

Whatever the other qualities of the earlier literary biographical
eulogies, they failed to provide sound critical defences against the
"ultimate revolt" prophesied by Dukes. Therefore, when it did come,
would-be detractors found it easy to give their own bias to the vague
critical terminology hitherto applied to him. For them, his comic,
imaginative and emotive strengths became the weaknesses of "whimsicality", "fantastical escapism" and "sentimentality".

An eerily exact prophesy of the fate which awaited Barrie
appeared in the *Times Literary Supplement* of 26 June 1937, shortly
after his death. The anonymous writer began with a blunt statement.
"No dramatist has been more perilous to criticism than Barrie within a
week of his death". Although he agrees that claims of genius on his
behalf are appropriate, he, like Dukes, fears they have not been
soundly constructed so far. While Ibsen, Shakespeare and even Shaw
(as political irritant!) are guaranteed immortality because they have all
been the subject of informed critical debate, Barrie has no such

assurance. Indeed, being an idiosyncratic writer in the first place and one whose greatest strengths are particularly theatrical, he may well be doomed to the status of odd outsider. "Europe has taken little notice of him. He has influenced none of his contemporaries except, vaguely Mr. Milne […] he has flattered no political dovecotes, set up no banners, beaten no drums" (*Times Literary Supplement* 1937: 1–2).

Unfortunately, of course, any successful appeal "within the theatre" to his mastery of dramatic communication implies the very kind of precise critical and modal awareness which had been only occasionally evident in the period of enthusiasm. The reviewer, aware of this, prophesies that "those who look deeply" into his works will soon be in a minority. They will be greatly outnumbered by those who take his plays at face value as "polite matinees" designed to "send everyone home to a comfortable tea". Viewing only the surface story and doing so with realistic expectations, they will miss the visual and poetic artistry which suggests darker and deeper concerns. The reviewer concludes, "It is probable that an influential part of modern criticism will dismiss him as a pot-boiler for the bourgeoisie and no more" (*Times Literary Supplement* 1937: 2).

The article is entitled "The Divided Mind" and its author correctly accepts that both views contain some truth. Like all of his contemporaries and most of his successors, however, he sees this as part of Barrie's unique and ultimately inscrutable genius. In fact, the research evidence described in the last section of this chapter will demonstrate that there is nothing mysterious at all about the divided effects created. Even before he left Nottingham to begin his free-lance London career, Barrie had worked out a critical formula precisely designed to create this "divided" effect.

Restoring Barrie's Voice

Any attempt to restore Barrie's own voice is, therefore, hampered by the long period during which it has been silenced and by the gaps in coverage identified above. A more detailed overview of the route proposed is, therefore, necessary.

To do so, another peculiarity, this time concerning the relationship between biographies and criticism, has to be noted. Usually, the two lines work positively and in harmony. Shaw and Wilde have also attracted biographers whose sympathetic assessments have boosted their positions in the literary hierarchy. Why, then, is Barrie's case different? Why has biographical attention seriously subverted his standing as a writer?

It is in one sense Barrie's misfortune that *Margaret Ogilvy*, *The Little White Bird* and *Peter Pan* (Barrie 1896a, 1902a, 1904) were published when Freud was developing his theories of sexuality in *The Interpretation of Dreams* (1900), *The Psychopathology of Everyday Life* (1901) and *Three Essays on Sexuality* (1905). That he then became a major focus for Freudian criticism is unsurprising. The first of these texts is the most overtly autobiographical of all Barrie's fictional works. In it, the narrator, who is a lightly disguised version of Barrie himself, not only idolises his mother, he says she is the heroine and inspiration of all his writing. In Margaret's "mute blue eyes [...] I have read all I know and would ever care to write" (Barrie 1896a: 4). The memoir also provides a convincing psychological basis for his problem. It describes the death of his elder brother in a skating accident and young James's failed attempt to take his place during the mourning period. For convinced Freudians, this trauma already places him on an Oedipal couch, ready for analysis. The symptoms are also to hand. As Anthony Storr explains, "Men who continue to regard women chiefly or partly as mothers" are likely to exhibit "a variety of sexual difficulties including turning away from women altogether, partial or complete impotence, or the need for reassuring devices like sado-masochistic rituals or fetishes before intercourse is possible" (Storr 1989: 38).

Barrie again appears to fit the stereotype. During the period of his infatuation with Sylvia Llewelyn Davies (1897–1910) when playing games with her sons and attempting to displace her husband in their lives, he was also presiding over the failure of his marriage to the actress Mary Ansell. When that unhappy match ended in divorce on 13 October 1909, Barrie's prominent position in London society guaranteed that his sexual problems were widely reported. In journalistic accounts of the case, an interested world learned of the playwright's presumed impotence and of his wife's affair with their friend Gilbert Canaan. That the affair was mainly conducted in the same Black Lake cottage where Barrie had played his "Peter Pan" games with Sylvia's children was also noted.

The account of the trial offered in *The Globe and Traveller* is representative. It records that "Mr Jas. Matthew Barrie, the well-known author and playwright" had appeared in an undefended case at the London Divorce Court before Sir John Bigham on the previous day, Wednesday 13 October 1909. The reporter goes on to comment that

> Mr. and Mrs. Barrie were married on July 9th, 1894, in Scotland and afterwards lived at Lancaster Gate. There was no issue of the marriage. The parties lived happily together until about 18 months ago, when they became acquainted with the co-respondent, who came to the house from time to time. In November 1908, Mr Canaan arranged that he should use a cottage which the Barries had near Farnham. The co-respondent went down there and Mrs Barrie and some ladies also stayed in the cottage while he was there. Subsequently, from a statement made to him by a servant at the cottage, Mr Barrie taxed his wife with this, who admitted her conduct with Mr Canaan. (*Globe and Traveller* 1909: 4)

Details of witness evidence follow with that given by Mrs Hunt, the housekeeper, being the most pertinent: "She told the court 'I had often seen Mr Canaan coming out of Mrs Barrie's bedroom early in the morning.' 'That's quite enough,' remarked his Lordship. The case was undefended and a decree nisi with costs granted" (4).

The validity of an Oedipal reading of Barrie's personality will be discussed later. At this point, it is the reduced canonical focus encouraged by that belief which is important. The more *Peter Pan* and the Thrums-based stories became the major source of popular interest the more literary historians happily sidestepped Barrie in favour of "deeper" and more "relevant" authors. For example, Marshall Walker, in a recent history of Scottish Literature, decides that none of Barrie's works except *Peter Pan* is worth discussing because they "lack depth except as reflections of his complicated nature" (Walker 1996: 250). Barrie becomes an odd parenthesis whose immature Freudian image at once defines and dismisses him.

Walker's damnation of Barrie, albeit with faint praise, introduces the third major reason for Barrie's rapid descent from fame. This comes in the most unlikely of area of all – from among students of Scottish literature. One might well have thought that the rise of interest in that subject would guarantee a more positive view of Barrie among his own people. In fact, Scottish critics would add their own kind of extra-literary condemnation in simplification. Politics and patriotism drive their case rather than psychology but soon the two would combine to produce a view of Barrie which convicted him of literary treachery as well as immaturity.

The origins of this movement are older than its Freudian counterpart. In 1903, J.H. Millar, in his *Literary History of Scotland*, focuses primarily on Barrie's prose because Scottish scenes and dialect dominate there. From this base, he condemns Barrie as a cynical crowd-pleaser, who wrote below his best in order to make money. He is also the one who formally links him pejoratively with the so called Kailyarders or cabbage patch writers, which included Ian Maclaren and S.R. Crockett. They are all condemned for their sentimentality and parochialism but Barrie's greater talent is used to make his sins appear the greatest.

Millar is writing in 1903, when Barrie's dramatic career was just beginning to reach fruition. *Quality Street* and *The Admirable Crichton* have just been performed; *Peter Pan* is a year away. Therefore his concentration on the early prose works is understandable. He also, correctly, prophesies that Barrie will find the theatre a better vehicle for his satirical skills than the prose world of Kirriemuir's re-invented past: "Mr Barrie's real strength lies in satire; in satire of a unique and mordant flavour, quite distinct from that of the professional satirist but infinitely more pungent" (Millar 1903: 656).

Most Scottish critics watched the fulfilment of this prophecy with some pride as Barrie left behind the prose of his apprenticeship and found in drama his true métier. But fifty years later there appeared an abbreviated revival of its central negative argument. Composed by a realistic novelist, George Blake, it worked from the sophistic assumption that Barrie was trying to be one also. In addition, Blake substitutes a fiery, passionate tone for Millar's objectivity. The latter found the Thrums novels disappointingly parochial but re-directed attention to *The Admiral Crichton*. Blake disposes of the prose more forcefully: "This sort of stuff might appeal to a cockney commercial traveller as a true picture of the sort of thing that could happen in Scotland, where they all wear the kilt and eat haggis" (Blake 1951: 65). Of Barrie's drama he makes nothing at all.

Blake fails to be a serious critic because he writes in a populist manner, has done no research, substitutes abrasive certainty for open-minded discussion and works backwards from his initial conclusions. Yet his booklet, *Barrie and the Kailyard School*, remains the most popular student source for generalisations about Barrie. Multiple copies of that text dominate library holdings. His opinions, couched as in the vaguest of critical vocabulary and confined to the prose alone frequently re-appear in academic surveys of Barrie's entire opus. That so slight a book with so early a canonical focus has become the "Barrie Bible" demands further explanation.

Most obviously, Blake links his argument to the Freudian case but his methodology also prioritises "Scottish" over "Literature". Properly defined, that can be a valuable approach and indeed the successful move to establish Scottish Literature as a University discipline was based on a sensible, pragmatically defined version of it. As late as the 1950s and 1960s almost all Scottish schools and colleges taught "The Great (English) Tradition" of Leavis. Burns and Walter Scott were the only Scottish authors likely to make their way into the canon and even then they were assessed on English terms. This did not mean that counter-movements were non-existent. An older tradition tracing specifically Scottish traits did exist and was most fully expounded in T.F. Henderson's *Scottish Vernacular Literature: A Succinct History* (1910). This work did not deal with Barrie as it concentrated on writing before Burns but it established a literary methodology which defined Scottishness in a particular way and ruthlessly excluded those who did not meet that definition.

George Blake would follow these guidelines more rigidly. But the clearest explanation of its principles came later. During the 1950s, at a time when Scottish Nationalism was enjoying a resurgence politically, Kurt Wittig in *The Scottish Tradition in Literature* offered an appealing short-term solution to Scottish Literature's identity (or more strictly non-identity) problems. Like Henderson, Wittig proposed to start with the differences between Scottish and English Literature rather than the similarities. He was admirably honest about the biased and essentially non-literary vision this would produce.

In Scotland, a different set of traditions has created a society which in many respects (though not all) is very different from that which exists in England […] In expounding these values I have picked out the ones, which seem to me specifically Scottish and have largely ignored the rest. (Wittig 1958: 3)

One patterned arrangement of texts governed by nationalistically determined criteria was to be replaced by another.

But there are major problems inherent in this methodology. First, it starts and ends with a paradigm, the confirmation of which is the true end of any criticism undertaken. More insidiously literary quality becomes only the lowest common denominator for canonical consideration. Effective selection of authors and texts depends on those "added values" which determine Scottishness and, foreseeably, these criteria are drawn from other disciplines – notably history and politics.

A list of these preferences would certainly include –

Writing in Scots	(the most widely recognisable non-English dialect)
Writing realistically	(the down-to-earth Scot)
Writing on Scottish themes	(the patriotic Scot)
Writing on radical themes	(the socialistic Scot)

When non-literary criteria, from whatever discipline, dictate which texts should be studied in an introductory curriculum, some authors will be favoured and others lose out. Indeed, a curriculum based on down-to-earth expression in the Scots dialect of left wing patriotic themes is an extremely eclectic one. Those like Barrie who favour myth and fantasy are not likely to be welcomed, especially when their political views are conservative. As he soon gave up Scotland to live in England and compose comic plays for the amusement of English audiences, his claims for "Scottishness" according to this paradigm become even more tenuous.

Of course, the method is crude. Translated into English terms, it is analogous to centring all Shakespeare courses on the English History plays, while casting a veil over *Othello* and consigning *Macbeth* to outer darkness. Wittig carefully justified the method in interim counter-balancing terms but the broad principles he invokes do no service to Barrie at all. Most of the Scottish *literati* still think his career suspiciously mirrors that of the tradition's arch-traitor, James VI. That monarch's desertion of Scotland and Middle Scots according to traditionalists make him the "terminator" of his country's proud tradition in vernacular writing (Henderson 1910: 333). Now, albeit tardily, the injustice of both these assessments is being recognised. Alternative approaches have been formulated by, among others, Crawford (1992, 2007), Craig (1996), Pittock (1991), Whyte (2004) and Sassi (2005). But although some of these offer a more sympathetic approach to Barrie, the task of making these views effective canonically when patriotic radical realism has held sway for so long remains arduous. The fact that the new "genius" of Scottish literature, Hugh MacDiarmid, shared the left wing and Anglophobic principles anticipated by T.F. Henderson and Millar, did Barrie's reputation little good either. MacDiarmid damned his predecessor with faint praise, finding little to his credit other than his love of hard work (MacDiarmid 1943: 249). Most critics, accustomed as they were to following Wittig's programme and MacDiarmid's poetic primacy, fell into line.

Methodology and the Myth

This study of Barrie's critical "fortuna" helps to suggest the way forward for those who wish to re-assess his place in British literature. Both the extremity of his fall from fame's wheel and the major reasons for that fall have to be taken into account. So what features are shared by the literary, psychological and nationalistic routes discussed above?

(1) All three displace detailed analysis of the texts themselves with agendas derived from other disciplines. Biographical interests fill the gap left by the vagueness of early adulation. Barrie's personality replaces his texts as the focus of fascination. Whether he is appropriately "Scottish" outweighs objective discussion of whether he was a talented writer or not.

(2) They do so from a reduced canonical base. The Freudian case effectively reduces Barrie's canon to the trio of texts which form the minimal base for Oedipal analysis. The nationalist case is equally reductive but more insidious as it ignores his mature drama in order to highlight his early prose. Biographically, two periods can be distinguished. Originally, biographers covered the entire range of texts with "reductiveness" applying to the lack of critical depth implied. To-day, however, the biographical focus narrows as well, with those sections of his life which relate to the Scottish and Oedipal paradigms receiving most attention.

(3) Dialectically, the psychological and nationalist approaches tend to argue backwards from previously established premises rather than seeking out Barrie's own views and adapting to them. Generalised conclusions, admitting of no exceptions, are encouraged by and derive from this methodology. The critical by-pass discussed in the first section is also relevant. When equally absolute, if mysterious, claims for genius define the literary defence, would-be detractors are

provided with a hermeneutic carte blanche and so can move easily
from eulogy to rejection; replacing one set of universals with another.

This in turn suggests that one of Scotland's most effective literary mythmakers – the creator of so many characters whose names
have passed into general use – is in danger of being underestimated by
another kind of mythic logic, that which offers an appealingly simple
vision by excluding all contrary evidence. Certainly, the movement
away from dialectical precision and the historical perspective in
favour of synchronically defined extra-literary generalisations
detected above is identical with Barthes' definition of myth: "In passing from history to nature myth acts economically; it abolishes the
complexity of human acts, it gives them the simplicity of essences, it
does away with dialectics, with any going back beyond what is immediately visible" (Barthes 1984:143).

The real question, therefore, is not whether the Freudian and
nationalist analyses contain some truth – self-evidently they do – but
whether the norms and values on which they rely are consistent with
Barrie's own. This brings the argument full circle. Can the critical gap
described at the start of this discussion be effectively filled at so late a
stage? Does Barrie himself provide clear evidence of his artistic pri-
orities despite the failure of both critics and biographers to identify it?

If one is asking Barrie to be his own critic, clearly the crucial
place to begin is with his own education. Everyone agrees Barrie was
well educated. His eldest brother's position as classics master at Glasgow Academy and later as schools inspector in the Borders area which
included Dumfries Academy meant that James became a pupil at both.
He then went on to gain an M.A. degree at Edinburgh University
before benefiting the people of Nottingham with his accumulated
knowledge in his leaders and reviews for their *Journal*. The odd thing
is that neither the Scottish critics nor the biographers discuss the
"academic" Barrie in any detail. Blake even admits that his views on
the subject are derived at second hand – "Mr. Denis Mackail has fully
and shrewdly analysed all this in his biography" (Blake 1951:61).

Unfortunately, the Edinburgh University years from 1878–82
form a major exception to Mackail's usual reliability. The cameo he
presents in *The Story of JMB* is of a student who already has the
creative writer's contempt for critical parasites. Mackail's Barrie sees
University life as a prison. His erudite professors, including David
Masson, one of the leading literary critics of the day, were valued "not

for their learning but because of the keys they held". Barrie, therefore, "made his notes, he mugged them up, and bluffed his way through the examinations" in order to escape as quickly as possible (Mackail 1941: 60).

His grounds for supposing this are Barrie's brief notes in a diary composed during 1879 (BVS A/35). It is not a cheerful document but the constant repetition of the word "grind" within it does not, as Mackail presumes, reveal a dilettante student "getting by" with the minimum of work. The Notebook anyway pre-dates Barrie's attendance in Masson's classes and that enthusiasm for literary research recorded in Chapter X of *The Greenwood Hat* (Barrie 1930c: 117–24). Nor does Mackail test his theory against the academic honours Barrie later received or the troublesome fact that this "contemptuous" student hosted a retiral dinner for Masson in 1899.

From his early *Nottingham Journal* article to the speeches he gave to St. Andrews and Edinburgh students, Barrie confirms his pride in Scotland and in academic learning. He is every bit as proud of Scotland's comparatively democratic University entrance procedures as his fictional characters – notably John Shand in *What Every Woman Knows* (1908) and Cameron in *Mary Rose* (1920). The anguished cries of the medical student in Barrie's first successful full-length play, *Walker, London* (1892) are also relevant but not cited. In Act 2, Andrew McPhail is sure he has failed his final examinations. On learning that he has passed, he almost faints in "a transport of delight" (Barrie 1941: 27).

The terror felt by McPhail was justified. Pass rates at that time were very low and usually the candidate had to pass papers in *all* of his past courses in one finals diet. Students like Barrie, who could only afford to study during the Winter or the Summer Term, felt these pressures most acutely. Indeed the idea that he could "bluff his way" through the M.A. Ordinary (Pass) degree simply does not stand up against the evidence of the University Calendar. Neither the contents of the syllabus nor the regulations governing them give any hope to the dilettante. In Barrie's final year, he had to sit and pass double papers in Latin, Maths and Greek as well as single papers in Moral Philosophy, Logic and Metaphysics, Natural Philosophy (Physics) and Rhetoric and Belles Lettres. The set texts included major works on Algebra, Geometry, Conic Sections and Dynamics. These scientific volumes vied with Tacitus, Cicero, Thucydides, Homer, Berkeley,

Reid, Chaucer and Shakespeare among others. And he had to do this in full awareness of the economic sacrifices made by his parents.

Mackail's view, that all this was unimportant, is reflected in a lowering of his usually high research standards. He even omits Natural Philosophy from the list of classes Barrie attended. But his dismissal of that period in terms of artistic condescension and dilettantism is still accepted by most biographers.

In fact, few authors have left more enthusiastic evidence about his favourite subjects and professors. Certainly, the research route which opens out when one looks into the University Calendar and reads his lecture notes encourages further examination of the Kirrie-muir writers academic inheritance (EUC 1878–83, ADV 6648–57). Here is a thoughtful student who not only copies down what he hears but, may in side comments challenge or develop the arguments presented. The notes covering the course in Rhetoric and Belles Lettres delivered by David Masson are certainly the most important for understanding how he was introduced to literature but other teachers and courses will prove significant. In particular, the metaphysics and psychology lectures of Masson's colleague, Campbell Fraser. are enthusiastically recorded by the young Kirriemuir student in both his class notes and *An Edinburgh Eleven*. The latter course – one of the first psychology courses to be offered in a British university – also provides an alternative to the Freudian perspective on Barrie's personality.

It is only common sense for a student to read the publications of his professors. Certainly Barrie admitted later to Masson that such was his practice. Nor did he confine himself to the copies available in the University library. In an article describing the character of "The Sentimentalist" he records the time when Masson, browsing in a bookshop, found a copy of one of his own books with the name "J.M. Barrie" inscribed on the flyleaf. On their next meeting he upbraided his student, "'You must have sold me second hand,' he said twinkling" (Barrie 1890: 16).

The more developed arguments in these books are, therefore, another source of evidence. For Masson, the most relevant are the *Essays Biographical and Critical*, *British Novelists and their Style* and his daughter's 1941 re-printing of his Shakespeare lectures as *Shakespeare Personally* (Masson 1856, 1859, 1941). The 1878 revised edition of Fraser's *Selections from Berkeley*, with its lengthy, student-friendly Introduction was anyway a set text when Barrie took his logic and metaphysics. The Irish philosopher's views on perception and personality, as presented in that text by the most "difficult" of Barrie's teachers would also have a major influence upon him.

Chronologically, Barrie's work in Nottingham is the next obvious source of information. As he was at once leader writer *and* literary critic for the *Nottingham Journal* its pages contain valuable evidence of his political and literary views at this time. From the Irish question to the Napoleonic wars, from Darwinism to the Women's Movement, from Hardy's novels to the latest play opening in London, the paper's workaholic young employee was ever ready to provide his opinions. Yet this vast reservoir of evidence has been largely ignored allowing the claim that he had no interest in such matters sophistically to flourish.

Barrie's academic writings are similarly treated. He kept the option of an academic career open until he began to make his way as a creative writer in London. To that end he worked on a major critical work with a suitably grandiose title: *The Early British Satirists, with Some Account of their Influence on the Period and the Manner in which they Illustrate History*. Early chapters from this work were sent to literary journals, as the manuscript articles on Skelton and Nash, contained in the Barrie Collection at Yale's Beinecke Research Library bear witness (Barrie 1BVS T63, S354). These texts are of especial interest because in analysing these Renaissance authors, Barrie reveals a great deal about his own problems as a modern satirist.

Generatively, too, the would-be critic has a wealth of material to consult. Working first of all from the thin Notebooks where he noted his first ideas, Barrie advanced through manuscript to a variety of typescript drafts. At every stage he makes changes. In this way, when the printed evidence finally appears, it can be clearly contextualised in terms of its origins. The task of the next chapter is to explore these neglected areas of research.

Chapter Two

Filling the Research Gaps: Beyond Freud and the Kailyard

As the title of this book suggests, the central irony concerning Barrie is that a man who, as creator of *Peter Pan*, *Quality Street*, *The Admirable Crichton* and *Mary Rose*, could validly claim to be Scotland's greatest myth maker, has been misinterpreted by critical methods which could also be termed mythical. Both sides create a simple pattern out of complex facts. In using comic types and creating simplified countries Barrie is following a powerful, imaginative line in literature. Dickens and Shakespeare, Cervantes and Molière, in different ways, link realism and idealism in this way. They do so, not to avoid the real but to offer a simpler perspective from which the original, complex issue may be re-examined.

In critical terms, however, the attempt to reduce all of an author's work to one simple formula can only work for the most naïve writers of all. Otherwise, as in Barrie's case, the "simple" story will tend to omit or underplay any counter-evidence produced by research. Similarly, the "generalised" story may avoid detailed textual analysis and the "de-historicised" story omit diachronic and generative evidence. I believe this has happened to Barrie and happened in a peculiarly unsympathetic manner. As this chapter will prove, his own literary ideals and favoured sources were clearly formulated. Both his own natural talents and his University training encouraged him to imitate the mythic methods of Dickens and Shakespeare. Formally, as has been seen already, he protests that his work is not only complex but subversive. Diachronically, he leaves a vast body of generative evidence.

To assume that Barrie is a poor realist whose entire opus can be explained in terms of one rather outdated psychological tag without confronting his own claims to be deep and myriad-minded suggests Milton's "fugitive and cloistered virtue, unexercised and unbreathed that never comes out and sees her adversary" (*Areopagitica* 12). That this does not happen while the strange vision of Barrie it proposes continues to "define" him for many are the twin propositions which place the onus on modern critics to produce a proof where none as yet exists and do so in the early period where these sophistries first emerge.

The Greenwood Hat and *The Nottingham Journal*

The most obvious lacuna of all provides a particularly nice example of these avoidance strategies. It might anyway be assumed that Barrie's one and only effort at autobiography would be the most obvious place to begin testing one's critical assumptions. But, for those whose major thesis is based on his early writings, it is the structure of that book which makes consultation and comment practically obligatory. *The Greenwood Hat* was privately published in 1930 as a Christmas gift to a limited number of Barrie's friends. But it is not a conventional narrative. Barrie opens each chapter with an extract from one of his early works. He then uses that extract as a fulcrum for retrospective discussion of what he then was and has now become.

Even in this confessional and "private" context, he warns his chosen group of readers against taking all he says at face value. Focusing on the work's proposed sub-title, "Memories and Fancies" he admits that "despite the best intentions" the two will sometimes mingle – "the memories become fancies and the fancies memories" (Barrie 1930c: 5).

Nonetheless, this personal memoir of his past life does offer a comparatively clear statement of his early views on life and literature. As most of these are at odds with the assumptions behind the Oedipal-Kailyard case, it is difficult to understand why the leading exponents of that case, Blake and Geduld, never mention the text. Their arguments, though differently focused, largely support one another and so, in this introductory context, I shall limit myself to the shared claims they make about Barrie's personality and art. By facing these with the views Barrie presents in the *Hat*, the central areas of dispute will be uncovered.

The vexed question of Barrie's personality is the first area where major differences can be detected. Reduced to its simplest common denominator, the Oedipal case argues that all of Barrie's life and writing is coloured by one woman (his mother) and one trauma (the death of his brother David). But, in fact, neither David nor Margaret Ogilvy is individually mentioned in the *Hat*. Among Barrie's siblings, there are only references to Alexander and Jane Anne. Barrie mentions his "parents" once in order to disclaim, via their poverty, any personal claim to a knowledge of nurseries (160). Individual references, however, focus not on his mother but on his supposedly despised father. William Barrie's gift of a silver watch when Barrie first decided to make his way in London is gratefully recorded (9). And in Chapter IV, James remembers with pride his "splendid father [on] his grand visit to London". He also notes that William "could read the Bible with such aweful reverence as [he] never heard from a pulpit" (37).

The narrowness of the myth's foundations extends into his fiction. There are in fact only two definite references to David's death in Victorian prose. So how is the impression given that Barrie was traumatised by the event?

It is here that Blake's canonical eclecticism comes into play. He cannot, of course, be blamed for reducing his focus to the early prose. His book is part of a series on the English (sic) novel and his chrono-logical parameters – "James Matthew Barrie cultivated the Kailyard assiduously for eight years on end, from 1888 until 1896" - are defined for him (Blake 1951: 70). It is his extremely narrow representation of the field which calls his confident conclusions into question. Only four prose works, all of which are set entirely in Thrums, are analysed. These include the only two which do record David's death – *A Window in Thrums* and *Margaret Ogilvy*. By granting fifty per cent of his attention to them Blake makes it much easier to assume a traumatic Oedipal link than Barrie's own listing of his works within that period would suggest. In the *Hat*, he estimates that he wrote about 800 works in four of those years (270). Of these the manuscript which contains the shorter list of possible texts to be included in *The Greenwood Hat* lists over 250 prose pieces (BVS G65/2). I have read almost all of these without finding another reference to his brother's fate.

Nor does *The Greenwood Hat* support the associated implication that Barrie's Oedipal voice can easily be detected in his work. Indeed, that book opens with an entirely different model, drawn from his early childhood. This substitutes the positive idea of an artistic personality which "contains multitudes" for the single, artistically condescending, idea of immaturity:

When I was a very small boy, another as small was woeful because he could not join in our rough play lest he damaged the "mourning blacks" in which he was attired. So I nobly exchanged clothing with him for an hour, and in mine he disported himself forgetfully while I sat on a stone in his and lamented with tears, though I knew not for whom. (Barrie 1930c: 1)

The analysis of all Barrie's Victorian prose in Chapters Three and Five will firmly establish that this vision of the myriad mind is a major leitmotiv in Barrie's Victorian prose. As befits the exclusive methodology of critical mythologising, the Oedipal-Kailyard case either ignores that evidence entirely (Blake) or occasionally admits it parenthetically (Geduld).

The personality model described above is a particularly threatening one for those who adopt an essentially biographical approach to Barrie's work. Any attempt to find him, his family and acquaintances in his work assumes that these voices can easily be detected behind a transparent fictive veil. In *The Greenwood Hat* Barrie will deny that possibility mimetically and topically, but even on the basic level of narrative and character he raises difficulties. For example, his fullest prose depiction of "the artist-as-young man" is reserved for *Sentimental Tommy* and *Tommy and Grizel*. In these novels, it is clear that Tommy is the author's alter-ego. As his chameleon personality is very strongly emphasised, however, a wide variety of Tommies are paraded, fleetingly, before us. How can the reader decide which of these has priority? As Leonee Ormond points out, there being no norm, there is, strictly, no Tommy, let alone a clear idea of Barrie behind him (Ormond 1987: 79).

When seeking the origins of this histrionic personality in the *Hat*, Barrie uses names to underline these two interrelated sides to his literary identity. As "Anon", the anonymous contributor to journals and newspapers, he is nobody. As "M'Connachie" the inventive writer, who can imagine himself into the roles of "a doctor or sandwich-board man, a member of Parliament, a mother, an explorer, a child, a grandsire, a professional beauty, a dog, a cat" he already contains multitudes (29). But the two are not distinct.

Nor is their relationship totally harmonious. Chapter Three of the *Hat*, which describes "Anon trying to open doors with his pen" explains the paradox. This is where he lists the range of M'Connachie's assumed characters cited above. But he also notes that they were all "written though anonymously as the experiences of himself". He adds, "This is a sure sign that he was groping for a method" (29). This is an accurate assessment of the two conflicting forces in his work when first he came to London. The imaginative M'Connachie and the autobiographical Anon may later combine positively but at the moment their undefined co-existence adds another "vocal" difficulty for those who wish to read Barrie's life into his art.

If the older Barrie, looking back to his youth, finds different models for his own personality and its presence in his early writing than those currently attributed to him, he also gives a radically different account of his literary aims and methods. The "Kailyard" view of Barrie has three central tenets. First, he wrote to please the market and so lacked artistic integrity. He was, therefore, a light author, whose escapist sentimental fantasy could only please his own age. Thirdly, he had no interest in wider, political issues. When these views are allied to the Oedipal strand of thought, they become part of a static argument. Barrie cannot become a serious author because of subconscious forces. The synchronic and generalising methods of the myth are again in evidence yet are not tested against a text whose argument, by way of contrast, is dynamic and progressive.

Thus, when Barrie admits in the *Hat* that he has not found a proper balance between imagination and egocentricity, or when he accepts that he did seek to gain popularity, these claims only *appear* to favour the Kailyard view. They refer to a past point in time and are diachronically explained. The first charge, he explains in practical terms. As a free-lance seeking to make a living from his writing alone he was peculiarly vulnerable to the demands of the market (6–9; 16–20). Having given a practical answer to one mythic assumption, his subsequent account denies another. Not a dilettante escapist but a determinedly self-conscious apprentice anxious to test himself across as wide a modal range as possible is the story told in the *Hat* and confirmed in his Notebooks. This "Scotsman on the make" will write for the popular market but only to keep body and soul together until he can move on to higher things. Later, he will attempt to scale the higher ramparts of the house of fame where high seriousness and the immortality reserved for geniuses alone reside.

His clearest statement of these ambitions is contained in the introductory, "Apology" to the *Hat*. There he notes that he came out of Edinburgh University with "a worthy craving to be the heaviest

author of time" (6). This claim includes his academic writings. It is
also made in a gently satirical tone which suggests that the aim was
part of youthful naivety. But while experience may have caused to
him to compromise, the *Hat* confirms that this early aim was never
abandoned.

Barrie was trained in Rhetoric. He is therefore particularly
concerned with the different kinds of forms and figures, definitions of
which opened Masson's lectures (ADV 6652.1–57). In this area, the
Hat demonstrates the range of literary "kinds" Masson had defined
and Barrie later attempted during his apprenticeship. This procedure
means that in the 1880s he was already beginning to understand where
his natural strengths lay.

First and foremost, he is an imaginative writer. The "real" world
is part of his concern but it is via fantasy that he will explore its
concerns. He had after all "invented M'Connachie to share the brunt"
of imitating the possible as well as the actual (Barrie 1930c: 29).
Further, he admits to having trouble with facts. From these doubts
arise his undisguised contempt for those biographers who lack the
"fanciful" and "humane" dimensions which are his own source of
interest. This view, indirectly and satirically expressed in Chapter XV
of *The Greenwood Hat* (163–74) emerges more stridently in the curse
noted by Birkin in his *Notebooks* – "May God blast any one who
writes a biography of me" (Birkin 1979: ix). As he also admits to
finding the comic techniques of satire much easier to adopt than
tragedy, it is as a comic, imaginative idealist he sees himself. Blake's
determination to assess him *as if he were* a serious social realist is
therefore triply misguided.

The impropriety of applying realistic premises to Barrie had been
earlier anticipated by Max Beerbohm. When Massingham condemned
What Every Woman Knows in this way, Beerbohm protested that he
had

made excellent use of the best recipe of all, which is to blame your man for not having
set out to do something quite alien from his actual purpose […] If the play pretended
to be the key of sober, realistic comedy, I too should be awfully angry about it. But in
What Every Woman Knows the key of fantasy is struck from the outset and to that key
I attune my ears. (Beerbohm 1970: 386)

Despite this, he does decide *a priori* and on absolute grounds that
those who favour the fantastic and comic muses are second-rate.

Satire and Romance may have served past tastes, he argues, but serious, politically-focused prose is the only way forward to-day. Dickens, arguably the most poetic, comic and idealistic of English novelists is especially taken to task. Stock characters and the humour they invoke are inappropriate when serious political topics such as "social injustice" are concerned. "Even Dickens found it difficult to be funny in *Hard Times*", we are informed (Blake 1951:10).

Widening his scope, Blake finds Scottish writers particularly guilty of this sentimental, retrospective approach. Walter Scott's "high wall of Gothic assumptions" and "not very accurate" dramatising of the past is regretted. R.L. Stevenson is also condemned for his "elegant Romanticism". Both are tarnished by that mode's unfortunate interest in the marvellous and the improbable. On these grounds the Scottish "kailyarders" are relegated to a third division of aptitude below even Neil Munro and John Buchan. Blake's case becomes particularly emotive here. They "go on drooling about" the rural past he comments when the present urban crisis is what really matters (Blake 1951: 9–10, 18).

In the *Hat*, therefore, Barrie carefully presents a view of his art which is significantly different from the first two Kailyard assumptions. He gives practical reasons for initially courting the masses and sets that strategy within a plan which demonstrates the artistic integrity denied to him by Blake and his followers. His lightness and apparently simple surface message are similarly contextualised, this time in terms of an alliance between realism and imagination within an ambitious allegorical remit; Anon joins M'Connachie in serving the Imp.

It is the last of these characters who exposes the sophistry behind the third kailyard claim. If Barrie had no interest in wider themes, then why would he need to adopt the kind of layered techniques employed by allegorists over the centuries? In Chapter XIII, Barrie explains how this layered form originated. There, he presents the allegorical impulse first of all as a problem for Anon – "he was sometimes nervous over articles which meant the reverse of what they seemed to say, a kind of writing that the Imp referred to was constantly egging Anon to write" (152).

This is the Barrie whom Walpole identified – one whose deeper ideas are only detectable, subversively, under the surface of the text (Barrie 1938: 3). As noted earlier, Walpole did not go on to explain

how this allegorical method worked. The different demands made by
realism and idealism are, however, another leitmotiv in the early
prose. They finally become part of an analytic discussion in the most
determinedly metafictional of these works *Tommy and Grizel*. In that
book an academic debate conducted between Tommy and the old
editor Pym effectively opens the action (Barrie 1900: 15–19). Using a
form which anticipates the Romance structures of dramas such as *The
Admirable Crichton* and *Peter Pan* the questions raised in that episode
as then fancifully explored and a new answer offered finally after
Tommy's death.

This range and these intentions are illustrated in the *Hat*. It might
even be said that the book's main purpose is to remind his friends of
how many different worlds Barrie has entered, imagined and re-
defined. The tone he employs is light and the extracts he chooses are,
by definition, personal but they do offer insights into Victorian
politics and education, European history and culture. Far from writing
about himself alone, Barrie did have extensive knowledge of those
wider areas denied to him by the myth.

The major case against the solely egocentric Barrie is advanced
in another source which the critical myth excludes from attention.
From January 1883 until October 1884, Barrie was the leader writer
for *The Nottingham Journal*. In that role he did handle local topics but
his major duty was to reflect both national and world news. It would
be extremely difficult to do this without mastering the political and
sociological areas whose absence Blake particularly laments. In fact,
Barrie's range of reference is extremely wide. But whether he is
explaining local issues or expounding on world politics his erudition is
always on display.

As befits a man who got this job by sending an essay on *King
Lear* to his would-be employers, his coverage of a Trade Union debate
on Nottingham's shoe-making trade manages to bring Carlyle and
France into an analysis which mocks academic theory and advocates
practical solutions "Frenchmen" he argues, "though they have never
read Carlyle, have taken advantage of the technical schools open to
them and have become, we are told, so skilful that they can do their
work more satisfactorily and cheaply than less fortunate operatives"
(*NJ* 13 September 1883: 4). There are many other examples of his
interest in the Industrial Revolution, that area of concern which Blake
especially denies to him. Barrie's coverage is, however, British and

International rather than stolidly Scottish. In his leader of 4 October 1884, he can be found comparing the effects of over-production of lace in Lancashire with that in the United States concluding that in the former context at least it places small lace businesses in a vulnerable competitive position – "Any one can see that too much additional capital has been floated into it [the lace trade] in too short a time" (5). Elsewhere, and in the same confidently erudite manner, he continues to offer his opinions on current sociological issues. The limits of educational charity (food but not clothes), a Swiss statistician's views on population and the problems facing deaf mutes are all grist to his mill (see *NJ* 22 September 1883: 5; 14 February 1884: 5; 4 August 1884: 5; 11 October 1884: 5).

But he also involves himself in current philosophical and spiritual debates. On Monday 22 October 1883, his theme is religious. This time it is Oliver Wendell Holmes' definition of "surface Christianity" as "the wish and art to be agreeable" which introduces the argument. Church attendances are holding up in "Mayfair" but falling in "Seven Dials" because looking good is not a priority among the lower classes in an age of theological doubt (5). Blake seems as unaware of this evidence as of the *Hat* itself. But even if had read these journalistic articles and the associated autobiography, it is doubtful if he would have retracted his basic position. It is not *any* kind of political enthusiasm which he demands but those nationalistic and left wing views on which Wittig based his case for the Scottish tradition in literature. The Barrie who emerges from *The Nottingham Journal* and *The Greenwood Hat* may be patriotic and politically aware but like so many beneficiaries of the democratic entrance policies fostered by the Scottish universities, his politics were closer to those of David Hume than Karl Marx.

Only two possible excuses remain for those who remain unaware of the journalistic evidence. The first of these would be to argue that Barrie keeps his journalistic views apart from his fiction. In that case, he might still be a totally self-absorbed novelist and dramatist in spite of the wide knowledge he had to amass in order to be an effective leader-writer.

Those who read Barrie's contributions to *The Nottingham Journal* are soon disabused of this notion. The ideas behind *Walker, London, Quality Street, The Admirable Crichton, Little Mary* and *What Every Woman Knows* are all anticipated in that newspaper (*NJ*

25 February 1884: 5; 6 March 1884: 5; 23 June 1883: 6; 28. May 1884: 5; 24 March 1884: 4 respectively). Perhaps the most astounding of these "prophecies" is to be found in his Hippomenes column on Monday 17 December 1883. Taking Carlyle's sarcastic suggestion of a comic Bible seriously, Barrie goes on to suggest particular biblical characters and situations, which invite the comic muse:

The adventures of David have been strangely neglected by comic persons. Descendants of Leech, do you not see in the contest between David and Goliath a magnificent opportunity of setting the town in a roar? (4).

This is a scenario which he realise will, fifty-three years later, in his last play, *The Boy David*.

This says a lot about Barrie's planning. Any idea which occurs to him is set down in his Notebooks. These may be consulted at any time and older, forgotten themes be resuscitated when conditions make this desirable. In the case of *The Boy David*, it was the boyish look of Elizabeth Bergner which provided the particular impetus for this biblical story to be re-considered and developed as a new literary "kind" – the comic legend.

There remains one last excuse which could be offered for ignoring Barrie's journalism. All the texts cited above are dramas. Blake's sole concentration on prose may not excuse him from partiality but Barrie himself admitted that he found self-revelation to be more of a problem in his novels. To test this hypothesis involves identifying those themes which dominate Barrie's journalism. Some of these, for example his interest in the Irish question, *are* relevant to his drama alone. His riddle play, *Little Mary*, cannot be understood without some awareness of Barrie's intense interest in the relationship between England and Ireland (see Jack 1987: 134–8, 263–4). There are two major exceptions to this rule, however. As the selections from *The Greenwood Hat* illustrate, the nature of love is a major concern in Anon's prose. After all, five of the twenty two extracts in the *Hat* are used as a vehicle for discussing Barrie's early sexual problems. That all five of these extracts come from his prose confirms that his early narratives *rather than* his dramas are the place where Barrie works out the key question of his sexuality. A brief analysis of the *way* in which the older Barrie explains this in the *Hat* will naturally introduce the two relevant leitmotivs of his thinking as presented in *The Nottingham Journal*.

In the *Hat*, all of the extracts are presented as confrontations which Barrie loses. Physically, he is too small to be successful in the game of love: "Mr Anon found it useless to love, because after a look at the length and breadth of him, none would listen" (214). As a result he becomes an unwilling spectator. Faced with different kinds of attractive women in a carriage, he suffers the worst fate of all, to be considered "quite harmless" (125). Intensely attracted to "a tall poetical-looking girl" he sees in her eyes the "saddest word... Nevermore" (126). As superfluous lover with an overtly histrionic personality, he soon finds himself playing false roles to cover up his inadequacy. "By deputy or in a mask", he makes them listen to his opinions on the very passion from which, really, he is excluded (214). As Chapters XX and XXI illustrate, he even begins to assume a female voice. As "lovely aunt" or the wife of a would-be playwright he joins the gender battle, by changing sides and so is doomed to idolise rather than love.

These experiences mean that he has an unusually high view of the female personality. The fact that he idolises women, is in fact the first comment he makes about them. In Chapter III, he tells us that "Heroines" not only were an early obsession of Anon but would continue to be a favoured topic in his later work (27). One only needs to think of Phoebe Throssel, Moira Loney, Wendy Darling, Maggie Wylie and Mary Rose to see the accuracy of that claim.

These themes and characters were all current in Barrie's day. The "superfluous hero" was already well known from Russian literature while Darwin's scientific account of the battle between the sexes had been dramatised by Ibsen. Barrie now seems to be applying similar views to Anon. Certainly, in the *Hat*, Anon's personal disadvantages are associated with battles at the highest level of genius. Anon's smallness is weighed against his potential for greatness as a writer and associated, via Carlyle, with Napoleon, a contradictory figure who will return again and again as hero and villain in Barrie's art (207–14). He also confirms that natural selection is the most crucial principle in life. "The Saddest Word" leads Barrie into a hierarchical definition of human needs. Most basically, there is survival ("To earn a pound a day") then there is art ("To reach some little niche in literature") but most important of all is to be a favourite of the ladies. All the other cravings he would set aside for that (134). This is where Barrie's views depart from the Darwinian norm. Darwin believed men were

superior to women. Both Anon's articles and Barrie's memoirs reverse
that result. From Mary de Navarro defeating him at cricket to the
ladies in the railway carriage, from the kindly aunt to the resourceful
playwright's wife, heroines rule.

Yet the critical myth does not raise the Darwin issue at all. This
may be another example of inadequate research or it may be is a
deliberate exclusion strategy designed to keep the idea of Barrie's
retrospective sentimentalism clear from troublesome evidence. Either
way, it does involve the deletion of a major line in the Scotsman's
thinking. That he had read, and largely accepted, Darwin's theories of
natural selection is evident as early as Notebook A2/8. There, as notes
348–50, 352 and 357 reveal, he is reading Darwin in order to write an
article on the great man's student days at Edinburgh University. This
interest is confirmed in *Auld Licht Idylls* (1888). There the narrator
introduces us to Thrums via an account of Nature's battles for survival. A vulnerable bantam-cock is "found frozen in his own water
trough" while a weasel gripping a water hen is presented as "only
another fierce struggle among the hungry birds for existence" The
direct echoing of Darwinian terminology is no coincidence. Thrums
folk, the narrator comments, "need no professor to teach them the
doctrine of the survival of the fittest". They learn that from Nature
itself. In addition, the Scottish peasant's high regard for learning
means that even labourers in their bothy may supplement experience
with theory. Among their books, the narrator notes, is "one of
Darwin's" (Barrie 1888b: 1, 5, 49).[1]

It is here that Barrie's journalism provides important supportive
evidence. His *Nottingham Journal* articles on evolution and the battle
of the species are among his list of possible pieces for inclusion in *The
Greenwood Hat*. There they are described as "Two Darwin articles".
They are not chosen but, as noted earlier, their conclusions are in
harmony with his presentation of the battle of the sexes in the *Hat*.

The first of his Darwinian commentaries appears in his leader
article of 8 May 1884. There he accepts "the Darwinean method of
reasoning" on personal grounds. As an ambitious man, he welcomes a
thesis which, in the uncertain spirit of "this curious, inquisitive age"

---

[1] Unless otherwise stated, references to the prose works follow *The Uniform Edition
of The Works of J.M. Barrie*, London: Hodder and Stoughton. Individual volumes are
indicated by capitalised titles. Their original publication dates are given in both text
and Bibliography.

looks forward rather than back. Darwin's account of life is appealing because it "can be adopted for determining the man of the future as well as the man of the past" (*NJ* 8 May 1884: 4). He even uses Darwin's competitive thesis as a means of assessing his own quest for fame. If life is a battle for supremacy, the late nineteenth century has raised the standard for the determined and the gifted within a hierarchically defined society. That this competitive vision was indeed in harmony with the young journalist's world-view can be confirmed from earlier articles, most notably this comment on 16 April 1883:

It may perhaps be said, and we do not doubt with some truth, that men of genius can still fight their way through the rabble with the old celerity [...But] the fight for life, indeed, is now far sterner, far more serious than it used to be, and the ladder of fame can only, except in rare instances, be climbed by inches. (5)

A more detailed defence of Darwin is presented in the newspaper on 15 September 1884. The article highlights another of Barrie's duties on the paper. He did not only write leaders. He was also frequently used as the paper's book critic. It is in that capacity that he reviews recent Darwin research. Evaluating the recent work of two influential Darwinians, Frederic Harrison and G.J. Romanes, he demonstrates his broad acceptance of the scientific evidence. Christians, he argues, must now adapt their thinking to the new knowledge presented.

It was this hyper-competitive Barrie, looking to a doubtful future rather than confirming the values of the past, who was earlier detected in the *Hat*. Particularly when describing the battle of the sexes, Anon's search for genius confirms that his focus is on the highest levels of evolutionary development. This line, which is at extreme odds with the popular vision of Barrie, is also confirmed in the *Journal*. His interest in Carlyle's definitions of heroism is evident everywhere, not only in his leaders but also in his book criticisms and those articles he wrote as "Hippomenes" and "A Modern Peripatetic". One of these in particular fascinates him. He repeatedly deals with Napoleon Bonaparte in his journalism, an interest which will later transfer itself to his prose and plays. This is not surprising. Having read about him in Carlyle's heroic context he was pleased to find parallels between this military genius and himself. Both were ruthlessly determined to overcome the disadvantages of birth and height in order to prove supremacy in their chosen professions. The partly admirable, partly devilish Napoleon who emerges from the pages of the *Journal*, also nicely illustrates the unresolved doubts which define the age and re-define conventional ideas of faith and morals. To represent this divided world after Darwin and Nietzsche, a divided hero-villain is needed and that is the role Barrie gives to Napoleon. At once the double-dyed villain of Phoebe Throssel's imagination in *Quality Street* and the supreme example of lower-class, upwardly mobile genius on whom Barrie modelled himself he had many calls on Anon's attention.

Therefore, when the older Barrie begins the romantic line in *The Greenwood Hat* by revealing Anon's initial interest in heroines and the battle of the species and his own continued involvement with great women, he is making two quite radical claims. On their own and within the battles of life, his fictional heroines sign his continued interested in the major moral and metaphysical problems of his day. They are part of the new, competitive world described by Darwin and Nietzsche to which his youthful self subscribed. That these important, even dominant themes have effectively been silenced may be another tribute to the power of the critical myth but that does not mean we can continue to diminish Barrie by ignoring them.

Arguably there is an even wider gap fostered by the critical myth. The Barrie of the kailyard has no interests beyond past and self while the Freudian Barrie is mother-fixated both artistically and sexually. The mythic method determines that analysis beyond these limits is forbidden. To go further and suggest that Barrie was also an early supporter of the Women's Movement and believed the female to be better adapted to the Darwinian world certainly violates those limits! Yet, when the heroine figure in the *Hat* is considered, not on her own, but within the battle of the sexes that is precisely the impression given. If one then examines his journalism, the evidence is so extensive that suspicion becomes fact and The "New Woman" has to be added to the "New Science" in any consideration of Barrie's early writing.

Consistently and approvingly, Barrie describes the social advances made by women in the 1880s. When writing of the recent introduction, into English law, of the concept that man and wife should be legally regarded as one person, he comments, "A wife has now at one stroke achieved a position of independence which is a striking tribute to the progress of the modern spirit with regard to the status of women" (*NJ* 21 June 1883). Characteristically he balances this kind of enthusiasm against his sense that these advances are being made unwillingly rather than out of a spirit of male enlightenment. Thus, when he welcomes the Married Women's Property Act, he attributes this advance to a lack of male foresight: "Probably the authors of the Act little thought what a tremendous weapon they were putting into the hands of those who are fighting for the recognition of the political equality of women with the rest of the community" (*NJ* 26 June 1883).

Unfavourable comparisons with other countries are another method he employs to present positive and negative simultaneously. In the case of school and University education Scotland's open and democratic methods are often compared favourably with England's elitist and sexist system:

At the very moment when the children of the London poor were ignorant of an alphabet, their brethren of Scotland, though still worse off from a pecuniary point of view, were pushing their way forward by the hundred through the village school and making names for themselves as "scholars" in the neighbourhood. (*NJ* 26 April 1884; see also 24 April)

The Darwinian, competitive terms in which Scottish superiority is here presented ("pushing their way forward") provides a microcosmic refutation of both Blake's "unpatriotic" and "topically retrospective" articles of faith.

Wider comparisons are also offered. When supporting a recent English proposal to grant scholarships for poor girls Barrie draws in the American example to force home his point. Although those who benefit from these scholarships "will be able to develop natural talents and this must tend to the good of the community" such advances pale into insignificance when compared to the position of women in America. There, a really open society with women clergy and women lawyers is developing (*NJ* 26 June 1883). This awareness of a major cultural difference would later manifest itself in the different dramatic scripts Barrie produced for performance in the States. Especially plays which dealt with sociological issues (e.g. *The Admirable Crichton*) would offer radically different plots in New York and London.

If this establishes Barrie's broad sociological position, his specific supports both for Women's rights generally and the cause of Women's Suffrage in particular can be proved from the pages of the *Nottingham Journal*. On the first topic his view that women are better adapted to life's battles than men leads him to see final success as already guaranteed, *accompli*. "The one excellent reason why women should continue calling for their rights is that they are sure in the long run to get them" (*NJ* 14 December 1883). On Women's Suffrage, he is more divided, supporting the end but sometimes doubting the means. The more daring efforts for drawing attention to the movement he sometimes believes may be counter-productive. An extended leader on 31 January 1884 offers a detailed account of his reasons for believing that the cause warrants support. In this he questions whether Chamberlain's apparent support can be soundly based so long as he refers to the granting of the vote as a "privilege" for women rather than a "right". If Chamberlain is going to champion that cause

let it be an honest opinion and not founded on mere conventionality and prejudice. In the question of female suffrage the real onus of proof seems to us to be rather on those who oppose than on those who support it. No doubt anyone who proposes a change in the law must show some reason for the change. But in the case of female suffrage a *prima facie* at all events can be shown. Women householders have to pay taxes and submit themselves to the laws of the land; as women they have many interests distinct from those of men, and again and again their sex has been treated differently from that of men. All this being so, as we are only stating the plainest possible facts, there is at once a *prima facie* case in favour of granting female suffrage, in favour of allowing women who have such an intimate interest in the acts of the legislature to take some part in determining what those acts shall be. (5)

It could be argued with some justification that this study of *The Greenwood Hat* and *The Nottingham Journal* has also presented "the plainest possible facts" in order to establish a *prima facie* case against viewing Barrie in simple Oedipal-Kailyard terms. But in this instance, those who argue for "no change" are in an even weaker position than their Victorian counterparts. They at least knew the terms on which the debate was being conducted. Those who still advance the popular, mythic view of Barrie have either not read the counter evidence at all or, less probably, have opted to ignore the uncomfortable truths it conveys.

Barrie as Academic I – Masson and Belles Lettres

Study of *The Greenwood Hat* and Barrie's journalism suggests a very different vision of the man and the writer. For a supposedly Oedipal personality limited to childish themes it substitutes a histrionic mind, using layered texts to address serious topics in satiric mode. For the myth of a writer so obsessed with the past that he shows no interest in contemporary events, it substitutes an authority on the political issues of his day with particular interests in Darwinism and the Women's Movement. These ideas are supported in another area. Barrie's academic work and the influence of his Edinburgh University teachers upon him can be shown to accord with the more complex picture presented above. In particular, the influence of David Masson on his literary theory harmonises closely with that of the myriad-minded Barrie, preparing to face the major challenge of uniting real and ideal in the manner of Shakespeare and Dickens.

The reasons for one research gap leading into another were broached in Chapter One. Bibliographically, the usually reliable Mackail's vision of Barrie as unwillingly, "imprisoned" in academe was partly amended by Dunbar's more sympathetic account (Mackail 1941: 49–77; Dunbar 1970: 38–49). As the canonical focus had by then narrowed, the opportunity she offered to literary critics was not followed up. Barrie may rhapsodise in his journalism, fiction and speeches on the wonderful opportunity given to ordinary Scots by the democratic system of entry into that country's universities, but its irrelevance to his own personal growth is assumed without further examination.

This returns attention to the evidence led briefly at the end of Chapter One. It was noted there that Mackail's evidence rests on a Notebook kept by Barrie when he was in his first year. To carry the expectations of your family into an unknown, competitive, academic world where standards for success are high is not an easy task and there is little doubt that Barrie did find the transition difficult. But the witty tone of *An Edinburgh Eleven* (1889) does not suggest that he remained unhappy throughout his four years of study. Nor does the evidence support Mackail's dual contention that he had an artist's contempt for scholars and only did the basic work needed to pass. That policy would have been dangerous in a system where all papers had to be passed in the final diet of exams and the pass rate was around 50%. In addition, the quality of his class notes (ADV 1878–82: 6648–57) and the wide range of subjects examined in the final diet (EUC 1883–84: 112) argue against Mackail's view. That he did well in literature might be expected and he did gain fourth place in the

class of Rhetoric and Belles Lettres (EUC 1882–83: 201). That he also
secured merit certificates in Mathematics and Logic and Metaphysics
(EUC 1880–81: 190; 1881–82: 194) suggests all round diligence
rather than the dilettante spirit suggested by Mackail.

That Barrie especially appreciated Masson's course in Rhetoric
and Literature can be proved from *The Greenwood Hat*. In it, he tells
us of his love for Renaissance literature:

Marlowe and Peele and Greene and Gabrielissime Harvey and Tom Nash and all the
others, how I dwelt with them in the Edinburgh University library and edited them
with voluminous notes of import, the while with the other hand I reached out for John
Skelton, Dunbar, Marvell, Mapes, Donne, Prynne. (Barrie 1930c: 123)

The English Renaissance stood at the centre of Masson's syllabus.
That the principles of classical rhetoric which inspired that period and
were heavily stressed in Masson's opening lectures exerted a powerful
influence on the young Barrie can be clearly established by looking at
his own academic essays. That he did write such essays and indeed
kept the option of an academic career open until 1891 is an important
fact. 1891 saw the success of *The Little Minister* and with it financial
security. The fallback option of writing critical monographs, noted at
the end of Chapter One, was no longer necessary. While it had offered
an alternative aim, however, Barrie had embraced it with his usual
determined enthusiasm.

The two holograph articles which I shall use to exemplify his
academic work were intended to be chapters in the proposed academic
monograph entitled *The Early Satirical Poetry of Great Britain*. In
1885 when he first embarked on his freelance career in London, Barrie
had badgered publishers not only with his fiction but with the proposal
for that book, another for *A History of Universities* and a biography on
William Cobbett. These articles are of particular relevance, as they
perform a double function. First, they seek to prove the young postgraduate's authority as a scholar. But they also serve as explorations
of his own aims as novelist and dramatist. As both of these lines
reveal the influence of Masson's teachings, a brief prefatory account
of the professor's background and the background to the articles
themselves will serve to contextualise the argument.

David Masson held the Edinburgh Chair of Rhetoric and Belles
Lettres from 1865–95. There was only one course offered in Rhetoric
and Literature and Barrie's chosen curriculum meant that he could

only study it in the last year of his studies for the Ordinary M.A. In 1881, all of the professor's books were available in the University Library. Most were also available for devoted students like Barrie to buy. They included his critical monographs on *British Novelists and their Style*, his monograph on Drummond of Hawthornden and his three volume life of John Milton (Masson 1859; 1873; 1874). Among his printed essays, those on literary theory and the position of Scottish writers are of special value for any consideration of Barrie's art (Masson 1856). *Shakespeare Personally*, although it did not appear until after the professor's death, is also important as it is an extended, printed version of the Shakespeare lectures which Barrie attended (Masson 1914). Masson's personality and lecturing techniques were also appreciated by Barrie. In *An Edinburgh Eleven*, he depicts a lecturer whose class was "a delight" and whose delivery was so vivid that his student still "seems to remember everything that [he] said and the way he said it" (Barrie 1889b: 15).[2]

The two holograph articles "Tom Nash" and "The Rector of Diss" are held in the Barrie Research Collection at Yale BVS. Both initially bore the names of the authors treated. From internal evidence it is clear that the one on Nash is the earlier. The holograph is dated 1883 and is one hundred pages long (BVS T63). Later, the piece would appear in shortened and popularised form in the July 1886 edition of *Home Chimes*. The essay on Skelton (BVS S354) runs to sixty seven holograph pages and was sent to an academic journal from Barrie's 1884 Nottingham address in Birkland Avenue. References drawn from his Skelton research also appear as part of his leader in the *Nottingham Journal* of 23 July 1884. At that time it was called, simply, "John Skelton". Extensive cuts and an amended address (his London lodgings in Grenville Street) show that it was sent out for reconsideration in 1885. This time, the title was "The Rector of Diss". There is no evidence that it was ever published.

These essays were certainly intended for academic audiences. Erudite openings mark out the work a young postgraduate anxious to prove his authority. Detailed textual analyses dominate but these are only offered once Nash and Skelton's preferred literary modes, their position in literary history, their lives and philosophies have been established. This mirrors the disciplinary breadth of the Scottish

---

[2] The Masson section of this chapter is based on Jack 2003 "James Barrie as Academic: 'Tom Nash' and 'The Rector of Diss'" in *Swansea Review* 20: 1–22.

Ordinary M.A. It also follows Masson's practice. The very titles of his
books – e.g. *The Life of John Milton: narrated in connexion with the
political, ecclesiastical and literary history of his Time* – confirm this
disciplinary range. He explains his reasons for this approach in his
article "Theories of Poetry". There he argues that the best writers
combine the specific excellence of their own craft with "the most
extensive array of other intellectual qualities" (Masson 1856: 439).
So, when his student also places his textual analysis within a broader
disciplinary framework, he is imitating his professor's practice.

Barrie's choice of authors was also intelligently related to his
training. Both Nash and Skelton lie within the chronological parameters of Masson's "Chaucer to Dryden" course (EUC 1881–82: 101).
The major focus, however, lay within the Renaissance. Barrie's class
notes confirm that his professor saw Shakespeare as the zenith of a
Golden Age, anticipated by Skelton and shared at a lower level by
Nash. This is one of Masson's clear, hierarchically arranged, assessments. It is one which Barrie's essays share. In his Nash article he
declares that "The tree of English Literature […] has never grown so
stately as in the days when Elizabeth was queen" (97). As Skelton pre-
dates that time, as inhabitant of a "fairly productive" but not excellent
period, he faces gentler standards of critical assessment than Nash
(67).

Barrie is an astute literary historian, adapting the bias of background support offered to the specific needs of the author under
scrutiny. He has also done the necessary research. Skelton currently
stood at the centre of opposed critical assessments. Barrie uses past
authorities to explain how the two schools of thought originated (1–2).
Alexander Dyce had produced the most modern edition of Skelton in
1843. This is carefully evaluated as well (16 –17). The same approaches are more economically covered for Nash. His life among the
wider group of Elizabethan playwrights is a major focus of attention.
Barrie adds cameos of Shakespeare, Marlowe and Peele in this case
(15–32). Skelton's life and times are also outlined (3–6). And within
these biographical and sociological sections, a third reason for
authorial choice emerges. These authors anticipate many of their
critic's own problems.

In these essays Barrie overtly favours Renaissance writers whose
life and art share features with his own. Skelton and Nash were also
University graduates, who came from rural stock. Like Barrie they

lacked private means and therefore faced the problem of maintaining high standards while appealing to the widest possible audience. Skelton, we are told, stood outside the London establishment and "had nothing of the suave courtier in his constitution" (54). In practical terms, all three are unprivileged outsiders seeking acceptance among the London *literati*. He also provides a vicarious image of Barrie's own difficulty with amorous dialogue: "What is required of him [in 'Garlande'] is to say something pretty or sad of the fair garland wearers, and he does it by giving them a lesson in ancient history" (53).

But it is "Tom (sic) Nash" who vicariously faces the same financial problems as his youthful critic. A rustic with no monetary support, he too "[arrived] in London, full of hope and confidence […] plunged at once into the sea of letters, and gave early promise of being a prolific writer" (32). He too was especially attracted to the theatre. "It is the irrepressible cat which the master used to put in a sack and cast into the river but which, nevertheless, was always the first to greet him on her return home" (8).

Barrie's favourite literary sources are also revealed. At the top stands Shakespeare. But even he becomes a vehicle for examining Barrie's personal creative problems. The habit of addressing Shakespeare on his own behalf had already been established in *The Nottingham Journal*. Anxious to become a dramatist, Barrie sought advice from the bard. He concluded that Renaissance playwrights had two advantages over their Victorian successors. First, drama was then the most popular form. "When Shakespeare went to London all the literary free lances of the day were engaged on play writing, it was the recognised means when the end was fame and prosperity". Secondly, their audience was more refined – "Managers and public would not endure plays which were without literary merit". Imaginatively moving Shakespeare into the late nineteenth century, he concludes that the Warwickshire man "would probably never have written more than one drama" which "would have been returned by some manager as 'Not quite up to the mark of the Frivolity'" (*NJ* 24 April 1883). In his articles, this hierarchy of genius is sustained. Skelton and Nash may strive; Shakespeare has achieved and his practice embodies the ideal.

If Barrie is aware of the need to win over a popular audience, he is also guided by the Cowley quotation "To be for ever known And make the world to come my own" which, if *Margaret Ogilvy* is to be believed, focused him ambitiously on genius from childhood onwards

(Barrie 1896a: 40). As it happened, Masson, who had himself been a journalist, addressed this question regularly in his lectures. He also provided a clear critical framework which allowed writers to address both public and peers. This involved adopting forms which worked on two levels, combining realism and idealism (in both its Platonic and imaginative senses).[3]

The articles on Skelton and Nash also show that in the 1880s, he was already aware that his own genius was essentially comic and that this might work against him in the courts of fame. When discussing Skelton's current critical standing, he suggests that it would now be higher, if he had been less witty:

His Latin elegiacs prove that if his propensity to the ridiculous had not more frequently seduced him to follow the whimsies of Walter maps and Golias than to copy the elegiacs of Ovid, he would have appeared among the first writers of Latin poetry in England. (BVS S354:13)

The Nash essay reaches the same conclusion but concentrates on audience reception. The English, Barrie argues, would more readily "seek reputation at the cannon's mouth [than] espouse a cause which he sees all his neighbours laughing at" (BVS T63: 44). The temptation to turn to tragedy is, therefore, great and many "great comedians" have foolishly given way to "an inward craving to essay the parts of Hamlet and Macbeth" when tragedy was not their natural métier (23). At the same time, many of the satiric authors in Masson's "Chaucer to Dryden" course offered a possible way out. As Ben Jonson had noted in *Discoveries*, comedy need not remain a "fowling for the people's delight" (Jonson 1985: 589). In its more serious forms it might become a vehicle for moral and spiritual guidance. Barrie's proposed book on British satire reflects Barrie awareness that this was a form which might allow naturally comic writers to attain that high seriousness which was necessary for enduring fame.

As this evidence supports his later *Greenwood Hat* contention that Anon sought eternal fame from an early age, it is worth looking at the arguments he offers, in that context, for Skelton and Nash. Was either destined to be remembered for the universal ideas he presented or was each condemned to perish with the issues of his own day?

---

[3] Carlyle, one of Barrie's favourite authors, made the same case for Burns's enduring fame in his *Essays*.

Barrie uses both realistic *and* idealistic criteria to assess each case. On the realistic level, there is nothing to choose between them. Nash's excellence in "painting portraits of actual beings" is noted (70). But Skelton's mimetic skills in "Against Garnesche" are also recognised. Indeed his young critic finds that poem so accurately vivid that he "can fancy the King [Henry VIII] rubbing his hands in glee" as the rector's "envenomed darts" hit the "bleeding and staggering knight" (6). When he moves from immediate to eternal fame, however, neither author comes out very well. Skelton might be said to win the "idealistic" contest but only narrowly and infrequently. Barrie believes he did try to balance popular and profound but only got the balance right in "The Boke of Phyllyp Sparow". He sadly concludes that this may well be why, he "has waited a long time for some adequate recognition of his merits from the Queen of Fame" (66).

Barrie's critical methodology at once comprehends and transcends Blake's. While the latter idolises serious social realism, Barrie prefers the Romances of Shakespeare and the comically idealised humours of Cervantes and Dickens because they use imagination to explore ideas. This vision exactly mirrors Masson's as presented in his lectures and his published work. In particular, the distinction between real and ideal, which Barrie uses to justify writing on two levels is central to both Masson's lectures and his published works. As Barrie admits to reading the latter before selling them second-hand, he would have seen that distinction employed over and again by his professor, most notably as a means of categorising novelists in *British Novelists and their Style* and philosophers in *Recent British Philosophy*. In the former, he explains the difference clearly:

The question with the Realist artist with respect to what he conceives is "How would this actually be in nature?" the question with the Ideal artist is "What can be made out of this? With what human conclusions, ends, and aspirations can it be imaginatively interwoven?" (Masson 1859: 250)

Special attention should be paid to the word "interwoven". The highest kind of writing for Masson as for Barrie combines imitation and imagination. Behind Masson's definition of these two aims lies a rather naïve view of his major model, Aristotle. In both his lectures and in his early essay, "Theories of Poetry", the imitative side of Aristotle's argument is highlighted. In the latter he uses a long quotation from the opening section of the *Poetics* (where only first principles are being established) to highlight the different kinds of representation practised from Homer's time (Aristotle 1984: 2: 2316). In *Poetics* IX, however, the Greek philosopher had gone on to distinguish the poet's range from the simple, representational role of the historian (Aristotle 1984: 2: 2323). While the former only describes "the thing that has been", the poet may also describe "a thing that might be" In that imaginative role he can claim to be more "philosophic" and "universal" than his rival. Therefore, when Masson claims that "Aristotle makes the *essence* of poetry to consist in its being imitative and truthful", he is correct (Masson 1856: 410 [my italics]). But the fuller context of the *Poetics* and the opening arguments of the *Rhetoric* grant a wider "potential" range of coverage to the poet than the historian.

Pedagogically, this simplification of Aristotle's remit, has an advantage. It allows Masson to credit English Renaissance writers, in particular Francis Bacon, with extending the writer's imaginative remit: "we haven't got far beyond the antithesis suggested by what Aristotle said about it two thousand years ago on the one hand, and what Bacon advanced two hundred and fifty years ago on the other" (Masson 1856: 410). De Quincey, whose works Masson was editing, is also drawn in as an idealistic and imaginative counterpart to Aristotle. Authors are then evaluated according to their ability to harmonise these two strains effectively. That Barrie the youthful critic followed this method has already been illustrated in his discussions of Skelton and Nash.

Bacon's broad description of the word "Poetry" also met with Masson's approval. In *The Advancement of Human Learning* the Renaissance philosopher had argued that if history is definitively memorial and philosophy definitively rational, then *all* fiction is definitively imaginative (Masson 1856: 41–17). This he applies to the major kinds of writing – lyrical, dramatic and narrative – in his usual hierarchically gradated manner. In these terms prose is less highly regarded than verse because it is a medium more adapted to the real than the ideal: "It may be that the representation of social reality is, on the whole, the proper business of the Novel". This does not mean, however, that idealism should be banned from it entirely: "even in the representation of social reality the spirit may be that of the far-surveying and the sublime" (Masson 1859: 308). Unfortunately, he laments, most modern novelists forget the fanciful and thoughtful part of their remit. limiting themselves to "the regions of the comic, and the historically complex, the didactic and the immediately practical" (86).

From that base, he develops an approach which comprehends Realism but favours Idealism. This overtly artificial view of fiction allows Masson to anticipate Henri Bergson's view that comedy is for those who think, tragedy for those who feel. Because comedy deals in types or humours it is naturally designed to represent kinds and ideas. In this sense, Masson argues, most of Dickens's characters only exist conceptually – "There never was a Mr Micawber in nature, exactly as he appears in the pages of Dickens, but Micawberism pervades nature through and through" (Masson 1859: 251). Cervantes too is celebrated because of his "more truly poetic genius" (Masson 1859: 4). Thackeray, because he follows the satiric method but does so more realistically, joins this hierarchy at a lower level. Dickens' and Cervantes' high position in Barrie's critical hierarchy was noted earlier. Soon Masson would add Shakespeare as both their dramatic equivalent and the supreme example of the method. He, above all, could interweave realism and idealism seamlessly in both comic and highly serious modes (Barrie 1941: 134, 137).

The influence of Dickens, Thackeray, Renaissance drama and Shakespeare in particular can be traced throughout Barrie's prose and drama. That these authors and the idealistic brand of realism they represent are first highlighted in Masson's teaching is a crucial piece of evidence. As Shakespeare in particular will remain Barrie's supreme dramatic idol, influencing the forms he chooses and the range of techniques he employs, I shall return to his case later.

As so much theoretical ground is shared by professor and student and so little coincides with the ideas and the methodology of Oedipal-Kailyard analysis two more questions arise at this stage. Are Barrie and those critics separated at the most fundamental level by the very dialectical methods they employ? And if so, would Barrie have defined terms such as sentiment, whimsy and romance in the same pejorative way?

In fact, one of the most important results of research into Barrie's university education is that the simple antithetical dialectic of the critical myth is nowhere practised either by Masson or indeed within the Edinburgh M.A. Both instead foster an inclusive, differentiated mode of argument modelled on the classical topos, *varius sis sed tamen idem*. An imaginative writer may, therefore, be at once fanciful *and* naturalistic, sentimental *and* cerebral, comic *and* serious, depending on the defined terms of reference. Structurally, this is because the course was organised on Christian Humanist assumptions. It is particularly noticeable that it is Bishop Berkeley rather than Locke or Hume who dominates the approach of Barrie's favourite teachers, Masson and Campbell Fraser. Indeed, Fraser was an ordained Church of Scotland minister while Masson admits that "recognition of Christianity as the supreme principle" underlies his thinking (Masson 1859: 277).

The Christian element within that formula introduced another reason for an inclusive dialectics. Because the Christian God is a God of all being, all goodness and all knowledge, who exists beyond time yet contains humanity within His essence, there can be no such thing, absolutely, as a false way to truth. As Boethius argued, only our necessarily imperfect understanding of the interrelationship between major routes and tempting byways leads us astray.

The Humanist element provides the sympathetic educational model on which the Edinburgh M.A. was overtly modelled – that is, the hierarchically arranged and harmoniously integrated structure of the Seven Liberal Arts. Barrie's lecture notes show how lecturers regularly opened their courses by relating their specialisation's unique contribution to that overarching scheme. Thus the difference between the scientific *quadrivium* and the humane *trivium* is economically explained by Professor Calderwood at the start of the moral philosophy lectures Barrie attended in 1880: "Science may be defined in brief as that which teaches us to know, Art as that which teaches us to do" (*ADV* 6655: f.2v). A year later in Higher Logic, Professor Campbell Fraser would ask "In what are Mathematics and Logic akin and in what do they differ? Does one not enhance the other?" Barrie in a side-note writes, "This subject worthy further consideration" (*ADV* 6656: f.46v). Masson for his part opened his Rhetoric lectures with comment, "It is to Greek intellect that credit must be given of minutely naming and classifying the modes of living speech" (*ADV* 6652: 57).

The dialectical evidence not only suggests another troublesome gap between the way the critical myth is formulated and Barrie's practice, but also the importance it lays on accurate definitions opens up another area of unacknowledged diversity. Barthes noted that mythical analysis omitted the evidence of the past. And certainly sentiment, whimsy and romance, those characteristics which are commonly used to describe and condemn Barrie's art to-day, are all used in their modern sense. As Masson and Barrie defined them all more broadly and more positively their usage in Victorian critical debate has also to be considered.

For Blake, sentiment is unpatriotic, escapist and anathema to the practical Scot. Masson, however, first defines the word in a rhetorical context. As part of Aristotelian catharsis, sentiment is necessary for the evocation of pity within the art of imaginative persuasion. Sentimentality as the creation through imagination of "noble ideas" is also considered and it is here that the "sentimental" within the Scottish Enlightenment is defined. Hume and other Scottish philosophers may confirm ideas about the "rational" Scot. But that is not the whole story. In terms of literary genius, Sentiment becomes true sign of national genius. Burns, Scott and Carlyle confirm this by "drawing their essential inspiration from the sentimental depths of the Scottish character" (Masson 1856: 391–408 [396]).

Masson not only turns Blake's view of sentimentality on its head by offering a different critical perspective, he also questions its validity philosophically and politically. He accepted that "Part of every Scotchman's outfit in life is, or used to be, his Scotticism" (Masson 1859: 169). What he did not accept was an exclusive pursuit of that goal. In "The Scottish Influence in British Literature" he argues that "the sentiment [sic] of nationality is essentially negative". Those who embrace it cease to aspire to "the intellectually extreme" where "the highest genius" alone resides (Masson 1856: 398).

As a result, while he and Blake both view Walter Scott as falling just short of genius, they do so for exactly opposite reasons. Blake sees Scott's strength lying in his patriotism. His weakness is his choice of the unrealistic, Romance form. For Masson, the form is ideal (in more senses than one) but Scott is too much of a patriot and realist to make full use of it: "the only Scottish thing that Scott had not in him was Scotch metaphysics" (Masson 1859: 201). Once more the critical views of Masson and Barrie are radically opposed to those which sustain the Kailyard account.

Masson provides a similarly positive and inclusive model for "whimsicality" and "fancy" in this account. The words "whim" and "whimsical" are not seen as signs of escapism but related to the greater imaginative power enjoyed by the poet over historian and philosopher. It is here and in his earlier article, "Theories of Poetry", that the alliance between Aristotle and Francis Bacon, detected later in his lectures, is first detected. For Masson, Aristotle may suggest poetry's potential remit but his bias is realistic. For an understanding of "That mighty licence in the fantastic, that right of whimsy", Bacon's *Advancement of Human Learning* (one of Barrie's set texts) has to be studied as well (Masson 1856: 419). From these foundations he moves to the Romantic period, allying himself not only with De Quincey but with Wordsworth's positive views on fancy, invention and imagination in *The Prelude* and Coleridge's in *Biographia Literaria*. All of these writers see these qualities as extending the writer's range and allowing him to be more profound than the historian. The terms they employ are never employed in the context of irresponsible escapism favoured by George Blake.

Another chasm separates Blake from Masson and Barrie's definition of Romance. For the former, the term referred to a literary kind which was weakly retrospective and failed to tackle the real problems of the day. Masson traces that form back to its roots in classical and renaissance literature. Only then does he provide a careful definition of the form. Romance is "a fictitious narrative in prose or verse, the interest of which turns upon marvellous and uncommon incidents". It reached its poetic heights in the Renaissance with Sidney and Spenser. Unfortunately, to-day the historical context has been forgotten and so "Our wretched modern criticism" demands direct depiction of "human interest" and condemns the pastoral form "as an extinct form by filling our minds with an absurd conception of it" (Masson 1859: 26, 67, 68).

Having anticipating the sophistries of realistic assessment employed by Blake, Masson warns that such writing must be assessed according to the artificial, exemplary criteria which define it. These include

the voluntary and avowed transference of the poet himself into a kind of existence which, as being one of the few elementary conditions was therefore the best suited for certain varieties of that exercise of pure phantasy in which the poet delights. (Masson 1859: 68)

For him, the finest kind of Romance begins with a simplified vision of today's problems. It then returns to a more primitive state not to avoid them but to re-examine them in their fullest potentiality against an artificially simplified background. Actual and ideal, historical and metaphysical can be obliquely tackled in this, exemplary, way.

A more eloquent condemnation of Blake's critical method could not be imagined. The different premises from which Masson and his student work produce a different evaluative hierarchy. They also elevate the very authors who are lowered in the league tables of realism. A comparative view of Dickens illustrates this clearly. Masson deplores the sociological realism which dominates contemporary British prose. On these grounds, Dickens is raised above his rivals. His invention of comic types within a world "of ideal phantasy" fills the gap most of the others leave (Masson 1859: 251). Blake, starting from exactly the opposite premise that the novel *should* be realistic uses the same evidence to condemn him.

It was noted that Masson places Shakespeare highest in his league tables of literary excellence. His works are also hierarchically evaluated. The comic romances, which he divides into different categories, are highly regarded. Masson welcomes *As You Like It* and *A Midsummer Night's Dream* because they set the norms of real and imagined worlds against each other. The incongruity implicit in setting artisan, pastoral, noble and divine societies together on the stage not only evokes laughter but offers new insights into the way we view the world. Masson's highest praise is, however, reserved or another kind of Romance. For him the late Shakespearean Romances – *The Tempest, A Winter's Tale and Cymbeline* – form the apex of all artistry. They enter the all-important world beyond time, posing those ultimate questions which, he fears, most Scottish authors avoid. These assessments are of particular importance for Barrie as he would adapt that form for his most ambitious novels and plays.

Masson's reasons for granting this author and these plays the highest position of all are clearly presented. He begins his case with his usual test question: "Do realism and idealism co-exist?" In Shakespeare's case the answer is, "Always". At this level of excellence, another question follows. "Do they ever quintessentially merge?" And it is here that only the bard's late Romances pass muster. In the lectures which Barrie attended and Rosemary Masson later printed as *Shakespeare Personally*, he explains why this is so. Only in *The Tempest, A Winter's Tale* and *Cymbeline* do Realism and Idealism interplay across the entire allegorical spectrum. "Never was a world so pictorially real, so visually distinct as that of Shakespeare's plays". It is that accuracy, "the result of lifelong experience", which becomes the vehicle for his "final mood of masterly and contemplative calmness". "That intensely real world with that interpretation of the mysterious as forming part of it" has then to be examined imaginatively. To do so Shakespeare returns to earlier days as these provide a simpler, more essential background. This "real world [...] Shakespeare throws back [...] with ease and delight to any point of past time whether only a generation before himself or in extreme antiquity" (Masson 1914: 134, 155, 137).

If Shakespeare and *The Tempest* are established as the highest model for genius in Masson's lectures, the means of achieving these heights is also clearly outlined. The lectures, whose major headings are often italicised in the book, depict him as a rustic outsider who is also a workaholic, a pragmatist, shy of publicity but with his own literary theory clearly established (Masson 1914: 19–27, 37, 59). Widely read, the Bard of Avon was anxious by that means to rise above earlier self-confession and "occurrence literature" (the journalism of his own day) so that his "deepest moods and musings" might later be revealed (Masson 1914: 60, 66). Barrie, therefore, came from Kirriemuir as an already established journalist and self-confessed fame-seeker only to find one of the world's most renowned critics presenting a view of Shakespeare which was uncannily close to his own position.

But this was not all. Masson's view of Shakespeare was at once academic and progressive. By rejecting Jonson's view of his rustic rival as a poor scholar and instead raising him to a level of academic self-consciousness which allowed him to emerge as a worthy critical opponent he allowed Barrie to think he too might take the way of learning to fame (Masson 1914: 35–6). The different stages were clearly charted. By dividing Shakespeare's literary life into different periods and associating each with different literary modes the professor presented a clear overall picture of an ambitiously self-conscious Warwickshire outsider intent on scaling the heights of literary achievement by testing himself out on an ascending scale of difficulty. It is this modal ascent which leads Masson to his conclusion that the Romances represent the zenith of Shakespeare's achievement. Theoretically, they mirror the mysterious merging, beyond time, of real into ideal as dictated by the Christian belief in God who contains all being. Chronologically they are placed last, at the end of a linear ascent which tested itself on history and comedy and then tragedy but now finds its fullest fulfilment (Masson 1914: 75, 105). Chapters Three and Four will demonstrate how Barrie followed that model, testing his own literary potential against a range of different literary kinds.

Barrie as Academic II: Freud, Berkeley and Campbell Fraser

If Masson is the major academic influence on Barrie's literary theory, the contribution of one of his colleagues to his views on psychology and personality are also of relevance. Alexander Campbell Fraser emerges in *An Edinburgh Eleven* as one of Barrie's favourite lecturers. That he also taught one of the first psychology courses in a British University is also curiously overlooked by Freudian critics. It can, however, be proved that Fraser's teachings supported both the histrionic view of personality sustained by Barrie himself *and* the Kirriemuir author's belief that any movement from prose to drama should highlight the aural and visual elements which the latter form uniquely encouraged.

The route to these conclusions involves re-consideration of the Freudian side of the critical myth. This is most thoroughly argued by Harry Geduld, a highly reputable comparative critic whose only real fault, in Barrie's case, lies in his adopting the Freudian premise so loyally throughout. Geduld's psychological account of Barrie's work also carries Blake's simplifying, generalising and de-historicising methods beyond the latter's early prose focus. For him the Oedipal evidence can be traced in all of Barrie's work.

His argument assumes that Freud's Oedipal arguments can be taken as truth. It is here that the first major simplification of the mythic method shows itself. De-historicisation is also necessary to make his claims seem watertight. Unquestioning acceptance of Freudian theory involves ignoring the interim rise of clinical psychiatry and the many questions it has raised. This kind of opposition has, most recently, been expressed in *Le livre noir de la psychoanalyse* (Meyer ed. 2005). In that study, forty experts from ten countries explain why they have moved on from his theories. This is, however, only the latest expression of severe discontent as the earlier works of Eysenck and Wilson reveal (Eysenck and Wilson 1973; Eysenck 1985).

Secondly, those elements of his work which are especially relevant to Barrie – his theories on sexuality and childhood development – have recently come under particular scrutiny. (See Valentine 1942; Hall 1953; Borger and Cioffi 1970; Foulkes 1982; Eysenck 1985). This is in part because sexual problems and phobias were, for a long time, shrouded by taboos. When clinical studies based on large control groups and benefiting from increased medical knowledge did appear they formed a strong challenge to both his premises and conclusions. They also uncomfortably highlighted the fact that his "control group" was limited to his own family. C.W. Valentine, who imitated the "family" method by observing his own concluded that it was as idiosyncratic as it was narrow: "I failed to find any evidence for either the Oedipus complex or early sexual desires in my own five children" (cited in Eysenck 1985: 97).

Eysenck uses this example as part of two lengthy chapters, challenging the security of Freudian arguments (Eysenck 1985: 92–114). Later discontent with the Oedipal case has been such that most recent editions of British and American psychological encyclopaedias do not even include it in their Index or Contents. Yet, many literary critics who would feel duty bound to take account of more recent research findings within their own discipline seem content to deny the same rigour to their colleagues in psychiatry. The second revolt against Freud is contained in more narrowly based symptomatic studies such as Gregoire and Pryor's *Impotence: An Integrated Approach to Clinical Practice* (1993). This prefers an account which balances organic with psychological and interactive causes. Even the dwindling band of Freudian sympathisers has moved beyond the simple Oedipal line (see Storr 1989: 33–39; Kline 1973). As a result, modern psychiatric studies of *Peter Pan* usually offer a more discriminating view of Barrie's sexuality than that preserved in most literary histories (see Karpe 1955: 104–10; Meisel 1977: 545–64). The de-historicising power of myth is therefore as obvious in the psychiatric area as in the literary. Certain premises must be frozen in time, foreclosed to examination even in the most extreme of cases.

It is not only a question of excluding later psychiatric inter-pretations from consideration; the popular critical view takes another leap of faith when it assumes that Barrie's early childhood provides a perfect practical model for Oedipal theory. In fact, the experiences of the young Barrie are not so easily translated into Oedipal symptoms as is usually assumed. Far from seeking out older women, the young Barrie was attracted to young actresses. Far from cherishing home and his mother's company, he learned independence at an early age. From the age of eight he spent nearly three years in Glasgow at the Academy, living with his eldest brother who taught there. A brief time at Kirriemuir and Forfar Academy saw him off once more. His senior secondary days were spent at Dumfries Academy enjoying what he would describe as "the happiest days of his life" in later speeches and confirm in his autobiography (Barrie 1895: Chapter 11; 1938: 77). Independence and an obsession with literature characterise this individual. Only the brief references to his mother mourning over David and his University homesickness remain and of these one has now been canonically and the other evidentially questioned. Nottingham and London independence followed and with them acceptance of the challenge failed by Scotland's most renowned bard, Robert Burns – to leave home and earn your living by writing alone.

Nor does the popular belief that he saw his mother as a broken and melancholic figure after the untimely death of his brother, David, stand up. Replying to a letter of sympathy on Mrs Barrie's death from Sir Thomas Wemyss Reid, Barrie regrets Margaret Ogilvy's death but not her life. Indeed, not for the first time, he finds his major sympathies turning to Jane Anne:

I feel most the pain of losing my sister, who had been in fair health until she was so suddenly struck down while my mother dies full of years and honour. There cannot be very many such daughters as my sister was. (*BVS* A3: 17 September 1895)

In the face of all this evidence it is necessary to explore alternative views of his mother's influence on him personally and artistically.

Barrie as Academic III: Fraser, Masson and *An Edinburgh Eleven.*

Fraser's influence is not confined to his views on personality although these *were* welcome to Barrie because of his own early problems of self-definition. Masson's translation of this model into positive artistic terms was also welcomed as it derived from similar convictions. But it

is the *degree* to which Fraser and Masson shared each other's opinions, highlighted similar issues and even used the same sources which
is of prime importance. With two Christian Darwinians singing from
the same literary and psychological hymn-sheet in order to prioritise
the very kind of imaginative, idealistic art their young student aspired
to produce it is little wonder that they exerted a lasting influence on
his approach to life and art.

The harmonious links between these academics can first be
detected in the curriculum. Barrie studied Logic and Metaphysics in
the Winter term of 1880 and Rhetoric and Belles Lettres in 1881. This
meant that Fraser's views immediately preceded Masson's and did so
within an Ordinary M.A. course which itself was modelled on the
interlinked principles of the seven liberal arts with individual professors regularly defining the place of their discipline within the classical
trivium and *quadrivium*.

Personal evidence draws the two men even closer. Rhetoric and
Belles Lettres was taught within the Philosophy Department. David
Masson's application, therefore, recommended itself to the appointment committee in 1865 because he had philosophical as well as
literary credentials to his name. And on that committee as successor to
Sir William Hamilton as professor of Logic and Metaphysics since
1856, sat Campbell Fraser. An ordained minister, he found a kindred
spirit in Masson. Here was another committed Christian who faced
Darwin's discoveries honestly and shared his own interests in the
works of Berkeley and Bacon particularly.

Against this background the many similarities between their
courses make sense. Both lecturers start from an Aristotelian base but
prefer overtly Christian philosophers such as Berkeley to the more
radical voices of Locke and Hume. If this establishes the general background to their intellectual alliance, a more detailed assessment of
Fraser's lecturing techniques will help to explain both the appeal he
had for Barrie and why so many of his central ideas are later echoed
by Masson.

Fraser's lecturing style is wittily presented in Barrie's retrospective account of his University teachers. The respect he shows them
and the enthusiasm with which he follows his preferred courses is well
described in *An Edinburgh Eleven*. It also offers a happier and more
positive account of Barrie's academic journey than that conveyed by
the troubled first year notebook on which Mackail relies.

That Fraser's delivery of his psychology lectures were as much characterised by questions as conclusions could be put down to the new discipline he is professing. This he admits at the start of the course.

The name Psychology, tho' now in common use was introduced into this country only some thirty or forty years ago [...] Psychology may be defined as the science of mind on soul manifested directly or indirectly in self-conscious life" (*ADV* 6650: f.4).

Fraser's enactment of difficulty and doubt is not confined to his treatment of psychology. His method in all his lectures is to enact personal doubt in order to encourage self-questioning in his students. In *An Edinburgh Eleven*, Barrie graphically mirrors the atmosphere created:

"Do I exist," he said thoughtfully, "strictly so-called?" The students (if it was the beginning of the session) looked a little startled. This was a matter that had not previously disturbed them. Still, if the Professor was in doubt, there must be something in it. He began to argue it out, and an uncomfortable silence held the room in awe. If he did not exist, the chances were that they did not exist either. It was thus a personal question. (Barrie 1889b: 64–65)

That this was a troublesome concept for most is also confirmed:

Fraser was rather a hazardous cure for weak intellects. Young men whose anchor had been certainty of themselves went into that class floating buoyantly on the sea of facts, and came out all adrift – on the sea of theory – in an open boat – rudderless – one oar – the boat scuttled. How could they think there was any chance for them, when the Professor was not even sure of himself? I see him rising in a daze from his chair and putting his hands through his hair. "Do I exist?" he said thoughtfully, "strictly so-called?" (Barrie 1889b: 64).

When Fraser then turns to his class and asks "How many states of mind have you gone through within the past half hour?" another of Barrie's personality traits, that of the ever-changing mind is explained. He even adds one of his side notes at this point – "This subject is worthy [of] further study" (*ADV* 6656: f.16r). In Barrie's early prose, it is this self-absorbed artistic, ever-changing figure who will dominate rather than Barrie the dilettante, mother-worshipper will appear and re-appear, reaching its fullest fictional form in Sentimental Tommy and his sad appeal to Grizel, "'It's easy to you [Grizel] that has just one mind', he retorted with spirit, 'but if you had as many minds as I have'" (Barrie 1896b: 380).

The form of these notes confirms Barrie's involvement in the questions Fraser posed. They contain more parenthetic personal questions than any of the others. In *An Edinburgh Eleven*, he calls attention to this. When preparing to write is surprised to find that set of notes "scribbled over with posers in my handwriting about dualism and primary realities" (67).

Barrie as Academic IV: Bishop Berkeley Francis Bacon and Thomas Reid

The evidence so far has explained Barrie's enthusiasm for the course and its influence on his personality. It has not accounted for the extremely close similarity between the dialectical methods employed by Fraser and Masson. Nor has it explained why so many topics and sources introduced philosophically by Fraser in the Barrie's third year were rhetorically re-contemplated by Masson twelve months later.

Another quotation from *An Edinburgh Eleven* introduces the dialectical part of the argument. "Fraser's great work is his edition of Berkeley", Barrie notes. "It was a labour of love, that should live after him. He has two Berkeleys, the large one and the little one, and, to do him justice, it was the little one he advised us to consult" (Barrie 1889b: 66). Fraser was well aware of the complex ideas he was introducing and so his student anthology, which contains Part 1 of *The Principles of Human Knowledge*, as well as the *Essay toward a New Theory of Vision* and *Divine Visual Language: A Dialogue* sensibly concentrates on the major lines in Berkeley's thought. This journey into doubt begins by removing the rational security of Descartes' "cogito ergo sum" (I think therefore I am). Instead the student has to look within himself. This personalising stage "ego sum cogitans" (I am a thinking being) in turn gives way to Berkeley's central tenet – "esse est percipi". The external world, conceptually *and* actually, only exists in our mind and senses.

Fraser may have been a puzzling lecturer but in the successive Introductions to his "shorter" Berkeley, he shows his awareness that he is addressing students rather than his peers. In the *Selections* of 1879, the set text when Barrie took the course the Introduction concentrates on the value this "retreat to the senses" may have for student enquiry. Within his own discipline, the book is presented as "a good

companion for a student of philosophy at an early stage in his career"
(Berkeley 1879: ix). But he also places psychology within the wider,
interlinked pattern of trivium and quadrivium as mirrored in the Ordinary M.A.:

It may be used by the student as aids to reflective analysis on various subjects in Psychology among others: – the five Senses; the development of immediate *Perception
through Suggestion*; the nature and origin of *rational Necessity in the mathematical
sciences*; *the meaning of Law in Nature*, with the ground or origin of our expectations
of its consistency in the perception of individual things and in forming physical
knowledge, the *relation between Sense and Will or moral agency;* Suggestion or
suggested expectation as *the ultimate solution* of human knowledge or at least as a
factor in its formation and development. (Berkeley 1879: 149)

He goes on to explain that Berkeley is a good starting focus because
he "presents subtle thoughts in graceful language", offers a case for
theism against materialism and is a key figure in the history of modern
philosophy. Consequently, when he comes to the central question of
perception, he offers a much clearer, personal and practical account
than that presented in his "larger" Berkeley or indeed in the more
challenging style of his lectures.

When he [Berkeley] reflected upon our knowledge of the things actually presented to
our senses [...] and which are commonly called Matter, he could not find in them any
archetype of Locke's abstract idea of substance [...] Instead, he found sights and
touches and sounds and tastes and smells. He found also a self, percipient or
conscious of these sights and sounds and tastes and smells. (Berkeley 1879: xxvi)

The problem of vision may be central in the discussion but its interrelationship in space with touch and hearing, is defined in "useful"
terms before his students are introduced to the more complex,
theoretical implications of "esse est percepi".

Both the range contemplated in Fraser's "useful" account of
psychology's place among the disciplines *and* the method to be
employed for exploring it anticipate Masson's critical guidelines and
Barrie's practice. For Berkeley, psychology is the starting point for a
study of "truth", which comprehends all the major disciplines. The
italicised sections of the quotation which describes that range make
this clear. His own course becomes an emblem of that movement as it
moves from psychology to logic and metaphysics but the other relevant courses in the Ordinary M.A. – Maths, Natural Philosophy and

Moral Philosophy – are also included. Exactly the same claim will be made on behalf of rhetoric by Masson. Its laws lie at the foot of a similar interlinked chain whose ultimate aim is the exploration of those final mysteries which surround mankind. The same range, the same foundations and the same reasons have been traced in Barrie's academic writings. Berkeley, in *De Motu* 43, had after all condemned the mythic approach out of hand "To understand things in isolation rather than as interrelated" he observed "is a chimera" (see Ardley 1965: 18).

The second quotation is equally important. If Fraser has been seen to share the same interlinked dialectic method as Masson – he now offers his own psychological version of those hierarchical classifications which the professor of rhetoric loved so much. Where Masson graded disciplines, forms and authors in this manner, Fraser grades human modes of perception from the senses upwards. This is because he shares Berkeley's contention that there is no objective reality only different individual perceptions of the world beyond self.

That Masson shared these views is evident in his own approving account of the bishop's thesis. "Denying that the mind had any rights to pursue its sensations beyond its own walls, or to attribute them to any real external world of matter" necessarily transfers philosophical attention from the nature of the perceived to the nature of the perceiver (Masson 1865: 58). Barrie's notes confirm that he is following Fraser's arguments very closely. He sees the magnitude of the change the professor is suggesting: "Is not then our own conscious state or act of perceiving more dependent on us and consequently surer for us than anything we perceive outside us" he asks (ADV 6650: 2). He understands the "darkness" of a vision which first of all uses the human personality as its medium. "We find ourselves to be no pure spirits but rather spirit-minds, conscious persons connected with organised bodies" (ADV 6650: 20). He reminds himself of the positive, of the flawed power of the senses. "Seeing is an instance. It must be kept well in mind, it is only our having a self-conscious mental experience that produces these manifestations" (ADV 6650: 2) If this looks forward to Barrie's own emphasis on the senses in his theatrical writing, Fraser's account of reason, memory and the imagination, at once looks backwards to Bacon and forward to Masson's lectures on the same topic.

Like Bacon, Fraser asks which division of the Human Intellect can fill that gap. "But there would seem still to be some missing link in our division of the Human Intellect creative modes of perception", Barrie notes (MS 6650: f.25r). On the dual authority of Bacon with Berkeley, Fraser finds the first answer in memory, "without which our knowledge would be practically nil". Using Bacon's analysis of the different kinds of imagination in his essay "On Truth" he re-defines that faculty more precisely as the "needed medium between elaboration and sense perception" and "the power of mentally representing in absence what has been actually present" (ADV 6656: 25).

Masson's interest in Bacon's theory of the imagination has already been mentioned. In his lectures he uses the Renaissance thinker (in alliance with De Quincey, Hazlitt and Ruskin) to counter the Victorian tendency to prefer realistic art. His counter-case for imaginative contemplation of the ideal not only uses Bacon, it also echoes Berkeley. If both the abstract (meaningfully) and the concrete (spatially) are lacking, he asks, which intellectual faculty can aid the senses in bridging it? Like Fraser, and on the same grounds, he advocates imagination built from memory's foundation for that key role. In his lectures he sums up the faculty's "perceptive" importance memorably as "The power of mentally representing in absence what has been actually present is a needed medium" (ADV 6652: 25–26).

In his earlier article, "Theories of Poetry", Masson had offered a wide-ranging account of the different *kinds* of imagination available to the poet. Depending on the different perspectives from which that faculty's powers and limitations may be evaluated, it can be seen variously as "the power of intellectually producing a new, artificial concrete", as "a kind of allegory of the whole state of his mental being at the time" and "a piece of concrete taken from the inanimate world [and] wedded to a piece of concrete taken from the actual world" (Masson 1856: 421, 436, 441). Given that the bias of these ideas towards self-analysis and fanciful composition harmonised with Barrie's own vision of life and art and given that the origins and broad outlines of the case were confirmed powerfully and repetitively by Fraser and Masson, it is little surprise that they remained with him throughout his life. That "Memories and Fancies" is the sub-title of *The Greenwood Hat* is no accident. Rather it is a retrospective vote of confidence in those who initiated his interests in literary theory and the direction in which they channelled his thoughts.

These ideas continue to influence their approach when the different levels of the verbal building are drawn into the equation. The necessary relationship between surface story (*sensus*) and the ideas conveyed (*sententia*) has been discussed earlier. But beneath both lay the verbal medium (*littera*) and so, necessarily, both professors turn their attention to the strengths and weaknesses of language as a means of representing that inner world of the senses which has now become the focus of their philosophical attention. Masson's lectures with their long introduction on language forms and Fraser's consistent advocacy of Berkeley's "graceful and transparent language" as the basis for his precise thinking (Fraser 1878: ix) are only the most obvious signs of this concern. That Barrie will work with Roget at his side and create, in *Sentimental Tommy*, a characters obsessed by the need to find the *exact* word to express his meaning provides confirmation of another kind.

Part of Berkeley's appeal, he admits, stems from the clarity of his style – "Berkeley wrote perfect English. I am not sure that any one has written such English since" (Barrie 1889b: 67). Behind this positive praise, however, lies the darker view of language's ultimate inadequacy which Bacon described in Biblical terms. After Babel, human perception itself became dark and verbal confusion reigned. Absolute linguistic pessimism, however, went hand in hand with contingent optimism. The more refined your linguistic system, the more varied its word forms, the narrower the gap between sign and signified becomes. And so Bacon became involved in that quest for a "Universal Language" which later attracted Lodovick, Urquhart and others.

Berkeley begins from similarly pessimistic premises. Words, while always inadequate, are especially so when it comes to expressing abstractions. Or as Barrie's notes have it, "The invisible, intangible contents of conscience (such as joy, pain etc.) refuse to connect themselves as steadily with words as external objects do. The words of the philosopher are particularly liable to ambiguity" (ADV 66656: f.16r). As no one "will deny that there is an intellectual superiority in examinations of mind which is not to be found in the examination of external objects" (ADV MS6656: f.22v), linguistic darkness exists at the highest level of perception. Yet Berkeley, like Bacon, counterbalances this by striving to write as carefully and accurately as possible.

As lay preacher and ordained minister respectively, both Masson and Fraser shared these views. Masson's hierarchical classifications have already been shown to deny genius to any writer who does not seek ultimate truths beyond time. That weakness had condemned Scott. That strength had placed *The Tempest* and *A Winter's Tale* at the zenith of the Shakespearean canon. Fraser offers a different kind of proof when he uses Bacon's "Of Truth" and *Novum Organum* to illustrate the problems facing the Christian philosopher in the late nineteenth century. The first of these texts is used in his ninth lecture to explain the dark implications of the Fall for theories of perception. Fraser agrees with his source that we now exist "in a corrupt state of natural law and love" (ADV 6656: 6). Those human faculties which are the means of perceiving this world and seeking out the next are therefore fatally flawed. Add the apparently antagonistic metaphysical implications of Darwinism to this dilemma and there are surely grounds for giving up any search for understanding completely.

Fraser, however, had ended his eighth lecture on a more positive note. Difficulties do exist but "Who will deny that there is an intellectual superiority in examinations of mind which is not to be found in the examination of external; objects?" Lecture nine then links this comment to an honest account of the limitations within which that search operates. "The love of truth for its own sake must ever be one of the greatest ends for which man can strive and philosophy and philosophy is the means by which that end might be approached" (8). It is in this context that Bacon's gradated account of topical range is introduced. "Civill Businesse" is a proper area of concern but so too is "Theologicall and Philo[sophicall] Truth" (8). In lecture ten, Fraser will move on to Bacon's *Novum Organum* but only after defining the philosophy's aims in suitably "doubtful" terms:

Philosophy has to be called the art of doubting well. It assumes that our intellectual inheritance of beliefs largely consist of errors and prejudices (which are quite different things). New honest thoroughgoing criticism of any belief implies on the part of the examiner that he at least suspend judgment until his examination is over. (28)

That Fraser uses his set texts and favoured sources as a vehicle for explaining his own "professed" views was an essential part of the Scottish M.A. As individual professors were encouraged to present their personal views and to that end gave all the lectures in the course the setting of texts which supported their views was the norm rather than breadth of coverage. Certainly, that was Fraser's method as his choice of Thomas Reid's *Essays on the Intellectual Powers of Man* as the only set text beside apart from Berkeley illustrates.

The closeness of the links connecting Reid to Fraser, Masson, Berkeley and Bacon can be briefly demonstrated. In his Preface to his *Essays*, the Scottish leader of the "common sense" movement made clear that he too started from the premise that our own sensual and intellectual perceptions were the mean and ends of knowledge – "Body and mind are the only kinds of being of which we can have any conception". From that position, he too looked at the power and limitations of words and questioned the value of reason – "we are fallible in all our judgments and in all our reasonings". His division of the powers of mind with its stress on the compensatory power of the imagination is another link with Berkeley and Fraser as is his insistence that the ultimate mysteries of life are explicable in Christian terms but not in rational terms alone – "But although the existence of the Deity be necessary, I apprehend we can only deduce it from contingent truths" (Reid 1853: VI: 489; 420).

In that sense, Reid offers yet another perspective on the views of art and life propounded philosophically by Fraser, and translated rhetorically by Masson. If one looks at this from the student's point of view, the reinforcing power of all these authorities is even more dramatically uncovered. For Barrie's class, Fraser introduces the range of topics to be covered in 1880. He confesses the difficulty involved and the "doubting" status of philosophy at this time. His own lectures stand at the centre of this challenge. Their earliest sources, he explicitly states, are Aristotle mimetically and Bacon imaginatively. In opting for Berkeley and Reid as set texts, he effectively continues the chronological development of this philosophical movement. In the case of Reid, Barrie's class were faced with an unusually broad set of selections. Usually only Book VI of the *Essays* was set in Sir William Hamilton's 1853 annotated edition. In reading terms, this made Reid a lighter postscript to Berkeley.

Even those students who restricted themselves to the essays set would find written support for the generative scheme outlined in Fraser's lectures. In Essay VI, Reid defines the source of his views on the scientific foundation of philosophical judgment: "Lord Bacon first delineated the only solid foundation on which natural philosophy can be built" (VI: 434). Moving forward he sets himself in opposition to

Locke and Hume; instead he regularly praises Berkeley and prefers his approach (VI: 420–21, 441).

This background prepared Barrie for transition into Masson's class in the following year. Here was a literature professor who began his lecture course with Aristotle and Bacon and from that base advocated original thought and fanciful writing across the entire allegorical range. Here too was a trained philosopher who knew the psychological and metaphysical grounds for advocating this kind of fiction. More specifically, here was a man who had praised Berkeley as "beautifully minded" and had, graphically, defined the perceptual basis of his thought: "[Berkeley denies] that the mind had any rights to pursue its sensations beyond its own walls or to attribute them to any real external world of matter" (Masson 1856: 43). Reid, too, he had covered, identifying the central premise he shared with Berkeley (he also "fell back on [...] the very structure of the mind itself") but also the different bias of attention. For Reid "the supposed equipment of necessary beliefs or elements of knowledge" was of more importance than it was for Berkeley (Masson 1856: 47).

This study of Barrie's training as student, journalist and academic has produced a wide range of evidence some of which is at odds with to-day's popular assumptions about him. His critical awareness rather than subconscious traumas will inform the study of his Victorian prose and verse which follows. Psychologically, the major focus will be on the histrionic personality Barrie attributed to himself rather than the immature, mother-fixated personality imposed on him by others. As an introduction to the method, I shall end this chapter with an alternative analysis, in histrionic terms, of the only two texts which offer a fictive account of the supposed cause of his trauma, his brother's death.

Oedipal evidence: *A Window in Thrums* and *Margaret Ogilvy*

Between 1886 and 1896, the chronological definition of the "Kailyard" period according to George Blake, Barrie wrote over 300 literary and journalistic pieces, excluding reviews. Of these, only two describe the death of his brother. It is only because Blake chooses to represent that period by four works, including those two, that the event seems to occupy so much of Barrie's attention. This extreme canonical reduction confirms the simplifying bias of mythic logic. The generalising tendency of the method also becomes evident when his critical account of the tragic incident is more closely analysed. Blake's his discussions of *A Window in Thrums* and *Margaret Ogilvy*, though only two or three pages long, are the most extended pieces of practical criticism he provides for Barrie.

The order in which these texts are considered is itself interesting. Blake begins with *A Window in Thrums* as this is the earlier work of the two but does not, in this initial account, consider Chapter VI, in which David's death is described, at all. He concludes by admitting that it is difficult to find consistent real life equations in the book because it is "sorry stuff in terms of life" (Blake 1951:73). He is correct here. Fancy does invade memory in *Greenwood Hat* fashion. Margaret Ogilvy becomes nominally Janet Ogilvy but her life-story is given to another character, Jess. It is Jess who mourns the early death of a son, Joey, while admiring the successful career of his younger brother, Jamie. He goes to London and becomes famous but as a barber with no interest in books at all (176, 187). Again another character, this time "Jimsy", rounds off the autobiographical line. He is the ambitious writer who devotes his life to one great poem, which now no one ever reads (95). The dangers of assessing Barrie's fanciful claims to genius in the single-minded manner of Carlyle instead of openly, as the product of Anon, the Imp and M'Connachie seems to be accepted at this point by Blake.

He moves on to *Margaret Ogilvy* and here his Oedipal-Kailyard thesis re-asserts itself. This memoir apparently proves that "Barrie really (sic) wrote [...] out and from his mother" (Blake 1900: 73). As he has not mentioned the earlier version of David's death, he does not need to tackle the fact that it is also a variation on an earlier, *fictive* account of David's death. Only after the more convincing case in the Memoir has been provided does he return to Chapter Six of *A Window in Thrums*. In the interim, that book has undergone a strange transformation. From being "sorry stuff in terms of life", the David episode at least has become a secure basis for direct biographical connections – "Perhaps the acute reader has already guessed the identity of Margaret Ogilvy and Jane Ann Barrie with Jess and Leeby of *A Window in Thrums*" (Blake 1951: 73).

The same reader might instead question the sophistry of his approach before going on to ask whether *Margaret Ogilvy* is so important or reliable a text as he makes out. Originally intended as a prologue to *Sentimental Tommy* it was composed hurriedly (the manuscript shows none of Barrie's usual stylistic corrections) at a time when the Tommy novels occupied most of Barrie's attention. This is reflected in his Notebooks. Preparations for the memoir are not recorded at all. The five Notebooks covering the period from 1892 until 1899 on the other hand contain many suggestions for the Tommy novels (BVS A2/14, A2/18).

In Barrie's own day, critics were not so naïve. One reminded readers that *Margaret Ogilvy* "lives in the borderland between imagination and fact" (*Critic* 26: 377– 8). Another perceptively praised the artistry of the book in terms, which Masson would have appreciated, as a blend of real and ideal. The young author artistically presents "a picture in which every line is ideal yet every touch absolutely true" (*Blackwood's Magazine* 161: 481–33).

If this provides a warning against easily identifying story with facts, biographical research raises further problems. The Oedipal case is centrally based on a supposed trauma caused by his brother's death. In both *A Window in Thrums* and *Margaret Ogilvy*, the reader is led to believe that David died almost immediately after the skating accident. Yet, as David's death certificate confirms, he was taken to hospital and retained there for seven days. Signed by Dr. Bruce Goff on 29 January 1867, it identifies the cause of death as "Inflammation of Brain". The accepted "factual" account is therefore based on an artistic "lie" which Barrie as a good Aristotelian created to increase the pathetic-cathartic impact of his story.

The same Victorian critics were in no doubt that the Tommy novels rather than the early Thrums tales were the place to search for evidence, however obliquely presented, of Barrie in the role of artist as young man. Interestingly one group of modern critics have returned to that belief. I refer to those who include him in broader, gender-based studies of Victorian and Edwardian writers. Humphrey Carpenter and Eve Kosovsky Sedgwick are among those who use these novels to provide alternative, challenging visions of Barrie's sexual identity (Carpenter 1985; Sedgwick 1991). In some ways the fact that these writers are not primarily concerned with Barrie works to their advantage. Unaware of the popular critical preconceptions about him they find the most interesting evidence beyond the kailyard. When they do refer to the "key" texts, it is to echo Jacqueline Rose's position. Carpenter's discussion, for example, begins with a timely warning about *Peter Pan*. Calling it "that terrible masterpiece" and referring to the funeral account in *Margaret Ogilvy* he highlights the dangers of "accepting his account of himself as the literal truth [...] We must be on our guard, therefore, when examining his writings for clues towards the personality behind them. It is all something of a circle" (Carpenter 1985: 171).

His analysis of Barrie's prose is carefully conducted. Moving quickly beyond *Idylls* and *Window*, he finds in *Sentimental Tommy* the clearest evidence of Barrie's artistic and sexual problems. These, he believes, mirror the self-conscious, egoistical, ever-changing personality which introduces *The Greenwood Hat*. He concludes that the only true passion in Barrie's life was not his mother but his art and the power it gave him over other people:

All his sexual energies seem to have been diverted from their usual course into this passionate desire to manipulate other people. He wished to stand above them and pull their strings rather than be on stage alongside them. He was alternately cold, remote, distant, god-like [...] a writer constantly on the look-out for copy. (174)

Carpenter does not deny Barrie's sexual problems but relates them positively to his dramatic strengths. A histrionically defined multi-personality is arguably well suited to theatrical composition. And behind that mask there lurks a darker figure, whose supreme egoism, competitiveness and desire to manipulate are well suited to the age of Darwin and Nietzsche.

Sedgwick also stresses the importance of role-playing and manipulation in her book. She does mention Freud but only as the major facilitator of a view of gender which is based "on the protean mobility of sexual desire and on the potential bisexuality of every human creature" (84). She also opposes the simple binary distinctions on which the Kailyard critics rely. Of Oedipal influences on Barrie she says nothing. Instead, she focuses on ideas of masculinity in the late Victorian period. D.H. Lawrence's early praise and later dismissal of the Tommy novels is cited as an example of this "subtlest, most intimate warfare" as it affected the masculine psyche. Barrie became an uncomfortable ally for Lawrence, she contends, because he "was also interested in the mutilating effects of this masculine civil war on women". She believes Barrie may suffer from homosexual panic although the aggressive artificiality of his writing makes it particularly difficult to know where art ends and biography begins. Unconscious of Masson's critical methodology, she nonetheless applies it to Barrie, finding Tommy to be at once individual and type, real and ideal. To this critical view she adds a sad psychological assessment. Behind "these astonishingly acute and self-hating novels", she finds a sad man who has "crippling moral and psychological defects". Far from believing that these weaknesses doomed him to immaturity and obscurity, however, she joins Carpenter in defining them in histrionically painful terms. For her, therefore, Barrie's personality represents "the very type of the great creative artist" (182, 195).

I believe that *Margaret Ogilvy* does reflects these views. Indeed, if there is a heroine in the Memoir, it seems to me to be Jane Anne. Mrs. Barrie is more realistically presented as Barrie's alter-ego, the source of both the good and bad sides to her son's personality. Barrie's love for her, which is not in doubt, would therefore stem from his recognition that he is truly his mother's son.

Certainly, Margaret is introduced in histrionic and manipulative mode, using her six new chairs as dramatic props to establish herself as living proof of what the work ethic can achieve. She then sees herself in imaginary roles – as a nurse "doctoring a scar" and a queen showing them off "regally". Next they become characters in a play as she enjoys "withdrawing and re-opening the door suddenly to take the six by surprise". She is now producer, director and entire cast (Barrie 1896a: 1–2). Precisely the same abilities will be attributed to Sentimental Tommy and the same desires remembered by Barrie in *The Greenwood Hat*, when recalling his own first play.

The events surrounding David's death also suggest one actor attempting to upstage another. After the funeral, Margaret adopts the part of the heroically pathetic invalid. Her emotive prop is the family christening robe "with its pathetic frills". Just as the chairs became characters in a self-focused drama so the robe "becomes" the dead David. Her emotions also move swiftly from one extreme to another in true sentimental manner. So, when the young James succeeds in making her "laugh suddenly" and calls in his sister to view his success, "the soft face was wet again". Genuine love is here played out against a darker, self-interested, manipulative backcloth. James may have a "crafty way of playing physician". But Margaret's swift movements from one emotional extreme to another guarantee he will lose the ultimately self-centred battle – "Thus I was deprived of some of my glory" (9–11).

Once the possibility of an alternative reading is established another unspoken assumption behind the Oedipal case may be disposed of. So much weight is given to the episode of David's death that one assumes it must be recounted in great detail. In fact the skating episode is recounted in one paragraph while the funeral takes place "offstage". As David's death has also been shown to be inaccurately speeded up in order to achieve a more powerful cathartic effect, the idea of art as Barrie's true ruling passion cannot be easily cast aside.

Chapter Three

Filling the Textual Gaps I: "Kailyard" Prose 1877–90

Filling the research gaps left by Freudian-Kailyard critics has high-lighted the narrow scholarly base on which the critical myth depends. But the narrowness of the textual base on which the Freudian case depends has also been revealed. Factually, only *A Window in Thrums* and *Margaret Ogilvy* directly refer to the supposed trauma of David's death and even their accounts are imaginatively rather than realistically configured. As these short narratives along with *Auld Licht Idylls* are the only early memoirs and tale collections which meet the kailyard premises they have also become the only ones analysed by Blake and his followers. The prose version of *The Little Minister* also meets these premises. It therefore becomes the fourth and last of the early narratives to be analysed by that school. As a more ambitious work with claims to be a well-constructed three volume novel as well as being the only one of Barrie's narratives to be translated into full-length dramatic form it raises different questions and will be discussed along with the play-translation in Chapter Five.

In the immediate context I shall concentrate on those of Barrie's early prose works which precede the publication of *Margaret Ogilvy* and are generally ignored by both Kailyard and Oedipal schools. Filling these textual gaps does, I believe, offer a radically different account of Barrie's art and personality. The works to be discussed are highlighted in the table below:

Prose Works	Theatrical Works
1877: *A Child of Nature*	*Bandalero the Bandit*
1880:	*Bohemia*
1883: *Vagabond Students*	"Caught Napping"
1887: *Better Dead*	
1888: *Auld Licht Idylls; When A Man's Single*	
1889: *The Superfluous Man*; *A Window in Thrums*; *An Edinburgh Eleven*	
1890: *My Lady Nicotine*; *Young Men I have Met*	
1891: *The Little Minister*	*Richard Savage;* "Ibsen's Ghost"
1892:	*Walker, London*; *The Professor's Love Story*
1893:	*Jane Annie*, "Becky Sharp"

The parallel chronological list offers a different kind of contextualisation, reminding us of Barrie's theatrical output at this time. In addition
to establishing the fuller canon, the table offers a new perspective on
the enduring power exerted by George Blake's prose-centred analysis.
When I asked a group of honours students for a brief account of
Barrie's Victorian output, most believed that he began with prose and
later changed to drama. That neat view stems from reading Blake's
account of the narrative works without fully realising that drama is
beyond his remit. As the only dramatic text he *does* have any interest
in is *Peter Pan* another simple, discrete pattern replaces a more
complex, intertwining one in the minds of those who use him as an
introduction to Barrie. As the power of the myth has already dis-
couraged any re-opening of critical enquiry, it is that misleading
pattern and the doubly reductive opinion of the author it encourages
which remain the basis for future non-enquiry.

Early Prose 1877–87

1. *A Child of Nature* (1877)

Along with the articles he wrote when resident in Dumfries, Edinburgh and Nottingham, Barrie records two longer works completed in
that period. The first of these was called *A Child of Nature* and was
composed during those happy days in Dumfries when he was voraciously reading the adventure tales of R.M. Ballantyne and Fenimore
Cooper. No copy of it remains. If its author is to be believed that is
because he "gently tore it up" himself (Barrie 1938: 81). The source of
this information is the speech he delivered on 24 December 1924
when receiving the Freedom of Dumfries. In that talk, he also
mentions the novel's length. It was 100,000 words long. This reminds
one of just how productive he was, especially in his early years. In his
Nottingham and early London days he wrote furiously and constantly.
This was done, as he himself repeatedly tells us, out of necessity.
Having neither reputation nor money to support himself, he had to
attract the popular market.

   If *A Child of Nature* offers the first literary example of this
ability, it also calls attention to one of the most damaging myths about

him. George Blake's reiterated claim that Barrie was *only* a populist is frequently repeated today. This is because he advances it as if it were a general conclusion rather than one which derives from analysis of the period before Barrie's reputation and financial security had been achieved.

Another sin of critical omission follows. Blake and his successors assume that Barrie chose commercialism without considering the higher claims of art. In fact, as the sources revealed in Chapter Two illustrate, few writers have tackled the problem of would-be literary genius constrained by a lack of funds so thoroughly and in so many different contexts as Barrie. If the anecdote in *Margaret Ogilvy* is to be believed, it first raised its head in his childhood with Cowley's quotation. Whether this be true or not, the problems involved in attracting the popular market while striving to make "the age to come [your] own" are certainly evident at each stage of his literary career. He had, of course, then heard Masson's eloquent lectures on the problem as it affected the literature of his own day. He had himself analysed the difficulties involved in achieving the desired balance between the immediately attractive and the universally significant in his essays on Skelton and Nash. His "Letter to Shakespeare" is only the most dramatic example of his journalistic interest in the problem. As we shall see he will also address the problem in some of his early narratives. More detailed analysis of the same problem will then appear in the Tommy novels. All of these works, however, are excluded from the kailyard canon. Finally, *The Greenwood Hat*, offers a nice conclusion to the subject. This has already been shown to distinguish carefully between the problem as faced by the impecunious Anon and its gentler formulation as it affects Sir James, the commentator. Usually, the Kailyard case is mythic in the oversimplified context defined by Barthes. In this instance, the alternative definition of myth as "lie" is more appropriate as the validity of a belief in Barrie as arch materialist depends on the erasure of so much academic and textual evidence.

A Child of Nature not only anticipates Barrie's determination and productivity, its topic offers an initial example of that enduring interest in women which he had highlighted in the *Hat*. "It was a tale of Dumfries and practically an exposure of the ladies therein", he tells his audience (Barrie 1938: 82). The other major features of Barrie's early "romantic" experiences as they appear in these autobiographical reminisccnces were discussed earlier but may conveniently be recalled at this point. Essentially, he saw himself as an unattractive, diminutive outsider who dearly wished to be the object of affection but was deemed irrelevant. In his writing he compensated for these deficiencies by fancifully taking on the role of expert in an area of activity about which he knew nothing. In that "borrowed" role, he advised and wrote letters for those who knew much more about passion than he. Variations on this scenario would appear in his later novels. But the immediate justification for recapitulating the major lines within it relates to *A Child of Nature* itself. Remarkably, Barrie's account of it suggests that, as schoolboy, he was already playing most of these roles.

Here is an example of the youthful writer rejoicing in that supreme challenge of the imagination – writing convincingly about things you know nothing about. The schoolboy Barrie's contacts with local women was, by definition, superficial. He did, however, very much wish to be appreciated by the girls at Dumfries Academy as his 1893 speech at the school's Prize Giving revealed. Indeed, the story of his winning their plebiscite for the "boy who had the sweetest smile" (Barrie 1938: 5) which he recalls on that occasion is his most frequently repeated Dumfries anecdote. His need to be highly regarded by the opposite sex along with his fear that he might not gain it is early established and lately remembered.

When Barrie describes the circumstances in which *A Child Of Nature* was composed he admits this. He introduces the book by confessing that when he read his heroes Burns and Carlyle he was quite ignorant about "how they made love". All he is sure of is "know[ing] which did it best". Having attributed similar insights to his audience, he translates the "love" problem to Dumfries Academy and the case of a schoolboy friend of his who had also fallen in love:

In his dire need, he consulted me. At that time he had a gratifying faith in me in affairs of the heart, partly because he recognised that I should be a poor rival. But still more because I was then writing my first novel. (Barrie 1938: 80)

Already the "irrelevant and ignorant but imaginatively superior" persona has emerged. The boy's reverence for Barrie, it then emerges, derives from hearing him read aloud the most romantic parts of the book. These, he admits to his Dumfries audience, were almost entirely derived from "novels by sparking young ladies which I read with my eyes standing out of my head in Anderson's library" (81). On these dubious grounds he then acts as the boy's guide in matters of love.

The histrionic, artistic and romantic positions which Barrie establishes here will remain leitmotivs in his later writing. But in *A Child of Nature* most of them are related to the drama surrounding composition rather than the book itself. Further, Barrie's speeches are notoriously fanciful. In one he describes a meeting between Napoleon and Jos Sedley from *Vanity Fair* and another between himself and Robert Louis Stevenson, which concludes with Stevenson chasing him "for hours that snowy night through the streets of Edinburgh, calling for my blood" (Barrie 1938: 71). The Dumfries speech is not set in this key but how much its account of his first prose satire owes to memory and how much to fancy can never be determined.

2. *Vagabond Students* (1883)

In Nottingham he composed his second lengthy prose work, *Vagabond Students: Original Sketches of Life at a Northern University* (Barrie 1883). It was serialised in the Saturday Supplement of *The Nottingham Journal*. I have been unable to trace copies of the Supplement but the daily paper contains lengthy advertisements of its form and content. From these one can establish that the first two chapters – "The End of the Session" and "A Students' Supper Party" – were published on 2 June 1883. An insight into the book's major characters is also provided. These will be "Four Academic cads and one Academic gentleman". In twenty chapters and eleven serialised parts they will take a Punch and Judy show round Scotland during their summer holidays (*NJ* 22 October 1883: 3).

Earlier advertised Supplement serials adopted the same picaresque form. *Vagabond Students* immediately succeeds *The Adventures of a Gentleman Tramp* and is followed by Mrs. J.K. Spender's *Recollections of a Country Doctor*. Obviously the format adapts well to serialised publication. Indeed Mrs Spender's rural "Doctor" stories are called "articles" which, for that reason, will "always have plenty of customers" *(The Academy* cited in *NJ* 5 December 1884: 3).

His choice of this form is consistent with Masson's critical views and the hierarchy of authors he recommended. Historically, he had taught his students to revere a form whose origins lay in Medieval and Renaissance Romance. Critically, he had argued its potential as a vehicle for quests of one kind or another, placing it in the category of the "Art and Culture Novel" within which "a mind of the thoughtful order, struggles through doubt and error towards certainty and truth" (Masson 1859: 266). That Dickens, who had gained Masson's first prize as Victorian novelist, had begun his career with a masterpiece in that form provided another kind of authorisation for Anon. And, of course, Barrie's choice of that book, *The Posthumous Papers of the Pickwick Club*, as deathbed reading proves beyond doubt his enduring affection for this form in lighter, comic guise.

The voice he adopts in *Vagabond Students* is also consistent with his critical training. Masson's preference for broad, loosely related categories over neat and discrete ones has been traced from its philosophical and conceptual origins (Masson 1856: 439) via his discipline's place within the interlinked, classically derived disciplinary pattern of teaching in Edinburgh's general M.A. to his mistrust of neat generic divisions in literary criticism itself. This concern is explicitly revealed at the start of *British Novelists and their Styles*. Beginning with a definition of all fiction as different branches of the art of imagination and therefore, in essence, sub-divisions of Poetry, he rejects generic divisions as "unscientific" preferring to explains this vision in terms of the medieval theory of voices. In this interlinked classification, priority is given to works of fiction which accentuate the Poetic (i.e. imaginative) by embracing all available voices, lyrical, dramatic and narrative (Masson 1859: 4). And which book is used to exemplify the attainment of these virtues? Why, the European equivalent of *The Pickwick Papers*. In Masson's lectures and critical writings, Cervantes ranks beside Dickens and Don Quixote's adventures beside Mr Pickwick's. Now, he gives ancient authority to the "new" (novel) form, which he fears has become too prosaic, by tracing its lineage back to the "truly poetic genius" which informs the story of that benighted knight (4).

When Barrie began to contribute regular columns to the *Nottingham Journal* he also adopted different "voices". To the voice of the leader writer, he added columns under the pen names of "A Modern Peripatetic" and "Hippomenes". These names are significant. The former recalls the Greek foundations of Barrie's critical training. Hippomenes, who used trickery to win his race against Atalanta, conjures up the creative wiles of the Imp and M'Connachie in *The Greenwood Hat*. It is Hippomenes who is credited with *The Vagabond Students* and imitates the mode of Cervantes and Dickens.

The advertisements for *The Vagabond Students* prove that it did combine all three Poetic voices. The narrative, we are informed, will consist of a series of *dramatic* sketches related by a *story-teller* with strong *lyrical* tendencies. He even meets Masson's concern that versification is in itself is a higher form of "Poetry" and the novel, on these grounds, a "lower" mode by inserting rhymes into his student tales. The standard of these verses, if the "Advertisement" examples are anything to go by, make the effort self-defeating:

Grind, grind, grind!
With eyelids heavy and red,
A student sat in his lonely digs
With a wet towel round his head. (*NJ* 26 May 1883: 5)

Barrie would become a highly imaginative prose writer and therefore a "poetic" novelist in the sense advocated by Masson and practised by Cervantes and Dickens. These verses, whatever the motivation for their inclusion, are arguably more prosaic in another sense than any of the prose extracts offered in the Advertisements.

3. *Better Dead* (1887)

Before Barrie reached London, then, he had written two lengthy episodic narratives. After he began his free lance career he produced another. This was *Better Dead* (Barrie 1887b). It was planned and written in 1886 at a time when he was beginning to warrant recognition as a writer of promise. While he still spent most of his time with friends from the past such as Riach and Gilmour, his favoured position as one of Greenwood's protégés on the *St James's Gazette* meant that he was invited to meet the great names of the time at the Garrick Club (Dunbar 1971: 63). While Barrie enjoyed his acquaintanceship with Thomas Hardy, George Meredith and others, he must also have been uncomfortably aware that he was now 26 and had neither a major novel nor drama to his credit. Certainly this was the gap he strove to fill.

Only after the book had been refused by several publishers did Barrie take the unusual step of having it published, at his own expense. Like its predecessors, it is a series of loosely linked dramatic sketches, based on Barrie's own life. He even overtly purloins the names of his friends (e.g. the hero is Andrew *Riach*). But the episodes themselves are satiric sketches of the great and good and so develop well beyond the more personal interests of its predecessors.

The structure, too, is different. The journey form employed in *Vagabond Students* was loosely organised around the adventures of the male group in the manner of one of his literary idols, the Dickens of *The Pickwick Papers*. For *Better Dead*, he chooses another model and another admired source. Stevenson's detective stories, *The Suicide Club*, had been published in 1878 in the *London Magazine*. In 1882, along with another cycle (*The Rajah's Diamond*) they were re-published in book form as *New Arabian Nights*. While the form itself was not invented by Stevenson, Barrie's admiration for his fellow Scot is well known. In 1886, moreover, Stevenson was enjoying a period of great popularity. Three years earlier, *Treasure Island* and *The Black Arrow* had securely established his reputation. Most recently *Kidnapped* had appeared in 1886.

Stevenson's method as adapted for Barrie's "Society for Doing Without Some People" means that different members set out to kill off different Victorian celebrities. As these discrete comic cameos from Chamberlain to Labouchère are separately conceived and discretely examined *Better Dead* is more tightly structured than *Vagabond Students*.

The book received some good reviews and gained a short-lived notoriety. That is all Barrie hoped for as its treatment in *The Greenwood Hat* suggests. An extract from it, recounting the club's programme and purpose is the second extract selected for retrospective commentary (Barrie 1930c: 21–26). There he describes the book's appearance as "lightening the gloom" of a particularly dreary April. Clearly, he regarded the £25 he spent on it as well worthwhile. Certainly, he had chosen his topic intelligently. In choosing to focus on the leading lights of Victorian society, he astutely relied on the rule that people love to read satirical attacks on great men and women while the celebrities themselves must appear to take such attacks in good spirit. Lord Randolph Churchill, for example, wrote to say how amused he had been by the "impertinent account" of his own death (31).

In qualitative terms, the older Barrie accepts that it is a melo-dramatic pot-boiler which relies on journalistic techniques. Only in one area could its chosen theme be said to offer the opportunity for an advance on his earlier practice. Inevitably the celebrities his society sought "to do away with" were involved in the major issues of his day. There was an opportunity here to make use of his journalism in a different way. The action of the novel may be a mixture of melodrama and farce but the chapter titles (e.g. "The Great Social Question?"; "Woman's Rights") remind the reader of those underlying social issues which Barrie, as leader-writer, had more seriously discussed. And so, for the first time, there is evidence of Darwinism, the nature of heroism and the rise of the "New Woman" becoming topics for concern in Barrie's imaginative fiction. George Blake's claim that Barrie had no interest at all in current social problems has been dis-proved by the factual evidence advanced in Chapter Two. Now, however, there is support for the counter argument within the mode and time with which he is specifically concerned. Canonical omission, whether innocently or conveniently adopted, is needed to keep this first exception concealed. For its author's total disinterest in serious issues to be maintained, it too is better dead.

Bachelor Prose 1888–90

If Barrie's earliest prose is of interest to biographer and literary critic alike, one would imagine that his bachelor prose would be of even greater importance for those seeking to prove Oedipal influences and hence artistic immaturity. That his mother and family problems should loom large in the Thrums collections is after all hardly surprising. In them, according to the premises of the mythic argument, he is mirror-ing his own early days in a mother-centred home environment. True signs of retarded development would only reveal themselves if Margaret Ogilvy in particular or mothers generally dominated these bachelor novels as well.

The relevant period is mirrored in four works which were composed at the same time as *Auld Licht Idylls* and *A Window in Thrums*. These are *When A Man's Single*, *The Superfluous Man*, *My*

Lady Nicotine and *Young Men I have Met*. Chronologically, they all come within Blake's Kailyard timetable. But as only the first is set in Thrums (and then only partly) Blake ignores them. As they also offer a number of clear challenges to the Oedipal view of their author's developing personality this omission is doubly worrying. That concern increases when Geduld seems to share Blake's reluctance to explore less "friendly" evidence. Awareness of Blake's strict geographical-critical premises might have led us to anticipate his canonical eclecti-cism. Contrariwise, Geduld's thorough textual testing of his Freudian argument in other areas makes his cavalier treatment of the bachelor narratives very surprising indeed.

Of the quartet he only analyses *When A Man's Single*. *My Lady Nicotine* is dismissed as "a piece of ephemeral journalism" (Geduld 1971: 23). That may be true but is no argument when the author's per-sonality rather than literary quality is your central thesis and the texts concerned offer a direct challenge to the psychological model you have proposed. *The Superfluous Man* and *Young Men I have Met* are not mentioned at all.

1. *When A Man's Single* (1888)

Geduld's case for the bachelor novels, therefore, rests on *When A Man's Single*. The hero of this work, Rob Angus, is imaginatively based on Barrie but only mentions his mother twice. The presence of Mrs Angus's sampler on his mantelpiece and the memory of her bringing him his dinner in a basket are hardly strong reasons for believing his creator never advanced beyond mother-worship (Barrie 1888c: 19, 265). Like most bachelors of his age, Rob is too obsessed with his present love for Mary Abinger to have much time to remem-ber the past.

Geduld ignores this problem but is determined to find signs of the trauma behind Barrie's supposed complex. This requires some critical ingenuity. The opening section of the tale does not mention the death of a younger brother any more than it recalls the death of young David. Instead it concerns Rob Angus's dutiful guardianship of his young female cousin. From this Geduld derives his prototypical interpretation. The girl's early death and Rob's subsequent departure from Thrums became Barrie's subconscious attempt "to jettison his brother while expressing his awareness that David's death is the *raison d'être* of his [own] creativity" (24). This is an ingenious rather than obviously convincing thesis as the story told in *When A Man's Single* seems to contradict rather than support it. Rob Angus *does* give up his ambitions to look after his dead sister's child but only out of duty. The only guilt he does express centres on the relief he feels when recognising that the girl's death allows him to escape from Thrums.

Geduld continues his ingenious argument by identifying Dick Abinger, Mary's brother, as a "representation of" Barrie's brother David. Even inanimate objects are drawn in to support the Freudian case. Rob Abinger's stick, for example, "represent[s] Margaret Ogilvy's staff". The staff in turn becomes a "symbol of her invalid state after the death of David". On these grounds Barrie is seen to identify "with the cause of his mother's condition" (33).

If the dislocation between interpretation and narrative raises direct problems, even in a subconscious context, the narrow focus of attention implied by the search for Oedipal evidence alone is also of concern. The a priori assumption that each of Barrie's texts can be read as a sign of the real world is not only at odds with the author's philosophical views on perception, it runs counter to his clear state-ment in *The Greenwood Hat* that all of his autobiographical memories are fancifully presented. When the number of problems encountered in Geduld's interpretation are also taken into account it would seem that an alternative approach to *When A Man's Single* is called for.

The de-historicising aspect of mythic argument is highlighted when one begins to formulate that approach. If literary critics do wish to match in nicety the detailed evidence provided by his biographers, then generative research must replace the synchronic vision of the critical mythologisers. This task involves considering the different successive drafts of Barrie's works. In the present case, it is a simpler, bibliographical issue which needs to be resolved in this manner.

Two different publication dates (1887 and 1888) are recorded for *When A Man's Single.* This was a time when Barrie's circle of influ-ential friends had widened to include W.E. Henley, the editor of a new sixpenny weekly, *The Scots Observer.* Barrie would soon be contrib-uting to that journal. But it was an older friend, W. Robertson Nicoll, a member of the influential group of Scots in London's publishing world who offered to serialise *When A Man's Single.* The 1887 date refers to that serialised format. The first episode was published in autumn 1887 with the last appearing in spring 1888. In substantially revised book form it was published in October 1888. Both pre-date the first (January) chapter of the next bachelor novel, *The Superfluous Man*, in 1889. Indeed, each of that book's twelve monthly chapters was headed "By the author of *When a Man's Single*".

The other contribution to that journal, *Young Men I have Met*, comes next in bibliographies. The first of its six, two-monthly chapters appeared in January 1890 while Hodder and Stoughton did not publish the collection of "tobacco tales" until April of that year. Actually, there are grounds for granting, *My Lady Nicotine* chronological priority. The series of youthful "kinds" in *The Young Man* did not end until November of 1890. That is why the supposedly earlier work can contain a review of its supposed successor. The September 1890 issue of *The Young Man*, which contained the fifth study of *Young Men I have Met* contains Frederick Atkins' nicely balanced judgment on what was and what was not offered by the story of the pipe-smoking club. Yes, these are "brief brilliant papers that are full of genuine humour" but no, "*My Lady Nicotine* is not a novel" only a series of articles (Barrie 1890a: 133).

If this reaffirms the interlinked planning which enabled Barrie to launch his energetic assault on the publishing world, neither the aims nor the structure of *When A Man's Single* suggest that he is yet trying to impress his peers. It continues the episodic narrative form of *Vagabond Students* and *Better Dead* and, if anything, relies more heavily on autobiographical material. Like his creator, Rob Angus is a lower class Thrums/Kirriemuir man with writing ambitions. Like Barrie again, this "literary saw miller" becomes a journalist in an English provincial town (Nottingham/Silchester). One might also argue that, as the book starts and finishes in Thrums, Barrie does for the first time mirror the circular form whose artificiality and connections with Shakespeare's pastoral comedies and late romances had been so highly valued by Masson.

The idea of conservative experimentation appropriate to a time of unfunded apprenticeship is also borne out thematically. Serious themes addressed but in the lightest manner possible mean that *Better Dead* does suggest a consistent world-vision but one which is still overtly a vehicle for comic effects. The medium should not, however, blind one to the message of *When A Man's Single*. In it, Barrie for the first time brings together in a Darwinian context those gender battles in love and art which will become central to Barrie's world-view and be more profoundly examined in his later prose and drama.

The titles of the opening chapters set the scene and reject his childish life. Far from longing to remain in Thrums, Rob is "Not a Free Man" (Chapter 1) when confined within the village. He only "Becomes Free" (Chapter 2) when he can escape from his responsibilities there and advance "Into the World" (Chapter 3). It is only when he has cast aside that confining world, that he identifies the twin challenges of life. Artistically, he must establish himself as a great writer; romantically he must vanquish his rivals for the hand of Mary Abinger.

The feminist bias to his own brand of Darwinism is also evident. Rob's battles against his male rivals are clearly fought and won. Artistically, a sustained and witty satire on the present state of British journalism ends with Rob seeking the high ground of eternal fame while his rival Noble Simms (Mary's brother in disguise!) remains contented with "finishing something really little" (154). In what is, by far, Barrie's most optimistic vicarious exploration of his own artistic and sexual future, Rob also wins the hand of Mary Abinger against rivalry from the more handsome and more socially favoured Sir Clement Dowton.

At the same time, while Rob may heroically defeat Simms and Dowton he yields to the greater creative powers, natural and artistic, of the authoress Mary Abinger. Before her the great orator becomes speechless. The great critic, having earlier damned her novel, now finds "things in it so beautiful [...] that they caught in his throat and stopped him reading!" (52). And, in case the comparative power of the two sexes is not coming across explicitly enough, the narrator confirms woman's superiority both on his own behalf ("probably no woman can live with a man for many years without having a natural contempt for him") and by interpreting the thoughts of his characters ("[Mary] knew however that if it were not for her sex men would never learn anything" [194]).

If this confirms the differentiated Darwinian line in his thought as detected in *The Nottingham Journal*, the novel's characterisation is also both realistic and idealistic in the manner advocated by Masson. Rob may be a shadow of Barrie but he is also literary "kind" defined by determination and genius. As the narrator puts it – "With most men affection for a woman is fed on her regard for them". Rob, however, will only woo where greatness is: "Greatness in love is no more common than greatness in leading armies" (95). Both that statement and the military metaphor which accompanies it echo his earlier essays on Darwin. The essential evolutionary battles exist only at the highest level for Barrie as for Darwin.

2. *My Lady Nicotine* (1890)

My Lady Nicotine offers a variation on these themes. Its hero offers a counterbalance in pessimism to Rob's sanguine personality. Again the hero is a native of Thrums with literary ambitions but he is also the tale's narrator. In that role, he proves as uninterested in his past or his mother as Rob Angus had been. She is only mentioned once and on that occasion her warning against theatregoing is defied by her son (Barrie 1889b: 37). But as these facts represent a direct challenge to the Oedipal case at a critically relevant time they cannot be ignored.

That the narrator-"hero" is never named is itself significant. Barrie believed that accurate characterisation depended on nominal exactitude as anyone who has read the long lists of possibilities in his Notebooks will realise. By keeping his main character nameless, Barrie is able to develop the idea of the irrelevant, harmless outsider in the game of love as discussed in Chapter XI of *The Greenwood Hat.* Passive in the battles of love, even his marriage has little to do with his own choice. His domineering wife makes that decision on his behalf and finally emasculates him entirely when depriving him of his last masculine passion for his pipe. And it is this melancholy figure "drifting towards a sad middle age" (1889b: 1) who opens and closes the circular structure of the book.

In both works stereotypes are used to represent the problems of life, love and literature, which Barrie was beginning to encounter in his own life. Here, too, variation is evident. Rob is the major character in *When A Man's Single*. Essentially the story is organised around his development as he meets one minor character after another. Rob Angus, as essentially the Barrie persona, meets individual challenges from Dowtown romantically, Simms artistically and Mary as representative of female power. In *My Lady Nicotine* a wider range of characters offer themselves as the idea of the "gentleman's club" re-

emerges from *Better Dead*. This in turn alters the book's autobiographical focus. Not only the narrator but other characters will
from time to time mirror Barrie's known life and characteristics. Not
only Barrie but bachelor friends are "translated" into this tobacco-
filled Arcadia. As Mackail notes, "he calmly helped himself to
Riach's surname and Gilmour's combination of callings" (Mackail
1941: 120). Lightly disguised portraits of his youthful London friends,
including Marriott Watson ("Marriot") and Tom Gilmour ("Gilray")
become members of the fictitious, pipe-smoking club.

At the same time, the merging of individuals into types and the
overtly fanciful nature of the work make the search for exact equations
between any one fictional character and his "real" equivalent an
ultimately fruitless task. For example, Marriott Watson, the most
confident of these young would-be lovers in real life becomes Marriot,
the "sentimental member" of the Arcadians (61). As literary type he
becomes a very unsuccessful lover indeed. Instead he anticipates
many of the characteristics later possessed by that much more complex sentimentalist, Tommy Sandys. In particular, he looks forward to
Tommy's intellectualism and the self-absorption which goes along
with it. Marriot has the *theory* of love at his fingertips. He even offers
lengthy philosophical analyses of the passion. In practice, he is sadly
aware that too much thought is the enemy of "that surging tempestuous passion [which] comes involuntarily" (64).

For the Sentimentalist's histrionic tendencies one must turn to
Gilray. He appears initially as a happy man determined to be sad –
"Gilray, as I soon saw, was a man trying to be miserable, and finding
it the hardest task in life" (53). This is only the first of many roles he
enthusiastically assumes in order to attract female attention. Unfortunately, as he is constantly forgetting which chosen *persona* he is
meant to be inhabiting at any one time, the strategy only promotes
farce and failure.

It could also be argued that the novel draws its strengths from
Dickens and Shakespeare, Masson's two icons of prose and drama. As
an innocent in love himself Barrie wisely made his Arcadians mirror
the naïve idealism of the pastoral world evoked in Shakespeare's
"sylvan romances" (Masson 1941: 90). This is married to the naïve
idealism of the Pickwick club and the picaresque form of their story.
Marriot for example, worships a woman having seen her act heroically. His passionate idealism only dissipates when he realises that the

object of his affection is not the one he saw at all. He does not fare any better in the theatrical world. Mirroring Barrie's tendency to idolise actresses, he fixes on one in particular and designates her the "lady of his life". Unfortunately she turns out to be a male actor in female guise!

3. *The Superfluous Man* (1889)

These works continue the saga of textual omissions revealed when the Oedipal case is measured against the crucial evidence of Barrie's bachelor novels. In this case, however, there is an excuse. Even Mackail, that most fastidious of biographers, draws the line here. "*The Superfluous Man*", he remarks, "may still be mouldering in the British Museum but if so it is no part of a biographer's duty to dig it out". This does not prevent him summing it up dismissively, as "a pot-boiler, on the twice-tried formula of the young hero seeking his fortune in London" (Mackail 1941: 151). Unfortunately for him, it does exist in the British Library and offers at least one major challenge to the Oedipal case.

When attempting to evaluate *The Superfluous Man* and relate it to Barrie's development, the details of planning and publication again prove important. The narrator in *My Lady Nicotine* was seen to be an onlooker in love. At the same time as his character was being planned in Barrie's Notebooks for a work which appeared in 1890, Barrie was working on his first contribution to *The Superfluous Man*. That novel was scheduled for publication in the 1889 January edition of *The Young Man* as the first of twelve monthly episodes.

Rob Angus had represented one kind of sentimental masculinity. *The Superfluous Man* introduces Barrie's readers to another variation on this type. In creating Dan Moore, he appears to have looked beyond these shores to Russia for a depiction of disaffected, self-analysing genius. Russian literary histories trace the tradition from the days of Onegin, Pechorin and Bel'tov. The hero or anti-hero in question is succinctly described by Iu. D. Levin as a "literary type, with such characteristics as the shunning of officialdom, spiritual lassitude, scepticism, self-questioning, a disharmony of word and deed, and social inactivity" (Levin 1995: 171).

Barrie's chosen title suggests a more specific source. Henry Gersoni's 1894 translation of Turgenev's short stories, *Dnevnik lishnego cheloveka* and *Mumu*, had called the first of these, *The Diary of a Superfluous Man* (Turgenev: 1894; 1968). As an avid reader of literary journals, Barrie is likely to have known at least the basic plot of this story as recounted in the reviews of the day. The playwright Arthur Barker gives such an account in *The Academy* of 28 June 1884. In it he comments on how easy it is to get hold of English translations of Turgenev – "Mr Henry Gersoni has contributed two more of Turgenev's tales to the large stock which the enterprise of English and American publishers has accumulated" (Barker 1884: 453–54).

In some ways Turgenev's hero, Culkaturin, anticipates Barrie's Sentimental Tommy more closely than Rob Angus had done. For example, like Tommy, he joins "excessive cerebration" to "agonising perceptiveness" and so becomes incapable of acting spontaneously (Kagan Kans 1975: 11, 41). Dan Moore, Barrie's "superfluous" hero, also gives up on the battles of life but does so in a more down to earth manner than that portrayed in the Russian tradition. His sense of "superfluity" is firmly based on the Calvinist work ethic as the following plot outline illustrates.

A young man, Dan Moore, deserts his village of Ballyhewan in Ireland to seek his fortune in London, where his father stays. In so doing he deserts his faithful love, Norah. On arriving in London, he discovers his father's success has been invented for the benefit of the residents of Ballyhewan in the letters he writes to them. Norah bravely follows Dan to London and herself finds work as a music teacher. After a series of adventures, their paths converge. Dan's kindness to a terrified young man-of-means enables him to find work. He marries Norah and even takes Dan's father as a lodger.

Essentially Barrie has used whatever knowledge he did have of the superfluous man in the Russian tradition to highlight the solitary, sad side of his own sentimental predicament. At the same time he had translated the intellectual agonies of Turgenev's hero into more practical terms as another version of the "youthful odyssey" theme.

If *The Superfluous Man*, in that sense, is just another imaginative chapter in Barrie's life, its emphasis on the hero's personal ambition and its lack of a maternal dimension sit uneasily with Oedipal theory. Dan does not dream of his mother and home; instead, the narrator tells us, "[n]o ambitious young man nears the London that is to become his home without a quickening of the pulse" (20).

But it is another uncomfortable piece of biographical and psychological evidence, which makes Mackail's failure to seek out the text regrettable. Like most biographers he subscribes to the view that William Barrie was as thoroughly expunged from his son's fiction as his wife dominated it. If he had read *The Superfluous Man* he could not have made that claim.

In that novel, Dan's father, Michael, not only vies with his son for heroic status, he is also established as the artistic, fanciful member of the duo. Dan it is who possesses Barrie's work ethic but lacks his imagination: "Had he had the journalistic instinct he could in afteryears have turned his fruitless search into money by writing sketches on London landladies" (85).

Later, in *Sentimental Tommy*, Tommy's mother will write fanciful letters to her home village so that they may appear to be thriving. In this earlier version it is the father Michael who anticipates both motive and method. He too creates a totally false vision of his and his son's success in London for the benefit of those who remain in the Irish equivalent of Thrums– "'Though I should starve,' he said grandly, 'I was determined to leave behind me a name in Ballyhewan'" (21). Nor is Michael's ultimate heroism in doubt. Indeed, it is his more liberal spirit and the resilient optimism accompanying it which rouses Dan from that spirit of moral defeatism which has left him "superfluous" and returns him to the battles of life. When his son, bowed down with Christian guilt, "turns his shamed face to the wall" it is his father who encourages him to start again (102).

This returns us to the question of the audience addressed. An overt description of the hero's major humour indicates one new direction in which Barrie moves for this reason. Describing Dan's early days in London, the narrator comments, "He felt like a superfluous man. It has its temptations, this city full of wickedness and sin; but those of the more garish kind do not entice young men whose aim is to avoid starvation. That December he looked at nothing, in the roaring streets he felt that he alone was without an occupation" (Barrie 1889: 37 [March]). "Temptations", "wickedness", "sin" – these words provide a much clearer description of Christian morality than any which its author has hitherto provided or, indeed, will ever provide again.

This is because *The Young Man* was a major organ for the propagation of muscular Christianity, a movement which stressed the need for energetic Christian activism in combination with an ideal of vigor-

ous masculinity. In each edition, the same hortatory sub-heading –
"Quit you like men – be strong" – is printed beneath the title. A high
percentage of the journal's contributors were protestant ministers, all
intent on urging the principles of moral and physical courage on their
youthful readers. These aims are conveniently summed up in an article
describing the "Ideal Man". According to its author, he should be
"physically strong [...] intellectually powerful and agile [...] always
controlled by a high moral purpose" (1889a: 56 [April]).

Barrie, as disciple of Darwin, does not need to renege on that
position in order to meet these editorial principles. He simply extends
the battle context in a way which includes both. Indeed, some of his
clearest statements on the physical and spiritual battles facing
Christians at this time are contained in *The Superfluous Man*. And it is
in these explicit terms that the narrator introduces Dan's entry into
London – "He is on the point of being shot into the fiercest struggle
the world now knows, and his greatest danger is that he may lose his
head and be trampled out of sight" (1889a: 20 [February]).

The protestant work ethic is also consistently promoted. Dan's
superfluity has, in fact, more to do with his inability to find work than
any failure he displays as a lover. It is the desire to find a better job
which brings him to London. Throughout the novel his sense of self
worth rises when he finds a position and falls when he is made redun-
dant. To underline this, the narrator self-consciously ends the story in
an unusual manner:

Stories generally end to the sound of wedding bells, and this is no exception to the
rule. But marriage is a profession with an income attached to it and the superfluous
man married is in a worse plight than the superfluous man as bachelor. It remains to
be told how Dan at last joined the army of bread-winners. (Barrie 1889a: 182
[December])

The novel's heroine also differs from her predecessors. Norah may not
be a "New Woman" but she is certainly more active and resourceful
than Barrie's earlier heroines. She dares to follow Dan into London
and energetically seeks him out when she arrives. In making her seek
work, Barrie strikes a new and radical note. Two years before, in a
manuscript called "Women who Work", he had compiled an account
of actresses' pay-scales, discovering that only three out of every two
hundred earned a working wage (BVS W67). In this spirit, Norah
comments on the gender pay-differential illustrated in the London

newspaper advertisements she consults. Sadly, she concludes, that the post of governess she seeks is as poorly remunerated as it is ambitiously described. Such a person, she concludes, "must be a female Admirable Crichton for a second cook's wages" (1889a: 53 [April]). Her early reference to that heroic figure is an example of the kind of relevant evidence which is bypassed if *The Superfluous Man* material is not taken into account.

4. *Young Men I have Met* (1890)

The May 1889 edition of *The Young Man* contained an article entitled, "Such a Jolly Girl" which discussed various types of women from the demure to the impulsive girl, from the sarcastic prig to the jolly girl (68–9). In the following year, this time at two month intervals, Barrie produced six male cameos under the title of *Young Men I have Met* (Barrie 1890a). That he was simultaneously working on his Arcadian types for *My Lady Nicotine* is relevant as are the identities of the types chosen.

Unsurprisingly, January's opening cameo defines "The Sentimentalist". It includes the dominant modern sense of excessive emotionality but extends into Masson's broader definitions of that trait. These include the actor's ability to inhabit many personalities. "When attacking a person or a custom at eight o'clock in one company, and becoming defendant at nine o'clock in another, he was equally in a glow". The tension between life and art for the creative individual, already broached in *When A Man's Single*, is again addressed here. While changeability is a potential disadvantage in life, its particular suitability for writers is highlighted. A young man of this kind may well turn to the imaginative arts where he can convincingly assume a range of imaginary personae. "He drew a pathetic picture of an old woman at an apple stall, and in moving language compared her soul to that of the proudest member of the aristocracy" (1890a: 6–7 [Jan]).

The remaining cameos tease out other strands of Barrie's character as defined in *The Greenwood Hat*. His egotistical inability to act spontaneously is anticipated in "The Prig". "The Student" in valuing class medals over the pursuit of knowledge for its own sake, embodies his superior, competitive side while "The Comic" and "The Dreamer" re-work, idealistically, those preferences for humorous and imaginative writing which he confirms in his academic essays.

Conclusions

At this stage, any conclusions regarding the alternative Barrie – the one who *does* write positively about fathers, whose literary models are Dickens and Shakespeare rather than purveyors of psychological realism, who defines his personality in positive histrionic rather than negative filial terms and whose highest aims as a writer are neither materialistic nor populist but directed towards impish difficulty and imaginative coverage of the fullest possible topical range – have to be tentative.

Yet, he can already be seen testing himself out in different modes while initiating a number of constant themes and interests, all of which will later be explicitly identified in *The Greenwood Hat*. There, his youth and lack of money force him to concentrate on the popular, transient side of Cowley's equation for genius. The tone of light comedy allied to unambitious themes and structures are therefore favoured in all the juvenile and bachelor narratives. This does not mean that preparation for more adventurous work has been put on hold. While all of the stories might fairly be called episodic there is much more variety in the specific forms chosen than is generally recognised. *Better Dead* and the four bachelor narratives, for example, are all artificially organised in different ways. In each case the specific form is designed to act as the best possible vehicle for the narrative concerned. *Better Dead* and *Young Men I have Met* both use a discrete cameo format suited to their mode and topic. The first seeks to appeal by linking celebrity satire to the charms of the adventure story while the second is conceptually conceived and designed to satirise *kinds* of men. Nor do the odysseys of Rob Angus and Dan Moore follow the natural order of time. Appropriately, but in different ways, both employ the anticipation and recollection devices of classical epic.

As *My Lady Nicotine* encloses the adventures of the pipe-smoking group within a circular form one can see that from the shared base of personal, episodic narratives a wide range of different structures emerge. These are all overtly manneristic and rely on different sources and literary kinds. This is, of course, consistent with

Barrie's belief that only a limited number of essential story types exist
(Jack 1991: 85–86). The task of the writer is to re-create them in as
many different modes as possible. Later the Peter Pan story will be re-
translated from photograph collection to novel, to full length and one
act play, to ballet, film, children's tale and speech (Jack 1991: 164).
The early prose, more timorously, anticipates this methodology.

The essential and universal story type which provides the basis
for such variation can also be detected. Hegel, in the section of the
Phenomenology of Spirit entitled "Human and Divine Law: Man and
Woman", had defined the battle of the sexes in these universal terms.
Barrie's acceptance of that proposition in Darwinian terms has been
illustrated in his journalism and the opening chapters of *Auld Licht
Idylls*. While this is transmitted in the spirit of muscular Christianity,
it also has a distinctly Nietzschean bias. The young Barrie is only concerned with the highest personal battles of heroism while his literary
conflicts centre on the nature of genius. Sexually, he finds for woman
rather than man in the newly-defined battle for social supremacy.

These tendencies are again confirmed in *The Greenwood Hat*.
There, the mystery of woman and Barrie's fear of inferiority as
primary, sexual creator is stressed along with his fear that the
"weaker" sex may even beat him in the secondary artistic conflict.
Among his juvenile prose, only Rob Angus's defeat by Mary Abinger
mirrors woman's natural and artistic victory. The idea of life as a
struggle in which women dominate is consistently advanced in the
bachelor novels. Only the mode and the bias of attention vary – from
the indirect satire in ignorance of *A Child of Nature* to the direct
support offered for the Women's Movement in *Better Dead* via
Norah's heroism in *The Superfluous Man* to the reductive visions of
men offered in *When A Man's Single* and *My Lady Nicotine*.

If the version of the story Barrie presents clearly shadows his
own views and experiences, the artificial forms he chooses warn his
readers that simple autobiographical interpretations must first pierce
the veil of literary convention. When they have done this they enter
another artificial realm whose inhabitants unite realism and idealism
in the manner recommended by Masson and do so imaginatively in
the manner of Dickens. All the "heroes" of the bachelor novels are
presented in terms of a "sentimental" type whose broad range of con-
trasting characteristics are explicitly analysed in *Young Men I have
Met*. It is this ability to be at once noble and ignoble, selfish and

altruistic, childish and mature which Campbell Fraser's vision of the ever-changing personality encouraged.

It might have seemed strange that *The Greenwood Hat*, focussing as it does on Barrie's apprentice works, opens with a vision of the artist's power to live many lives vicariously while defining self in terms of changeability alone. Not so. At an early age Barrie had accepted his need to express imaginatively, through the lens of variable selfhood, the challenging, frightening world of Darwinian doubt and conflict which confronted late Victorian Britain and the emerging role of women within it. What place psychological realism and autobiographical identifications based on its premises can have in this learned yet fanciful realm is the real difficulty. And that problem does not become any easier when Barrie's juvenile and bachelor drama is drawn into the equation.

Chapter Four

Filling the Textual Gaps II: "Kailyard" Drama 1877–93

So far, the discussion of Barrie's apprenticeship has been limited to his prose. Full coverage in that area has been linked to a demonstration of the fragile foundation of the Oedipal-Kailyard case. That was necessary because Barrie's early tales *are* the basis of the entire psychological-literary myth. But he did, at the same time, write plays in accordance with a desire to test himself across the widest possible range of literary kinds compatible with this essentially populist stage of his career. This chapter not only examines these plays in accordance with the critical principles established in Chapter Two but it also highlights the many links which exist between the theatrical and narrative lines of development. The plays are more thoroughly treated because, even in his apprenticeship, the theatre was "the irrepressible cat which the master used to put in a sack and cast into the river but which, nevertheless, was always the first to greet him on her return home" (BVS T63: 8).

If this approach continues the positive vision of Barrie as thoughtful, learned imaginative writer it also exposes the largest and most complete gap in the evidence advanced on the reductive Oedipal/Kailyard side of the argument. Even Geduld's most thorough presentation of that argument tacitly ignores the existence of the early drama. Yet in that material, it is very difficult indeed to find evidence of a mother fixation while the idea of the artist's naturally histrionic, all-embracing personality is creatively presented in the eleven, literally histrionic, productions which he offered between 1877 and 1893. I shall examine these in turn, beginning with those which precede his decision to move to London.

Schoolboy, Student and Journalist: Drama 1877–84

Date	Title	Mode	Place
1877:	*Bandalero the Bandit*	Melodrama	Dumfries
1880:	*Bohemia*	Pastoral	Edinburgh
1883:	"Caught Napping"	Commedietta	Nottingham

Given so much interest in Barrie's early life, it is surprising that later biographers pay so little attention to his earliest dramas despite the fact that *Bandalero* and *Bohemia* are discussed at length in his account of the origins of the powerful spell cast upon him by the theatre in *The Greenwood Hat*. True, he has a low opinion of them. Barrie rejoices that his first schoolboy play has been lost: "No page of it remains" (Barrie 1930c: 67). In a way, *Bohemia*'s epitaph is worse. He had forgotten its existence entirely until it turned up at auction. Offered the chance of reading it, he declines. But he does remember that its title page described "A glade in Brighton". This, he cynically remarks, proved that Anon " knew at that time about as much about Brighton as he did about Bohemia" (Barrie 1930c: 182). "Caught Napping", the product of his Nottingham years, he never mentions at all.

1. *Bandalero the Bandit* (1877)

Despite Barrie's protestations, the manuscript of *Bandalero* does exist as BVS B34 in the Beinecke collection. It was composed for and performed by the Dumfries Academy dramatic company when he was only seventeen. In Chapter Six of *The Greenwood Hat*, he remembers that it "played for less than half an hour". He himself acted a "charac-ter [...] who was a combination of his favourite characters in fiction" (Barrie 1930c: 67). Later, in 1924, when accepting the Freedom of Dumfries he called attention to his innocence of stage practice at that time. As egotistical author, he "kindly" allowed a friend to play the title part because he thought his own multi-character would be more attractive. In fact this desired outcome was thwarted – "I had to be constantly changing my clothes, with the result that I was scarcely ever on stage" he records (Barrie 1938: 87).

Barrie's memory of the play is an exaggerated one. He took the role of Smike, named after the character in Dickens' *Nicholas Nickleby*, but had only two costume changes. The one which is vital to the plot is when he disguises himself as the priest, Father Dolan. But Barrie's other claim, that he drew heavily on his schoolboy reading, is fully confirmed. And while the play is at times naïve, the parodying of these sources is cleverly done. Most of them are not themselves dramatic but drawn from their young author's favourite novels. As well as Dickens, the voices of Walter Scott, R.M. Ballantyne and J.

Fenimore Cooper can be heard. Shakespeare is the dramatic exception with Barrie relying on his audience's ability to detect Smike's echoing of serious Shakespearean lines in a low, farcical context. Thus, he wonders whether he is in fact dead in the words of Hamlet via Mark Anthony, "Am I killed or not killed, that is the question for Benshaw is an honourable man", and ends the play with a low-style version of Shakespeare's final appeal for audience appreciation in the comedies: "And as for you (to audience) if you're pleased we'll maybe ask you to the weddin'" (BVS 34: 26, 28).

Nonetheless, the first words ever spoken in a Barrie play are enough to confirm its author's later concerns over general quality. Bandalero enters "pale and bloody". He then addresses the audience in a high poetic manner which unfortunately also calls up the image of dogs with human hands:

BANDALERO: (pale and bloody): I am come to keep my appointment with my beloved Alice! Much I fear 'twill be our last meeting! My footsteps dogged by these bloodthirsty hounds of Sir Richard Vernon what chance have I to escape their fell hand. (1)

Perhaps the major lesson Barrie learned from this play had more to do with theatrical politics than anything else. Consultation of the text and the circumstances of production proves that he began his theatrical life as he ended it as a team-worker; one who would discuss his scripts with actors and stage hands and adapt it to their needs when he felt they had made their case.

That this was one of the few occasions when he was on stage himself is also relevant. Already he understood (in a personally painful situation!) that writing for the stage is not the same as writing stories. A playwright needs to "think through" the words to the action. Forgetting the practicalities of costume changing the young Barrie learned that there was no exact correlation between the length of speeches given to a character and the theatrical impact he has on stage. Awareness of this differentiation would become a major principle when Barrie began to adapt his own prose for the theatre.

Another kind of teamwork is evoked by the dramatic sources for these plays. Here, Barrie himself provides the necessary background in Chapter Six of *The Greenwood Hat*. There, in an affectionately mocking tone, he recalls his introduction to Shakespeare on stage in the intimate surroundings of "The Smallest Theatre" in Dumfries.

Rural repertory, he records, produced "A public that takes its Shake-speare four plays a night" (1890c: 61). It also allows you to meet last night's *Hamlet* wandering like an ordinary man on the streets the following day. But it is the commentary on this memory which reveals another aspect of teamwork.

Knowing the right people has always been crucial in theatrical circles. In this area, Barrie was fortunate from the outset. His village Hamlet-Macbeth-Oberon was the actor J.H. Clynes. That great man occasionally brought "star" companies from London and in this way Barrie met the renowned London comic actor J.L. Toole. Toole also happened to be the manager-custodian of the Williams Street theatre which bore his name. As biographers note, Barrie would later find this brief acquaintance with Toole of great value. Certainly, knowing the man made it easier initially for Barrie to find a theatre for the two comedies which first launched his West End career – "Ibsen's Ghost" and *Walker, London*. Toole's historically famous theatre with the equally famous Toole in the major comic roles guaranteed that the opening nights would be sold out. The rest was up to the playwright and Barrie did not fail.

Of biographers, Hammerton offers the fullest explanation of why an apparently unimportant schoolboy troupe so "impressed" Toole. First, it had a prestigious group of patrons, including Henry Irving and the Duke of Buccleuch. Toole was introduced to the Duke and other civic dignitaries. On stage he had received the uncritical worship of a rural audience. Then, when he came to see the boys' three one act plays, his notorious ego must have been further satisfied. And what *did* he see? He saw that the two major movers in the group, Barrie and Anderson not only knew his work but had made them their "stage favourite". *Bandalero* was accompanied by shortened versions of two plays in which he had starred. Little wonder that the great man was encouraged to return and watch the troupe repeat their homage the following year (Hammerton 1929: 46–50).

2. *Bohemia* (1880)

The movement from *Bandalero* to *Bohemia* takes us from Dumfries and Barrie's happy schooldays to the more competitive arena of Edinburgh University. While it is better than its predecessor, Barrie's anxiety to forget it remains understandable as a plot outline will confirm.

Act I: Vanity Ray, a foundling, is adopted by Mme de Rue, manageress of the Hilarity Theatre eighteen years before the action begins. Now at the height of her acting powers she is secretly in love with Sandilands, a leading playwright. She confides this to her friend, Hannah before flirting with two other "type" suitors, a professor and a peer.

Act II: The central act moves to a wood where she promises love to each of her suitors, uniquely. Sandilands is a concealed conspirator-observer during the game. After it, they agree to marry. Sparks, a musician, provides a lyrical background to their happiness. This is short-lived. Hannah enters with a letter from Mme de Rue, revealing the two lovers to be brother and sister. On Sandilands' return he is astonished to have his overtures of love rejected. The curtain falls as Vanity faints and Sparks recognises Hannah as someone called "Christobel".

Act III: Christobel proves to be the assumed name of a "handwriting imitator", who has forged the letter because of her own concealed passion for Sandilands. Exposed and driven off, she reacts cynically but later returns, having herself found love. As Sparks now loves Vanity's maid three marriages are celebrated as the curtain falls.

This is exactly the kind of play one would expect from a student reading an English course centred on Aristotle and the Renaissance. It has a Greek chorus and, in Sparks, a character who formally describes himself as the "*deus ex machina*" of the piece. Its mode is anticipated at the outset when Sandiland quotes the commercial principle on which Mme de Rue kept her theatre thriving. "'Light comedy,' she said, 'has brought full houses to the Hilarity during the whole twenty years of my management. I depend upon it; the moment you place a heavy piece on the boards, will that success decline'" (BVS A2/1:1).

The choice of a young playwright as the hero of a Renaissance comedy makes this play the creative counterpart of the academic articles which Barrie was formulating at this time. Sandilands, like Lyly and Nash, becomes a vehicle for probing vicariously the problems he is himself facing as would-be comic playwright. The form he adopts is also significant. Many of Barrie's finest, mature plays follow a circular structure which has at its centre a wood or island. *Bohemia* is the first of his plays to adopt these methods. In the later cases, his model would be Shakespearean Romance. To meet the lighter demands of Mme de Rue, he does not desert Shakespeare but prefers to draw his inspiration from the comedies. The mistaken identities in the wood remind one of *A Midsummer Night's Dream* while the idea of a "comedy" within a "comedy" recalls the gulling of Malvolio in *Twelfth Night*. *As You Like It* is also echoed. Barrie was at this time a dramatic critic for the *Edinburgh Courant*. He had in that capacity recently seen Glasgow's Gaiety Company revive the play and, as Leonee Ormond notes, that production "caught Barrie's imagination from the start and had a marked effect on his later work" (Ormond 1987:42).

Masson's championing of the currently unpopular pastoral form may also be relevant. Having completed a major study of Scotland's finest Renaissance pastoral poet, William Drummond of Haw-thornden, he urged revival of interest in the mode (Masson 1873). The possibility of direct influence on Barrie does not rest on the fame of that work alone. The ways in which Masson advocates a revival of pastoral writing and the place it occupies in his account of Shake-speare's development are also relevant. The printed version of his lectures shows that he taught his students that the use of simpler rural worlds in the comedies led to a more serious employment of that device in the late Romances. The wood in *A Midsummer Night's Dream* allowed him to develop his "dream ideality, his natural Spensereanism, his delight in sylvan phantasy and romance" while the pastoral element in *As You Like It* offered scope for a more reflective consideration of "the problems of meditation" (Masson 1914:148ff).

Masson argues his case for every one of the voices he had defined as sub-categories of Poesie. The narrative voice joins the poetic and dramatic analyses of Drummond and Shakespeare in *The Art of the Novel*. There the retreat is used as part of an argument designed to urge modern novelists towards imaginative, idea-centred composition. As simplified, elemental focus it is "best suited for certain varieties of that exercise of pure phantasy in which the poet delights" (Masson 1859: 68).

The title, *Bohemia*, is also of interest. Later Barrie will return to that world, so successfully dramatised in cantata form by John Gay and Robert Burns. It will inform his picaresque novels and re-appear in dramas as formally disparate as "Becky Sharp" and *The Little Minister*. The demands of the form may also account for there being no record of *Bohemia* being performed. In his student play, Barrie naively anticipated the grand scale demands he would later, more appropriately, make as established author for *The Admirable Crichton* and *Peter Pan*. The cast demands a chorus but also a dancing troupe, headed by the gloriously named "Première danseuse", Viola Pratt! The songs of Sparks add a lyrical element which is present in the Shakespearean source but whose more formal development here suggests a cantata model. Together the presence of dancers and a professional songwriter suggest that Barrie may seek to claim novelty for his work on the ground of its hybrid form. Lost in ambitious theorising of this kind he forgot that such a play far exceeded the practical resources of a student production.

3. "Caught Napping" (1883)

Nottingham and *The Nottingham Journal* succeed Dumfries and Edinburgh as the background for Barrie's third drama. Like *Bohemia* it seems never to have been performed. The text appeared in the weekend Supplement to *The Nottingham Journal* for Saturday 26 March 1883. Although I have consulted advertisements for it in the daily newspaper I have failed to find a copy of the Supplement. Barrie also had it published in booklet form. Later consultation of a copy of that text (NLS Rb.s. 2797) served to confirm the evidence of these advertisements.

Together advertisements and pamphlet offer guidance on Barrie's early theatrical education. The first discovery is biographical. The play was written for an actress he admired and whom Chaney identifies as Minnie Palmer, an American actress, whose successful tour of Great Britain in 1883 and 1884 coincided with Barrie's stay in Nottingham (Chaney 2005: 64). Barrie's infatuation with Miss Palmer emerges earlier in his reviews of her British performances in the *Journal*. From her first Glasgow performance through the various stages of her tour he is unrelievedly (and uncharacteristically) enthusiastic about the talents of "this clever little lady" (*NJ* 11 July 1883: 3). When she returns to Glasgow, he uses the *Journal* to offer his own sad farewell:

It was at the Princess Theatre, Glasgow, that Miss Minnie Palmer made her first appearance before an English audience some fourteen months ago – and she is true to her old love insofar that at Glasgow she bade farewell, to English folk. She has just completed a three week engagement there, and it speaks volumes for her popularity, that, with the thermometer at 90°, she has been able to attract more people than the theatre would hold. (*NJ* 18 August 1884: 4)

If *Bohemia* anticipates the Romance structures of Barrie's mature drama, so "Caught Napping" is the first example of that actress worship which will include Mary Ansell and end with Elizabeth Bergner's appearance as the title character, fifty three years later, in *The Boy David*.

Mackail calls the play "Short, crude, peppered with appalling puns, and quite atrociously bad" (Mackail 1941: 85). This is confirmed by the plot description and occasional quotation offered. If Shakespearean comedy is still Barrie's major influence, then he seems to be unwisely attempting imitation of the verbal virtuosity of a Touchstone or a Benedick in this offering.

The advertisements offer another important insight into the range of his duties on *The Nottingham Journal*. They confirm that his by-lines extend beyond the poetic and narrative personae of "A Modern Peripatetic" and "Hippomenes" to include dramatic comment as well. The advertisements which preceded the publication of the play in May 1893 identify him under a third theatrical by-line as author of "The Dramatic notes of Pelham".

It is under *that* name he praises Minnie Palmer. This mixture of voices is consistent with the interlinked view of "Poesie" as advocated by Masson at the outset of *The Art of the Novel*. Pelham shares that vision. When reviewing a comic opera, he comments "It is perhaps a good thing to be a playwright, but it is still better to be both a playwright and a poet" (*NJ* 25 May 1883: 6).

Barrie's first three dramas confirm the view of him as a complex personality whose earliest plays appropriately invoke all three poetic voices, lyrical, narrative and dramatic. They place him in the ranks of participator-dramatists willing to discuss their scripts with actors and stage directors. Their major sources are Shakespeare and Dickens, both of whom stand at the zenith of Masson's critical hierarchy.

The study also suggests new links with Barrie's past and future. *Bandalero* proves that he had read Dickens, Scott and Shakespeare before entering university. It looks forward to a much finer parody,

"Ibsen's Ghost" while offering his first fictional version of the role-changing personality which would soon become a leitmotiv in his work. *Bohemia* is the first example of Barrie following Shakespeare's use of rural-fantastic retreats as a means of presenting lovers' concerns in a simpler, elemental manner. It therefore precedes Thrums in that role and looks forward to *The Little Minister.* Dramatically, he begins on the progressive route marked out in Masson's account of Shakespeare's development as a playwright. This begins with precisely the kind of light, pastoral comedy mirrored in *Bohemia.* "Caught Napping" for its part not only offers the earliest example of actress-infatuation but also provides a theatrical preface for those gender battles which will later be so powerful an element in Barrie's prose.

Early Drama 1885–93: Collaborations and "Translations"

Tracing the development of Barrie's critical thinking highlights the complexity of his mind. It also confirms the varied criteria he uses to assess his own work. In this section, while continuing to study what he learned of the dramatic craft, I shall concentrate on his most basic beliefs about the ways in which prose and theatre interrelate. Following Masson, he starts with modal distinctions and allies them with his own conviction that there are very few story types. The power of mode to re-invent meaning is therefore the first key to his thinking. As his method remains comparative and comprehensive, drama and narrative are not defined separately but in relation to each other on the classic principle of similarity and variation. The second area highlighted is, therefore, that of translation, in both its linking (prose sources) and its dramatically definitive senses (theatricality).

Barrie's search for literary glory has now taken him from Nottingham to London. Against the advice of Greenwood and without financial backing he entered the centre of the competitive literary world in 1885. Aided by Gilmour who had become his naïve Scottish friend's unofficial banker he survived the next five years and even impressed the London *literati* with his publications. With the aid of Meredith he was accepted as a member of the Garrick Club. Look more closely, however, and you will find that this reputation rests on

eight prose works, from *Better Dead* to *My Lady Nicotine*. There are
no dramas at all. Why has Barrie apparently given up on the theatre?

One of the reasons for this choice was financial. In his Nottingham letters to Shakespeare, in his academic essays and in Masson's
lectures he learns and accepts the difficulty of making money by
writing for the theatre before he even enters London. Other practical
considerations played their part. It is easier for an unknown outsider to
sit down, write a novel or a poem and get it published than to break
into the somewhat incestuous theatrical world in order to find financier, director, venue and cast. In fact, Barrie only really revived his
interest in drama when his novel, *The Little Minister*, freed him from
commercial concerns.

The popular view, based on Blake's eclectic evidence delays
consideration of the movement from prose to drama until the turn of
the twentieth century when *Tommy and Grizel* gave way to *Quality
Street*. The plays listed below are all ignored when the evidence for
the Oedipal-Kailyard case is presented. Whether this is intentional or
not I do not know but it is certainly convenient as they completely
upset the notion that Barrie starts with apprentice prose and then
advances to mature drama. Between 1891–93 there is only one prose
entry (*The Little Minister*) while there are six experimental plays,
none of which is noticeably autobiographical nor much interested in
mothers!

Year	Title	Mode	First Performance	Opening Run
1891:	*Richard Savage**	Tragedy	Criterion, 16 April	1
1891:	"Ibsen's Ghost"	Burlesque	Toole's, 30 May	27
1892:	*Walker, London*	Light Comedy	Toole's, 25 February	49
1893:	*The Professor's Love Story**	Comedy	Comedy Theatre, 25 June (> Garrick)	144
1893:	*Jane Annie*†	Opera	Savoy, 13 May	50
1893:	"Becky Sharp"	Farce	Terry's Theatre, 3 June	6

* Collaboration with H. Marriott Watson
† Collaboration with Arthur Conan Doyle

In assessing the literary goals Barrie sets himself, the evidence of the
Notebooks is as important as that of performance or publication. The
jotters covering 1885–90 are dominated by plans for the major novels
centred on Gavin Dishart and Tommy Sandys. Those for the next
three years are more balanced generically. Therefore any clear

transition from early prose to mature drama proposed on psychiatric and kailyard premises finds no support there either.

1. Collaboration: *Richard Savage* (1891)

If the Notebooks offer an insight into the generative side of Barrie's work, modal definitions are the normal starting point for the critical methodology he himself favoured. All of the non-collaborations are in that sense very conservative, being variations on a comic theme. They are, therefore, in harmony with his earlier critical comment that his talents confined him to presenting serious themes indirectly, through laughter (BVS S354: 13). At the same time the principle of collaboration introduces a new, authorial perspective on the idea of teamwork, which he saw as a quidditative distinction separating dramatic from narrative compositions. A tragical history and an opera are forms respectively rejected and unanticipated in his critical essays. In the first case, he had suggested that tragedy was beyond him and so should not be attempted. In the second, his refusal even to consider providing a libretto is unsurprising. As he remarks in the *Hat*, at that time he "had no musical sense" (Barrie 1930c: 183).

The collaborations, nonetheless, enter these forbidden areas. Of the two, *Richard Savage*, written with Marriott Watson, is the more surprising as it was described by critics as "a tragic history". Barrie as comic-idealist was therefore entering *two* unlikely realms in the one play. The opera *Jane Annie* was composed with Conan Doyle and although it demanded musical knowledge at least it returned to the comic norm.

In the *Hat*, Barrie concentrates on the lessons he learned from these radical experiments (Barrie 1930c: 181–85). While condemning the quality of both he does see them as justifiable parts of a young author's need to test himself to the limits of his range. This principle in relation to the quest for genius is explicitly introduced in the article which immediately precedes consideration of tragedy and opera in Chapter XVI (175–81). There, Carlyle's simple definition of genius as "an infinite capacity for taking pains" is regarded as simplistic. There are many different ways of looking at genius, Barrie counters. Different combinations of work and talent have to be considered and only those who have explored these fully can understand what genius means. It is in this context that he describes the valuable lessons he snatched from the jaws of collaborative disaster.

Richard Savage, he remembers, had only one performance and that was at the expense of the authors. As a vanity publication, it is therefore the theatrical equivalent of *Better Dead.* Its disastrous opening matinée also helps to explain Barrie's later reluctance to take curtain calls. Marriott was over six feet tall and the contrast in their appearance allowed the press to end strong criticism of the performance with variations on the dismissive phrase, "and that was the long and the short of it" (182). *Jane Annie: or The Good Conduct Prize* also offers valuable biographical evidence. Importantly, it disproves the general belief that Margaret Ogilvy was the first member of his family to be given eponymous fame. It is also anecdotally ridiculed. D'Oyly Carte, he recalls, asked one theatregoer why he hadn't clapped. "I didn't like to, when no one else was doing it", he replied (Barrie 1891a: 184). A fuller account of Barrie's interest in these "failures" is therefore warranted.

The first reason for his agreeing to record Richard Savage's tragic story is the vulnerability of young authors to flattery. The idea for the play was suggested to Barrie by Marriott Watson. Henley, one of Barrie's literary idols, supported the idea and even offered to write a prologue for the drama. Barrie and Marriott showed their confidence in another way. An expensive privately printed copy of the text rather than the usual printed draft (ADD 53471B) was sent to the Lord Chamberlain for his approval. *Jane Annie*, for its part, resulted from Richard D'Oyly Carte's surprise choice of a young dramatist with only "Ibsen's Ghost" and *Walker, London* to his West End credit to fill a gap in his Savoy programme caused by the recent quarrel between Gilbert and Sullivan. But where the Barrie of *Richard Savage* was overly self-confident, despondency and insecurity would characterise his first venture into opera.

Self-evidently, collaboration presents a new kind of challenge. Barrie was learning how to adapt to the needs of actors, producers and stage directors. In *The Greenwood Hat* he records the different problems he faced when authorial collaboration was demanded. In recalling these productions, he also stresses how different the collaborative relationships were. Marriott Watson had come up with the idea for *Richard Savage*. The collaboration covered the entire period of composition. Geographical distancing had been the main practical problem – "My recollection is that I wrote bits in Scotland and Marriott wrote bits in London and that we then re-wrote each other's bits" (Barrie 1930c: 182). For *Jane Annie*, the plot and, initially, the authorship was Barrie's alone. Conan Doyle was only drawn in towards the end of the process when Barrie's poor health meant he could not meet the production deadline on his own. The major practical problems this time centred on reconciling two different styles and personalities at a late stage of composition.

When Barrie broadens his teamwork survey to include impresarios, directors and actors the two cases remain different. His account of *Jane Annie*, centres on Doyle's inability to resist actors' pleas to have their own parts lengthened. An entirely different lesson is learned from *Richard Savage*. It might simply read "When West End theatre managers *en masse* reject a script they are usually right". On the other hand, the benevolent side of West End collaboration among actors is also revealed. The single matinée production of *Richard Savage* at the Coliseum was made possible by the fact that *The School for Scandal* was currently running in the evening. As both plays belonged to the same period the costumes for one could be used for the other. And so, on one Saturday afternoon and with Wyndham's permission, Bernard Gould and Cyril Maude appeared as Savage and Richard Steele respectively only to resume their major roles as Sir Bernard Partridge and Sir Benjamin Backbite at night.

In *The Greenwood Hat*, Barrie fails to follow his own rule that good criticism implies discrimination. He ridicules both plays. But in fact *Richard Savage* is clearly inferior to its operatic counterpart. In accepting Marriott Watson's invitation, Barrie may have thought that interest might be revived in a bohemian minor writer of the past. And certainly Savage held the same extreme, criminal position in the Kit Kat club which Marlowe had earlier claimed among Elizabethan dramatists. If this were Barrie's hope, reviewers were quick to dispel it. Almost all agreed with *The Times* correspondent that "The personality of Richard Savage is not one which excites general interest to-day" (17 April 1891: 12). They also agree with his own earlier critical judgment that tragedy was not his métier. This was neither a good tragedy nor an accurate history. "Staginess" replaced seriousness and accuracy gave way to "glib distortion of the facts" (*The Stage* 23 April 1891: 13).

For Barrie whose narrative endings had met with more than their share of critical vitriol it must have been particularly galling to find that the conclusion of this play was judged the worst of all its many inadequacies. And indeed Savage shows such a disinclination to die quickly that the audience's reaction as described by *The Era* reviewer seems fully justified. "The poet's magnanimous suicide", he notes, was witnessed "not only without a pang, but even with some sense of relief". He even detected "some tittering" as Savage's farcical death effectively killed off the play itself (8 February 1891: 11). No other Barrie play would fail so quickly and disastrously.

That *Richard Savage* is a bad play is incontestable. At the same time it fair to ask whether it was meant to be the "tragical history" assumed by its critics. Given the importance of exact modal definitions in the rhetorical tradition, another problem has to be faced. The play in its privately printed form (BVS R53/1) is simply called "A Play". Nor is it unrelievedly serious. The central love triangle is often comically presented. Type characters intent on duping each other with the assistance of screens and disguises recall the Jonson of *Volpone* and *The Alchemist*. The melodramatic spirit is also all-pervasive. Violent conflicts, sudden revelations and extreme characterisation (e.g. the arch-villain Jocelyn) are the stuff of the play. As accurate modal definitions were so important to Barrie, it is worth reconsidering the dénouement in these terms.

Measured against serious and tragic expectations the ending has strong claims to be ranked the worst of all attempts in that mode. Savage doesn't just take ages to die, the fact is commented on, or more accurately exclaimed upon, by others while he is engaged in that process. Repetition of the word "dead" and the drawing in of Jocelyn's demise increase this curious emphasising of the very weaknesses which caused its own critical death knell.

STEELE: (*feeling* SAVAGE's *heart*) Fainted! He is dead!
LADY MIDDLETON: Died! (Falls into chair. TONSON tending her.) Died!
STEELE: Dick!
[Much affected. Puts screen up between sofa and the others and then joins them. SAVAGE is thus shut out from their view but in full view of the audience. ENTER PRUE CENTRE.]
PRUE: He is dead!
SAVAGE: (overhearing): Jocelyn dead!
PRUE: How's Mr. Savage?
TONSON: Hush, he is dead too. (BVS 53471/B)

Alternatively, Barrie and Marriott Watson might have been trying their hand at tragic parody using the comic conventions of Jonson. This would be consistent with the neutral title "play" given in the script and with Barrie's interest in mixed modes. In that case, those who laughed at the ending might have been meant to do so while those who assessed it as bad tragedy could be criticised for using an overly simplistic model for assessment. In the last analysis, however, Richard Savage's theatrical death only proved one thing – that the young authors had entirely failed to carry their audience with them.

2. Collaboration: *Jane Annie* (1893)

Jane Annie (Barrie 1893c) has also been judged a failure but has more redeeming features than its predecessor. First of all, it had a reasonable run from 13 May until 1 July 1893. Barrie's *Greenwood Hat* anecdote notwithstanding it was greeted with sustained applause on the first night. It then went on a short tour of other English cities. Most reviewers voiced disappointment but were not entirely unimpressed. George Bernard Shaw's scathing dismissal was, therefore, atypical. He called it the "most unblushing outburst of tomfoolery that two respectable citizens could conceivably indulge in publicly" (*The World* 24 May 1893: 26–27).

Obviously opera introduces a new challenge. For the first time Barrie had to work with a musical associate. This was not Sullivan. The great man had read the libretto and decided it was not for him. That he passed it to one of his students, however, suggests that he did see some merit in it. His choice was Ernest Ford. Ford was already known as a composer of operettas and had experience of working at the Savoy. His one-act operetta, *Mr. Jericho*, had preceded Sullivan's *Haddon Hall* at the Savoy in Spring 1893. Ford provided a score which would later meet with faint praise. *The Era* reviewer's assessment that it was adequate "without being distinguished or original" was widely shared (20 May 1893: 11).

There must have been some contact between Ford and Barrie if only to agree on the ways in which his libretto might match the different musical styles in the score. Ford's allusions to other composers were, indeed, one of the features of his music which critics really liked with the echoes of Wagner's *Die Meistersinger* at the end of Act One being especially welcomed. Barrie, of course, had no musical training and so his only recorded comments on that aspect of the collaboration reflect the lack of musical "sense" he refers to in *The Greenwood Hat*. At the same time, for a writer who had committed himself to highlighting the aural as well as the visual aspects of drama, the opportunity to extend his experience lyrically must have had some appeal. At this stage, the best he could do was study and imitate Gilbert's methods. But later, in 1920, when he collaborated with Sir Arnold Bax for *The Truth about the Russian Dancers*, he showed himself a more knowledgeable and active collaborator.

An account of *Jane Annie's* plot will demonstrate its centrality to Barrie's creative and critical planning.

Act 1 is set in a girls' seminary while Act 2 is on a golf green. The tone is, throughout, farcical with women academics, male "warriors" and the New Journalists being produced at a nearby male college all being subjected to light satire. Bab, described as a "bad girl", plans to elope, but cannot decide whether to marry Jack the lancer or Tom the student journalist. Jane Annie, the school's "good girl", schemes to take one of them (Jack) off her hands, and calls on her powers of hypnotism to help her. In the end all four are happily united, Jack with Jane and Tom with Bab.[1]

How does this evidence relate to the major lines of Barrie's professional development traced so far? In it he continues to develop those essentially theatrical qualities within texts which combine the dramatic voice with its narrative and poetic equivalents. But only the first of these aims is successfully realised in *Jane Annie*. The theatre's visual strengths are realised in the contrast between Act One's expected (seminary) setting as in *Princess Ida*, and Act Two's unexpected (golf-course) one. The latter was greeted with spontaneous applause by the first night audience. Both Barrie and Conan Doyle played golf and were therefore able to introduce and sustain the vocabulary of the game. For the first time on the London operatic stage, "niblicks", "brassies"[2] and the dark arts of the "caddie" were

---

[1] I have used the text on the D'Oyly Carte home page (http://diamond.idbsu.edu/gas/other_savoy/htm/jane_annie_home.html; accessed 21 November 1997) for all quotes. The Lord Chamberlain's text (ADD 53526A) reflects the rush for completion and even, unusually, bears the word 'Proof' across its opening pages.

[2] Historical golfing terms for obsolete clubs, roughly equivalent to the modern 9-iron and 2-wood respectively.

lyrically celebrated (*JA* 20). Even the most cynical of reviewers saw little to criticise here and some offered unreserved praise to the scenic director and choreographer – "In its dances […] its costumes and scenery, and its interpretation, there is so much deserving high praise" (*The Stage* 18 May 1893: 10).

Unfortunately, neither Barrie nor Conan Doyle was able to sustain the high quality of Gilbert's comic verse. At best their attempts are strained; at worst they are doggerel of the sort Babs uses to express her fear of aging:

BABS: Now my figure – once like this –
Droops like autumn berry;
Pity me, my secret is,
Me is sleepy very! (Barrie 1893c: 4)

Thematically, Barrie's choice of a farcical and fantastic story line allows him to escape the additional problem of writing on two levels. This is, after all, *light* opera with current social trends being farcically presented in Gilbertian manner. Here Barrie shows a sure hand. *Jane Annie* is certainly up to date. It is for example a clever idea to profit from current interest in the New Journalism by showing the first *paparazzi* armed with Kodaks competing for celebrity pictures. The decision to make Jane Annie a hypnotist at a time when Mesmer's views on that subject were being challenged by Liebault and Braid was also intelligent (Winter 1992).

The research Barrie had done on Gilbert is obvious throughout. In setting the story in a ladies' seminary, he recalls the plot of *Princess Ida* although the battle between male students and military men for female hearts also echoes *Patience*. Most of the defining characteristics of the Savoy Operas are retained. These include the lengthy "patter" songs and the unexpected revelation of the heroine's identity as baby-hypnotist at the end of Act One. Individual songs and verbal echoes also bear witness to the breadth of his research. The Proctor's song, "I am a man of erudition" with its refrain "And I don't know why!" echoes in an academic context Prince Gama's famous "benevolent" defence of misogyny in *Princess Ida* (31) while Miss Sims' lament on aging, "A girl again I seem to be" with its refrain "Though I'm an old schoolmistress now" (21), is closely based on Dr. Daly's similar lament in *The Sorcerer*.

Even in this farcical context Barrie manages to re-introduce the "creative-competitive" themes he had been developing in his prose. The battle between the sexes, the rise of the New Woman, the difficulties of uniting journalism with serious writing are all re-visited in a musical context. Barrie's feminist inversion of Darwinian theory is also re-established. Gilbert's satire in *Princess Ida* had been quite even-handed; Barrie gives the victory in every battle of minds to the woman. The stage directions then confirm his desire to underline these ideas visually: "[The GIRLS put on the caps and gowns of the STUDENTS, and swagger about in a manly way. The STUDENTS look shy and mincing]" (23).

The related question of artistic power, trivial or profound, is also lightly introduced. The nearby college (Oxford in disguise) has set up a Chair of New Journalism. The scenes in which these students, in pursuit of good copy, invade the girls' seminary are among the best in the opera. They also translate another topic dear to Barrie's heart. As in *When A Man's Single* and *My Lady Nicotine*, the serious artistic quest for enduring fame is set against the trivialising trends of current journalistic practice.

Jane Annie also offers an insight into Barrie's critical perfectionism. As Darlington notes, his mental exhaustion was in part due to his recognition of real deficiencies in the opera (Darlington 1938: 66). So much did these weigh upon him that he tried to stave off criticism by anticipating it. The first night audience were not only handed the full libretto. Academic footnotes were also provided. These were attributed to Caddie, the youngest character on stage, a device which would later be adapted in *Peter Pan* when the child actress Ela Q May was listed in the programme as "author of the play".

The role of Caddie, played by the child actor Harry Rignold, had originally been a minor one but was significantly expanded in subsequent versions. Caddie begins by calling attention to the structure of the work:

PRESS STUDENTS: School aristocratic,
                         The scene most dramatic,
                         Plot unsystematic
                         And very erratic. (14)

In a footnote to this passage, he reveals that cast members have had "a bet that the critics will quote the third and fourth line here, and say that they apply to the opera".

In the event, they did just that. Correctly seeing that this strategy suggested a lack of confidence, they saw the "inconclusive conclusion" in similar terms. Measuring the opera's open-ended dénouement against Gilbert's witty tying up of all ends they find it wanting. If one thinks instead of Barrie's modernist tendencies the "uncertain" ending of *Jane Annie* might alternatively be seen as his one attempt to impose his own mark on a Gilbertian model which elsewhere he had faithfully imitated. Certainly, a variety of moral and not so moral endings are presented. First Milly and the female chorus offer a conventional ethical directive – "You mustn't do this, you mustn't do that!" Then the men discover they haven't any idea what "that" is – "We mustn't do that, we mustn't do which?" Next the proctor, in offering to resolve their differences, finding he's forgotten his own "conclusion", regretfully, turns to the audience and tells them it's hardly important anyway.

PROCTOR: But just this point I can't recall,
         So, though it's most material,
         You'd best go home without it.
ALL: You'd best go home without it. (35)

Last of all, Caddie in his footnotes offers a fourth, suitably amoral, reaction – "No more good conduct prizes" (37).

Caddie's remark wittily rounds off a four-way exercise in inconclusiveness which was, apparently, well-received. This is interesting as Barrie's equivalent attempts to imitate Victorian doubt via open endings had been misunderstood and criticised in his prose and drama so far. Overall, however, the work lacked comic and poetic power. It is, therefore, fitting to give the last word on it to the reviewer who elsewhere commended its choreography, its costumes and scenery. Turning Caddie-Barrie's own wit against himself, *The Stage* reviewer accepts there was some humour on offer but found more of it in his programme (Caddie's notes) than on the stage (18 May 1893: 10).

These two collaborations continue the story of Barrie's self-conscious and self-critical dramatic apprenticeship. By definition they emphasise teamwork as one means of distinguishing theatrical composition from the narrative mode and so re-confirm his basic belief that an artist should start from the qualities which separate one mode from another. But they also continue to widen the range of dramatic kinds attempted in his apprenticeship as he tries to evaluate his own strengths and weaknesses. Here, there is further evidence of his beginning to distinguish between the artistic challenges he *must* overcome to attain the high artistic goals he had set himself and those which can be sidestepped. While no individual tragic studies followed *Richard Savage*, music would play an increasing role in his dramas after *Jane Annie*.

3. Translation: "Ibsen's Ghost" (1891)

Barrie's rhetorical training with its emphasis on Classical and Renaissance criticism encouraged him to follow the principle of imitation and invention in his early writing. Shakespeare, after all, had used sources, narrative, poetic and dramatic, for *his* plays. It is, therefore, no coincidence that Barrie's first London plays, while not collaborations, all rely to a greater or lesser degree on other sources. Indeed the wide range of techniques implied in these "translations" suggests that he may be seeking to discover the limits of imitation as well as mode.

The earliest of the four plays and the only one to rely on another dramatic source is "Ibsen's Ghost". It was performed in 1891 at a time when the Norwegian playwright was dividing critical opinion on the London stage. *The Doll's House* was presented in that year. It was condemned on moral grounds by most critics but predictably attracted crowds because of that notoriety. This encouraged two actresses, Elizabeth Robbins and Marion Lee, to invest in a limited matinée run of *Hedda Gabler* at the Vaudeville. Unlike Barrie's similar venture with *Richard Savage* they were rewarded. The play was moved to the evenings and enjoyed a long run.. The majority of London critics, led by Clement Scott, continued to condemn – "It was like a visit to the Morgue […] There they all lay on their copper couches […] false men, wicked women, deceitful friends, sensualists, egoists, piled up in a heap behind this screen of glass […] What a hideous play!" (see Griffin 1979: 61–3). But audiences have always been attracted to the forbidden and so continued to attend. Barrie, who was currently preparing *Walker, London* for production at Toole's, saw an opportunity here. He would break off from the major task in hand and produce a shorter, comic work taking advantage of the Ibsen debate by offering a one act parody of the Norwegian's best known plays. This would coincide with and act as a rival to the serious performances at the *Coliseum*.

The success of his efforts can be gauged by the reviews the play received. *The Times'* "Review of Drama for 1891" went so far as to see "Ibsen's Ghost" as a sign that England had found a new Molière (7 January 1892: 7). Less ambitiously and more accurately it was assessed in terms of its defined mode and welcomed in those terms: "A return to the true theory of burlesque" (*The Gentlewoman* 6 June 1891: 5); "As clever and amusing a parody of some of Ibsen's dramatic peculiarities as any playgoer might wish to see" (*The Era* 6 Jun 1891: 8).

To begin your career by mocking Ibsen is unlikely to gain you a reputation as one of his disciples. Even to-day, Ibsen scholars continue to see Barrie as unsympathetic to that dramatist's ideas and methods. This is another effect of the "rustic escapist" myth. When Barrie is defined in sentimental, retrospective terms there seems no way in which he could have admired or shared ground with the creator of *Hedda Gabler*. But he did admire and imitate Ibsen, a fact which will be variously confirmed in the succeeding studies of *Walker, London*, "Becky Sharp", *The Wedding Guest* and *Tommy and Grizel*.

The moment one moves from mode to form and matter in accordance with the structure proposed for this section, the dangers of reading Barrie's mockery of Ibsen at surface level becomes obvious. A major editorial problem also emerges. Barrie's MSS and rehearsal drafts are usually close to the Lord Chamberlain's MS. "Ibsen's Ghost", however, proves an exception to this rule. ADD 53475/L35 is not in Barrie's hand and differs markedly from the five versions of the play preserved in the Beinecke collection as BVS Ib 6/1–5. These vary among themselves and belong to different stages of the play's evolution but are not in chronological order. Ib 6/1 is the earliest version and accurately represents Barrie's first draft. Ib 6/2, however, as its holograph introduction to Cynthia Asquith reveals, was composed in 1932 when Barrie was revising the play for publication by the Corvinus Press.[3] The précis below follows this text.

---

[3] In a limited edition of 16 texts. None survives, probably because the Corvinus Press lost most of its stock in a fire.

George Tesman sits at his desk. He is so totally absorbed in his writing that his wife, Thea, who wishes to leave him can only get this message across by writing him a letter and sending him off to post it to himself. Her grandfather, Peter Terence, then suddenly enters from *Ghosts*. He brings with him that play's central themes of heredity and guilt and accordingly blames himself for Thea's inherited nature. At this point Thea turns into Hedda Gabler. In her new role she looks forward to a new age when heredity will count for nothing. Peter's wife, Delia, now returns from seeing yet another play, *The Doll's House*. It has turned her symbolically from Peter's "duck" into the rebellious *Wild Duck* of yet another play. She bitterly blames Peter for never giving her the opportunity to be disreputable –"Did you ever take me into low society?... Did you ever bring home a disreputable man to dinner?" (15). The two women urge Peter to kill himself in the nobly aesthetic manner intended for Løvborg in Hedda Gabler. After some delay, they do all shoot themselves. George returns, still wrapped up in his own concerns, dismisses their bodies as "rubbish" and continues to write.

Even this brief account shows how seriously Barrie has taken the task of the parodist. To echo and interweave material from four Ibsen plays demands careful reading of the original. And later, it will emerge that he in fact admires the man he mocks. In the letter attached to BVS Ib 6/2 he claims "Ibsen's Ghost" as "his first play" but also regrets having "having made 'play' even for twenty minutes with the dramatist I have always known to be the greatest of his age".

The reason for the strange disparity between authorial intentions and the play received by the Lord Chamberlain is also explained to Cynthia:

As here presented [his 1932 version] in its winding sheet the burlesque, so far as my reading of it recalls is much as I posted it to Mr. Toole but not as he despatched it to the Lord Chamberlain. Between these two events it received many emendations which I have now struck out, all pressed on me in his wistful way by Mr. Toole […] I reduced a speech of about 100 words, now lost for ever, to five or six because he said wistfully that long speeches were hard to learn. I added a sub-title "Toole-up-to-Date" because he said it would make him feel more at home. I let him turn suddenly into Ibsen because Miss Vanbrugh turns into Hedda. (Intro. Ib 6/2)

This comment confirms the suspicion that the Lord Chamberlain approved Toole's revision of Barrie's play. Foreseeably, his version highlights his own part as Peter and introduces a series of those farcical devices on which his reputation had been built. Unfortunately, as Barrie tells Cynthia, he was mystified by the deeper purposes of the play: "As for Mr. Toole, he wandered through the thing, searching vainly for what it may be about". As a result there is a major difference between the seriously acted presentation of Ibsen which Barrie had intended ("because nonsense acted gravely was at that time an innovation" [Intro. Ib 6/2]) and the totally farcical offering which was licensed for performance.

The same source suggest that, in 1891, Barrie did manage to restore some of his own material at rehearsal stage. Certainly the first night production as described by Walbrook was not quite so farcical as wholesale adoption of Toole's text would imply. But if he won that battle, Barrie did not win the war. For him, Toole was still the schoolboy idol of past days. That the actor-manager used this influence to manipulate him is even evident in the first night programme. This does not mention Barrie by name but does faithfully record Toole's involvement as actor and manager.

Barrie's memorially reconstructed 1931 text cuts out most of the concessions he made to Toole forty years earlier. In it Peter no longer turns into Ibsen while the farcical final song and dance are also excised. An additional sheet contains that song and is enclosed with the earliest typed text Ib 6/1 in the Beinecke Barrie Collection. But Toole's own MS as given to the Lord Chamberlain pre-dates even this text. It contains an even more blatant piece of self-advertisement for the actor-manager. Its light tune, the crude device of bringing the stage-dead back to life and its eulogising of Toole and his theatre were all at dramatic odds with the clever but restrained ending proposed by Barrie.

In the Lord Chamberlain's version Toole himself sings the first stanza and so brings his actors back to life:

PETER: Just fancy that! – It is my cue.
        Well I don't fancy them – do you?
        I think that all the Ibsen ladies
        Should find a place and go to Hades.

Equally inevitably, the final cameo centres on him. In the revised version of 1891, as described by critics, it would appear that Barrie did manage to spread the character focus more evenly. But this was only a minor concession and if he had later harboured any thought of including "Ibsen's Ghost" in the *Collected Plays* his awareness that it was every bit as much a collaboration as *Richard Savage* or *Jane Annie* must have despatched it immediately.

Nonetheless, it does remain one of his finest early works. It made his name on the London stage while his experiences with Toole taught him valuable lessons about theatrical teamwork. The burlesque form also offered him an ideal opportunity to develop his interest in visual and aural effects as Moult and Hammerton confirm (1928: 204–5; 1929: 239–41).

London critics were especially impressed by the young dramatist's use of aural and visual effects. Key phrases encapsulating themes from Ibsen are repetitively employed and act as aural clues. "Just fancy that", "vine leaves in your hair", "mad, mad, mad" and "so the bolt falls" all fall into this category. By way of contrast, mime scenes offer visual signs alone while the physical transformation of Thea into Hedda is accompanied aurally by an exaggerated stylistic transition from plain speech to high style apostrophe (13).

The exaggerated "comic cameo" form as practised in his early novels also finds its natural theatrical equivalent in burlesque's one-sided comic presentation of action and ideas. From *Hedda Gabler* and *Ghosts* the ideas of free love and the power of heredity are presented through Thea's exaggerated nymphomania – "It is in my blood, I cannot look at a man without wanting to kiss him" (Ib 6/2: 8) – and grandfather Peter's melodramatic acceptance that he is their source: "Ah! Revile me, Tia. It is I who have made you what you are! Brandy! Ghosts!" (10). The device of repetition even becomes the focus for explicit comment when Peter asks Tia whether he is "saying Ghosts too often?"

The "immoral" Ibsen who so outraged English opinion is also ludicrously represented. Thea's listing of her daily flirtations ("Parson Greig kissed me on Tuesday and Henrik Barsam on Wednesday and Baron Kleig on Thursday") is one example of this (7). More unexpectedly, Peter's elderly wife returns from seeing *A Doll's House* demanding to know why her husband has deprived her of all disreputable company. This leads into mockery of Ibsen's use of symbolism as she determinedly turns from being his "doll" into a new more troublesome role as his "wild duck".

If closer definitions of mode and teamwork reveal Barrie's relationship with Ibsen in a new light, study of the play's position within his range of translation techniques helps to explain why that influence endured. Two features set it apart from the other three works considered in this section. As noted earlier, the other three all have prose narrative sources. Only "Ibsen's Ghost" re-translates the work of another playwright Secondly, the other plays in this section will make different "translation" demands. For another, more respectful, imitation of the major features of a source's style, one has to move two years on and turn to *Jane Annie*. Although in that case the imitation is not satirically intended, Barrie's careful study of Gilbert's artistry *was* noted in the discussion of the opera. That professionalism had been anticipated in his approach to Ibsen.

"Ibsen's Ghost" is also the first of his plays to work on two levels. Appreciation of parody depends on a knowledge of what is being parodied. By choosing to exaggerate the most obvious features of the Norwegian's style Barrie makes sure that even the most superficial reader of Ibsen will recognise the focus of his wit. Yet, when one reads the particular plays he parodies, it becomes clear that Barrie mocked in excess on stage the very themes in Ibsen which he was simultaneously himself advocating in his prose.

When Brian Johnson, in his analysis of *A Doll's House*, cites Ibsen's concern with those social forces which prevent women realising their massive potential, his comments could be applied to Barrie with equal justification (Johnson 1974: 97). When Ibsen made his famous speech in Stockholm on the power of Darwinism to change people's personal, social, moral and metaphysical outlooks he was advancing a view of gender conflict very close to Barrie's own. Ibsen's plea for imaginative addressing of this broadest referential range possible was also one of the tenets Barrie had inherited from Masson (Boyesen 1894: xx). Further, both playwrights return to past ages in order to reformulate the present and so explore worlds beyond time. Barrie's acceptance of that formula has been fully discussed. The same ambitious aims are critically attributed to Ibsen:

The great themes [of Ibsen] are the recollection of the Past and the search for a new spiritual direction in the present which the entire spiritual history of humanity is resurrected for a judgement day upon the soul. (Johnson 1974: 263)

While one writes serious, the other comic drama they also shared a belief in texts which not only work on more than one level of relevance but may strive to conceal this. Certainly, when Holtan notes that "[t]here is more beneath the surface of Ibsen's drama than is immediately apparent" he unconsciously echoes Horace Walpole's assessment of Barrie (Holtan 1974: 7, 3; Barrie 1938: vii).

The first sign of what will become a strong metanarrational strand in Barrie's work also appears in "Ibsen's Ghost". The opening scene cleverly counterpoints vocal and written communication. The discussion between Peter and Tia starts with a debate on the relative values of dialogue and miming. And, as noted earlier, the suicidal ending turns to the instability of the text. In a desperate effort to avoid theatrical suicide, Peter scans the different translations available:

TIA: So well, that is your cue how
PETER: No; "other women" is my cue. I am using Gosse's translation, you know.
TIA: I am using Archer's.
PETER: This is very awkward. (8)

Only when he is doomed textually, does he agree to die.

There is even a meta-theatrical dimension for, of course, the play's success in part depends on specific parodying of its serious, Coliseum rival. Toole's leading actress, Irene Vanbrugh, was therefore encouraged to study and parody the acting styles of her "serious" rivals Lea and Robins.

This crossing of the bounds between actors created by scripts and their supposed "real" existence is a modernist technique. But Barrie's critical sophistication means that, from an early stage in his career, he challenges his audience in the same way. Later, his pursuit of this line would be met with bewilderment on all sides. The original MS of *Peter Pan* which translated its "original" theme in both dramatic (*commedia dell'arte*) and histrionic (imitation of past actors) terms is only one example of this (Jack 1990: 101–13). In that case, Barrie reacted to the incomprehension by deleting both sections but later resuscitating the former in one act form as "Pantaloon". No such difficulties existed for the simpler, meta-dramatic coding of "Ibsen's Ghost". But as a play which at once re-translates Ibsen and offers its own critique on play-making, it defies simplistic definition.

4. Translation: *Walker, London* (1892)

The evolution of this play is a long one. It opened at Toole's on February 25th 1892 but planning begins as early as 1886. Notebook 6 (1885–88) and Notebook 7 (1887–88) show its gradual development from the basic idea of a houseboat setting and a flirtatious barber. Therefore, the relationship between it and "Ibsen's Ghost", in the Notes, anticipates that between *Margaret Ogilvy* and *Sentimental Tommy*. A shorter work, occasioned by outside events (interest in Ibsen and Margaret's death), appears before a longer, more carefully considered counterpart.

Usually it is called a comedy, occasionally a farce and sometimes, as in the Lord Chamberlain's text (ADD 53493F), it is not defined at all. This evidence accurately describes a play whose action is often farcical but whose author recommended that it be played with restraint. Within that field, Barrie's most immediate rival was Pinero whose *Lady Bountiful* and *The Times* had recently enjoyed minor triumphs at the Garrick and Terry's respectively.

Barrie forsakes any attempt to use comic action as a vehicle for serious ideas in *Walker, London*. His invention is instead focused on techniques of translation. In a sense, therefore, *Walker, London* is lighter than "Ibsen's Ghost" whose parodic remit *does* imply dual plotting. Critics correctly saw the houseboat play in these terms. For them it was "a trivial story" and "a box of frivolous theatrical tricks as ephemeral as yesterday's newspaper" (Wright 1976: 53; Geduld 1971: 101). The prophecy implicit in these remarks has proved accurate. Its ephemeral storyline condemned it to popularity within the period it described. But its first uninterrupted run of 511 consecutive performances was the longest any Barrie play enjoyed throughout his career. Subsequently, it went on tour before returning to Toole's on Boxing Day for a further month of festive performances.

Why was this story so captivating? The undemanding tastes of those who frequented Toole's theatre only take us so far. There were, after all, many trivial plays in London at this time, none of which enjoyed the continued success of Barrie's offering. A brief account of the plot will again aid enquiry.

The leading role belongs to Jasper Phipps, a barber, who in disguise gains entry to a houseboat party. The leading female members of the party are the Girton bluestocking, Bell Golightly, and the outgoing Irish girl, Nanny O'Brien. Along with Jasper's fiancée, Sarah, they provide one side of a light, undemanding comedy centred on three nicely differentiated love affairs. Bell's flirtations with the cricketer Kit Upjohn are used to satirise excessive reliance on either brains or brawn. Nanny and her Scottish partner, Andrew McPhail, offer another neat personality contrast, this time in terms of nationality. The circumstances surrounding the third lower-class pairing, however, provide the major catalyst for the drama. Jasper decides to have his honeymoon before his wedding to his fiancée, Sarah. In accordance with that aim, he jilts her and flirts with the upper-class women on the houseboat. Playing the part of the African adventurer Colonel Neil, a customer whom he physically resembles, he easily wins the affections of both Bell and Nanny with his invented tales. Finally, he returns to his own class and Sarah.

The plot, then, is conventional. The only original idea is Jasper's decision to have his honeymoon before his wedding. Barrie has already studied the clash of different worlds and conventions in Shakespeare's comedies. He now profits from that training, gaining maximal comic effect from the principle of incongruity which underlies the mode. Structurally, as his Notebooks reveal, he has worked hard to interlink the three romantic plots and reduce the action to a single day. Act One depicts the houseboat in the morning, Act Two is set at midday and Act Three in the evening. Light the plot may be but it obeys Aristotle's definition of the Unity of Time!

If one places *Walker, London* within the wider contexts of Barrie's literary ambitions and his prose works an important fact emerges. In this light comedy he has achieved theatrically what the earlier Thrums tales had proved prosaically. In popular terms, and at a very early stage in his dramatic career, he has shown that he can meet the first – popular but transient – stage in the quest for genius as defined by Cowley and critically developed in his own Skelton and Nash essays.

Behind the three interlinked plots lie three of Barrie's own prose works. *When A Man's Single*, *My Lady Nicotine* and *An Edinburgh Eleven* are all echoed in the houseboat drama. In *The Road to the Never Land*, I offered an extended account of the ways in which he uses these sources (Jack 1991: 32–38). That evidence shows him progressively compressing the descriptive side to his narrative while sharpening the dialogue. Only the most immediately powerful dramatic situations are exceptions to this general rule of increased economy as manuscript gives way to typed drafts and printed texts.

Barrie would later test out different ways of translating his prose theatrically. Soon, in *The Professor's Love Story*, he would move from light echoing of many sources to detailed employment of one. But the key principles of modal translation were learned as, stage by stage, he imaginatively moved the houseboat he shared with Gilmour away from the pages of his novels and began to re-construct it, literally and metaphorically, for the theatre.

Barrie's major reason for making the move from prose to drama was the one he confessed to Cynthia Asquith – his inability to keep himself out of his novels. When translating the houseboat from narrative to theatrical use, he made a particularly important discovery. In *When A Man's Single*, the houseboat's real existence remained obvious. Its theatrical equivalent, given drama's autobiographical distancing powers, lost this personal connection. Giving distinctive personalities to different physically visible characters on the houseboat was one way of diminishing the biographical links in the original plot. But the process of source adaptation also taught him that the first material to go when drama imposed its own tighter demands was indeed the autobiographical content of his narratives.

Walker, London, then, represents a major step forward in Barrie's exploration of the nature and range of modal translation available at a time when plays based on novels were enjoying a vogue on the London stage. Considering it in relation to another prose text, *The Little Minister*, strengthens this conclusion. The planning for both ran parallel in the Notebooks and *The Little Minister* was published only four months before *Walker, London* opened. To compare them is, therefore, chronologically justified although they stand at different stages of modal development, the one being a late ambitious prose work, the other an early, relatively undemanding foray into drama.

The most obvious similarity between the two is their shared narrative structure. In each case a number of dramatic situations are linked. For Barrie, this is as much an innovation in the "old" mode as the "new" as his prose had been until then characteristically linear and episodic. Unlike *The Little Minister*, however, all of the *Walker, London* plots are lightly conceived and executed. This means that the problems of reconciling narrative and allegorical logics which had bedevilled the novel were avoided in the play. The particularly enthusiastic reception which greeted the ending of the drama illustrates this important difference. At the same time as critics were condemning Barrie's failure to reconcile real and ideal or provide a satisfying conclusion to Gavin Dishart's romance they were reserving particular praise for Jasper's last farewell to the houseboat.

Barrie may well have found these reactions darkly amusing especially as the last scene in *Walker, London* owed its form to last minute desperation rather than long term planning. His Notebooks initially show him changing the title over and over again. Finally, he decided upon *The Houseboat,* only to discover that it had been used before. At the last minute the idea of calling it *Walker, London* occurred. "Walker!" in Cockney slang has the sense of "You must be joking!" It would be known, in that sense, to Barrie from Dickens' *A Christmas Carol*, where it was used by the boy whom Scrooge sends to collect the Cratchits' goose to express doubt about the old man's seriousness.

But Barrie also revised the ending to include the phrase. Having escaped, Jasper outwits the upper class group on the barge for the last time by making the play's title his unattainable contact address:

MRS. GOLIGHTLY: He gave me his telegraphic address yesterday. Oh, I have lost it. [*Goes to back of saloon.*] Colonel, what did you say is your address?
JASPER: (*in punt*): What's my what?
MRS. GOLIGHTLY: Your address.
JASPER: (*off*) Walker, London.
ALL: Walker, London. (Barrie 1942: 52)

The new title and text were rushed to the Lord Chamberlain and the licence for performance granted one day before the play opened.

If interlaced structures were one of Barrie's major interests at this time, the ideas of Ibsen also continued to influence him. That influence extended to *The Little Minister*. In the case of the novel, Ibsen's example affected the mythic, allegorical levels of Gavin's story. *Walker, London* is just a light comedy, however, and one might therefore suppose that any influence from Barrie's most radical source would disappear. But there is one exception to that rule. Barrie's training meant that he was likely to share Ibsen's desire to balance realism with poetic techniques. If that is so, he is (not for the first time) critically ahead of his time. This view of the Norwegian's art, as Holtan notes, was not common in Victorian Britain. There it was the socio-critical Ibsen as interpreted by Brandes and Bernard Shaw who dominated thinking. "Until very recently it has been in these terms, reformer, moralist, problem dramatist, that Ibsen's reputation was represented to the world" (Holtan 1974:3; see also Brandes 1899; Shaw 1981).

If, with this in mind, one returns to the generative account of *Walker, London* at the late stage of composition which coincides with "Ibsen's Ghost", an interesting possibility emerges. Walbrook's lengthy analysis of the play in *Barrie and the Theatre* is entitled "J.L. Toole and the Cuckoo" (Walbrook 1922). This cuckoo does not exist in the early drafts. It first makes a modest appearance in Act 2 of the Lord Chamberlain's text, when Jasper is trying to sustain his fraudulent role as African adventurer against close questioning. As he feigns dizziness to cover his ignorance, the bird calls out three times:

NANNY: Listen to that cuckoo.
MRS. GOLIGHTLY: Yes, we never heard it till you came to us Colonel and now we hear it a dozen times a day. (ADD 54393/F Act 4.15)

Its call is heard later in the same act when Jasper vows to shoot it. This was the version witnessed by the first night audience. But in the course of the first run subsequent revisions made it central to each act.

It seems probable that Barrie was seriously adopting Ibsen's symbolic techniques in *Walker, London* while mocking them in "Ibsen's Ghost". In the one act play Delia's sudden change from loyal wife to rebellious "new" woman is hilariously presented as a "doll" (*A Doll's House*) turning into a "duck" (*The Wild Duck*)! Barrie's serious critical interest in symbolism is further confirmed in both early and later texts where the implications of Jasper as cuckoo are not only enacted but explained to the audience by Old Ben when he says to Jasper "you're the cuckoo in the hen's nest and that's your mate a-calling to you" (Barrie 1942: 17). The wider implications of the symbolism are also poetically extended. The houseboat and the punt become, imaginatively, the nest which Jasper as cuckoo has entered, pretending to be of the same "kind" as its other inhabitants. When nature reasserts itself and he finally sails off the link is again made. He and Sarah are of the same class and so belong to one another. The initial timing of these poetic additions (in the Lord Chamberlain's text) and the thoroughness with which they are later confirmed does suggest that Barrie's current interest in Ibsen extended from *The Little Minister* and "Ibsen's Ghost" to *Walker, London.*

Walker, London is also the first play in which Barrie makes a clear practical statement about the kind of theatre he wants. That he sees drama as a collaborative effort is clear from the changes made in the successive drafts of the first acting text. Most of these alterations have been made in the theatre as he watched and listened to the cast. He had done the same for *Richard Savage* and "Ibsen's Ghost" and was, as a result, gaining a name as the actors' playwright at precisely the time when two of the accepted "greats" of London theatre were convicted of using the stage as a vehicle for their own, essentially undramatic talents. *Lady Windermere's Fan* opened five nights before *Walker, London* and was condemned in *The Times* as less a drama than a convenient means of communicating the wit of this "literary artistic trifler" (26 February 1892: 2). In the same year, Shaw's *Widowers' Houses* was similarly criticised in *Lloyds* as "in no sense a drama, but a succession of dialogues in which the author sets forth his views concerning Socialist questions".[4]

But Barrie was still under Toole's influence and so the problem of who captained that team remained an issue. The first night programme suggested slight progress. Barrie's name is there but only once; Toole's appears three times in larger print. The play is billed as the actor-manager's triumphant return from illness. Toole it was who played the comic lead and made the final curtain speech.

But the evidence, this time, suggests that Barrie allowed him these apparent victories only after he had won the war. Joseph Harker, the scene painter, notes the clarity of the young playwright's directions and his quiet, efficient way of getting his wishes across.

Barrie was very quiet and undemonstrative [...] save in a few instances where his dictum was important. On these occasions he would assert himself with a sudden access of vigour, impressing on you his wishes in a way that quite plainly indicated that he knew exactly what he wanted and that he was capable of seeing that he got it". (Harker 1924: 246)

George Shelton, who would later play Smee in *Peter Pan*, had the role of Jasper's ally Ben in *Walker, London* and he noted the playwright's

---

[4] I consulted this in 1990 in the Theatre Museum. The heading with title and date was cut off.

particular resistance to any sign of Toole's "thickening": "As the gags came along Barrie in his quiet way, said 'Out,' and so it went on until every gag was banished" (Shelton 1928: 110). In this way, he turned the "patronage" tables on Toole before rehearsals had even begun.

Irene Vanbrugh confirms this. Having decided that she preferred the role of Nanny O'Brien to her assigned part as Bell Golightly, she

approached the shy little author, confident at seventeen that my position as Toole's leading lady would intimidate him into giving me a choice of either part. How young but how foolish I was and how quiet but firm he was!" (Vanbrugh 1949: 29)

The truth here is that Barrie had already met his future wife, Mary Ansell. The kind of romantic attachment he had shown for Minnie Palmer dictated that no one else would play Nanny's part.

The same evidence, in Notebooks and personal reminiscences, confirms his principle of highlighting the unique powers of the theatre. Both its aural and visual potential are pushed, successfully, to extremes. Characteristically, the first hint of the play focuses on a visual effect – "Flirtation scene through blind in a houseboat" (A2/6:72). This will in due time become part of the dramatic climax as recorded in the Definitive Edition when Jasper makes his escape in Act 3 (48). George Shelton's memories of the production also begin with the visual. The cast, he confides, initially feared that the set was too complex but Barrie's detailed understanding of the challenge quickly reassured them: "[as] the dialogue proceeded, Barrie indicated where the speaker should be upon the stage, whether upon the upper deck or in the saloon, or in the punt alongside; and all went well" (Shelton 1928: 110).

Arguably, Barrie's interest in drama's distinctive visual and aural power originates with Campbell Fraser's "sensual" introduction to Berkeley's theory of Vision and Masson's emphasis on Shakespeare's "visual distinctiveness" (Fraser 1878: "Introduction" *passim*; Masson 1914: 134). Practically, it is put into play in an uncompromisingly ambitious way at the very start of Barrie's West End career. The Property Plot in the Acting Edition illustrates this. Its long list of settings – deck, saloon, cabin, punt, bow, water – is accompanied by an even longer list of the props associated with each. Particularly difficult movements from one section or level of the stage to another provide another kind of proof. For example, at the same time as the original miming scene is being enacted, the crane, set up for cricket practice,

has to move the sleeping Sarah in her chair from the upper deck down
to a punt on river level.

The sounds of a minuet form the background to Jasper's furtive
exit, reminding us that aural effects as well as visual ones contributed
to *Walker, London's* theatricality (48). Aural effects are also highlighted, as the opening Stage Directions for Act III in the 1907 Acting
Edition illustrate:

ACT III. CURTAIN rises on evening moonlight. Houseboat precisely as when curtain
fell on Act II except that Sarah is now asleep in her chair on deck. From a distance is
heard a piano with whistling accompaniment. Light splashes; as if of water rats, rus-
tling in branches and "wheep wheep" of birds settling to sleep. Next the sound of oars
and a cockney voice, "Look when you're shoving your blooming canoe." A shadowy
boat with one light goes by, a bat flaps about, and disappears. A distant clock strikes
nine. Next a punt passes, containing a male and female figure. Man exclaims "My
darling, let us glide on like this forever and ever!" Woman answers, "But what would
mum say?" Then someone is heard singing a verse of a song in distance. The singing
fades away into distance, then the sound of punting.
    [KIT and BEN enter R. on bank.]

Every character is precisely pictured and given a distinct area of the
stage. The penny whistle adds atmospheric sound. The drawing of the
blinds reveals in turn the breakfast table and then, in depth, the distant
bank. That the result was extremely successful is remembered by the
play's scene painter, Joseph Harker. There, he identifies *Walker,
London* as the most satisfying experience of his entire career and pays
glowing tribute to the young playwright's clear visualisation of what
he wanted (Harker 1924: 239). Another tribute to the set was provided
by Clement Scott who devoted much of his review to its effectiveness:
"[a]s if by magic, we are carried right away from dull, unromantic
London to the lovely reach of pure Thames scenery under the Cleve-
don Woods at Maidenhead" (*Illustrated London News* 30 June 1892:
156).

Walker, London may be outdated but its importance for Barrie
should not be underestimated. In it he first successfully grappled with
the unique challenges of the theatre. In translating his early prose
dramatically he also proved that the new form could (as he had critically anticipated) reduce the autobiographical tendencies which
continued to mar his narratives. Indeed, especially as he did not share
the public's general enthusiasm for *The Little Minister*, he might well
have begun to consider making drama his main artistic focus even at

this early stage. As he was also, by now, working on the Tommy novels and would have to wait some time before he could make the stage "pay", any such plan could not immediately be put into force. After all, the "failed" prose version of *The Little Minister* poured £20,000 into his bank account while Toole's tight contract meant that he earned precisely £250 for the "successful" *Walker, London* and its record-breaking run. One does not need to be an out-and-out materialist to find those figures persuasive.

5. Translation: *The Professor's Love Story* (1892–93)

Variations on a world in which women outthink men define Barrie's early drama as well as his prose. Lightly based on Darwinian theory and relying mainly on different versions of Shakespearean romance, these plays make little attempt to be "heavy" in *Greenwood Hat* terms. They do, however, allow Barrie to extend his expertise. From an original, essentially feminist, base he can present different versions of this "battle" narrative while at the same time setting himself different structural and "translation" challenges.

This principle of variations on a theme is consistent with Barrie's view that a limited number of stories exist and that the artist's task is to re-translate them inventively. The relationship between *The Professor's Love Story* and its immediate predecessor, *Walker, London*, provides a good example of this. Viewed as light romantic comedies on sexual rivalry, there does not seem much to choose between them. Perhaps, as the *Sketch* reviewer comments, *The Professor's Love Story*, may be the more serious of the two – "*Walker, London* was farce with a tendency to comedy; the new piece is comedy with a strong leavening of farce" (4 July 1894: 510). But in it Barrie seeks to consolidate on his earlier success rather than attempt radical change. In a letter of 1916, he supports that view when he calls it "An old conventional, harmless play of mine" (Mackail 1941: 496).

That letter comes at the end of the play's very strange stage-history and will add another, unexpected, chapter to Barrie's determined attempts to maintain his belief in theatrical teamwork. Meanwhile, a brief description of its plot will illustrate how it is at once similar to *Walker, London* and very different from it.

Professor Goodwillie, an absent-minded academic loses interest in his work and assumes he must be the victim of some illness. In fact, he has fallen in love with his secretary, Lucy White, who is also romantically attracted to him. As an intelligent, liberated New Woman she easily serves and manipulates him. The barriers in her way are two other female "types". First, there is her delightfully useless rival, the young Dowager Lady Gilding, whose hierarchical view of the world prevents her from suspecting she has a lower-class rival. She makes Lucy her confidante, confesses her tactics in advance and so is easily overcome. More threatening is Goodwillie's spinster sister. Another theatrical type – the "grande-dame" in Miss Havisham mode – she nearly persuades Lucy to give up her suit. The arrival of a long-lost love-letter finally restores Miss Goodwillie's faith in men and allows the professor's love story to end on a suitably idyllic note. There is also a rustic sub-plot, in which the professor's maid, Effie, attracts two suitors, Pete and Henders. Both are "slow" wooers and so are easily manipulated by her. In the end, it is Henders who proves himself less passive and so wins her hand.

When the play opened in London, critics placed it in the same "light-fantastic" category as *Walker, London*. While some shared the *Sketch*'s view, others thought its central premise drew it closer to farce than its predecessor. Darlington found the idea of a man at once deeply in love yet unable to recognise the passion "crudely incredible" while the Scotsman placed him "on the verge of insanity" (Darlington 1938: 63; *Scotsman* 26 June 1894). William Archer, who had hoped Barrie would write a serious Ibsen play to build on "Ibsen's Ghost", was the most scathing of all. For him the plot was simply absurd: "Of the four chief moments or motives in the play, two are psychologically impossible, one psychologically improbable and the remaining one materially improbable, not to say miraculous" (Archer 1971: 186).

This criticism and the comparative similarities noted are proper reactions to the question, "What's the play about?" The evidence adduced so far for Barrie's early development as a dramatist suggests that three additional questions have to be asked. The first of these concerns the play's place among Barrie's experiments in converting prose narrative into drama. Here, radical differences emerge both particularly and generally. In terms of translation techniques *Walker, London* and *The Professor's Love Story* offer an extreme contrast. The houseboat drama used a variety of prose works as sources for its interrelated plots but never drew heavily from any one. In the double (upper and lower class) plot of *The Professor's Love Story*, Barrie instead chooses to adapt thoroughly, and in the sub-plot alone, a single chapter from *Auld Licht Idylls*.

Moving "The Courting of T'nowheads Bell" from book to stage was not an easy task but Barrie was by now quite experienced in this area. "Ibsen's Ghost", it should be remembered, had presented another different and difficult challenge – the parodic distillation of four full length Ibsen plays into one act. He, therefore, shows a sure hand when importing into Professor Goodwillie's tale, those most unromantic of suitors, Pete and Henders. In particular, he shows his awareness of the tighter demands of theatre over drama by economically translating his early tale in every way possible. Minor characters are excised, the time-scale shortened, the two chases in the original, coalesce into one. Barrie also avoids what must have been a great temptation – to lift rather than re-write most of the dialogue – as the chapter in question is so dominated by direct speech that it already reads like a chatty playscript.

Trained as he was in classical rhetoric, the relationship between form and meaning was an essential element in Barrie's critical thinking. It is not, therefore, enough to define his skills in the sub-plot alone without asking how they fit in to the structure of the work as a whole. This, the second "developmental" question, diverts attention to another source – Shakespeare. The general influence of the bard on *The Professor's Love Story* is not in question. Indeed Leonee Ormond claims that it "is the most Shakespearean of his early comedies". In making this assertion, she sees *As You Like It* as its prime source. A Victorian tale is played out in "the forest of Arden, a place in which the strictures of city life can melt into pastoral idyll" (Ormond 1987: 50).

This is obviously true. Masson had made a special case for Renaissance pastoral writing generally when he argued that it worked subversively on both realistic and idealistic levels of reference. Later critics have agreed. Walter R. Davies, for example, notes:

The heroes of the Renaissance Pastoral romances are always *sojourners* in the Arcadian preserve, never shepherds. This fact, together with the continuing contrast between the pastoral land and the other places necessary to exhibit its meaning, makes the setting of the Renaissance pastoral romances always *multiple*". (Davies 1965: 34)

This is because they become part of a poetic synthesis which at once comprehends and re-creates them.

To be poetic and subversive was the ambitious aim of Barrie's *Imp*. *The Professor's Love Story* cannot, of course, claim to realise that ideal. Simply and popularly conceived, it may, nonetheless represent a first step in that direction. There is an interesting biographical parallel here also. Masson's account of Shakespeare's life drew him close in rusticity, ambitiousness, critical astuteness, pragmatism and hard work to Barrie's vision of himself. The chronology adopted in the professor's lecture course has Shakespeare leave the countryside for London to embark on a process of financially unaided artistic self-discovery. *As You Like It* and the group of "sylvan romances" according to this scheme were assigned to Shakespeare in his thirties at the end of an apprenticeship which saw him forsake verse and narrative for theatre alone. *The Professor's Love Story*, therefore, adopts one of Shakespeare's comic forms at the equivalent time in Barrie's career and prophesies the modal choice he too would make.

Ormond's sense that it is the *most* Shakespearean of all Barrie's works can be accounted for by looking at the variety of Shakespearean models and techniques it employs. Only *Bohemia* had earlier attempted to offer so wide an imitative range and its artlessness only serves to highlight how skilfully the older Barrie translates the many-world comedy of the Renaissance into the Victorian era. But of course, this time, he introduces another Shakespearean convention. What distinguishes *The Professor's Love Story* is its conscious employment of the double plot, which counterpoints the main, upper-class story at lower-class level.

Against a set which accurately mirrors Victorian life and in a plot which nicely reflects the manners and conventions of that age, Barrie re-introduces his audience to the eternal battle of the sexes as fought out, in mythic manner, between contrasted character types. At both levels he also re-introduces his feminist inversion of Darwin's model. An upper class triangle in which two cunning ladies energetically pursue the affection of an almost totally ineffectual man is set against a lower class triangle in which two passive, unromantic men fail to pursue the smart, worldly woman of their supposed affections. The strategies he employs to link the actions – turning Effie into Lucy's confidante and allowing Henders to discover Miss Goodwillie's letter – are also economically effective.

The third question concerning the play's place in Barrie's artistic apprenticeship arises from this account. While neither *Walker, London* nor *The Professor's Love Story* is, in any sense, a philosophical play the narrative as well as the structure of the later work is designed to present Barrie's thesis of female superiority in a clear and exemplary manner. In terms of Darwinian powerfulness and evolutionary adaptability, Goodwillie, Pete and Henders exist at the lowest level of masculine impotence. Their houseboat equivalents, Kit and Andrew, may not be a match for Bell and Nanny but they are not entirely outclassed while it is a man, Jasper Phipps, who outwits everyone and whose final triumph gives the play its name.

Is Barrie consciously thinking of the implications of Darwinian theory for those involved in the women's movement and does a minor line of serious social comment exist within *The Professor Love Story*? His Notebooks offer the answer. The wider Darwinian context is initially mirrored in Notebook 13 with an indecision over titles. Will the play be called "The Bookman" or "The Self-Made Woman" (Beinecke A2/13)? This serious line of argument is then developed in Notebook 14:

183) Realising love better than books & fame.
185) S.M.W. (Act 1) Stupidest woman is more than match for cleverest man.
203) S.T. (Elspeth's Lover) "her father a baker" – Mine was a fishmonger. (BVS A2/14)

Other contemplated titles such as "Look for the Woman", "Find the Woman" and "The Eternal Feminine" reinforce Note 185's view of woman's superiority within the debate. More specific references to the Women's Movement were also contemplated. Note 220, for example, suggests that Lady Gilding's father might think of supporting the ideals of the Reform League.

What follows, as the final title choice anticipates, is a loss of political courage. Very few of these suggestions are carried through into the 1892 text which Barrie offered to Irving (BVS P66). By then the comic focus has moved to Godwillie's farcical situation. While these changes reduced the political line significantly, it would still be fair to see the play as a comic enactment of Barrie's main reasons for supporting the Women's Movement as earlier revealed in his journalism. Certainly, the formidable Bessie Hatton, co-founder of the Women Writers' Suffrage League, seeing Lucy White as a kindred spirit, accepted that part for the 1894 London revival with more than usual alacrity.

The long and troubled evolution of that text is the next area in which Barrie was to extend his theatrical experience. The key issue here is, again, that of teamwork and the practical difficulties of balancing openness to the advice of actors or directors with the retention of overall control. That belief had only recently survived Toole's efforts to usurp him as leader of the theatrical team. As the play's production history reveals, he now had to face a different challenge.

Three West End managers, Henry Irving, George Alexander and John Hare, turned it down. Their reasons are not recorded but they may well have shared Archer's doubts about the absurdity of its central premises. Whatever their reasons, as Janet Dunbar explains, Barrie became so depressed with rejection that he sold the rights for £50 to E.S. Willard, an English actor whose early career included a period with the Wilson Barrett company. He now ran his own company which specialised in tours of America. Under Willard's direction it opened in New York on 19 December 1892. There it had a short run at the Star Theatre before transferring to Boston's Tremont Theatre in April 1893 (Dunbar 1970: 98–99).

This meant that, for the first time, Barrie did not see one of his plays develop on the rehearsal floor or attend its first night. When it transferred to London in 1893 he was convalescing in Kirriemuir and about to marry Mary Ansell. Willard was quite happy to have his input at rehearsals but Barrie felt too frail to come to London.

It is only in the last chapter of the play's evolution that he regained control over his text. He also proved the theatre managers' doubts about the play's power to please to be unjustified. *The Professor's Love Story* is usually called a box office failure because it did not match the opening run of *Walker, London* and was generally damned with faint praise by critics. Yet it enjoyed extended runs in America and in London. Goodwillie and Lucy acted out their romance in New York from 19 December until the end of April when it re-opened in Boston. Critical reaction was positive – "Mr. Willard has won golden opinions at the Tremont Theatre in Boston, in Mr. Barrie's new comedy" (*Atheneum* 29 April 1893). Indeed, Willard would turn it into America's *Mousetrap*. For over twenty years it remained in his repertory. When he opened a revival in 1904, the opening night programme records that he is playing Goodwillie for the 892nd time!

Although the London critics, anxious to prove that they had higher standards than their American counterparts, were at best luke-warm about it, an unbroken run of 144 performances does not exactly suggest a popular failure. That this was generally recognised by those impresarios who had earlier rejected it becomes evident later. In 1916, when the management of the Savoy were seeking a light, unchalleng-ing work, appropriate for wartime, they remembered *The Professor's Love Story* and so allowed the Professor to wander the West End stage mistaking love for illness for another 235 nights.

The fact that Barrie re-writes his plays so often is another impli-cation of this view of authorial teamwork which is expressed in its most extreme form in the Dedication to *Peter Pan*. If each production has to be re-defined by group discussion for a different cast at a differ-ent time, then the relationship between any printed text and the stage of development it represents has to be defined. In the present case, it is important to realise that the Definitive Edition of the plays reproduces the revival text. The opportunity of revising the plot and becoming part of the production team had been restored to Barrie in 1916 and he took full advantage of the opportunity.

Interestingly his revisions reversed the trend noted in the play's progression from Notebooks to first production. Now it was Good-willie's part which was diminished and Lucy's which was developed. The dialogue became more pithy and most (though not all) of the autobiographical material was excised. Changes designed to mirror the advances gained by women in the intervening years were also inserted. The *New York Times* critic, who had seen both the first American production and the London revival, confirms this. Barrie, he says, had altered the text considerably, "amputating most of the asides and soliloquies" and, generally, "modernising" the play (27 February 1917: 219). It had taken Barrie twenty-two years to win this "theatri-cal" battle. Whether he took additional pleasure from the fact that Goodwillie's part was played by H.B. Irving, the son of the man who had first rejected it, is not recorded.

It remains to consider another of those quintessentially theatrical principles which Barrie the critic formulated and Barrie the playwright built upon. In *The Professor's Love Story*, he continued to experiment with those visual and aural effects which, for him, distinguished enactment from narration. Critical enthusiasm, withheld from the play as a whole, greeted the technical skills involved in this area. The visual power of the rural settings for Acts Two and Three were as highly praised as *Walker, London*'s houseboat. *The Theatre* critic lyrically congratulated the production team on having "achieved a masterpiece of Dutch painting on the coarse and baffling canvas of the stage" (*The Theatre* 1 August 1894: 306). Even those who damned the play made an exception in this technical arena. *The Theatre*'s reviewer saw "his remarkable instinct for stagecraft" as practically the play's only saving grace (73). His opinions were echoed in *The Sketch* (16 December 1893: 306).

One novelty in this area is his echoing, with variation, of the shadow play in Act Three of *Walker, London*. At the same structural point which had witnessed Jasper's escape from romantic entanglements, the background dancing and musical accompaniment are repeated. This time, however, it is the romantic union of Goodwillie and Lucy which is signed in a shadowy embrace, which was so passionate in the London production that some critics objected to it on ethical grounds (*Sketch* 4 July 1894: 510). Most, however, saw it as an ingenious proof of Barrie's desire to stretch stagecraft to extremes in the imitative yet inventive spirit of the Renaissance.

The Professor's Love Story can, therefore, claim to be at once a conventional, sentimental comedy whose central character is the victim of a particularly strange obsession *and* to occupy an important part in Barrie's development as a dramatist. It also anticipates a number of ideas and motifs which will return in his later plays. The comedy of the long slow love affair, treated in the Thrums sub-plot, will soon reappear as the main plot of *Quality Street*. The hypocritical attempt of Lucy's upper class rivals to embrace democratic values will be retranslated by Lord Loam in *The Admirable Crichton*. The framing device of having two old men illustrate their sex's inadequacies in the opening scene of first and last acts will be re-employed in *Mary Rose*. George Gilding's attempt to hitch his parliamentary career to the Women's Movement looks forward to John Shand in *What Every Woman Knows*. One is even tempted to wonder whether Shand's loss of political nerve, so severely satirised there, is Barrie's covert confession of his own timorous revisions in *The Professor's Love Story*.

6. Translation: "Becky Sharp" (1893).

Assessing the early comedies as part of their author's developing theatrical craftsmanship has not turned "Ibsen's Ghost", *Walker, London* and *The Professor's Love Story* into early works of genius but it has allowed their individual strengths to be acknowledged in relation to the themes and techniques which would later define his mature drama.

"Becky Sharp", chronologically the last of these plays, received the harshest criticism of all, however, and might initially seem to be the indefensibly awful exception that proves the rule. After all, it only ran for six days and was almost universally damned both as a play and as a translation from Thackeray's *Vanity Fair*. Archer in *The Theatrical World of 1893*, unites these lines of attack. Calling himself "a good Thackerayan" he strongly objects to Barrie "making a stupid and vulgar farce out of the conclusion to *Vanity Fair*" (Archer 1893: 153). Comparatively too, the play was damned. Presented on a five drama bill devised by the actor-manager Charles Carrington at Terry's theatre it was generally held to be worse than the one act offerings of Conan Doyle, Thomas Hardy, Lady Colin Campbell and Mrs. W.K. Clifford (Mackail 1941: 210).

But the evidence is not as clear as this suggests. Indeed, if one pursues Masson's critical method and first asks what *kind* of play it is. a complication arises already. Archer's assumption that it was a farce was generally accepted and the play damned against the conventions of that mode. But Barrie never described it in these terms. The manuscript has no modal definition at all (BVS B42) while the version sent to the Lord Chamberlain (ADD 53528/151) is called "A Comedy in One Act". Moreover, in these texts, the cast are specifically warned against playing their parts in a farcical manner. Understatement, as Moult explains, was to be favoured (Moult 1928:122–24).

These instructions as well as the desire to use light comedy as a vehicle for serious comment are consistent with Barrie's aims. Serious playing of ludicrous material follows the model adopted for "Ibsen's Ghost" and *Walker, London*. Radical tonal contrasts were part of the subversive formula of his Imp. They had already been proved successful in the Ibsen parody particularly while the farcically-tragic dénouement of *Tommy and Grizel* was already being planned in his Notebooks.

The contemporary theatrical context provides another motive. This was a time when different approaches to the Theatre of Ideas were in vogue. But, as George Rowell comments, the efforts of Barrie's predecessors, Thomas Robertson and Henry Arthur Jones, though different, had both proved inadequate. Robertson's serious realism had failed to impress because his ideas were largely superficial. Jones, who was at his most prolific in the 1890s, anticipated Barrie in using oblique comic techniques but "his ambitious pieces [...] fell seriously short through sensationalism and a ludicrous lack of genuine humour" (1978: 77, 119).

That there is a serious line in "Becky Sharp" is first suggested in the Notebooks. There, as early as 1891, the idea that "Becky Sharp is the Napoleon of fiction" appears. A later proposed plot offers a more detailed idea of what that parallel meant. This "poor Becky Sharp has had a hard upbringing". She has also had a baby and, as a confirmed Bohemian, fears "a dreary future if she does not marry" (BVS A2/14.47). As a result, when Carrington approached Barrie about the five-play project a completed manuscript already existed. But what is implied by the Napoleonic comparison? Does the connection between Thackeray's Machiavellian heroine and the "dark Corsican" of *Quality Street* suggest not only another variation on the theme of woman's potential for power but a radically different one also? Until now Barrie had concentrated on the power of the "New Woman" for good. Is he turning to the "immoral" side of the equation and asking his audience to consider what will be the effect on society when the Becky Sharps of this world are emancipated from patriarchal control?

Transfer of attention from the written text to the "play produced" introduces two other questions. Was the critical reaction influenced by the auspices of performance and, more pertinently, was the play the audience witnessed the one Barrie intended them to see? Certainly Carrington's new format met with critical hostility. *The Times* commented that the format, though "novel to the stage", had been "a hotch-potch" and should never be tried again. (12 December 1893: 6). Therefore, all six plays suffered from being part of an unpopular experiment. But crucially, some of those who judged "Becky Sharp" to be the weakest of all did not blame Barrie alone. Charrington's production came in for criticism as well. He had cast his wife in the part of Becky and some critics thought she was not up to the task. Further, the playwright's guidelines on understatement had, yet again, been totally ignored. The *Atheneum*, for example, found it "most disappointing" but was inclined to blame "the exposition rather than the dramatist" (10 June 1893: 744).

The emphasis Barrie places on theatrical effects makes him especially vulnerable to misdirection of this kind. If "the play produced" is the valid focus of judgment then "the play badly produced" is unreliable and "the play which exactly contravenes the stage directions" even more so. It is, therefore, necessary to re-open "Becky Sharp" and re-consider its qualities, beginning with an outline of the plot and an assessment of its qualities as a translation.

In Barrie's adaptation of Thackeray, we first meet Becky Sharp towards the end of the novel. In Germany, in a garret room, she is in the Bohemian stage of her adventures, literally and metaphorically. While drinking with two German students she explains her past history to them. They leave when Joseph Sedley enters. Becky soon convinces him that she has always loved him. In this deluded state, he brings Amelia, the friend she had betrayed, and the faithful Dobbin to the garret. Skilfully, Becky at once tricks Amelia into trusting her again while estranging her from her only true friend, Dobbin. Later, in a moment of unaccustomed generosity, she disabuses Amelia of her faith in her dead husband, George Osborne. In so doing she dooms herself to feigning love for the foolish Sedley as her only means of returning to high society.

That Barrie was misguided in attempting to reduce such a wide-ranging novel into thirty minutes playing time is incontestable even in the context of those extreme translation challenges he was setting himself at this time. He has, however, made a number of intelligent choices. The first and most obvious of these is his focus on the ending of the novel. By introducing us initially to the Bohemian Becky of Chapter 64, he provides a psychologically convincing reason for her bringing the audience up to date on her past history, warts and all. The German students with whom she is drinking do not only share her lodgings, they share her anarchic attitudes as well. And so, as they pass the bottle round, their continued interest in the unexpected revival of her old life and its challenges is made plausible.

Nonetheless, almost a quarter of the play is given up to recapturing the essence of the sixty-three preceding chapters for that section of the audience which did not know the novel. And all this effort, as the reviewer in *The Stage* shrewdly noted, was in danger of providing

too little information for the ignorant and too much for the knowledgeable: "[For those] without a knowledge of *Vanity Fair* the sketch
would be unintelligible, and with a knowledge of the book it appears
nothing but a clumsy desecration" (8 June 1893: 13)

The conventions of farce aid the economising process. Use of the
aside at once establishes Babbie's superiority over Joseph and Amelia
and explains the background situation. When about to clinch her
domination of Jos, she confides "[over Jos's shoulder] He's mine!"
(BVS B42 f.11). Before claiming Amelia as her own, she invites the
audience as conspirators to appreciate her artistry "[aside] Now to
pluck a goose!" (f.16).

Becky's position within the Darwinian struggle is also cleverly
established. Both Jos and Amelia are fools, we are told, whom she can
"twist round [her] fingers" (f.5). To establish intellectual power, she
will use her multi-personality to create a deceptive moral and spiritual
role, "This angel Engländerin must be a good little girl to-day" (f.4).
While the material for these battles is present in his source, Barrie's
focus remains on Becky alone and therefore these rivalries are viewed
from her perspective. As his intention is to explore, at the edge of
imaginative potentiality, the ethical implications of granting social
equality to the self-seeking Beckies of this world, Jos and Amelia
have to be more easily dominated than in the source.

When he wishes to highlight the ideas behind his drama, Barrie
selects carefully from the wealth of situations available in the novel.
Characteristically, he does not wish to present an easy moral contrast
between Becky as "bad" woman and Amelia as "good". Even in the
earlier and similarly farcical *Jane Annie* he had blurred these distinctions. He, therefore, highlights Amelia's shortcomings. Indeed,
arguably, she commits the drama's most immoral action of all in her
cruel rejection of Dobbin and his confession of love. Barrie highlights
this movement by fully reproducing the Captain's lengthy speech in
the novel from "It is not what I said" to "We are both weary of it" (ff
22–23) rather than maintaining the reductive approach to Thackeray's
dialogue which elsewhere characterises his translation.

If asides and character interaction occasionally allow Barrie to
present Becky in a more favourable light than that prescribed and pro-
scribed by her character-type, her accuracy as moral analyst also
contributes to her ambiguous, "Napoleonic" status. Indeed, in many
ways she usurps the position of the novel's knowledgeable narrator.

Hedonistic and immoral she may be but her ethical assessments of others are totally accurate. Amelia is indeed "a simpleton" whose purity implies cruelty, Dobbin "worth a thousand of George Osborne" and Jos "a fool without being a good man". (ff. 5–6). But as they enter and fulfil her pre-portraits of them, in the manner permitted by the conventions of farce, the audience's laughter depends on them sharing, albeit temporarily, the vision of the "villain".

The tighter structure of the play does not, therefore, prevent Becky's Napoleonic dynamism being demonstrated. Nor does it detract from her histrionic personality. Like so many of Barrie's sympathetic characters, she moves from one role to another. In the opening exchanges, she turns from angel-Bohemian to helpless victim of man's tyranny to Joseph's love-slave to trustworthy friend to loving mother in less than ten minutes' playing time. In Barrie's "creative" agenda, however, the woman who opts for acting many parts must sacrifice her primary creative role as loving mother. Becky's use of assumed motherly devotion to gain power over Amelia as genuine mother as recounted in Chapter 65 of *Vanity Fair* is in close harmony with this vision.

Thackeray's symbolism in Chapter 64 may also have attracted Barrie. There, the narrator explicitly sums up his views on woman's divided nature and powers as "goddess-devil". The English novelist also uses the figures of siren and mermaid to suggest the gentler sex's hidden power for evil. And if he promises never to "show the monster's hideous tail above water" (Thackeray 1983: 812) neither he nor the Barrie of *Peter Pan* could expect their readers to take this protestation at face value.

Barrie's play is not, therefore, motivated by a desire to imitate the "vanity fair" of England. Its existence stems from Becky Sharp's suitability as a two-way vehicle for exploring the nature of the hedonistic actress-heroine. This is an especially important discovery as it explains a good deal about why the Scottish playwright chose Thackeray as a model and about the means he employed to "translate" Becky on to the stage at *Terry's*.

Almost all the major writers whom the young Barrie imitated ranked high in Masson's critical hierarchy. Thackeray is no exception. Indeed, in *The Art of the Novel*, Masson only narrowly awards Dickens superiority over him as the finest of all contemporary English novelists. Both combine the real and the ideal and so meet the professor's first criterion for excellence. When Masson judges the former ultimately inferior – "Thackeray is a novelist of what is called the Real school; Dickens is a novelist of the Ideal or Romantic school" (Masson 1859: 248) – it is in terms of bias within this shared unity. As a realist who also artistically explores higher moral and philosophical ideas the author of *Vanity Fair* may even be a safer initial model than his rival for young writers who wish to embrace both approaches. Indeed, Masson does recommend Thackeray to would-be writers in these terms:

[Thackeray is] as perfect a master in his kind of art as is to be found in the whole series of British prose writers; a man in whom strength of understanding, acquired knowledge of men, subtlety of perception, deep philosophic humour, and exquisiteness of literary taste, are combined in a degree and after a manner not seen in any known precedent. (249)

Barrie feels at home with Thackeray because both used the individualised type as a means of presenting clear ideas typically while frustrating them particularly. As one modern critic puts it, whenever Thackeray tempts you to oversimplify ideally, seeing Amelia as the passive loving obverse of Becky's manipulative, immoral mentality, unsettling qualifications are introduced (Peters 1987:157). The same could be said of Barrie's subversive, Impish approach. He is, therefore, naturally drawn to *Vanity Fair*.

Once the strengths of the play have been acknowledged, the reasons for its appearance at this time as well as its place in Barrie's artistic development become clearer. In the early 1890s women's rights had become a major topic of interest in England, as Barbara Caine confirms: "In the 1890s and more particularly the early twentieth century, the question of women's rights became a matter of intense public and political debate" (Caine 1977:131). Interestingly, she goes on to argue that this provided a reason for mothers and motherhood being so important at the time: "Social Darwinism, eugenics, and national efficiency which enforced the centrality of women's biology, elevating motherhood to an altogether new height, making it central in women's contribution to social health and prosperity" (133). The relevance of this to Barrie and Margaret Ogilvy need not be underlined.

Most Victorian critics now accepted that in Barrie's re-writing of Darwin, woman is the superior gender. As Harvey Darton puts it, everyone knew where "Mr. Barrie" stood:

By "woman" in any of Barrie's comedies, you do not mean what Mr Turveydrop meant by "Wooman, lover-ly woman". You mean (if you are a man) a creature of the opposite sex who has supreme insight and an uncanny, almost wicked, power of concealing the fact. (Darton 1929: 56)

Darton also covers the world according to the "third sex" as fought out creatively and sexually between histrionic men and women. Like the male actor-artist (Tommy Sandys) or even the male actor-trickster (Jasper Phipps) Barrie sees himself as sharing, atypically, the many-layered mind of women. This allows him to address, from the male side, the problems of sexual insecurity implied. The most extreme example of this is, of course, the actor or actress whose profession it is to inhabit roles imposed upon them by others. New manuscript evidence shows just how early Barrie began to explore this area. Beinecke BVS W67 contains manuscript notes under the heading "Women who Work". These were written in Dumfries between 1882 and 1885 (BVS A2/3). They are part of a research project undertaken by Barrie into the payment of women in the theatre of the day. Having worked out the scale of remuneration for the pantomime season across thirty British theatres, he discovers that roughly 4,000 women are required by managers at this period but only about a dozen are paid at the upper rates commanded by many male actors (BVS W67: 5). Most are hired on short-term contracts as offered in advertisements which emphasise physical beauty:

100 handsome and shapely ladies for the pantomime. Only the leading danseuse can attract a wage of about £40 a week; the rest will be at the basic rate, between 9d and 1s 6d. per night, and be laid off when the production closes. (4)

This, he suggests, drives many into prostitution and so brings the name "actress" into disrepute.

The importance of the "Napoleon" image, formally and philoso-phically in Barrie's mature work can be traced from *Little Mary* and *Peter Pan* onwards but its dramatic origins go back to "Becky Sharp". It was, after all, that image – Becky as Napoleon – which was first recorded in the Notebooks rather than ideas for a plot or theme. This focus on a central, defined character in its turn implied that it offers a different kind of structural challenge. Instead of the allegorical and romantic structures which were currently occupying his attention, a return to the older pattern of the individual quest, mirrored in the real-ideal manner advocated by Masson was envisaged. Becky's name itself signs the mode. As Becky rather than Rebecca, she will be individualised. As a type of "Sharpness" in all the senses of that word, her actions will extend beyond self to type.

The association with Napoleon also harmonises with the subversive mode of the Imp. Barrie had an ambivalent reaction to the little corporal. Opposed to him patriotically as "the Corsican ogre" he also admired him as one small, determined man to another. This is why he becomes a leitmotiv in Barrie's coded dramatic language. As supreme male model for those who raise themselves from obscure origins he is as passionately worshipped by Barrie as he is despised in the same writer's political journalism. Becky Sharp will be presented in the same open-ended manner.

Philosophically, the source for Becky as Napoleon is Carlyle, the author who ranked next to Burns in Kirriemuir's authorial hierarchy. It was Carlyle who placed Napoleon in the category of male, warrior heroes. And it was Carlyle who defined the criteria against which this kind of heroism was to be judged. Barrie for his part followed these categorical imperatives but translated and transcended them in female terms. Becky is dramatically evaluated against Carlyle's triple criteria of dynamism, persuasive power and truth to self but on a higher level of Darwinian adaptability which is Barrie's alone (Jack 1993: 60–76).

The translation tasks Barrie sets himself in "Becky Sharp" are all extremely difficult ones. Catching the essence of *Vanity Fair* in a brief drama whose farcical surface was intended simultaneously to conceal and convey serious ideas was an ideal which by definition was unattainable. But the play is also consistent with those lines of literary experimentation which Barrie has been consolidating throughout his apprenticeship. Topically, it presents yet another variation on the battle of the sexes and does so with a bias towards female power. The potential of the histrionic personality is again explored against a recognisably Darwinian view of life. Modally, the work at once justifies a translation from prose to drama by appealing to the overlapping concept of the voices *and* emphasises onstage those qualities which are quintessentially theatrical.

These are all strengths which will later emerge in more crafted form in the mature plays. But Barrie is, at the same time, becoming aware of where his talents will *not* take him. His acceptance that direct seriousness and clearly defined endings are beyond him had been anticipated in his critical essays. But while the tonal and modal experiments he has so far conducted to counter this weakness have demonstrated the nicety of modal definition which lay behind his academic training, he had still to translate theory into successful practice. The idea behind "Becky Sharp" – to use controlled farcical techniques to present a more subtle account of the moral battle conducted between the two "kinds" of women, as defined by Ibsen – may have made sense to Barrie in his study. It might, arguably, have made more sense in the theatre, had its author attended rehearsals or had the cast been of a higher quality. To play farce in a restrained manner is, however, one of the hardest tasks an actor can face and in this case the gap between Barrie's higher ideal of subversive com- plexity and the actuality of a poor production was exposed in a particularly disastrous manner.

This study of Barrie's early prose and drama has emphasised further major gaps in the case for his limitations as mother-obsessed personality and failed realist. Indeed, without denying Margaret Ogilvy's importance in Barrie's life, it has strongly suggested that the key to his work is not retrievable via studies of his psyche which regularly ignore his own contrary or differently biased views on the subject. This is a man who lives through his art and has at an early stage created his own artistic world. Centred on the Darwinian- Christian conflict of the day as anticipated in his *Nottingham Journal* articles and the opening of *Auld Licht Idylls* it will be developed imaginatively and topically in his later, mature dramas. But the sexual battleground and the literary skills needed to dramatise the different kinds of creative conflicts fought on it have already begun to appear in his bachelor prose and drama.

That all the themes and variations he develops at this time can be traced in "Becky Sharp" (itself a minor, flawed one act play) mirrors this consistency of critical purpose. Its origins, once more, lie in the Notebooks. This underlines the memorial function they played. By glancing through the earlier notes, he could quickly revive and return to earlier abandoned ideas and re-create them. Only when this economic and comprehensive method is understood can the broader consistent picture be retrieved. In the case of "Becky Sharp" it is the earlier note likening her to Napoleon which is later developed in a manner which confirms both the central Darwinian "battle" theme and the poetic, symbolic methods which he had developed in "Ibsen's Ghost" and *Walker, London*.

The figure of Napoleon had fascinated Barrie the journalist and the reader of Carlyle. His reaction to the great man was, on one level, that of hero worship. That a physically small man from unprivileged background could ascend the heights of fame was, for the equally small and unprivileged Barrie, a source of inspiration. But when these powers were transferred from a Nietzschean to a political, patriotic point of view he became as hateful and notorious as he had been adulated and glorified. Later, in *Quality Street, Little Mary* and *Peter Pan*, this ambivalent reaction to the "Corsican corporal" will be translated in Miss Phoebe's conversation with the recruiting sergeant, Mary's Napoleon Hat and Pan's transformation into the French hero on the Bellerophon in the tableau of Act 5 Scene 1 of that fairy drama.

This symbolic ambiguity is appropriate as a vehicle for Barrie's own divided, questioning reaction not only to Napoleon but to the wider battles of heroism which his example evokes. In the earlier analysis of "Becky Sharp" it was demonstrated how Barrie offers overall confirmation of a similarly unprivileged woman's histrionic powers to subdue men. In this way he confirms his "feminist" views. But, in Becky, he also offers his first exploration of the "bad", powerful woman. In this way, she becomes the predecessor of Lady de Winter in "Pages from Dumas", Leonora in *The Adored One* and even Kate in *The Ladies' Shakespeare*, his feminist re-working of Shakespeare's *Taming of the Shrew* (Jack 1993; Jack 1995). In neither of these battles between woman and man and between two "kinds" of women does the play provide a clear answer. Becky may easily manipulate the German students and the gullible Jos Sedleys of this world. But arguably the only ideal hero of the piece is a man. The modest, courageous Dobbin not only surpasses Becky, he also proves his moral superiority to the "good" heroine, Amelia. This is because the second battle has also been inconclusive in its moral judgments. Becky may return to her old duping ways finally but the major dramatic focus before this had highlighted her unaccustomed generosity against Amelia's cruelty to Dobbin.

Most of the early plays end neatly. In some of them, however, Barrie is beginning to favour non-conclusive endings of this sort. In the same year, he had after all offered four different "conclusions" to *Jane Annie*. Towards the end of his apprenticeship challenging, questioning endings would dominate his major dramas (*The Wedding Guest*) and novels (*The Little Minister, Tommy and Grizel*). That movement, however, had been anticipated in the "failed" opera and one act play of 1893.

In tracing the development of ideas and methods at the end of Barrie's apprenticeship an awareness of the interrelationship between prose and drama is necessary. This is partly because he does not see the two in polarised fashion but as different kinds of vehicle for presenting his own world view. As the study of the drama has shown, it is also because the majority of these plays are translations from either prose or theatrical originals.

The second area of necessary awareness concerns the stage of development reached. While the range of models chosen is as wide as is consistent with attainment of Cowley's populist principals it is only very slowly and carefully that Barrie begins to introduce the higher areas of imaginative and allegorical exploration which Cowley and Masson associate with the universal, eternal definitions of genius.

In this context, the two versions of *The Little Minister* assume peculiar importance. In practical monetary terms, the prose version of the story was so successful that it freed Barrie from the economic necessity of emphasising the transient and trivial. In terms of practical composition, the drama comes at the end of an ambitious range of inventive imitations and is, arguably, Barrie's most ambitious work so far. Conceptually, this is not a "part" translation but the rendering of his own three volume novel in its entirety into the narrower form of theatrical performance. For these reasons, and because that transformation will show Barrie attempting to answer ultimate questions in mythic form, a more detailed and comprehensive account of these works will be offered in Chapter Five.

Barrie's Later Criticism

Given the importance of these texts and as the methodology employed in Chapter Five will rely on the critical and psychological conclusions reached in Chapter Two, I shall preface study of *The Little Minister* with an enquiry into Barrie's later criticism. If his basic views on the histrionic personality, on women and Darwin, on realism and idealism, on theatrical teamwork and on the nature of genius had changed since his entry into London, an adaptation of critical methodology would be called for.

Fortunately, Barrie is still doubling as a critic and his continued acceptance of these basic critical ideas can be confirmed. Between 1888 and 1890 he contributed three articles to *The Contemporary Review*. These provide a later, prose-focused continuation of his literary theory as earlier illustrated, dramatically, in his studies of Nash and Skelton. The subjects of the first two are conveyed in their titles – "Mr George Meredith: Novels" and "Thomas Hardy: The Historian of Wessex" (Barrie 1888a: 575–86; 1889d: 57–66). In the third ("Brought back from Elysium") he uses the device of an imagined railway journey to cover a range of current theories about the novel (Barrie 1890c: 206–14). A Realist, a Romanticist, a Stylist, an American Analyst and an "Elsmerian" happen to share the same carriage but not the same views on how the Victorian novel should develop. (Jack, I.L. 1998).

The Contemporary Review was a respected journal and Barrie's articles are among the most wide-ranging and critically astute within it. They also confirm that his essential views on literature have not changed. Masson's prime emphasis on literary kinds is reflected in the structure of "Brought back from Elysium". The comparative approach it adopts, stressing links and differentiations among the various schools, is that encouraged in the Ordinary M.A. and followed by all professors across the disciplines. The Meredith and Hardy essays follow the same lines.

Indeed both explicitly use Masson's favoured Real-Ideal spectrum as a basis for judgment. Meredith ranks higher on this scale, being overtly artificial. The first sign of this is, for Barrie, linguistic. "Phrase making is Mr. Meredith's passion. His books are as overdressed as fingers hidden in rings" (Barrie 1888a: 575). Despite this tendency to excess, he approves of the value Meredith puts on style. He also praises his complex ideas going on to explain why he is a more "difficult" writer than either George Eliot or Thackeray. Concluding that Meredith's novels are "an intellectual exercise like chess" he argues in favour of this approach to art *despite* the lack of financial success implied by it. Echoing Masson, he regrets that the trivial tastes of its readers threaten to draw the form into disrepute, as "[t]he majority reads novels not to think, but to keep themselves from thinking" (577).

This elitist argument continues by highlighting those features which differentiate prose and drama. His continued search for those features which quintessentially divide one mode from another is another bridge between the periods. Using that method, he concludes that Meredith is the best comic writer of the day only once he has distinguished carefully between comedy and tragedy. In arguing that comedy is at once a more artificial form *and* less highly regarded, Barrie is again on tried ground. Even the way in which he revives the case, using links between the three voices to explain Meredith's uniqueness echoes his earlier academic and journalistic views. In these terms Meredith is seen to be a naturally *lyrical* novelist like Dickens while Richard Feverel appeals especially to this reviewer because "It is Mr. Meredith's most *dramatic story*" (580).

His views on the battle between the sexes and his favouring of women's power within it have not changed either. His assessment of Meredith's characterisation uses a comparative method which underlines the breadth of his own reading. Thus, "The countess in *Evan Harrington* is a Becky Sharp without Becky's bohemianism" (582). But the female characters are also considered first and at greater length than the men. The confident qualitative judgements he makes between one author and another and the hierarchy of literary kinds on which such comparative assessments are made continue to echo Masson's methodology. For example, among the men, Harry Richmond's father is granted the accolade of being Meredith's most "brilliant creation" but only after his literary type (the adventurer) has been defined and compared with Dickens' practice. Once the specific kind has been defined, a close rival's claim for "best in class" is advanced. Thackeray's Barry Lyndon is almost as fine a representative of the type, but Dickens' greater imaginative power means "Richmond is, I think, a greater".

The erudition shown here largely derives from texts which Barrie had read at University. Chaucer and Milton are also drawn in as extremes of objective and subjective writing, so that Meredith may be placed, nicely, between them as "less subjective than he seems" (585).

The Hardy article confirms this continuity from a different perspective. Meredith was valued as an artificer. As the article's title suggests, it is Hardy's realism which Barrie values. The principle of refining modal definition which Masson taught and practised begins at once. What kind of realism are we talking about? Literary comparisons are again introduced to demonstrate the range of possibility. The "historian of Wessex" has his narrative mode compared first of all with William Howells' *The Lady of the Aroostook*, then with Wilkie Collins and finally with Henry James. Only then is Hardy's definitive claim to fame identified – "Mr. Hardy is the only man among them who can scour the village and miss nothing" (Barrie 1889d: 56: 59).

When describing Hardy's rural world, Barrie offers a different view of the "village retreat" from that espoused on his behalf by George Blake. Hardy's realistic skills, he argues, are limited to the country. Transfer him into an urban setting and he loses his touch. He is lucky, therefore, that he is writing at a time when society and the town are *not* affected by the Industrial Revolution. "The face of society has changed but little since Thackeray represented it". It is the rural world and not the urban, then, which has been transformed by "the arrival of railways and machines" (59).

It would be strange if Barrie, the advocate of artifice and the imagination, made claims for Hardy on realistic terms alone. As he thinks of all arts as branches of imaginative rhetoric or "Poesie" he starts from a unified view of "word making" which allows Hardy's realism to be defined in narrative, lyrical and dramatic terms. Having stressed how thoroughly he creates the actual narrative foundation for his stories, Barrie goes on to credit him with the lyrical voice as well – "Only a poet could have put Egdon Heath so wonderfully into *The Return of the Native*; only a poet described the thunderstorm of *Far From the Madding Crowd*" (60). Their dramatic power is also welcomed with the highest accolade in that context being awarded to *The Mayor of Casterbridge*. It is in this wider rhetorical sense of "realistic Poesie" that Hardy is judged, Accurately observed actuality, imagistic ingenuity and powerful dramatic effects on this understanding can all reinforce the Real effect. Only the stylistic seal of approval needs to be provided before the overall qualitative judgment is delivered and here Hardy is judged to "reign supreme".

The basic method is that attributed to the classical rhetoricians in Masson's lectures. To them goes the credit for "minutely naming and classifying the different modes of living speech"(ADV 6652.3). In similar manner, the good critic nicely defines the exact literary "kind" practised by modern authors before demonstrating his own erudition by comparing other practitioners within the same school. When Barrie concludes that "Mr Hardy stands higher than any contemporary novelist" he is not, therefore, contradicting the similar conclusion he had come to for Meredith. That judgement is delivered within the more realistic category to which Hardy has been assigned after a thorough comparison with other eminent authors of the same persuasion. And here it would appear that this has been a tightly run race with Hardy narrowly "beating" Stevenson to the laurel wreath – "His [Hardy's] writing has not always the air of distinction which sometimes catches one's breath when reading Mr. Stevenson, but it is clear, terse, without self-consciousness" (66).

As in the Meredith essay, female and male characters are separately considered. In this case, however, women not only precede but do so as part of a wider claim that British novelists have proved themselves much better at producing heroines than heroes. Scott and Dickens are used to substantiate this; the former through his own confession to that effect, the latter via Barrie's own claim that "Pickwick is worth all Dickens's other heroes" (62).

These studies confirm that Barrie's critical methodology, while it is constantly developing, remains firmly on the rhetorical training he had received at University. More generally, his academic essays present a strong case for his learning and his continued desire to reach the highest level of artistic attainment. Yet, while the critical works of Shaw, Stevenson and Wilde are highly praised, the existence of Barrie's much more extensive and equally perceptive articles and essays is, in practical terms, denied so that the myth of his naivety-in-immaturity may flourish undisturbed.

Chapter Five

The Little Minister

In the Introduction I listed five major aims. The first three were designed to counter the remarkable power of the Oedipal-Kailyard myth to withstand the academic case raised against it. The first four chapters defined this problem and offered a more thorough, more positive, more inclusive account of Barrie's mind and artistry based on new research and wider canonical coverage. If these aims were essentially corrective and looked backwards to Barrie's apprenticeship, the two remaining goals can be combined in the following question: "If this alternative, progressive and cumulative vision is accepted why as his apprenticeship comes to a conclusion with the Tommy novels does he seem to despair of prose and only write one, apparently tragic play (*The Wedding Guest*)?"

There are two issues here. The first is a thorough testing of the critical methods I have employed so far. *The Little Minister*, as the only instance in which Barrie translated one of his own major prose works into a full length play provides an ideal focus for that enquiry. With the methodology clearly established the various transitions between Barrie's Victorian and Edwardian periods can then be addressed more economically in Chapter Six.

The Little Minister's "exemplary" qualities were discussed at the end of Chapter Four. At this transitional stage of the argument it is the positive vision – that of Barrie testing himself across a wide range of literary modes and methods which warrants prime consideration. As his most demanding translation test and as the most overtly mythological of his work so far *The Little Minister* is an ideal focus for this kind of discussion. At the same time, while the counter-case has been thoroughly challenged, personal and biographical views of Gavin and Babbie's romance remain relevant. To meet these challenges an account of the Oedipal and Kailyard approach and the question which most worries biographers precedes a thorough, generative analysis of both novel and play.

The Little Minister in both modes made Barrie's name and filled his hitherto slim wallet. Yet he consistently expressed his dislike for both. Can a different approach, denying critical myths and embracing creative ones solve that enigma?

The Little Minister

1. Origins and Oedipus

At the mid-stage of his apprenticeship, Barrie returned to Thrums for inspiration. In that setting, as George Blake claims, he sets out to compose "the big novel of which every writer dreams, to which every critic continually urges him" (Blake 1951: 67). It will in fact be a financial success beyond his wildest imaginings. Yet he will never like the book, nor be satisfied with the full-length drama which re-translated its tale into the more economical theatrical mode.

The novel is analysed at length by Geduld and Blake. Both accept that Barrie has forsaken his usual linear, episodic plot for a many-stranded structure. This they mirror via long descriptive accounts of the different story lines. They both then state that Barrie lost control of this ambitious plan and that the book was a failure. They are, of course, committed to a thesis which explains why Barrie was *not* a great writer and so any "successful" conclusion is excluded *a priori*. For Blake, the key premise explaining that failure is his fanciful escapism. For Geduld, he cannot achieve genius because everything he writes reflects his troubled sub-conscious.

It is no coincidence, therefore, that their accounts bypass the possibility that their form is at once allegorical and imitates Shakespeare's pastoral romance for this introduces artificial and ideological complications which defy realistic analysis of the surface alone. The *Scottish Review* did recognise these facts – "[Babbie] belongs not to Scotland but to the realm of Oberon and Titania", he comments (1894: 42). This was not the first time Barrie had used these comedies creatively. His University drama, *Bohemia*, had earlier confirmed his recorded appreciation not only of *A Midsummer Night's Dream* but of Lyly's *Endymion*. By refusing to enquire into Barrie's own favourite literary sources the proponents of the critical myth avoid having to counter additional, troublesome evidence. By keeping their parameters narrow they can re-design the book in a way which re-confirms the major premises on which their theses are, respectively, based.

Blake, for his part, accurately defines the various story lines – rustic, romantic, historical, spiritual and mysterious but makes no attempt to relate one to the other. Without explaining his reasons, he simply states that the book is a "hopeless – and utterly impossible – tangle" (Blake 1951: 68–70). "Hopeless" confirms his *a priori* belief that Barrie is a failure; "utterly impossible" reflects the realistic norm against which he is assessing an overtly artificial work. Geduld finds even more. For him there are "six or more sub-plots" (Geduld 1971: 39). There is, however, one foreseeable difference. Blake had ignored, in his account, the story line dealing with the Narrator and the Little Minister's mother. As Geduld's thesis depends on finding "real" Kirriemuir parallels for individual characters, he concentrates on that story line alone.

When it comes to characterisation Geduld cites Blake as an authority for applying solely realistic criteria to characters who, self-evidently, are personalised type. He therefore finds many of the characters unbelievable (Geduld 1971: 39–40). This is a misunderstanding noted throughout their analyses of the early novels. In this case, however, Barrie is also playing one level of reference against another in the manner of his Imp. This counterpointing device is one of his most basic critical tenets. Its leitmotiv status has been traced from the Cowley anecdote in childhood to his recalling of Impish subversion in old age. The need it implies to be both real *and* ideal in order to have eternal as well as transient appeal is also consistently mirrored in his critical essays.

This does not mean that Blake and Geduld are necessarily wrong in their broad conclusions. Nor does it mean that the novel lacks any autobiographical background. The characters' names, the Thrums setting, the little minister as Edinburgh graduate, his testiness over his diminutive size – all of these reflect Barrie's own experiences. Yet, as his letter to Asquith, cited earlier, confirms, he was anxious to move away from personal material in his prose writing. If this is so, why does he seem to cling to it still?

The major reasons for this will be discussed in the broader, structural discussion which follows. But even in story terms some signs of distancing do exist. Most commentators accept that his choice of a clerical alter-ego rather than his usual artistic persona marks a movement away from self-examination. More fundamentally the multi-stranded plot provides a broader character focus than the earlier odysseys of Rob Angus and Dan Moore or the later spiritual journey of Tommy Sandys allowed. From Babbie herself to Lord Rintoul and Rob Dow each has a major part to play in the novel.

None of these considerations are raised by Geduld. In one sense, this is unsurprising as his acceptance of six story lines for *The Little Minister* makes his task of reducing it to a single Oedipal prototype quite difficult enough anyway. He begins the reductive process by offering a survey of critical assessments. Despite the fact that there were more contemporary enthusiasts for the book than detractors, only the latter class is represented.

As "finding the mother" is his prime aim he at once concentrates on the narrator's love for Gavin's mother. Here he quite fairly finds the nominal evidence needed to connect Margaret Ogilvy with both the narrator (Gavin *Ogilvy*) and his wife (*Margaret* Dishart). These links are only suggestive, however. They do not establish clear one to one links between fact and fiction. Geduld assumes they do and so allows the logic of the sub-conscious to take over. By this process, the little minister becomes a type of Barrie's tragic brother. He is even introduced as the "David hero of the novel". To complete the proto-typical cast-list the narrator then becomes "the dominie father" (40). "A more complex version of the prototypic story" then "splits" Margaret Ogilvy in two so that she may be both "Margaret Dishart, the Little Minister's mother and his would-be lover, Babbie". The paternal side of this traumatic equation involves a parallel split in the significance of Babbie's father. According to this thesis William Barrie is subconsciously reflected first of all in the figure of Lord Rintoul, Babbie's father. Then Adam, Gavin's own father, is seen as "a reincarnation of the William Barrie figure" (40–43). Only the original prototypical logic is advanced as proof of these indirect connections.

If one looks at biographical studies of *The Little Minister* a more detailed and convincing picture emerges. The earliest biographers are intrigued by its monetary success. Their research is again supported by Mackail and, although Dunbar has little to say about it, Lisa Chaney has offered an intelligent survey of the novel in its final form (Chaney 2005: 87–93).

In focussing on Mackail's contribution, I am again acknowledging the normally high standard of his evidence. That he is the last to enquire into the evolution and reception of the novel is of particular importance because Barrie's Notebooks provide evidence which bears directly on the central problem of the novel's structure. This kind of enquiry only seems unnecessary when one accepts at face value the proclaimed tenets of the myth instead of following Mackail through Barrie's Notebooks via the serialised form of the novel in *Good Words* to publication in three-volume form (Mackail 1941: 143).

Checking Mackail's generative evidence confirms his thoroughness. He correctly points out that *The Little Minister* was planned over a much longer period of time than any of the bachelor novels. From 1888 until 1890, over four hundred notes are devoted to it (Mackail 1941: 143; BVS A2/9–11; A2/45). There is only one area in which he fails to see the implications of his own research. As he does not profess to be a literary critic he does not relate the evidence he has uncovered to the problems Barrie encountered in turning his theoretical ideals into practice.

So what can additionally be deduced from the Notebooks? The earliest entries give its original title as *Gavin Ogilvy*. Another "odyssey" is proposed, this time featuring a young minister whose mild disposition causes concern among his congregation. The idea of another man returning from the dead is also contemplated at this stage. As the returning man will behave "masterfully", a re-run of the Darwinian battle between masterful, mysterious figure and his meek, good counterpart is also considered but later disappears (BVS A2/9. Intro. 1–5). When, instead, a battle between the minister and a gypsy girl surfaces it is couched in clear ethical terms. She is to be the power of passion destined to bring disorder within his rational soul. An atmospheric meeting with her "in the dark" (A2/9.3) is initially proposed. "When Gavin talks of law and order, suppose she says she hates them" is added later (A2/10.34).

The imaginative energy behind these notes also shows Barrie enthusiastically introducing other story lines. The major problem here is his speedy accumulation of historical, romantic, political, moral, spiritual and even metaphysical lines of reference without any clear idea emerging of how they might relate to each other. Individual plots *are* carefully thought out although some cause more trouble than others. The narrator's position is one such. In one note it is even suggested that he might be Babbie's tutor (A2/10.14). The decision to make him Gavin's father only surfaces at a late stage and after a variety of alternative hypotheses.

It is also at a later stage that specifically critical concerns emerge. In A2/11, the whole form of the book is at last considered. Until then Gavin has been the proposed narrator of his own story. The reasons for making the change and critical implications implied by it are then addressed as A2/11.31 illustrates – "Revise (book form). Would not LM be better if it were compiled from gossip (not got from G.) thus freeing self from analysing G's feelings […] realism heightened in this way".

Mackail, in his analysis of the Notebook material, intelligently highlights a problem for the critic rather than the author when he cites the overlapping form of the Notebook entries. For example, he uses A2/45 (Barrie's first year University Notebook) to point out that planning for *The Little Minister* begins before *Auld Licht Idylls* and *When A Man's Single* were published. On the dramatic side he is equally enlightening. "Ibsen's Ghost" and *Walker, London* are in this sense contemporary with the invention of Babbie and her little minister – "Yet again that isn't all in the little pocket-book. We turn it round, so as to start at the other end and here already are notes for a play about a house-boat and a barber" (143).

The fact that the Notebooks show Barrie simultaneously planning different kinds of writing is important for understanding the modal range he is covering. Yet when Mackail comes to discuss the evolution of *The Little Minister*, he replaces the interlinking principles he had himself identified with a neat line of chronological analysis devoted to the novel alone. It is this reduction of different modes and influences to single generically distinct lines of analysis and simplified time-structures which produce, for *The Little Minister*, the now generally accepted biographical view that it was yet another of Barrie's increasingly despairing failures to write a properly structured novel.

Mackail concludes in this way – "And there was to be a plot. There had got to be a plot if he was to escape the previous blind-alleys and pitfalls" (143). By so doing he implicitly dismisses the possibility that Barrie may be attempting to reach higher literary goals and addressing the *literati* on their own terms. When he calls it Barrie's "big novel" (143), he is only referring to its length and its additional story lines. That it might be a new and more challenging *kind* of novel is not considered nor is the fact that *two* major novels, following different structural patterns, are being prepared simultaneously. Instead he uses sales figures to claim that it was another proof of Barrie's materialistic populism:

Look at *The Little Minister*'s sales for the first fourteen months – at the end of which they were still almost as active as ever – there's something pretty solid in the record. Well over a thousand in the three volume edition, nearly ten thousand at seven shillings and sixpence, over six thousand at six shillings, and the best part of seven thousand sent out to what we still call the colonies […] No wonder we are nearing the end of the journalism, and that long, tremendous and exhausting spurt. (Mackail 1941: 185)

If Barrie's aims were solely materialistic, then the sixty four thousand copies of *The Little Minister* in circulation by 1898 should be the beginning and end of a triumphal story. Yet, as everyone from Mackail himself to Cynthia Asquith records, he proved remarkably sensitive about it, refused to explain his disappointment and finally re-wrote it as a play.

This dilemma cannot be resolved so long as *The Little Minister* is viewed as only a collection of loosely intertwined stories. The generative and critical evidence, however, has suggested that the book is designed to raise the questions which Cowley had defined as the higher goals of genius. On those grounds the reaction of his peers becomes as important for Barrie as his popularity with the ordinary reader of novels. Indeed, if he *does* value invention over imitation, the opinion of the new audience for whom the book's structure had been re-formulated would be *more* important to him.

In fact, *The Little Minister* puzzled and frustrated as many critics as it impressed (Cutler 1989: 180–96). And among those who did object were men whom Barrie admired. When Shaw, Stevenson and Quiller Couch found it unsatisfying Barrie was left with a problem. Was this primarily his fault as author or theirs for not coming up to the reading standards he had assumed on their behalf?

Nor could he fail to see the irony of his position. Having satisfied his established, popular audience more effectively than ever before he had failed to convince the *literati* for whom the book was specifically designed. Some of these anticipated Blake and Geduld in ignoring the obviously artificial and imaginative form of the book. Sophistically assessing the personified types of the novel on these terms they of course found them "impossible" or "exaggerated". But others, including Andrew Lang, accepted artifice but still found the elemental, faery world too much to take – "When it comes to the story, my power of credulity, which is huge is staggered and declines to do its office" (*Illustrated London News* 5 December 1891: 5). Francis Adams in *The Fortnightly* Review also saw that the book represented a more ambitious kind of novel writing, praised individual lines within it but still found it "utterly wrong as a whole" (*Fortnightly Review* 1892: 5: 17-19).

And there were many who shared Adams' view. The *Forum and Century* reviewer for example declared it "exquisitely finished, though failing of complete success as a novel with unity and cumulative effect" (*Forum and Century* 1892: 12: 814). Yet, as anyone who has traced the novel's growth from its Notebook origins onwards will understand, cumulative unity was precisely what Barrie was struggling to achieve.

If the Notebooks show him slowly becoming aware of the need to control the different plot lines, the novel's next stage of evolution demonstrates the painstaking efforts he later made to draw them together. Barrie had, in 1891, produced both a "serial" and a "novel" version of his 150,000 word Romance. John Gordan has confirmed that the "type was set from the 490 page MS [of which] hardly a page is without emendation" (*Bulletin of the New York Library* 1965: 69: 317–29, 396–413). This is consistent with Barrie's relatively late realisation of the structural problems he faced as revealed in the Notebooks. It also shows him working hard to recover control. Unfortunately the implications of Gordan's research have not been taken on board and so the idea that Barrie continued to make changes to the novel at a later stage continues to confuse matters. In fact, if one compares the story as published in *Good Words* from January to December 1891 with the three volume version published in October of that year, it is the closeness of the two which impresses.

Barrie does not, in this case, differentiate between the form appropriate for serials and that for novels. The *Good Words* text may be divided into four or three chapter episodes but there are no signs of an attempt to keep the reader on tenterhooks until the next issue. Even the two endings, supposed to be of great concern to Barrie, are practically identical. Barrie *will* make one major "translation" of his story –

from prose to drama. It is not preceded by another focussed on the prose versions alone. The serial and three-volume forms remain essentially the same.

Anyway, in practical terms there was little time to make later changes. Barrie was at this time making his name on the London stage with "Ibsen's Ghost" and *Walker, London*. As the casting for *Walker, London* began so did another of his "actress" infatuations, this time with his future wife Mary Ansell.

The last, and strongest, reason for assuming that the essential story *and* the structure employed to support it had already been established in January 1891 comes from the first chapter as it appeared in *Good Words*. The teacher-narrator begins his tale by using the image of the looking glass to explain how he will tell his story. As he existed before the major characters of the romance were born and now tells their completed story to their daughter, a circular structure is adopted, appropriate to his godlike position. But that is not all. In the first *Good Words* episode specific references to the first and last locations for Babbie's meetings with Gavin are present – "the Jaws of Death (Chap XLIII) and the well of Caddam, where Babbie went one day for water (Chap IV)" – suggest that Barrie had planned the overall structure of *this* word building before he laid the first line of words. In circular fashion, the story thus returns to its origins as a sign that its entire narrative had been played out before the dominie picked up his pen to "make" it suitable as guidance for his granddaughter (*Good Words* January 1892: 52).

For the rhetorically trained "word maker" the circle signs not only serious but ultimate themes. Is Barrie for the first time offering a romance which poses those metaphysical questions which for Masson were the supreme test of artistry? Whatever the answer to that question may be, the answer to the structural planning query has become clear. The revised manuscript of 1891 has been as carefully structured as Barrie could manage in the time at his disposal. Consequently, he would consider criticism which lacked awareness of these principles especially unfair.

The idea that form should underline meaning is a basic tenet of Aristotelian criticism. As the evidence has so far suggested that the romantic story of *The Little Minister* was used as vehicle for raising political, ethical, spiritual and ontological issues it is unsurprising that Barrie uses another common rhetorical topos to prepare the reader for the ambitious imaginative challenge awaiting him. Masson had presented the "novel" as, literally, the "new" prose version of early verse Romance. Among the major conventions employed in that tradition is that of the "sententia". This offers an initial overview of the major themes to be addressed and of the methods employed to convey them. Hammerton, despite his reservations about the novel as a whole, recognised Barrie's use of this device – "The author had begun with the clear intention of holding his characters in leash" (Hammerton 1929: 165).

While Barrie had already flirted with those ultimate questions which Masson saw as the final test of literary genius it is only in *The Little Minister* that he first attempts to represent the world beyond time. And it is that world which the Narrator signs most clearly in his introduction. At once he sets the highs and lows of Gavin and Babbie's tempestuous relationship within the reassuring, regenerative patterns of nature. In the first three chapters he introduces four generations, beginning idealistically with his own earlier career as a minister and "the beautiful face that God gives to all who love them" of his predecessor. That man who "embodied the highest ideals of the Christian life" is the first to draw attention to ultimate questions. His accession all those years ago seems a brief moment within God's resurrective patterning of time. As an example he gives the cherry-tree which will later have the same eternalising function in *Mary Rose*. The first thing he made up his mind to do would be to cut it down. Yet it is still there. The fourth generation is equally idealistically presented. The daughter of Gavin and Babbie is at once an innocent who harmonises the conflicting characters of her parents and the "reader" for whom her grandfather's book is intended.

In this way, the human drama of Darwinian struggle and the pagan world of folk-tale and faery are initially framed within an optimistic regenerative vision of the world beyond time. As these hopeful signs will return finally, the potentially tragic human drama is effectively (and affectively) framed within a more hopeful "ideal" vision.

If Barrie addresses metaphysical questions directly in the novel, the passionate and volatile love affair between Babbie and Gavin presents yet another variation on his favoured theme of Darwinian sexual conflict. Here, the narrator's role is that of the "good" but less "magerful" contestant for the hand of Gavin's mother. Darwinian logic dooms him to defeat. Lacking enough of the "old Adam", he meekly gives way to another Adam in Adam Dishart.

The ethical and spiritual levels of reference, which initiated the idea for the novel in the Notebooks, are also confirmed in the opening chapters. There, the threat Babbie represents to Gavin's rational soul is introduced as a battle between reason and passion in the manner of Dunbar and Lydgate, both of whom he had studied at University. Reason again combats sensuality as the narrator fears "His [son's] love may now sink into passion, perhaps only to stain its wings and rise again perhaps to drown" (4). The historical and political framework of Gavin's romance is also confirmed in the opening chapters when the Chartist riots are described (19).

Most of these worlds have been individually represented in the bachelor novels. In this translation they all come together in the character of Babbie and the world of myth and faery she represents. For that reason, the opening chapters introduce this realm with particular care. The resolution of apparent opposites in her ever-changing personality and her mysterious origins are especially stressed. As "bare-legged witch" and "phantom woman" (3–4). Babbie also enters the tale as a threat to faith and order. In an age of doubt the certainties of the Christian faith cannot go unchallenged. Babbie as angel-witch, saint-devil is, therefore, regularly compared to supernatural figures of good and evil. She also carries ambivalent natural signs such as the rowan and is frequently associated with the changing moon.

If the circular structure of the opening chapters anticipates microcosmically, the circular structure of the novel as a whole, the narrator also continues to give critical guidance throughout. For example, he goes out of his way to explain the mystery of Babbie's world by relating it specifically to past legends and superstitions. The lovers do not just meet in any wood but in an ostensibly mysterious wood which has a dark, legendary history which he proceeds to explain. "The mystery of woods by moonlight thrilled the little minister. His eyes rested on the shining roots, and he remembered what had been told him of the legend of Caddam" (34). The lovers encounter each other at a well and at once the dominie reminds us that "Children like to peer into wells to see what the world is like at the other side" (146). Nor is his audience conditioning confined to glosses of this sort; his imagery also suggests the way in which he wants us to see Babbier and her world – "In the fairy tale the beast suddenly drops his skin and is a prince, and I believe it seemed to Babbie that some such change had come over this man, her plaything" (179).

If Babbie reigns supreme in the faery world and represents the mysteries of Nature and the folk tale, Gavin's Christian vision of the world beyond time is formally marked out in a series of sermons each of which warrants a chapter title. Chapter Ten's "First Sermon against Women" and Chapter Fifteen's "The Minister Bewitched – Second Sermon against Women" give way to Chapter Nineteen's "Sermon in approval of Women". While these demonstrate the growing power of his love, they also mark a retreat from strict Calvinism. And that counterpointing technique had itself been anticipated two chapters earlier. Chapter Eight is called the "The Monstrous (sic) audacity of the Woman". The adjectival echo of Knox's sermon against female rule, "The first Blast of the Trumpet against the Monstrous Regiment of Women" provides the context and foreshadows the dilemma.

Not only the Narrator but the Auld Licht chorus offer their inter-pretation of his spiritual journey. That the latter group are presented in a comic yet curiously dignified manner represents yet another attempt at the mixed tonal effect most recently, if less successfully, adopted in "Becky Sharp". Ontologically, however, Rob Dow is the key Christian figure. That is why his story as well Gavin's begins and ends the cir-cular structure recommended for representing divine truth. As "drucken, cursing, poaching" parishioner he becomes the first exam-ple of Christ's power to transform (24). Centrally he loses faith and returns to his old ways only to sacrifice his life for his human saviour in a manner which mirrors Christ's own death. (333).

If highlighting those instances in which form *does* sign meaning in *The Little Minister* helps to counterbalance the popular view that it is just an uncontrolled mess it also offers a new perspective on the autobiographical line in Gavin's story. Once the relationship between Gavin's story and the artificial structure of the novel as a whole has been accepted, it becomes virtually impossible to find secure links between the fictional narrative and "real" people. That is because the particular shape taken by the various stories is often determined by their position as appropriate vehicles for the ideas represented on the upper storeys of the tiered word-building.

The Darwinian role of Margaret Dishart was briefly noted in this connection earlier. As the mother figure is of such importance in Oedipal terms, a fuller study of her "*exemplary* tale" will repay attention. First of all, and confining attention to the story line alone, no psychological significance can be claimed just because a mother is present in the narrative. It is only when she *unusually* dominates her son's attention that any Oedipal implications may arise. Margaret Dishart satisfies neither of these requirements. When the question of her place within the central Darwinian theme of the book is posed the evidence does not support the autobiographical thesis either. After all, her story is not at all similar to Margaret Ogilvy's. The latter did not marry a "magerful" man and suffer exile from Thrums because of it. That pattern has more to do with Darwin than David Barrie. Margaret *has* to be presented in this way as an early example of the sexual demands made on woman by the evolutionary process. In accordance with Darwin's "law" that modern men like their primitive predecessors must "wrestle for any woman to whom they are attached; and of course the strongest party always carries of the prize" she must reject the good but passive suitor for the one whose masculine power will advance the species (Darwin 1871: 562). That is why the dominie spends so long explaining his own passivity when faced with a "magerful" man – "I would hang back, raging at his assurance or my own timidity" along with Margaret's reluctant subjugation to Adam's aggressive male sexuality power (271–73) at the same time as an even more explicit version of the same conflict was being worked out for Mrs. Sandys in *Sentimental Tommy*.

But it is not only Margaret's character which differs from Margaret Ogilvy's. In the earlier bachelor novels, the major male protagonist usually matched his female opponent in the artistic, if not the natural, side of the creative contest. But Gavin is a typical single-minded male pitted against an extreme, because partly supernatural, example of woman's natural powers of adaptability. "Chasing a spirit" he has no chance at all (186).

Barrie employs a variety of techniques to explain Babbie's histrionic powers. Most obviously, the narrator believes this to be so He therefore introduces her as a – "girl, who was a dozen women in the hour" (186). Her possessing of mutually exclusive personality traits as gypsy *and* lady, devil *and* angel, witch *and* fairy is also insisted upon. In anticipation of divine harmony these seem mysteriously reconciled in her alone. The ambiguous associations of the rowan berries she often carries conveys her mystery in another way.

Statement soon gives way to enactment. Visually her change-ability is underlined by the cloak she wears and casts off. Aurally it is applied to the decorous changes she makes in her linguistic register when moving from one personality to another – "You saw she could put on and off the Scotch tongue as easily as if it were a cap" (111).

Of course, Gavin must have his own claims to greatness. Other-wise he could not be Babbie's partner at the pinnacle of natural selection. That claim is established as early as Chapter Two. "According to Margaret, Gavin's genius showed itself while he was still a child" (8). Its ethical and faithful foundation makes nobility his defining quality and the ministry his destined profession. These are undeniable strengths but, in the youthful innocent state described in the earliest Notes for the book, they still leave him totally at the mercy of an experienced, intelligent woman who practically embodies the spirit of mental adaptability.

The other, *naturally* creative power which women possess is of course childbirth. As the Women's Movement gained support, moth-erhood *per se* became a major focus of attention for that reason. Barrie was by no means the first male writer to address the current debate by drawing birth, the primary form of creation, into the comparative equation when wishing to highlight woman's unique and superior nature. And it is in this spirit, Barrie creates a heroine whose appeal is the spirit of youthfulness. Her own motherhood remains a hypothesis beyond the time scheme of the novel, making Margaret's presence just as necessary for completion of the "natural" as for the "artistic" argu-ment he presents in favour of women's greater potential power.

If any lingering doubts remain about *The Little Minister* being the most thorough statement so far of Barrie's own brand of feminist Darwinism, three of the narrator's many statements to that effect may dispel them. The first reveals his general view of the battle. "Woman", he observes, "is not undeveloped man but something better" (105). The second is another general observation but it refers specifically to that youthful stage of romance which Babbie and Gavin embody from the earliest Notebook jottings onwards. Female guile, he remarks, will conquer *all* young men not Gavin alone – "At twenty-one a man is a musical instrument given to the other sex". The last example moves the argument for superiority from womanly wiles to male pride. An honourable but egotistically naive man such as Gavin may even be more vulnerable to female wiles than his less gifted male counterparts, he argues. This is because his underestimation of his opponent blinds him to the very nature of the game he is playing. As the father-narrator shrewdly comments his blindness derives from "never realis[ing] that Babbie was a great deal cleverer than he was" (172).

2. Sources and Voices

The introduction of two more of Barrie's basic critical principles will continue this enquiry into the simultaneous success and failure of *The Little Minister*. That there are as many literary sources as there are worlds and perspectives in *The Little Minister* reminds us that he accepted the principle of imitation and invention. For Barrie, as for the Renaissance writers he admired, older material was welcome so long as it was transformed into something new. In this particular case, when he was trying to impress his peers, that principle had the additional value of conveying his own status as a learned writer.

His major prose sources – Scott and Dickens – are precisely those we would expect to find, given the nature of his academic training. Critics also recognised dramatic influences. These, inevitably, begin with Shakespeare. His many-world comedies are the model on which the entire structure is built. The classical unities are also evoked in the twenty-four hour scenario described in Chapters XXV to XLIV. If Shakespeare could have a play within a play, Barrie could have a play within a novel. (The periodical version even has detailed stage directions.)

But Andrew Lang also sees Ibsen's influence when regretting Babbie's tendency to sound like Norah in *The Doll's House* (*Illustrated London News* 5 December 1891: 739). As Tennyson's poem, *Enoch Arden* was also suggested as a source, it is clear that the range of Barrie's learning was generally assumed.

Barrie's easy welcoming of poetic and dramatic influences into his prose also takes us back, this time to his preference for the interlinked theory of voices over more discrete generic categories. This view, as demonstrated in his critical assessment of Meredith and Hardy, is directly linked to his interest in both those features which unite and divide these, essentially poetic, modes. As he explains to Maude Adams in 1920 when discussing the difference between dramatic and cinematic performance – "I think it [a film] only worth doing if one can have the many things shown that can't be done on stage, for we may be sure that what can be done on the stage can be done much better than on the screen" (BVS A2 14/11/20).

Never again would Barrie write a novel which so successfully united the poetic, dramatic and narrative voices as *The Little Minister* nor one which subtly employed such a variety of outside sources. Evidence for this imitative-inventive strain begins with Shakespeare and Masson's advocacy of the many worlds of *A Midsummer Night's Dream* as a perfect vehicle for comical incongruity. The hierarchy of worlds presented in that play from that of the Elizabethan artisan at the foot to the pagan gods at the top, Barrie translates into his own terms. Nanny waiting to be taken to the poor house takes Bottom's place at the foot of the scale while Babbie occupies the supernatural world of Titania at the top. And just as laughter accompanies Bottom's translation into the fairy world, so Nanny's Presbyterian values clash comically with Babbie's presumptions of her own superiority, when the two women have Gavin to tea!

"Yes," said Babbie, "you take this chair, Mr. Dishart, and Nanny will have that one, and I can sit humbly on the stool."
But Nanny held up her hands in horror.
"Keep us a'! she exclaimed; "the lassie thinks her and me is to sit down wi' the minister! We're no to gang that length, Babbie we're just to stand and serve him and syne we'll sit down when he's risen." (119)

Barrie re-invents the intermediary worlds of Renaissance comedy also. He re-creates, on his own terms, the pastoral, amorous and noble worlds of Lyly and Shakespeare via, respectively, the Thrums elders, the young lovers and the upper class world of Halliwell and Rintoul. And he does so from methods he has tried out before. The inevitable Thrums chorus may have a different role to play within a different medium but it still relies on the same social and national incongruities for comic effect. One line follows in the tradition of Burns's Kirk Satires as it is directed against the extreme Calvinism of the villagers. Another returns us to one of Barrie's oldest comic devices – the pitting of genteel English attitudes and the English language against the darkness of the Scottish temperament and the density of the Scots dialect.

But once more the novel's serious and mysterious themes introduce a new twist to the old formula. Just as Babbie comprehends many personalities, so she is mistress of both Scots and English. This power extends the range of comic contrasts but also has more serious connotations. Whichever linguistic register she offers to others conveys only that side of her mysterious personality which she wishes to convey at that time. Barrie's use of clothes imagery in this context underlines the darker, deceptive and manipulative background to this verbal comedy. Usually it is her cloak which is used as objective correlative but when McQueen explicitly makes the link between her use of language and her mysteriousness, he chooses a different item: "But who can she be? You saw she could put on and off the Scotch tongue as easily as if it were a cap" (111).

In *The Little Minister* the poetic strain extends well beyond images of this kind. Masson had placed imaginative novelists higher than all others. Barrie the critic had also used the same cumulative vocal criteria when defining Hardy's supremacy as rustic novelist in poetic *and* dramatic terms. In particular he had admired the "historian of Wessex's" powerfully evocative descriptions of locations and weather. In *The Little Minister* Barrie offers his most thorough and most skilful attempt to imitate these effects. To confirm this one need only think of the imaginative links he creates between the mysteries of Caddam Wood and Babbie's own mysterious nature or the close association between the dark, tragic personality of Rob Dow and those Jaws of Death in which he meets his doom.

Walter Scott offers a different kind of poetic and personalising influence. In his historical novels Scott had placed his unknown heroes and heroines within past times of conflict – the Jacobite Rebellion in *Waverley*, *Old Mortality* and *Redgauntlet*, the Porteous Riots in *Heart of Midlothian*. This technique allowed imagined characters to invade the "reality" of history and meet those famous heroes and villains whose actual contribution endured in historical records. That methodology, naturally commended by Masson, is now adopted by his student when he places Gavin at the heart of the Chartist Riots. Scott's practice of reviving old ballads and folk songs he also imitated. By giving most of these songs to Babbie he re-inforces her connection with the world of Scottish folklore:

"How did you get up there?" [Gavin] asked in amazement.
"On my broomstick," Babbie replied and sang on –
The lady looked o'er her window sae high,
And oh! But she looked weary,

And there she espied the great Argyle
    Come to plunder the bonny house o' Airly. (131)

If there are particular influences from Hardy and Scott, Barrie's major model for imaginative narrative remains Dickens. As a piece of poetic prose *The Little Minister* outdoes its predecessors as the opening to Chapter III illustrates:

> The dog-cart bumped between the trees of Caddam, flinging Gavin and the doctor at each other as a wheel rose on some beech-root or sank for a moment in a pool. I suppose the wood was a pretty sight that day, the pines only white where they had met with the snow, as if the numbed painter had left his work unfinished, the brittle twigs snapping overhead, the water as black as tar. But it matters little what the wood was like. Within a squirrel's leap of it an old woman was standing at the door of a mud house, listening for the approach of the trap that was to take her to the poorhouse. Can you think of the beauty of the day now? (99)

As Lang saw, Barrie's current theatrical involvement with Ibsen also influenced his prose at this time. "Ibsen's Ghost" and *Walker London* were performed in the same year as *The Little Minister* was published. Research for the first of these meant that Barrie knew a good deal about Ibsen's techniques. He immersed himself in the work of an author who, as Holtan remarks, uses "traditional stories [to present] an existential posture, a means of relating to the universe and of being in the world" (Holtan 1974: 7, 3).

This vocal and imitative approach to the texts is consistent with Barrie's own critical methods. As such, it helps to explain why some aspects of the novel were given a positive, even rapturous reception. It remains to be seen why the book as a whole was greeted with less enthusiasm.

In Aristotelian terms the original, material and formal causes of rhetorical composition have been covered. The result of this enquiry has been confirmation of all the topical and technical preferences identified in Barrie's early plays along with a clear desire to extend the Darwinian and sexual conflicts imaginatively and allegorically. Psychologically too, the earlier findings have been confirmed. The histrionic rather than the mother-obsessed personality continues to stand at the centre of the gender battles in the prose version of *The Little Minister.* Here too a more ambitious example is proposed than before. Women, with their Russian doll minds, are still seen to be naturally more adaptable than men and so gain power in the evolutionary contest. But Babbie as mysterious embodiment of the principle of changeability has to carry these battles into the semi-divine area inhabited by Oberon and Titania so that ontological concerns may, for the first time, become part of the debate.

Only the "final" cause, the reception of the work by its audience remains to be considered. There are a number of good reasons for leaving analysis of this until a rhetorical analysis of the play's origins, themes and form has been completed. First, there are major differences between the conclusion of the novel and some of the dramatic endings proposed.

Second, endings – especially theatrical endings – have already become a centre of concern for Barrie's critics from the time of *Richard Savage* and *Jane Annie* onwards. That debate will heighten when the play of Gavin's book is "finally" considered. This introduces the third reason for treating the reception of both together. Barrie's disaffection with the novel and the translated play stems from critical dissatisfaction with each individually but also with the relationship between them. As he had transferred *The Little Minister* to the boards in order to meet those criticisms of the novel which he thought were justified a comparative consideration of that transference is needed.

From Prose to Performance

1. Origins and Outside Influences

Before the conclusion and reception of both modes can be assessed the same generative, formal and topical criteria employed for the novel have to be applied to the play. The first of these enquiries returns us to the personalised, psychological focus which dominates to-day. That this account, fair on its own terms, is not accompanied by any re-examination of the literary evidence once more bears witness to the power of the critical myth in making such an enquiry seem superfluous. And, without that aid, modern biographers find it difficult to explain the story of *The Little Minister* fully. Any attempt to fill that gap has, therefore, to begin with the apparently unanswerable enigma couched in personal terms which earlier biographers placed at the centre of their argument.

That the questions modern biographers ask were also posed by Barrie's friends and contemporaries underlines their fairness. All centre round the paradox of why the financial success enjoyed by both book and play met with apparent distaste from their author. The novel, after all, had made him financially secure while for the first time the box office profits for his play had not been largely diverted into other hands. Cynthia Asquith, as Barrie's secretary in the years when the play was revived sums up the dilemma nicely – "He spoke disparagingly of the play, *The Little Minister*, which he said he didn't intend to include in any future edition of his works. Ungrateful of him, for it earned him eighty thousand pounds in its first ten years!" she notes. Indeed, when it became a film, starring Katherine Hepburn, in 1935, he refused even to walk the ten minutes from his door to *The Tivoli* to see it!" (Asquith 1954: 21). Clarification of the premises behind Barrie's reaction will help enquiry into whether an account of his artistic problems will explain his disappointment more adequately.

In its simplest, de-historicised form it is neatly summed by one of the earlier biographer when he comments

He [Barrie] knew, he must have known, that of all his writings for the stage, it was the one in which he had been most hampered and least at liberty to go his own way. Bright had begun it, Frohman had knocked it about; the early view of the Auld Licht legends had gone further and further out of sight. It was a manufactured article, and much of it painfully manufactured at that. (Mackail 1941: 267)

The simplifying tendency of mythic argument is well represented here. The quotation which sums up popular opinion to-day comes from Mackail but is, in fact, a simplified, de-historicised view of the more complex generative evidence he himself presents.

Return his statement to its fuller generative context and the first thing to emerge is that he is at this point primarily referring to the American production of the play alone. This preceded the London production. Barrie crossed the Atlantic with an unfinished script which he presented for the approval of the impresario, Charles Frohman, and the proposed director, Addison Bright. They did at this point put pressure on him to revise it radically. Their aim was to use it as a vehicle for Frohman's latest actress protégée, Maude Adams. If Barrie did turn *The Little Minister* into *Babbie's Tale* as the extracted quotation suggests then there would be no need for further discussion.

There is no doubt that this *is* part of the story. Mackail and Asquith were personal friends of the playwright. Doubtless, they heard him express his discontent in these terms. Barrie's decision to exclude it from the *Collected* edition also confirms that his sense of failure, however based, was genuine. To reconstruct the full story generatively it would seem that the play's theatrical history is the natural place to start since the conditions of production are Barrie's principal expressed concern.

When Barrie crossed the Atlantic to discuss the possibility of opening the play in Washington, he was not the naïve young playwright, who had allowed Toole to re-write "Ibsen's Ghost" in his own image. Nor had he forgotten the difficulties caused by his selling the rights of *The Professor's Love Story* to Willard. This time, he would ensure that copyright for any London performance remained with him. And so, after initial conversations with Frohman *but before the first Washington performance* he sent a completed script to the Lord Chamberlain (ADD 55635A) and arranged for a single matinée performance as a further guarantee of his rights. He also, at this time, became involved with Cyril Maude in rehearsals for a London run at the Haymarket (Mackail 1941: 247–60).

That this was part of a plan to delimit outside control supports the "interference" case but also demonstrates Barrie's determination to prevent these pressures getting out of hand. Someone who had learned to cope with Toole's ego and witnessed the fate of "Becky Sharp" knew only too well the dangers of giving directors and impresarios a free hand. And so, when faced with Frohman's demand that his script be massively changed in order to become a vehicle for Maude Adams, he at once negated the more extreme implications of that plea. (The title, for example, did not become *Babbie* as Frohman wanted!) Finally, he heard of Bright's proposed directorial changes and arranged for both American impresario and director to come to London before the Washington opening. At that meeting, he heard of the changes the director wanted and made his own holographic revisions where applicable (BVS L54/3).

He had also made sure that he was involved in the cast selection both at home and abroad. *The Professor's Love Story* had been presented by two comparatively untalented repertory companies, chosen by Willard. It had suffered from the limited acting talents this implied. *The Little Minister* was played by excellent casts on both sides of the

Atlantic. In America, John Drew had been brought in to play Gavin after the play had puzzled rather than pleased Washington audiences. He and Maude Adams went on to head an unbroken New York run of 300 performances while Cyril Maude and Winifred Emery proved equally successful in the London production which began on 9 November, continued until July the next year and was revived for another two months after the summer recess.

This does not suggest any radical loss of authorial power. Frohman, Marbury and Bright did not take advantage of a naïve, young author and force the actress of their choice upon him. Indeed, Barrie was invited to watch Maude Adams performing at the New York Empire and had been suitably impressed (Mackail 1941: 247). If this suggests harmony on the acting level there s little sign of friction in financial and directorial areas either. Indeed, the friendship with Frohman which would result in his funding *Peter Pan* when British theatre managers remained doubtful about it, began here. Bright, for his part, shared many theatrical convictions with Barrie. In particular he shared the Scotsman's obsession with visual effects as his holographic additions to his copy of the rehearsal text illustrate. For example, In Act 2 Scene 2, when Gavin shuts the window of the manse on Babbie and sets off for his prayer meeting, Bright underlines the dramatic symbolism with directions to the lighting crew, "Begin to slowly check red batten behind transparency, and simultaneously bring up blue batten. When red is quite out and blue full on check white line" (BVS L54/3: 16).

The London rehearsals which Barrie attended offer puzzling evidence. From the director's point of view they were a source of joy. This was the first time Cyril Maude had collaborated with Barrie and the actor-manager's account of their relationship is almost breathtakingly enthusiastic.

I loved every minute of the work on it. Barrie sat with me on a little platform we had rigged up in front of the stage and worked and helped in every minute of the stage-management, and we lunched and tea'd together and nursed the lovely thing into the perfection everyone seemed to consider it six weeks later [...] The cast was *perfect*. Winifred's Babbie was exquisite. Why shouldn't I say so? – everyone said the same. (cited in Dunbar 1971: 111)

Winifred Emery was Maude's wife and Barrie, according to all accounts, flirted with her in a very obvious manner throughout rehearsals (Dunbar: 113). In showing no concern about this, Maude gives powerful support to the playwright's own view that he was a romantic irrelevance. What Mary Ansell, who attended some rehearsals, thought about her husband's behaviour is another matter entirely.

At the same time this is when Barrie's concerns about the play having got out of his control are first regularly recorded. As he was now on hand and busy revising the script it is difficult to see why he felt this way. A possible solution to this dilemma will be suggested when the play scripts for the New York production are analysed at the end of this chapter. Until then, the enigma remains.

Barrie did, therefore, face outside pressures in the early negotiation stages for *The Little Minister* and it may well have been those which he reflected on and exaggerated when in despondent mood. But the evidence tells another, more optimistic story. His clever handling of actors, director and financier suggests that he now knew how to maintain his ideal of theatrical teamwork without abdicating authorial power. The play's later theatrical history confirms this. There were two revivals – one in 1914 at *The Duke of York*'s, the second at *Queen*'s in 1923. In these texts there are some signs of revision. But these do not return to the harsher views of the original. Indeed, partly due to the changed expectations of a different days and a wartime context, the play becomes even lighter.

For all its achievements, financial and artistic *The Little Minister* (play as well as novel) had failed to achieve the more ambitious artistic aims which were in a sense the justification of each. As such, they might provide valuable lessons in the later stages of his apprenticeship but it was in that preparatory context they remained.

2. Translation and Adaptation

When Barrie saw both play and novel as "overall" failures, therefore, the epithet did not have the sense of "everywhere and entirely". Instead, it means "measured against the highest standards". It could not be otherwise. Barrie, like Gawain in *Gawain and the Green Knight*, condemns his own efforts against the absolute standard of perfection at which he aimed. The critic, like the Green Knight, has the contingent opportunity of interpreting his achievements contingently and benevolently. Some did grasp this opportunity; some even claimed

that *The Little Minister* had rescued a proud British stage tradition
from extinction:

> Had he [Barrie] failed he would, as they say, have put the hours of the British drama a
> long way back. Luckily for the British drama he succeeded. From that memorable
> night [the Haymarket opening] dates the brilliant chapter of stage history in which the
> names of Clemence Dane, John Galsworthy, Arnold Bennett, W. Somerset Maugham,
> Morley Roberts, Thomas Cobb and other men of letters, so happily shine. (Walbrook
> 1922: 50)

With play as with novel, however, there were just as many who found
it wanting:

> To those ignorant of the novel it [the play] will appear as a rather confused, ill-
> digested medley built around an incident in the lives of two people. Its construction is
> open to improvement and there is an inclnation to childishness in it at times that
> cannot readily be accounted for in a man of Mr. Barrie's attainments. (*Stage* 11
> November 1897: 14–15)

The continuation of the mixed reception accorded to the novel does
offer one plausible reason for Barrie's frustration with both of these
commercial successes. This was a particularly important stage in his
artistic development. In the novel he had for the first time ventured
into the higher, universal realms of genius. He had worked tirelessly
to achieve that recognition of high seriousness which that transition
implied for both Cowley and Masson. That he had achieved much was
not in doubt. Yet, he had persuaded only half of his audience. The
play, in these terms was a second effort, which involved massive
structural changes. Yet while many saw the translation skills needed
to effect that change, essentially it too received a mixed reception.

It is in this sense – a frustrated awareness of how hard he had
worked and how nearly he had achieved his goals – that the intensity
of his anger is most plausibly interpreted. Even after he had made his
name he would react in the same way when difficult plays met with
shallow responses as the stories behind *Little Mary* and *The Adored
One* illustrate (Jack 1993: 60–76; 1995: 137–67).

The implications of this view for critical analysis make recognition of what he did achieve a necessary preliminary to analysis of that
cumulative failure which he seems himself to have recognised in *The
Little Minister*. For example, his translation skills and especially his
awareness of the economies demanded by stage production were

almost universally praised. Of course he now had considerable experience in these areas. *Walker, London, The Professor's Love Story* and "Becky Sharp" had posed the same challenges before he faced the more ambitious experiment implied by translating all three volumes of *The Little Minister*. And he would continue to argue the principles of stage economy throughout his career. In 1928, for example, his Dedication to *Peter Pan* opens with an admission to the lost boys that the stories they played out on Black Lake Island had to in their imaginations had to be "clipped […] small to fit the boards" (Barrie 1928: 3). Even as late as 1935, he would write to Cynthia Asquith confirming the belief that plays were different and "easier" to write because they were "shorter" (BVS A3/ 5.9.35).

There are two ways in which comparative analysis underlines these economies of style, characterisation and plot. The first and more obvious derives from direct comparison between novel and play. The second concerns different stages of dramatic revision. As intelligent enactment often relieves the need for narratorial explanation each stage of theatrical revision relies more heavily on the ability to translate imaginatively what had been made explicit in both novel and earlier drafts. This process affects Babbie in particular as this early example illustrates. In the novel the gypsy-lady had clearly explained her conduct to Cruickshanks at the outset. In the early typescripts for Act One, she is still explicit, albeit more briefly:

BABBIE: They were so eager that I thought it would be fun to outwit them – I mean, I felt sorry for the poor weavers and so when my father thought I was in bed I disguised myself in this dress and slipped in by the secret door that – that my father has the key of! (Gaily.) And oh! It has been such fun. (BVS L54/2)

At the equivalent stage in the Definitive version she also says nothing. Barrie is content to let her motives remain mysterious.

In making this movement Barrie relies on the visual and aural powers of drama to compensate imaginatively for what has been lost explicitly. Many critics do recognise this. Walbrook comments, "He succeeded by bravely altering his story and its characterisation to meet the requirements of an art-from in which everything depends on dialogue and 'situation'" (Walbrook 1922: 52). Howe supports him:

There is no part of the theatre's art which is more frequently foregone by the novelist in the theatre than what we may speak of as its visual possibilities [...] and there is no part of the theatre's art which, by Barrie, is more surely seized. (Howe 1913: 120)

And it is, of course, true that *seeing* Babbie change her clothes, enter the wood, linger at the well, carry the rowan berries and drop the rose are all more powerful ways of suggesting her otherworldly nature. Barrie's university training in the psychology of perception as well as his practical experience knew this just as well as he knew that *hearing* the sounds of the trumpet blown or hearing Babbie's changes of linguistic register were unique dramatic effects and as such to be highlighted at every possible opportunity. Walbrook's comments all stem from an awareness of the specifically theatrical dimension to Barrie's drama. He had been one of the observers who had earlier noted the visual and aural strengths of *Walker, London*. For him, therefore, the colourful setting with Babbie at its centre, wordlessly reinforces the mysterious world she opens up for Gavin. Winifred Emery, he comments, "barefooted and barelegged among the red-dened leaves of Caddan [*sic*] Woods, in her dress of leaf-green serge, loose bodice, leather belt, scarlet berries in her flying brown hair" was contrasted visually with Gavin's "trim, black-coated shyness" (Walbrook 1922: 55). Hammerton makes the same point more concisely, "Unlike other authors who failed as adapters, JMB took his successful novel's main theme and wrote a stage play around it, not merely a dramatisation of the novel" (Hammerton 1929: 231 –37). Together they offer valuable guidance for later critics. First, a Barrie play has to be seen and heard in the theatre. Secondly, Masson's criti-cal prioritisation of "matter" along with his warning that that no writer should set pen to paper unless he had something new to say were positions which Barrie accepted and tried to satisfy throughout his literary career.

In *The Little Minister*, therefore, he uses tried translation tech-niques to carry his latest theatrical version of sexual and artistic conflict further into the world of myth. As Ronald Bryden points out, that movement prepares the way for his later dramatic triumphs. Here is an early example of his interest in "half-dreamed figures who try to share, if not to take possession of, the lives of living people", a list which will later include Peter Pan, the ghost of Mary Rose as well as the succubus in "Farewell, Miss Julie Logan" (Bryden 1969: 146). Others saw it as a clever variation on the Cinderella Myth. In Barrie's version, instead of the heroine being raised in worldly terms by the prince, she is the one to descend in class only to be raised spiritually and find her home in the manse. This interpretation most obviously anticipates *A Kiss for Cinderella* but also Phoebe and the ball scene in *Quality Street.*

If the different stages of dramatic revision emphasise economies of enactment as they apply to dialogue and dramatic presentation, comparison between novel and drama move the focus to economies of structure. And here another problem arises. The original, inventive justification of the novel had begun with its many-stranded narrative. But if this had to be reduced to "fit the stage" than a simplification or even a reversal of that experimental strategy was demanded.

So how did Barrie attempt to put theory into practice? The various plot lines in the novel told of the dominie-narrator's love for Gavin's mother; of Gavin's own struggles to be accepted by his Auld Licht congregation and especially of his saving the soul of Rob Dow. They told of his love for the mysterious Babbie and set that love affair in both legendary and "real" historical settings. Of these strands, the love affair and the mysterious, legendary world are expanded theatrically while the others either disappear or are considerably diminished.

The task Barrie sets himself here is more difficult than might appear. While the change of mode encourages narrowing, the broad aims of the novel – to raise questions about the creative implications of the Darwinian gender battle across the full range of allegorical exploration – had to be maintained. This goal has also to be kept in mind when analysing the translation techniques he employed.

A shortened cast list is likely to be the first difference noted by anyone seeing the play after reading the novel. Most obviously the dominie and his mother vanish. In one sense, this is inevitable. This plot had been the last to establish itself within the novel. It did so for two reasons which no longer pertained to the play. First, the narrator provided clear, commentating links among the various plots in the novel. As these were dramatically reduced, his utility as readers' guide lessened. Secondly, he had emerged in the Notebooks as the conventional third person narrator of the Victorian novel so that Gavin's subjective accounts of his own problems could be lessened. The transition to enactment solved that problem too.

Difficulties still remained. The narrator had played too extensive a role as commentator for his excision to leave no information gaps.

Audience complaints on the vagueness of the play's historical background and on Babbie's seemingly contradictory origins are examples
of this legacy. Thematically and structurally, deleting the narrator's
story had necessary consequences. Structurally, it opened and closed
the circle which signed the novel's regenerative optimism. Thematically, the Darwinian and hereditary lines in the play were threatened
as the four generations of the novel disappeared in the play. Barrie did
make formal dramatic changes and increase the Ibsenite, hereditary
line. These changes did much to maintain the idea of mysterious
cyclical patterns albeit in a darker, more personalised manner than in
the novel.

    While overall critical opinion was divided there was almost com-
plete agreement on the difficulty of the translation task Barrie had set
himself. His first overtly mythical novel had moved away from the
simpler, single-stranded structures which Olrik identified with myth
and fairy-tale (Olrik 1965). Now, in the theatrical version, he returned
to them.

    The simpler structure allowed him to enact more clearly the ideas
which the characters represented. Prose commentary on the *kinds* of
conflict Babbie and Gavin represent may disappear but on stage their
existence as clearly differentiated counter-types is underlined, not
only in dialogue but visually and aurally as well. These specifically
theatrical techniques are consistently employed to strengthen the
polarised contrasts which lie behind the romantic narrative. Gavin's
solidly sombre black suit is, therefore, set against Babbie's colourful,
aetherial costumes. The moral contrasts which first suggested the
novel are also theatrically re-instated with greater force in the
dialogue. Ethically, the little minister represents orthodox religion,
obedience to authority, convention, reason, seriousness and responsi-
bility. Babbie, on the other hand, is a pantheistic free spirit,
passionate, anarchic and humorous. Against this background we see
and hear a simplified version of the love-contest between the two.

    As Barrie's formal entry into the mythic world brings to the fore
those ultimate questions which exist beyond time the way in which he
translates these mysteries also becomes particularly important. That is
why deletion of the narrator's plot has to be resolved in both romantic
and transcendental terms. The same two criteria have to be met when
characterisation economies become necessary. The most obvious
example here is Rob Dow. In the Notebooks and the novel, he had

been the arch-representative of Barrie's earlier, faithful self and those Christian ideals which Babbie threatened. In that text, his fall into doubt and near madness ended in imitation of Christ's own unselfish death-in-sacrifice.

It is that death which first disappears from every one of the extant dramatic texts. In the novel his "flinging away his own [life] for the minister's" [333] had been at once his last action and the one which most clearly embodied Christian metaphysics. As early as the Lord Chamberlain's text (ADD 55635A) that sacrifice has gone and Dow becomes only one among the group of Kirriemuir worthies Aesthetically, this is a sensible move. The mixing of romantic comedy with high melodrama had been one of the least successful movements in the novel. If one consults the full range of texts from the earliest drafts to the revival of 1923 a simpler structure conveying a darker, less overtly Christian message is evident from the outset. The narrator, who provided most of the Christian commentary disappears from all the dramatic versions while Dow's role is significantly diminished. In particular his Christ-like death disappears from all dramatic versions of the plot. That Barrie's audience were the patrons of the London stage rather than the readers of *Good Words* is relevant here. They could be expected to appreciate the change without being offended by the new dominance of natural and pagan images of regeneration over religious ones.

There is a difference, however, between excising a character's death however dramatic and significant and deleting another from the dramatis personae entirely. It is necessary, therefore, to trace Dow's fate in successive versions of the play. In 1897 in the Lord Chamberlain's text, for example, he is still the central focus of attention in the visual cameo which rounds off Act 1. After Gavin challenged Whamond's authority, it is on Dow shaking his fist at Babbie and declaring his murderous intent that the curtain falls:

DOW: You flisk-mahoy, if I catch you near the minister again, I'll wring your neck like a hen's (ADD 55635A).

But in the interim dramatic drafts he has less and less to say. In the Definitive Edition he is silent.

Different Senses of an Ending

By transferring attention away from Barrie's personality to the
problems he faced in his art, the preceding analysis has offered
answers to the initial question posed over Barrie's disappointment
with both versions of *The Little Minister*. On the one hand there is the
novel – multi-stranded; circularly structured as a mirror of divine
regeneration, turning attention away from Gavin and Babbie at the
end. On the other, there is the drama which deletes the divine strands
to concentrate on human love in an explicitly Darwinian context. It
concludes less certainly.

But if they are so different why do modern critics habitually
extend Stevenson's brief comment – that "it" should have ended
unhappily – to cover the drama as well? There is a simple answer.
They are reading only the latest available texts in each case. For the
drama, especially, that is a dangerous approach. A clear idea of Barrie's original plan for the drama must begin with the earliest texts and
the Washington production. Changes made between that production
and the play as produced in London and New York are also of crucial
importance while the later revivals of 1914 and 1923 on which the
"Definitive" Text is based reflect different times and lighter auspices.

Much of this has been discussed earlier but the majority of radical changes centre on the play's conclusion. As the endings to both
novel and play were also singled out for particular criticism Stevenson's focus for discontentment is a fair one. "We all know it did (end
badly) and are grateful to you for the grace and good feeling with
which you lied about it" was all he wrote (Colvin ed. 1901: II.268).
For the novel he had the support of many. *The Atheneum* critic was
only one of many who found "The arbitrary fashion in which the
dénouement is brought about" to be the book's worst feature
(*Atheneum* 14 November 1891: 645). I shall, therefore, begin discussion of what Stevenson meant by his comment with the novel as the
proper object of his concern.

My point of departure is a double question which is never, to the
best of my knowledge, asked. What did Stevenson mean by his criticism and did Barrie agree with it? Stevenson has, for so long, been
regarded as the better critic of the two that it is now assumed that
Barrie would defer to his "elder brother in the muse". Yet, in *An
Edinburgh Eleven*, Barrie is less than enthusiastic, accusing his

brother Scot of "complacency" and "indifference to the affairs of life and death on which other minds are chiefly set" (Barrie 1889b: 111–20). Moreover, Stevenson does not explain his reasons for distinguishing between what Barrie ought to have done and what he actually did. Nor does he explain what kind of ending he is referring to. Critics, if they say anything about this at all, assume that "it" means the love affair and that Barrie is aiming at a neat ending. That Stevenson might be reading from an entirely different script or that Barrie might be aiming at something quite different are suggestions conspicuous by their absence.

If one goes on to think of Stevenson's friendly references to Barrie's grace and goodwill another area of doubt opens up. Does he believe this lying grace was free or prevenient? The end of good oratory is, after all, successful persuasion of an audience on its own terms. And Barrie was writing his novel for *Good Words*, a periodical originally designed for a Sunday readership created by the limited activities permitted on the Sabbath. It was first edited by Norman Macleod, a moderator of the Church of Scotland. In an early article he described its aims as those of "a general magazine designed to be suitable [...] for family reading" but which would also record "the literature of respectable bourgeois England" (*Good Words* 1860: 782; see Sullivan 1984: 145). The highly intellectual nature of many articles in the journal warns us against condescending to the audience as thus described. A highly knowledgeable reading public is assumed initially and the contents designed to encourage them into even more challenging areas of enquiry.

When Barrie wrote for *Good Words* control had passed to Macleod's brother who also was a clergyman and maintained these principles. Theological contributors dominate its pages along with prominent scientists and philosophers. The literary contributions are also usually both conservative and Christian. Margaret Oliphant's *The Marriage of Elinor*, which was also serialised in 1891, directed its satire *against* the "New Woman" and had a heroine whose love for her child was thought to foreshadow the Madonna's love for Christ.

Such a journal was in some ways ideally suited to this stage in Barrie's development. He was, for the first time attempting to mirror worlds beyond time but doing so lightly and romantically. A middle class audience who shared these interests might well enjoy such a story. Yet the distance to which contributors could go in questioning

Christian metaphysics was significantly foreshortened by the auspices under which the magazine was produced. Indeed, by introducing Darwinian themes within a world of superstition and folk-tales, Barrie was already stepping into a dangerous area.

The moral and theological convictions of this audience also delimited the way in which the ending could suggest sadness rather than happiness. Study of the novel's evolution confirms this and is at odds with Stevenson's apparent assumption that Barrie wanted a sad ending from the outset. For *at no stage was an unhappy ending planned.* Even when Barrie's discontent made him revise his manuscript, there are no signs of a reversion into misery. At the same time (and in the same spirit as *The Superfluous Man*) it is the spirit of muscular Christianity which defines the book. This means that final joy is only won after the hardest possible spiritual battle. That this is consistent with the mythic method is confirmed by Lévi Strauss, "Myth adopts a pleasing narrative form [...] precisely in order to make palatable certain truths about the human condition which men have always found it difficult to contemplate" (cited Scholes 1974: 44).

The second question raised by Stevenson's comment takes us from novel's audience to the kind of ending the author proposed. It might read in suitably Impish fashion, "Was the novel meant to end in either happiness or unhappiness at all?" Both novel and drama, are after all, layered texts. Therefore, while all levels ought to arise naturally from the story line and be harmonised mysteriously the logic of ideas on the intermediary levels need not be harmonious.

Further, the earlier analyses of *When A Man's Single*, *The Superfluous Man*, "Ibsen's Ghost", *The Professor's Love Story*, *Jane Annie* and "Becky Sharp" have proved Barrie's interest in open endings in both modes. This desire to leave his audience with questions to solve applies especially to Barrie's dramas as he sees the continued audience involvement implied by that technique as one of those "essentially theatrical" strategies which he sets out to highlight. It would also be in his drama that he continued to refine and develop the method employed in *The Little Minister.* One has only to think of the apparently happy ending of Phoebe Throssel's marriage in *Quality Street* to see that Barrie develops this ambiguous model in the Edwardian period. Phoebe with her hair down as a sign of newfound freedom and wearing the wedding dress which signs her escape from the bird-cage of Quality Street which her name suggests may escape from the constraints of a paternalistic society but the dress she wears belongs to her spinster sister and signs her failure to share that escape. In the final cameo, the sister is there, her hair still tied up, to remind us that Phoebe is the exception which proves the rule. Most spinsters remain encaged in a male society and in their own gentility.

In general terms these tendencies place Barrie "conclusively" in the third category of writing practice as described by Brian McHale:

> Endings constitute a special case of self-erasing sequence, since they occupy one of the most salient positions in any text's structure. Conventionally, one distinguishes between endings that are closed, as in Victorian novels with their compulsory tying up of loose ends in death and marriage, and those that are open, as in many modernist novels. But what are we to say about texts that are both open and closed, somehow poised between the two, because they are either multiple or circular? (McHale 1987: 109)

In the particular terms of *The Little Minister*, they mean that even the predominantly Christian novel leaves doubts open for those who are capable of thinking beyond the narrator's religious interpretation of the story he tells.

But the full extent of Barrie's questioning challenge is reserved for the drama. Here, both practical and theoretical reasons for Barrie's discontentment have been provided. For the drama in particular, the disappointment begins with another failure to convince a significant proportion of his peers that his major theme of Darwinian conflict was being presented in a radically new, mythic and questioning manner. That many did fail to see this is not surprising. Neat endings and clear generic distinctions were the norm in Victorian theatre. Yet Barrie refused to think in a neat, compartmentalised manner especially when it came to comedy. A letter he wrote to Irene Vanbrugh in 1902 illustrates this point. The actress had been urged not to waste her time on comedy as she had shown her ability to be a tragic actress. Barrie urged her against abandoning the supposedly lighter mode. "The comedy of life", he wrote, "is only properly understood by those who feel the seriousness of it also and such only can interpret it in the right way" (BVS A3: 12.3.02). This confirms theatrically the tonal ambiguity detected in *The Little Minister*.

Only one line of enquiry remains. But it is an important one and brings into play the generative analysis of the drama's final scene as

promised at the start of this section. A confession Barrie made to
Cynthia Asquith will define it. "I'm apparently so constituted, that I
can't possibly sit out a month's rehearsals without meddling and
tinkering with the script" he said (Asquith 1954: 37). The revisions he
made to his earlier plays have been examined in Chapter Four. But the
need for close generative analysis to prevent misunderstanding is
particularly acute in the case of *The Little Minister*.

To demonstrate why this is so, I will look at the different endings
of the play as it progresses from the Lord Chamberlain's text and the
first Washington production via the later rehearsal scripts held in
Beinecke to the revivals of 1914 and 1923.

A comparison between the last movement in the 1942 edition and
the Lord Chamberlain's 1897 text will provide an idea of the parameters within which we are working *and* explain why concentration on
the later text alone suggests a much more conservative movement
from novel to drama than was originally contemplated.

Definitive Edition 1942

LORD RINTOUL: Mr. Dishart, if you would just let me bring this about her
shoulders for once, I think I might forgive her in time.
[GAVIN *smiles*. LORD RINTOUL *goes into manse*. GAVIN *and* BABBIE *who are
some distance apart, are arrested in their desire to rush into each other's arms by a
boy-and-girl shyness.*]   5
GAVIN: Babbie, my wife.
BABBIE: [after a pause]. Eleven days.
[*They embrace.*]
GAVIN: I do like being married.
BABBIE: So do I – to you I mean.   10
GAVIN: That's what I mean, too.
BABBIE: [*a little tremulously as she looks at the church*]. Is that it?
GAVIN: Yes, my dear church.
[*Lights in Manse appear.*]
BABBIE: I can't think what father men when he said, "I wonder."   15
GAVIN: Babbie, that is the window of your drawing-room.
[*She blows it a kiss.*]
Just come a little nearer this way.
BABBIE: Was it from there you threw the rose?
GAVIN: Yes, it fell there; no, a little farther to the left, there.   20
BABBIE: I shall plant a rose tree there. [*Places her hand on his breast.*]
GAVIN: My dear wife, it is a beautiful May evening and before we go indoors I
should so like to walk you once round the premises as if I owned you, you know, to
let the stars see us.
[*He shyly crooks his arm and she puts her hand in it. They make a brief turn of the
garden and he is now strutting while she is shy. They get to Manse door.*]   25

Babbie!
[SNECKY, ANDREW, WHAMOND, SILVA, *and* DOW *kneel behind the wall, with arms on wall.* GAVIN *and* BABBIE *run into the Manse.*)
CURTAIN

(1942: 211)

Lord Chamberlain's Text 1897

GAVIN: Ah, Lord Rintoul, I am her husband, you see no one must cane her except myself.
(*Her appeal that he repeat himself is this time answered.*)
BABBIE: Oh! [*she stands looking in horror at audience while GAVIN unaware that he has said anything startling opens door to let LORD RINTOUL exit into manse.*]
GAVIN: [coming joyously to Babbie] Babbie–my wife! [*He is surprised to see her looking agitated.*] 5
BABBIE: Yes, but – what was that you said just now to father?
GAVIN: [innocently] What did I say?
BABBIE: Well?
GAVIN: I only said I am your husband [*with rapture*] your husband!
BABBIE: But after that?   10
GAVIN: And that no one must cane you now – except myself.
BABBIE: Did you mean it? That you – that you would –
GAVIN: Only if you deserve it.
BABBIE: [*after making a face*] Gavin, I – I feel sure that you are the right man for me.
[*They are about to embrace when heads of NANNY and MICAH pop up over the dyke 15 watching them. They enter the manse hand in hand.*]
CURTAIN

(LCP53635/A)

The first point of comparison is the caning incident. It was earlier observed that all versions of novel and drama make some reference to Babbie's desire to be physically humiliated. The reason for this was topical. Barrie continued to emphasise this physical reversal of her mental superiority on stage because the ethical, Darwinian and spiritual messages of the play demanded a "magerful" Gavin re-asserting his power as, variously, a rational soul, a vehicle of evolutionary progress and a good minister to his flock. That image of submission had also been the originating idea for the play:

Play – Girl crouching before man because clothes + stockings off. Taken against her will. Yet they captivate her, as she wishes man to subdue her. First her independence, 2nd hates herself at feeling it go, 3rd proud to be his slave (A2/9.10)

In the 1897 text, the battle between Gavin and Lord Rintoul for the right to thrash Babbie is briefly enacted, leaving the audience to make of it what they will. There is no accompanying symbolism to guide them indirectly while only the friendly Nanny and Micah look on from behind the wall in a spirit of loving concern the couple enter the manse.

This ending is in harmony with Sheila Kaye-Smith's view of Barrie's mature comedies: "He [Barrie] has been inspired to see that the greatest tragedy of human life to-day is that its tragedy cannot be faced, that it can only be shown us by a trick – the trick of laughter" (Kaye-Smith 1920: 108). It is also in accord with the radical changes Barrie first proposed for the translation of his novel. And it was this ending, with only slight variations which was seen on the first night of the trial run in Washington at a time when the ideas of Darwin were a major topic of the day.

The Definitive text, on the other hand, is based on the second revision of 1923. That is, it addresses a different audience twenty six years later. While Barrie's feminist views on the Darwinian gender battle have not altered, the social and political context had. Women had gained many of those rights which were still unattained in 1897 and Barrie's prophecy that they would prove a major rival to men once those freedoms were granted had largely been realised. Changed theatrical auspices were also relevant. In 1914, the revival of *The Little Minister* was partly motivated by the perennial need for light drama in days of austerity and military conflict. The changes made for the later 1923 revival if anything increase that spirit of comic optimism and so distance that production even farther from the dark, questioning play offered to the first Washington audience.

The different way in which in the caning incident is handled in the Definitive text can be explained in these terms. It continues to be the major focus for the last movement of the play in 1923 as in 1897. This is because both the ethical and evolutionary themes of the play demand that reason dominates passion and the most talented of women guarantee the continuation in advancement of the species by giving herself physically to a "magerful" man. The context, however, has changed. The most obvious sign of this is the comparative length of the passages. Barrie's dramatic scripts usually become progressively shorter as he follows the principles of economy by shortening dialogue and relying more and more on visual and auditory effects. The opposite process is in evidence here. Twenty seven lines replace seventeen because he now wishes to introduce a lighter, comical and romantic finale without sacrificing either the male battle for caning rights or Babbie's apparently strange but allegorically necessary enthusiasm to be thrashed.

In these ways he is, of course, returning to the regenerative optimism of the novel. That movement is strengthened when the imagery and symbolism of the last scene is considered. In both plays, roses are used as a sign of the hope and transience of young love. Only in the 1914 text does a rose tree enter the final movement (21). It remains for the 1923 production and is therefore given "Definitive" authority in 1942. But nowhere, even in the fourteen or fifteen different versions suggested for the last scene in the intermediary dramatic scripts does a rose tree appear. Its presence, of course, justifies comparisons between its regenerative promise and that offered by the cherry tree in the novel. But the latter is introduced at the start of the story. The narrator tells us it was there before his story began and would still be there when it was over. It is therefore part of the integral planning of a Christian story. On the other hand, the rose bush in the play was no part of the original text nor the early revisions of it. One cannot therefore validly use these symbols as a means of comparing novel and play as originally conceived. Yet many, unaware that the definitive text differs radically from the Lord Chamberlain's and the Washington script, do just that.

Another motif confirms both the positive moral message in the Definitive text and a return to the techniques of the novel. In the novel, the state of the battle between reason and passion in Gavin's soul is regularly signed by the manse light (14). When it is on, he is spiritually awake. When it is off, he is overcome by passion and worldliness. The stage directions to the Definitive text call for this to be enacted visually. The Lord Chamberlain's text does not.

The replacement of the concerned Micah and Nanny with a comic chorus of elders in the final cameo is, therefore, only the last in a series of changes which diminish the more serious, questioning techniques which had justified the original translation. They also provide the clearest evidence so far of the reasons for his disappointment with the play. He did go on seeking for a "better" ending. His 1923 letter to Cynthia Asquith revealing that he has "Just had an idea for what I think is a better ending for *Little Minister*" confirms this (BVS A3). But "better" in this context does not mean best. If, as seems possible, the letter was occasioned by his participation in rehearsals

for the 1923 *Queens* revival the major battle for integrity had already
been lost by that time. The changes might make for a better play than
in 1914 but both of these remained sad compromises which would be
denied entry into the Collected Edition.

It remains to consider the acting scripts held in the Beinecke.
Their precise provenance is at times difficult to assess. The first of
them (L54/1) does seem to be the unfinished text Barrie first showed
to Frohman. As such it lacks a final act. L54/2 and L54/3 bear the
names of Frohman and Bright respectively. Frohman's copy even
identifies time and place – it reads "Empire Theatre, New York.
27/91897". That they are the impresario's and director's copies for the
post-Washington rehearsals is, therefore, certain. I am inclined to
think that L54/4, however, belongs to the London rehearsals. This is
because there are more written corrections in Barrie's hand. It also
contains the following post-Curtain direction:

[For PICTURE the ELDERS etc are still looking over wall, BABBIE and GAVIN are
talking in doorway. The light in the MANSE is up.] (BVS L54/4: 18r)

So far as I know the idea of using this picture as a means of advertising the play originated in London. Originals and cartoons abounded
and caused Barrie even more trouble. Many Scots were offended at
him apparently mocking his own people. Sensitive to this, he would
later add compensatory comedy designed to show the Thrums elders
in a more positive light (Jack 1991: 49–51).

While it would be good to know the exact progeny of these
manuscripts it is clear that they all reflect an immediate reaction to the
failure of the Washington text to convince or please. This means that
essentially Barrie sacrificed the darker play which had been his main
artistic goal at a very early stage in the drama's evolution and did so at
a distance as part of a panic reaction. Certainly this scenario offers a
plausible way of accounting for Barrie expressing disappointment
with the play while actively revising it for the London opening.

Anyone who wishes to know whether he accepted the Washington judgment need only look at the key texts. BVS: L54/ 2–5 are all
covered with emendations. The endings in particular have revisions
over revisions. The range of suggestion is also amazingly wide. Some
retain Micah and Nanny or even Nanny alone "watching them with
beaming face" (L54/4.17v). Others, including the alternative version

offered on the facing page, encourage comic byplay and include the chorus of elders:

[At the same moment Dow, MICAH, the ELDERS and NANNY who are hiding behind the wall unknown to Audience, suddenly peer over it gazing with delight and curiosity. GAVIN sees them, pulls himself up with dignity and EXITS into Manse primly with BABBIE on his arm. This effect should be quick and sharp, the ELDERS etc. bobbing up being a surprise to Audience as well as to GAVIN and BABBIE.] (L54/4 17r).

Barrie's holograph on Frohman's edition confirms that he did have some part to play in the revisions for the New York production. But these were only attempts to make a failed play saleable by making significant compromises with the darker vision earlier proposed. In these terms, he could at once correct and adapt yet realise that his major aims were already sacrificed in the name of audience satisfaction.

Given those revisions which immediately followed it might not be an overstatement to say that Barrie's great dramatic revolution had stopped before it began. Certainly generative analysis offers a more securely based answer to the questions raised by biographers. It only remains to apply these methods to the last period of his apprenticeship and pose one final question. Do the works of that period – most notably *Tommy and Grizel* and *The Wedding Guest* – anticipate *Quality Street* and the other "mature" dramas? The assumption that Barrie planned a conscious assault on genius on terms spelt out by Cowley and Masson suggests that they should. Yet the biographical consensus on these works will again paint a different picture.

Chapter Six

To The Never Land and Beyond: A Dramatic Route

To argue that the last two plays and the last two novels in Barrie's apprenticeship look forward to his mature plays will seem strange to those who accept the conclusions of Oedipal critics and later biographers such as Geduld and MacKail. For them, in the theatrical context, "A Platonic Friendship" instead of anticipating later works looked back to burlesque and the Scottish playwright's earliest London production of all – "Ibsen's Ghost" – while *The Wedding Guest* is a last despairing exercise in Ibsenite realism. Geduld calls it the "Ibsenite play reduced to melodrama" (Geduld 1971: 105). This group argues that Barrie unwisely returned to a model which deprived him of his natural comic talents. Since he had also warned against this practice in his critical essays, his last Victorian dramas appeared to have ended in a cul de sac rather than pointing the way forward to the confident artistry of *Quality Street* and *The Admirable Crichton*.

A similarly dark account is offered for the Tommy novels. Both Mackail and Geduld see them as despairing, unsuccessful conclusions to his apprenticeship. The former finds two major retrogressive signs of Barrie's dilemma. First, they return to the older, episodic model of the bachelor novels and second, they rely heavily on autobiographical material. The structural and (comparatively) impersonal advances made in *The Little Minister* have indeed been short-lived.

Tommy and Grizel especially offended Mackail. "The second part of this psychological study was so personal and morbid – that's to say when it wasn't just being melodramatic or absurd that, even with the proofs before him, you would have thought that he would have tried to suppress it or draw back" (Mackail 1941: 294). One endemic fault leads to another. For Mackail, Barrie has never really known how to end his novels properly. And, after so many attempts, comes arguably the worst of all. What purpose can possibly be served by killing Tommy off in a humiliating and accidental manner? "And he oughtn't to kill his hero like that. It wasn't fair. Or if he insisted on that why, in Heaven's name, couldn't he kill his heroine too?" (303). His own critical conclusion is clear enough. *Tommy and Grizel* proved that Barrie should give up novel writing entirely:

Yet if he had written a dozen more so-called novels he could only, in all probability now have used the same methods again. The medium was too loose and treacherous, he couldn't, even in fiction, conceal himself and his secrets under any other name. (303)

This neat negative judgment still prevails to-day.

I have three reasons for considering the opposed point of view. First, the negative judgment is reached without reference either to the rhetorical principles which informed Barrie's view of art *or* to the layered subversive forms he employed. It also ignores his ultimate concern with the "original" questions of creativity. Second, the consistently negative account fails to address the most obvious question of all. How can such a disastrous "rehearsal" lead seamlessly into the confident craftsmanship of *Quality Street* and *The Admirable Crichton* less than two years later?[1]

The third objection is the most powerful. Once more a neat mythic pattern emerges for works which were, in their own day, at the centre of extreme disagreement. In Barrie's day there were many who dismissed *The Wedding Guest* in the same terms as those which generalise the situation now. But in fact 1900 saw as deep a division of opinion over Barrie's Ibsenite drama and Tommy Sandys' story as with any Barrie work at any time. Walbrook makes this case for *The Wedding Guest*. Having read first night reaction, he imagines the author chortling with laughter, when he sees his play "described on the same day by one expert as an evangelist of goodness and by another as an ogre of sin"! (1922: 60). Current positions in the Ibsen debate also determined reaction, with William Archer foreseeably praising it and Clement Scott condemning. The same oppositions appear concerning the Tommy stories. Where many anticipate Mackail's condemnation of *Tommy and Grizel* especially as looking backwards and ending miserably, for Moult "His later writings are, as it were, born in these books" and "Tommy's death is the most masterly contrivance of the story" (1928: 134–35).

In approaching this important debate and reconsidering the alternative case, I will again raise only the most basic questions which informed Barrie's own rhetorical training. Before I do this, however, there is one major canonical issue to be considered. Those who see the

---

[1] Indeed, *Quality Street* was being planned in the Notebooks at the same time as *The Wedding Guest*.

prose and drama of this period progressively do highlight *Peter Pan* but that play does not overshadow the others. "To the Never Land and Beyond" is therefore an accurate statement of the way they see the start of his major assault on genius.

To remind readers who are used to the reductive "Famed for Pan alone" thesis an account of the very different climate of opinion in his own day will act as a valuable counterbalance. Here is how one experienced critic viewed his literary legacy. James Agate wrote this overview on the day of the playwright's death:

Barrie died suddenly this morning. His was an irritating genius, which never left one doubt either about the genius or the irritation. *Dear Brutus* and *A Kiss for Cinderella* are pure gold. *Mary Rose* is enormously helped by O'Neill's music, and I always succumb to it even when poorly acted. I have come to hate *Peter Pan*. The ideal audience for this would be a house composed entirely of married couples who have never had any children, or parents who have lost them all. (Agate 1976: 82)

It is fair to say that the reductive view of Barrie as a one-play author is slowly going away. But it is certainly taking its time. This is because the major advances in our knowledge and understanding of Barrie over the last ten years tend to remain in the academic realm alone. To achieve this advance has meant re-interpreting in today's critical terms the largely intuitive viewpoints of Barrie's enthusiastic contemporaries and doing so in recognised opposition to the unsympathetic Oedipal assessments of the intervening years. Even when reduced to basic propositions the counter-case being argued is complex and its initial premises notably different from those currently adopted by biographers.

Essentially, the new critics start with the qualities which make Barrie's fictive world of Thrums different from the "real" world of Kirriemuir. They do so by embracing the comprehensive and inclusive dialectics encouraged in *The Greenwood Hat*. Psychologically this means acceptance that Barrie *has* a streak of childishness but only as one strand in that ever-changing histrionic personality which marks out the *type* of the sentimental artist. Inspirationally, they accept that his mother, like Betty Davidson for Robert Burns, could offer him folk material drawn from Kirriemuir's actual past. But Burns also read the classics voraciously while Barrie profited from the major authors he was introduced to at University. Formally, they accept that, at this late stage of his apprenticeship, his major aim is the satisfying of public and peers in the kind of layered composition described in *The Greenwood Hat*. If these premises are complex, however, the means of exploring them are not. Following classical and Renaissance practice, Barrie must imitate as well as invent but do so in a way which makes the novel treatment of his topic clear. Mode and message are therefore the first areas to be defined. The textual analyses which follow will open in this way.

Unfortunately, despite the academic advances made and the restoration of Barrie to a central position in British literary history, a more difficult form of persuasion is still needed if the new critical vision is to establish itself more widely. A personal account of my own peripheral part in the ambitious plans made for the 150 years celebration in Kirriemuir on 8 and 9 May 2010 will make the point more forcibly than any number of generalisations. A great deal of work and effort went into this celebration, which was a great success. I was, however, given the opportunity to see advance copies of the notices for the exhibition as planned by The National Trust for Scotland. These unapologetically "celebrated" the Oedipal Barrie of old. My urge to have major alterations was met politely with the argument that "This was what people expected". The Trust's periodical, *Scotland in Trust*, had an essay by Alan Taylor which I found more comforting as it did make claims for wider reading of his work. Nonetheless, he too concludes that, albeit "for good or ill Barrie's reputation rests chiefly with Peter Pan" (Taylor 2010: 22). This is unfortunately true.

I depart from Taylor, however, when he adds, "To-day, no apology for this is needed". What he revives here is the critical consensus of ten years ago and with it the particular problems of the one volume being *Pan*. To recapitulate – it is one thing to make a "single work" case for an author who died early or who exhausted his talent in one moment of rare insight. It is quite another to link an author whose childish, mother-fixated personality is assumed and has become of more interest to most people than his art to the one work which apparently defines his immaturity. Certainly, to use Masson's hierarchical methods, this was why he was relegated two academic divisions below his erstwhile partners in genius – Wilde and Shaw. It is also why it has been so difficult to re-establish him by their side.

I had hoped that the most recent Barrie biography, Lisa Chaney's *Hide and Seek with Angels*, would accept Hollindale's challenge and in some way mirror the equal importance of Barrie's life in literature. This hope was in large measure fostered by her generous acceptance that she was "indebted to" Birkin's work to Leonee Ormond's and my own (Chaney 2005: v). The trouble I have with this book is well exemplified in her treatment of *The Wedding Guest* and the Tommy novels. On the positive side, her critical analysis of the former is intelligent, though characteristically brief. This is sometimes the case and she does admit that some of the more complex areas of Barrie's thought are beyond her remit.

Indeed, it may be that my only problem arises from her reassurance that she is indebted to some of the works which raise Hollindale's challenge most clearly. But in fact, beyond saying that she has profited from those books, it is difficult to see where any influence comes in. I naturally regret that my own arguments, for example on Darwin's influence, the "waiting" ending of *The Admirable Crichton* and the quintessential allegory of *Little Mary* are simply sidestepped.[2] But surely Jacqueline Rose's highly sophisticated analysis of Barrie's authorial invisibility must also be met on its own terms? Even more troublesome is the fact that the gender critics have not been consulted. They, after all, work in a sympathetic biographical-psychological manner but approach Barrie's writing (and particularly the *Tommy* novels) in modern theoretical terms.

This principle of avoidance is particularly obvious when she treats the Tommy novels. A general acceptance of the books' complexity opens the discussion: "These extraordinary books are much more complex than that. *Sentimental Tommy* in particular, is a profound meditation on the nature of fantasy, reality, childhood, the passage of time and, by implication one's own end" (Chaney 2005: 129). There is no refining of the items in this list only the conclusion that the clash between reality and fantasy is stronger in these books than elsewhere in Barrie's work. She then, without further proof, pronounces *Sentimental Tommy* to be the best of his novels.

The initial acknowledgement of complexity is not therefore explained, making it easier for her to return to Margaret Ogilvy as the books' ruling spirit, "As the words flowed from him, Barrie discovered that, instead of finding it painful to write about his mother, Margaret had become the subject of his book" (138). The publishing

---

[2] This is, arguably, Barrie's most ambitious work of all and the one which proved his genius to Shaw. It is only mentioned in passing.

links between *Sentimental Tommy* and *Margaret Ogilvy* are then used to support the Oedipal line despite the fact that the opening chapters of the former and the relevant passages in the latter offer more obvious support for the alternative thesis that mother and son are co-conspirators in verbal manipulation and power-play.

The most disturbing gap of all is the lack of any reference to Leonee Ormond's account of the Tommy novels. This is certainly the most detailed account to date of why the Tommy books *are* so complex. Far from reducing them to Margaret Ogilvy's influence, Ormond proposes the most ambitious allegorical range of all for these books. For her they cover all levels but lay prime emphasis on the ultimate mysteries while adding a further layer of metanarrational reference. And at the root of these allegories lies Tommy as histrionic type, not the child Barrie and his supposed traumas (Ormond 1983: 72–79).

A full literary biography remains the best way of re-defining Barrie to a wider audience. But despite some advances made by Chaney, we still await that *rara avis* – the writer who has as much understanding of his art as his life.

Mode and Meaning

1. "A Platonic Friendship"

The turn of the nineteenth century presents this challenge in a particularly acute form. National change was under way. On 22nd January Queen Victoria died in Osborne House on the Isle of Wight. She had reigned for sixty three years. In this context it is not misleading to use the terms Victorian and Edwardian to indicate the division between those plays which satisfied Barrie and were published in the Collected edition and those, ending with the *Wedding Guest*, which did not and were not. The Barries' marriage was also undergoing a significant change. This was the time when Barrie's sentimental infatuation with Sylvia Llewelyn Davies was becoming more and more obvious. It was also the time when he was completing *Tommy and Grizel* and obliquely signing his failure as a husband to Mary. That she became actively involved in buying a personal retreat at this time is scarcely surprising. That her acquisition of *Black Lake Cottage* in Surrey would later become the setting for her husband's games with the "lost boys" *and* her own affair with Gilbert Canaan could not then have been foreseen. The basic "plot", however, had the potential for the doubly ironic outcome which was, in fact, realised.

I use a literary metaphor because one of the major reasons for so many people becoming engrossed in Barrie's life is because it does, regularly, read *like* fiction. The period we are about to discuss is one of the most dramatic. As such it inevitably warrants lengthy bio-graphical analysis. Even when some of his contemporaries valued the Tommy novels highly and accepted *The Wedding Guest* as his most serious apprenticeship play to date the tragic events surrounding his personal life justifiably warranted more extended coverage than his fiction. Yet Barrie was, at the same time, facing one of the most daunting crises in his literary life. And later, when the quality of both *Tommy and Grizel* and *The Wedding Guest* were questioned in terms which turned them into additional symptoms of his disturbed psyche, the imbalance increased.

It is from that position which Rose, Ormond, Carpenter, Sedgwick and, most recently, Andrew Nash have rescued us. It is to develop their contribution via a detailed account of the equally intense battle Barrie faced in the world of fancy that the rest of this chapter is designed. To that end, the table below includes all Barrie's prose and drama after *The Little Minster*. It also accommodates itself to the overlapping process of preparation mirrored in the Notebooks by including *Sentimental Tommy* for analysis.

	Novels	**Plays**
1896:	*Sentimental Tommy*	
1897:		[*The Little Minster*]
1898:		"A Platonic Friendship"
1900:	*Tommy and Grizel*	*The Wedding Guest*

Among the four texts to be considered, it is "A Platonic Friendship" which makes the most obvious claim for prior consideration. It does so chronologically because *Sentimental Tommy* is best analysed as the prequel to *The Wedding Guest*. But it also does so as the work which most obviously challenges that general movement towards greater seriousness and complexity implied by the progressive view of Barrie's apprenticeship.

The Little Minister had, after all, established high standards of
intent both structurally and topically. In adopting the methods of
myth, it had been the clearest literary expression so far of Barrie's
belief that there are only a few basic story types whose potential for
varied development lies in the choice of different expressive modes. It
had also re-confirmed that his own artistic world centred on that gender conflict which Hegel had earlier defined as the basic underlying
theme behind modern ethical thinking (see Benhabib 1992: 23–67). Its
consistency in Barrie's thought has now been traced in Darwinian
terms from *Auld Licht Idylls* onwards while its unique development in
feminist and artistic terms, the features which make Barrie's world
unique, have also been revealed.

No matter how one regards the Tommy novels and *The Wedding
Guest*, they clearly conform to that pattern. They all are seriously
thought out in the Notes, they are all regarded as serious attempts to
re-present in new forms the sexual and artistic battles described above.
Their formal complexity is not only accepted but often claimed to be
the reason for their failure to please.

However, if one looks at the mode and plot of "A Platonic
Friendship" on the surface narrative level, one can see why it seems to
look backwards in time. After all, the play was composed in one night
as part of a celebration for Nellie Farren, the burlesque artiste who had
so attracted Barrie in his Nottingham days. After enjoying a long
tenure as leading lady and Principal Boy at the *Gaiety Theatre* she had
gone on a lengthy tour of Australia. On her return in 1889 she experienced an attack of rheumatic fever and developed a spinal disease.
This progressively crippled her, and by 1892 Farren was mostly
retired from the stage having become unable to work. This association
with burlesque takes Barrie back in time to *Toole's Theatre* and his
first London play, "Ibsen's Ghost" at a time when progressive complexity is the expectation raised in *The Greenwood Hat* and confirmed
by Barrie's work so far. The plot of "A Platonic Friendship" also suggests a return to earlier days and light comedy. The associations are
this time with *The Professor's Love Story*. A young philosopher takes
over the role of Professor Goodwillie while his pupil Winnie re-enacts
the romantic threat of Lucy White.

It is, of course, true that different practical opportunities call for
different kinds of play. Add to this Barrie's own belief in translating
the same basic story type across the widest possible modal range and

one can see that the idea of constant progression towards Impish complexity is a critical abstraction unlikely to be neatly mirrored in practice. That Barrie admired the contributions made by burlesque theatres to British drama is also well authenticated. To Violet Vanbrugh he wrote, "Evidently, you don't know that in the lovely and debased form of burlesque or parody you are of an excellence that no other actress can touch" (BVS A3.1927). And he would later compose, in *Rosy Rapture*, a full-scale burlesque of his own (Barrie 1915a).

It is, therefore, Barrie's apparently extreme return to the ways of the past which overtly challenges the progressive view of his apprenticeship. But a closer look at the key questions regarding mode and meaning reveals a more complex situation.

While Nellie Farren was primarily known as a burlesque actress, her artistic versatility is illustrated in the wide range of theatrical modes listed in her biography. These included starring along with Edward Terry and Kate Vaughan in *Thespis*, the first of Gilbert and Sullivan's collaborations. It is not, therefore, surprising to find Gilbert himself taking the part of the Associate in a performance of *A Trial by Jury* which formed part of the celebration. In this production, the principals included Barrington, Lytton, Passmore and Perry. The barristers were all played by well-known playwrights. The jury were principal comedians while the ladies' chorus contained both leading ladies and real chorus girls from the Gaiety. The influence she had exerted on the London stage was mirrored both by the number of "acts" (the celebration lasted six hours) and the prestigious audience, including the Prince of Wales, who gathered to honour her.

This reminds us that the burlesque form itself was more widely defined then than now. It also makes a distinction between auspices and mode. While the *Gaiety* was a burlesque theatre and Nellie's fame was founded on her burlesque skills, this celebration, which was held at the *Theatre Royal*, Drury Lane, mingled burlesque acts with a wide variety of other forms. A more detailed account of the plot of "A Platonic Friendship" will reveal that *its* form was in fact a new one for Barrie and one in which he continued to re-invent modally his own version of the battle between the sexes.

The Lord Chamberlain's text (LCP53655/A) reveals the new form. This is "A Duologue" to be performed by Cyril Maude and Winfred Emery for the Nellie Farren night at the *Gaiety Theatre*. The curtain rises on Mr Stanley, a young male philosopher. Despite being a disciple of Plato and therefore of reason's control over passion, he is first seen confessing his love for his pupil Winnie in *extremely* passionate language. Unfortunately he believes his manservant, Simpson, to be the recipient of his confidences. But, as the audience can see from the outset, Simpson is conspicuous by his absence. Stanley is in fact revealing the justification of his character description as "[a young man and a fraud]" to Winnie herself. By imitating the butler's "gruff voice" (LCP53655/A: f 1) she encourages him to dig an even deeper passionate pit for himself.

"A Platonic Friendship" was a successful play. It was revived for similar benefit performances at the *Comedy Theatre* and the *Haymarket* in 1900 and the *Prince of Wales* in 1901 (Hamilton 1920). At the *Theatre Royal* its first production was greeted with enthusiasm by an audience who saw Mr Barrie returning in a more controlled and focussed manner to the ethical centre in reason and passion of his current obsession with the battle of the sexes. Once more the upper hand is given to women but in a form which turns upside down Plato's model for the soul in the clearest manner possible. The central comic technique doesn't change. The young man over and over again protests male, rational control, having already enacted his passionate servitude. The play's comic variety derives from the different ways in which Winnie restates her power. Consistent with Barrie's emphasis on the aural and visual powers of the theatre many of these move-ments depend on mime. The opening action, for example, moves from one visual and aural confirmation of her power – the non- existence of the butler and her mimicking of his voice to another, her destruction of his first rational defence by repeatedly mimicking him screwing up his lips to kiss her when he thought she wasn't there (LCP: f.2).

The critical model for this kind of play is the one Barrie discussed at length in his academic articles on satire. There he defined the central problem in terms of two audiences – today's and tomorrow's. To attract the first you had to focus on the transitory interests of to-day. To ensure that your satire continued to interest future generations, you had also to evoke enduring ideas. Measured against these aims, "A Platonic Friendship" deserves to be a success. The serious, ethical focus on the gender battle, which had originated *The Little Minister* in Barrie's Notebooks is clearly enacted. The generic evidence, though slight, confirms this parallel on a broader planning level. Whether *The Little Minister* should, as its title suggests, be another version of the male artist's sentimental journey or become (as it did) a study of both genders in conflict was a major question posed in that drama. "A Platonic Friendship" was originally called "The Platonic Guest", a title which suggests that the controlling woman is its major focus. Winnie's story would be highlighted. The "Guest" remains the triumphant "Friend".

In arguing that "A Platonic Friendship" cannot be dismissed as a slight piece but as a light, economically presented example of Barrie's determination to make future ages "his own" I have necessarily highlighted the ethical theme and therefore the more serious side to the play. The skills Barrie shows on the popular level are of equal importance in explaining why the play was so highly regarded in his own time. Two examples will demonstrate his skills in keeping the whole audience amused.

Burlesque actresses were associated with different colours and young men indicated their preferences for one or other by wearing those colours. Nellie Farren's were light blue, dark blue and white. Barrie translates this tradition into his farcical duologue by having his "rational" philosopher exhibit a Pavlovian reaction to Winnie's colours, in this case green. Each time his powerlessness before her green scarf is farcically enacted, she reminds him of the assumed heights from which he has fallen: "A silly scarf! And you a philosopher!" (f.3).

At this time a flu virus was abroad and Barrie uses it to cross the footlights and draw his audience into the play. Having invented an infirm brother, the young philosopher impresses on Winnie the danger of illness if she stays. She defiantly replies that she is quite well but this time Stanley does not give in at once:

MR. STANLEY: Still, with all this influenza about –
WINNIE: Isn't it dreadful! My Aunt Grace has it just now for the seventh time.
MR. STANLEY: Winnie, dear.
WINNIE: It comes so suddenly too. All those people there, (*calmly pointing to audience*) so well and happy just now – isn't it sad to think that half of them may be down with influenza tomorrow!

If it is important to produce a detailed account of Barrie's literary life his status as the "dramatist's dramatist" means that it also has to be

theatrical one. Discussions of his work which lack that dimension are
unlikely to capture fully his aims and techniques.

2. *The Wedding Guest*'s Reception

The Wedding Guest marks the end of Barrie's apprenticeship in the theatre; 1902, the
year of *Quality Street* and *The Admirable Crichton* witnesses his advent as a mature
dramatist. (Ormond 1987: 85)

The major question posed for "A Platonic Friendship" was whether it
revealed Barrie's late apprenticeship in progressive or regressive
terms. Despite surface signs of a retreat into triviality its development
of the moral implications of the battle between the sexes made it yet
another variation on that theme. Almost exactly the same movement
from the appearance of retrogressive failure to evidence of an ambitious, forward-looking mindset can be detected in *The Wedding Guest*.

Critics of this, the last play in Barrie's apprenticeship, advance
four major reasons for seeing it as at once a failure *and* a return to
methods which had failed its author in the past.

[1] As Realistic Failure. In its own days, *The Wedding Guest* was
seen as an odd return to the kind of art Barrie had claimed he could
not master. This view still persists. Allen Wright, for example, defines
it as "as one of the few attempts he made to come to grips with "Life".
"Realism", he adds, "was never his forte" (Wright 1976: 54). These
conclusions appear to be confirmed by all we know about Barrie's
apprenticeship. He is, after all, the one who admitted that he preferred
to keep real life at a distance while all his criticism places him on the
side of fancy and the imagination, of Dickens and Shakespeare. Is
Barrie in any sense re-visiting *Richard Savage* his worst failure to
date?

[2] As Ibsenite Failure. Most critics began by defining it in Ibsenite terms. Geduld sums up this argument nicely when he sees the
play as Barrie, "avoiding comedy" and instead "set[ting] out to work
on a serious problem play, written in response to the Ibsen vogue of
the 1890s". It from this position that he advances the opinion cited
earlier, that it is really a melodrama in Norwegian guise (Geduld
1971: 105). Many earlier critics anticipated this reaction and there
certainly are melodramatic moments in the play. Barrie, they agreed,

wanted to appear to have "grown up" and so had decided to enter a
darker world and impress people with his daring.

Another group, while praising the play aesthetically against the
model of Ibsen's problem plays used that effectiveness as a means of
condemning it as *morally* repulsive. Clement Scott was the most powerful medium for this kind of ethical outrage. For him *The Wedding
Guest* contained so much "unpleasantness, painfulness and doubtful
morality" that one feared it might "encourage promiscuous seduction"
(cited in Walbrook 1922: 63).

These comments prove that the play was damned for being too
Ibsenite (by those who liked the Norwegian's drama) and for not
being Ibsenite enough (by those who did not). What was not at issue
was the theatrical coup Barrie had achieved in the short term by
advertising in advance the shock which awaited those who came in the
hope of light comedy. This produced full houses in the early part of
the run. As Walbrook puts it, "Here was their gentle ironist, their
sentimentalist ladling out scenes as harrowing and remorseless as
those of Ibsen himself" (Walbrook 1922: 60). But surely he had
gained that transient fame by denying those dramatic strengths which
elsewhere he had been nurturing and developing?

[3] As Original Failure? The opening scene, in repeating the idea
of the "Scotch wedding" looked backwards, not only to his recent
dramatic production of *The Little Minister* but to the very origins of
his prose in Chapter 4 of *Auld Licht Idylls*. This tension between the
modernism of Ibsen and the retrogressive direction of his own sources
led some to believe it was not his novels but his plays which were at
the end of their inspirational tether. Certainly, Walkley in *The Times*
saw *The Wedding Guest* as proof of his need to concentrate on
narrative – "The more we see of Mr Barrie's talent on the stage, the
more we sigh for his talent in the novel" (*The Times* 28 September
1900: 4).

[4] As "Final" Failure: There were other criticisms which
suggested that Barrie had lost his literary way at the very time he
should have been emerging confidently from his self-imposed apprenticeship. These related to repeated failures rather than apparent returns
to past ways. Continued failure to provide understandable endings was
the most consistent of these. The view of the play as descending
qualitatively from promising beginning to problematic middle and
awful end was common. *The Stage*, for example, found the first act

"charming, if sketchy" the middle acts "poignant [...] but unpleasant" and the conclusion "halting and inconclusive" (*Stage* 4 October 1900: 14).

These views dominated in Barrie's day. They strengthen and threaten to become the whole story in the simplified canonical picture presented now. It is here that Lois Chaney proves an honourable exception. Starting from recognition that a smaller group of critics were as thrilled by the play as others were disappointed or outraged, she looks at the key question – how did Barrie react? *The Little Minister's* success had caused him acute disappointment which continued to fester. Chaney reminds us that more usually he learned from his audiences. We know from Mackail and others that the perfectionist within him was intensely disappointed with *The Wedding Guest*'s failure to charm or persuade. He may have accepted Henry Irving's dictum that the drama must succeed as a business if it is not to fail as an art but, without doubt, he thought it was a good play. Chaney goes on to suggest that he was trying to use subliminal, poetic methods to present his case, citing the *Times* in order to explain the ambitiousness of his aims:

For the charm of a genuine Barrie, while it is undeniable is at the same time not very easily explicable. In the ultimate analysis we believe that the pleasure of a genuine Barrie will be found not so much in what the work – whether novel or play – says as in what it implies. *(Times* 1902 cited in Chaney 2005: 176–78)

These conclusions are consistent with Barrie's belief that he had achieved most of the ambitious aims he had set himself in *The Wedding Guest*. Unfortunately he had taken neither the stalls nor the *literati* along with him.

A Realistic Ibsenite Drama?

The play's, mainly antagonistic, reception having been covered, it is appropriate to give some idea of what the audience actually saw. At the opening night on 27th September 1900 the *Garrick Theatre* welcomed a distinguished cast and a full house. The curtain rose to reveal a problem play in its old, "eternal triangle" sense:

Act 1: [The Drawing Room at the Old Keep]. On the day of his marriage to Margaret Fairbairn (Dorothea Baird), Paul Digby (H.B. Irving) is faced with the unexpected return of Mrs Ommaney (Violet Vanbrugh), his former mistress and the mother of his child. We first see a Scottish butler (A.E. George) guiding the English couple and the chief bridesmaid (Ethelwyn Arthur-Jones) through the conventions of a Scottish wedding. Paul's reputation as an artist and Margaret's innocent love for him are then enacted. Margaret's optimistic, non-confrontational father (Brandon Thomas) is also introduced and the wedding goes through as planned until Mrs Ommaney faints and Paul recognises her.

Act 2: [Mrs Ommaney's lodgings at the Pans]. Before the honeymoon, Paul and Margaret visit Mrs Ommaney's house. Mrs Ommaney's extravagant behaviour leads Margaret to believe she is mad but on hearing she is a single parent her sympathy returns. Margaret's aunt, Lady Janet Dunwoodie (Kate Sergeantson) who has herself been let down in love learns the truth. Mrs Ommaney has a melodramatic on-stage breakdown and once more faints. Paul covers her up and waits with her.

Act 3: [Mrs Ommaney's lodgings at the Pans]. Mrs Ommaney awakes with Paul still at her side. They discuss the practical and moral implications of their situation and Mrs Ommaney makes a last desperate plea to return to their old days together. Unaware of the real situation, Margaret continues "generously" to excuse her rival. Lady Jane, however, retains her clear distinction between "good" and "bad". Paul's full confession, which brings the act to an end, is in harmony with this strict moral vision.

Act 4: [The Drawing Room at the Old Keep]. The act opens with Margaret's father and the minister childishly falling out over a game of draughts. Mr Fairbairn's determination to see no cloud in the emotional sky is enacted. But it is Lady Jane's discovery that her own lover had not let her down which acts as the catalyst for, at least, a partial resolution. The end of the play does not, however, mirror the idyllic ending to Act 1. Compromise defines the new alliance between Paul and Margaret while Mrs Ommany unwillingly accepts her new role.

This narrative account challenges two of the simple "retrogressive" arguments. First, it becomes clear that the darker vision of Ibsen is not the sole influence to be considered as it mingles with the lighter mode of English, love-triangle comedy. Barrie's enthusiasm for Pinero is well documented. On seeing *The Second Mrs Tanqueray*, he wrote enthusiastically to his rival, "The woman is a masterly study bound to hold her place in the annals of dramatic writing" (BVS A3/17/1/1913). Leonee Ormond links *The Wedding Guest* with that play and Wilde's *Lady Windermere's Fan* (Ormond 1987: 52). Others, seeing Paul's guilt as central to the love problem, relate it to the tradition of Pinero's *The Profligate*. It should be noted, however, that the original MS of the play (BVS T45) relies less on the opening Scotch-English comedy and omits all reference to the farcical draughts match between

Margaret's father and the minister. These only enter in the typed playscript T45/2.

For those who know the history of Barrie's interest in Ibsen, this hybrid evidence is, anyway, unsurprising. The evidence of "Ibsen's Ghost", *Walker, London* and, in a darker way, "Becky Sharp", argued a guilty desire to imitate the "greatest playwright of his age" but only in his own inventive way. This is precisely what Barrie offers in *The Wedding Guest*.

The second retrogressive argument to be challenged is the one which sees a return to *The Little Minister* in solely chronological terms. The narrative account of the play reveals that its sub-title, *Two Kinds of Women*, is borne out by the action. The implications of this in topical terms will be explored later. Even at this simple descriptive level, however, an alternative, continuous viewing of its place in the canon emerges. As another variation on the central theme of gender conflict it can be seen as looking back to *Sentimental Tommy* and "Becky Sharp" as well as reflecting the artistic themes of *Tommy and Grizel*, its contemporary in planning and production.

As major problems with regards to both the mode and basic meaning of *The Wedding Guest* have been raised, any guidance that can be derived from studying the play's origins is more than usually welcome. And that evidence does prove helpful. The MS of the play is the shortest and most serious of all (BVS T45). Most of the comedy between Scottish and English characters is added in the next, typed version. The title page mirrors this. No description of the play's mode or genre is offered. The printed text witnesses the added comic scenes by calling it "A Comedy" (BVS T 45/2). This evidence, while it does not deny the obvious fact that *The Wedding Guest* is a problem play, confirms that it was first conceived as a lighter adaptation of Ibsen's themes rather than a serious attempt to imitate them. The earliest signs of its topic also challenge the simple Ibsenite model for detraction. In the Notebook for 1897, note 187 reads "Play. Scotch Wedding. – The other woman steals in while it is in progress" (BVS A2.16). That is, both retrospective reliance on tried methods *and* an advance towards more serious themes are anticipated three years before the play was produced. On these grounds, it is fair to see the last play of Barrie's apprenticeship as sitting "On the boundary between his attempts to give the stage what it wanted and his attempts to give the stage what he wanted" (*Bookman* 1918: 55.104).

Barrie's formal and tonal experiments do become more daring as he comes to the end of his apprenticeship. Consequently the temptation for biographer or journalist to simplify the evidence becomes greater. Mackail, for example, calls the production a failure because it only ran at *The Garrick* for fifteen weeks. At that point H.B. Irving deserted, Martin Harvey took over and the production transferred to the *St James's*. Yet we are actually talking about a production which opened as a *cause célèbre*, endured cast and venue changes and ran for a hundred nights. It was withdrawn ten days before Queen Victoria died.

In his sad acceptance of this ambitious failure Barrie did spread the blame. As usual, he wanted an understated production. The chosen director was the youthful, up and coming star of the London stage, Dion Boucicault Jr. He, in common with most talented young producers then and now, wanted to put his own radical directorial mark upon it. That even the more mature, knowledgeable Barrie could not withstand this assault, is borne out by critics and playwright alike. The cast may have been good but, if Walbrook is to be believed

> *The Wedding Guest* suffered from an excess of the sort of acting which so blackens every shade and whitens every light that the whole of the dramatist's appeal to the imagination of his audience evaporates in a sort of orgie of histrionic obviousness. (1922: 66)

Little wonder that Barrie, for whom indirection and understatement were paramount, was heard to bemoan his "bleeding and broken play" (Mackail 1941: 300).

There is, of course, a sense in which *The Wedding Guest* tests Barrie's powers as a realistic writer to limits only earlier attempted in the disastrous *Richard Savage*. At points in the play, he even attempts to mirror the speech of adults in love, a task which, it will be remembered, he could only undertake when imagining himself chained to his desk. It is fair to say that at times he succeeds. There *are* moments when his lovers convince us of their passion. The dialogue between Paul and Mrs Ommaney, in Act 3, is one such. Here is Mrs Ommaney's plaintive appeal to return to their old relationship::

PAUL: Kate and our child will be well provided for.
(*Mrs Ommany turns away*)
You must take it. Oh, it is so pitifully little I can do.

MRS OMMANEY: (*eagerly but half afraid*) It need not be so pitifully little, Paul, if – (*Hesitates*) – I shall do whatever you ask of me, live where you please, go into the country far from her, be so patient. Paul, I need never again be as you have seen me to-day. Only my wild craving for you brought it on. It turned my brain. There shall be no more of that. I will be so contented; so happy; you will say I am my old self again – when you came to see me. (III: 253)

If this is good realistic writing in the sense that it is psychologically convincing, there is another kind of realism Barrie seeks to master – that which is associated with darker topics. Here, the modern reader has a problem. Today, it is difficult to see what could possibly offend audiences in a story about a single mother and her baby. This is to discount the high moral expectations of the Victorian London West End as described by Mackail: "In 1899 he (Barrie) was being pretty daring with his lawless Mrs Ommaney and the actual stage appearance, even in the form of a small doll, of her illegitimate child" (283). That Barrie had offended them and done so in an extreme manner is everywhere evident.

Further, his successful attempts at realism are sporadic. His use of childish language in Act 3 is positively embarrassing while, as the following stilted conversation between Paul and Margaret illustrates, the rhythms and vocabulary of love escape him as often as he catches them:

MARGARET: I don't know what to do. The world has slipped from under my feet, and I can catch hold of nothing. I am only a girl and I don't know what to do.
PAUL: You loved me once, Margaret.
MARGARET: The man I loved – he was not the real Paul.
PAUL: The real Paul needs you so much more than the other. (III: 270)

If the entire play had sought to appeal on realistic grounds, one suspects, this inability to sustain psychologically convincing dialogue would have become ever more apparent.

Probably aware of this, Barrie uses a variety of strategies to limit the realistic bias of the play. In critical terms these are justified by the model he is following. Barrie was reading Hardy at this time, an author whom he had praised for realism combined with poetry and drama. He had recently completed "Becky Sharp" and Thackeray was another author whose basic realism he had assessed as not denying idealism or imagination. If one thinks, then, of *The Wedding Guest* in balanced terms as an attempt to view the gender battle through the realistic-idealistic lens of *Vanity Fair* rather than the idealistic-realistic lens of Dickens a more accurate view of the play's aims is authorised by Barrie's own interests at this time. Certainly, study of the earlier plays and prose has shown that he never allows one vision to dominate, even in the basic Christian-evolutionary terms of his central theme. Instead, he counterpoints one form against the other in the subversive spirit of the Imp. And, if doubts still remain, one might ask "How does the play's prose contemporary *Tommy and Grizel* open?" Why, it opens with a debate between Tommy and Pym on the different kinds of art possible with specific reference to the realism/idealism debate (Barrie 1900b: 18–27).

So in what ways does *The Wedding Guest* limit the realistic side to the play? First, and most obviously, the play imitates staged reality as much as it mirrors actual individuals in love. The first act clinically prepares the way for another version of those plays about "a woman with a past", which were currently enjoying a vogue on the London stage. The innocent young bride, the bridegroom with a secret and the strange woman who invades the wedding are all quickly established in Act One. The conventional secrets and discoveries demanded by that mode soon follow. The revelation of Mrs Ommaney's true identity initiates the dramatic confusion while Lady Jane's realisation that her lover had been faithful after all initiates the semi-reconciliations on which the curtain falls

Nor are any of the characters consistently presented in a realistic manner. Even the lovers at times mirror the types demanded by the gender battles conventionally associated with the characters of Ibsen and the humours of Pinero. Among them, Mrs Ommaney moves from serious depiction of an individual in love to the extreme and extended theatricality of her "mad" scene (236–44). The introduction of Lady Janet as, specifically, a "Scotch Grande Dame" is another example of truth to theatrical traditions rather than life:

PAUL: She is said to be very formidable. A *grande dame.*
ARMITAGE: I thought there were no Scotch *grande dames.*
PAUL: My young friend, there are only Scotch ones (I.220)

Further overt humour comedy in the Bergsonian sense is provided by Mr Fairbairn. This ensures that another comic tradition, that of Molière is added (226). Variety of presentation and tone rather than tragic realism alone characterise the play.

While this may be construed as Barrie fittingly pushing to extreme limits the battle between real and ideal characterisation which also opened *Tommy and Grizel* it is easy to see how audiences could become confused by so varied and inconsistent an approach. It would probably have been wise, in this context, to offer a neat ending for an audience who were not really being helped to solve even the more immediate of the "problems" within the play. This was, however, a time when another kind of counterbalance affected all of his writing. While he was testing himself to the furthest extremes of his technical range, Barrie was also narrowing the topical focus of his work and determining the major formal and thoughtful principles which would mark out his uniqueness. These have now been firmly established. In terms of Cowley's formula for genius he has raised his aims to the "time to come" and so, underlying his major work, a consistent universal theme has emerged – that of the battle of the sexes in both natural and artistic arenas.

If this is so then the end of his apprenticeship should, in some measure, develop that theme. Two major approaches have already emerged – the "heroic" which focuses primarily on one character and the "embattled" which sets man and woman or different kinds of woman against each other. That bias and balance had been suggested in the alternative title of the duologue – "A Platonic Guest" vying with "A Platonic Friendship". It is true also for *The Wedding Guest* where that name highlights one character, Mrs Ommaney, but *Two Kinds of Women* highlights her battle with Margaret. The same choice of focus was offered as far back as *The Professor's Love Story* where "The Bookman" and "A Self-made Woman" were earlier suggestions in Barrie's Notebooks.

The "mature" plays which followed *The Wedding Guest* – *Quality Street*, *The Admirable Crichton*, *Little Mary* and *Peter Pan* – would also have open endings but have a clearer form and a consistent tone. By then Barrie's desire to refine questions rather than answer them was accepted by most and seen as appropriate for an age of doubt. When he chose to add a really complex ending to the mixed modes and moods of *The Wedding Guest*, however, the idea that he didn't end his plays neatly because he *couldn't* still held sway.

More than one practical consideration must have suggested caution to him but instead he offers an ending which could be interpreted in so many ways that it was discussed on these grounds in an essay entitled "Problems and Playwrights". There, the writer offers different accounts of what his ending might mean. Interestingly, he does anticipate Barrie's likely reply – "He (Barrie) might urge that the absence of a conclusion is actually a conclusion in itself" but cannot himself find such virtuosity dramatically effective (*Fortnightly Review* 1900: 74: 360).

The following analysis of *The Wedding Guest* while revealing those qualities which made it, in many ways, a suitably complex and ambitious final development within Barrie's apprenticeship, does not seek to deny the weaknesses just described. There *are* too many moods and kinds jostling for attention. As *The Stage* succinctly puts it – "Take it in art, take it in ethics, *The Wedding Guest* cannot be called a consistent piece" (4 October 1900: 14). A number of critics agreed. Hammerton is one such – "It is does not have the appeal of a sincere piece, but is rather an experiment in a new manner" (1929: 224) – and even the enthusiastic Archer has similar technical reservations: "There is ample cleverness in the play – indeed rather too much […] On the technical side, the clevernesses, it seemed to me, were rather superabundant" (*The World* 30 October 1900: 22–23).

Only those who have traced the mythic and the Ibsenite strands in Barrie's thinking from "Ibsen's Ghost" are likely to understand why mythic aim and Norwegian source should naturally come together at the end of Barrie's apprenticeship. At that time he was naturally trying to link his central social theme, the battle between the sexes, to those questions of origin and creativity which they ultimately embody. Walbrook saw this shared ground when he drew an apparently eccentric parallel between Paul Digby and the themes of *The Master Builder*. What he says specifically is

The psychology of its chief character seemed to have been inspired by one of Ibsen's most splendid plays, *The Master Builder*, which had been denounced seven years before as […] a bewildering farrago of tiresome rubbish. (Walbrook 1922: 61)

While the character comparison with Solness relates to the downfall of two creator-artists, one young and one old, who define themselves through their art and expect the worshipful service of women as their right, they also emerge as exemplars of a universal creative process in varying stages of completion. But, in choosing this example Walbrook, wishes to draw other parallels. *The Master Builder*, like *The Wedding Guest*, uses a compound of realism and symbolism to challenge his audience and was, especially in England, misunderstood and wrongly vilified.

In this way Ibsen helped Barrie to explore yet delimit his own realistic powers. He offered a darker and more intensely realistic account of the battle of the sexes than Barrie could ever achieve but in a way which denies the premises of the heading to this section. Barrie does not offer "a realistic Ibsenite play" because Ibsen himself did not write solely realistic plays. As Northam succinctly describes the case, he too set "limitations on his realism", which included "illustrative action", "visual suggestion" and "persistent suggestions of symbolism" (Northam 1953: 16, 17, 40, 218). This use of imagery and symbolism to offer a broader poetic and associative background to his plays was a route which Barrie already favoured and had developed from *Walker, London* on.

Barrie's closeness to Ibsen thematically can also be demonstrated. The most convenient way of advancing this apparently radical claim is to compare what has been revealed about his interest in heroic women with the account of Ibsen's earlier plays offered by Joan Templeton (Templeton 1997: 1–73). The fact that Templeton can write a book about Ibsen's women and validly claim that their variety is a leitmotiv in Ibsen's writing points to the most basic similarity of all. Just as Ibsen consistently explores different versions of women in their equally varied battles against men, so do variations on that theme dominate Barrie's writing from his Victorian apprenticeship onwards. Ibsen too begins with clear contrasts, the strong woman against the weak, the good woman against the bad. But even as early as *Catiline*, while "thoroughly absorbing the conventions of Romanticism by pitting a light, passive woman against a strong, powerful one, he begins to subvert that model" (Templeton 1997: 26). The neat, polarised patterns are replaced by shaded definitions of good and evil. In particular, influenced in part by his Darwinian view of life, Ibsen begins to show as much, if not more, sympathy for the strong woman in *Catiline*. As Templeton puts it, "In the first example of Ibsen's paradigmatic triad of a man caught between two women Ibsen turns one of Romanticism's and Western literature's favourite truisms on its heels as he makes the powerful woman his hero's conscience and the gentle woman the representative of moral conscience (26–27).

We have seen exactly the same triadic focus and the same form of questioning throughout Barrie's apprenticeship. From the naïve and explicit opposition between the "good" girl who is not so good and the "bad" girl who is not so bad in *Jane Annie* to the sympathetic portrayal of Becky Sharp's immoral "sharpness" in the play bearing her name. Barrie goes on to prove that the "eternal triangle", given a suitably imaginative artist can also become an eternally varied theme. One has only to place the long list of Ibsen's women offered by Templeton beside Barrie's to see the similarity of their basic themes and the very different stories they can derive from within different triadic forms of the gender battle. Barrie's first presentation of this battle is the fairly conventional contest between Lucy White and Lady Gilding for the hand of Professor Goodwillie. Even here, however, he does offer a female-centred lower class counterpoint in Pete and Henders' contest for Effie. It is in "Becky Sharp" that his radical tendencies first make their presence felt. As in *Catiline*, it is the powerful Becky rather than the passive Amelia who emerges as the true supporter of Dobbin. It is here that *The Wedding Guest* with its obvious debts to Ibsen comes in. But one need only list the future via a list of Barrie's "embattled" and "heroic" women to see how the Ibsenite influence remains with him, sometimes within the eternal triangle, sometimes as iconic heroines in their own right. Phoebe Throssel, is followed in turn by Little Mary, Wendy Darling, Maggie Wylie, Miss Thing in *A Kiss for Cinderella*, the "evil" Leonora in *The Adored One*, Kate in Barrie's revised feminist version of *The Taming of the Shrew* and *Mary Rose* herself. And that is to confine oneself to full length plays and so omit many others, including the actress Rosalind and Barrie's version of the evil Milady de Winter in "Pages from Dumas". But by this time he had clarified his views on structure and exchanged a clash of moods and voices in favour of a unified comic-satiric approach to those problems which also lay at the centre of Ibsen's more serious focus. That both were strong supporters of the women's movement and initially, at least, drew their inspiration in part from their own lives and in part from the history of their country are also consistent with a shared artistic vision.

It is, nonetheless, Barrie's experiment in realism which caused critics to praise or condemn *The Wedding Guest*, and so Barrie's success or otherwise in that area is of prime importance. Critics were naturally on the alert for signs of Barrie failing to meet the new demands on characterisation implied by his change of approach. Here was a writer firmly associated with comic types in Dickensian fashion.

But the "hero" of *The Wedding Guest*, Paul Digby has to be more of an individual than a type. *The Stage* journalist neatly explains what he had to achieve and then condemns him for not delivering it. Once an author decides to make his characters pass for real individuals, however, they must fulfil the laws of psychological probability at all times. Barrie, he feels, only make Paul *at some times* believable. Indeed, even at major dramatic moments "he gives us characters who in their critical action cannot be referred to life with much probability" (*Stage* 3 October 1900: 45).

In part this is because Paul also has an exemplary role to play in the play's presentation of the battle of the sexes. Here too the two levels, without Impish intentions, do not fit. Thematically too, Barrie is trying to be innovative. Here is a young artist-hero who has already won fame – the French government have, after all, offered to buy one of his paintings and "hang it in *The Luxembourg*" (I. 218). He is, therefore, already a success. Later, he will prove to be a father as well, thus combining both kinds of creativity. From these heights, he gradually and tragically falls. To begin with, the implications of his artistic talents are optimistically and idealistically addressed. The principles of "Art for Art's sake" are, for example, are described and embraced. But as the secretive, illicit circumstances of his paternity are revealed, he comes to see both his natural and artistic triumphs as signs of a fraudulent personality. By the final act, it is a much more melancholy Paul who attributes his failure as a man to his egoism as an artist:

PAUL: I lived too much in my art, and my solitary thoughts. I shrank from men's free talk of women, and yet when I left them it was to brood of the things they spoke of; theirs was a healthier life than mine. (IV.251)

These are among the saddest of all Barrie's dramatic lines when applied to himself. Even attainment of artistic success leaves the man of sentiment, "superfluous" and unfulfilled.

If this artistic vision cruelly exposes the bleakness of living for art alone it also leads into Barrie's most daring attempt to present art as the shadow of childbirth in the manner of *Hedda Gabler*. In that play Hedda specifically destroys the book-child of Eilert and Thea. The battle is fought out again in *The Wedding Guest*. The personal conflicts which lead into it are initially framed in the clear framework of god and bad which also opened *Jane Annie* and "Becky Sharp". The action then sets out to demonstrate that these moral categories can never be applied to human beings. In *The Wedding Guest*, the two women explicitly ask whether they *are* good or bad while the action provides its own more complex reply. Margaret's early generosity to the plight of the single mother (I.225) turns to rigid rejection as Mrs Ommaney's lack of a wedding ring and "possession" of Margaret's husband are revealed (IV.254). Mrs Ommaney herself swings more melodramatically from kindness to open malevolence.

The effect of this, as in the earlier plays, is to blur the issue of which of the "two kinds of woman" wins the sexual battle. What is added in *The Wedding Guest* is the battle between the women to be the source of Paul's inspiration. Margaret's claim is made at the start of the play. It is encouraged by Paul's equation between his best paintings and the best parts of his character and the repeated assumption that she is still a child. On these terms, she accepts his vision of art and idealistically claims she will be his support for ever (II. 218–19). Mrs Ommaney's counter-claim comes at the start of Act III when she has recovered from her fit of madness. It too is idealistically defined but derives its power from the real past rather than the imagined future. Opening with a variation on the "good"/"bad" theme she uses the claim that she had been a "good woman" until she met Paul, to arouse his sense of personal guilt. Revealing a tempestuous passion similar to Hedda Gabler's, she argues that only his fidelity allowed her to continue the belief that she was inspirer of his art: "I could exult in your growing fame, because of it; it made me a part of that fame for in leaving you I had made you ambitious again!" Showing him their child she argues that this thought gave her creative power twice over, as mother and inspiration. To that happy state they could return. (III.253).

The broader vision of woman's innate superiority over men, crucial to Barrie's view of the creative struggle, is also covered. He fills that gap in the manner of *The Professor's Love Story* by using the farcical sub-plot surrounding Mr Fairbairn. In Margaret's passive, idealistic and totally useless father, all of Barrie's reservations about his own sex are combined and written large. Fairbairn is defined by, often repeated, phrases which encapsulate his escapist passivity – "Let sleeping dogs lie. I dislike painful subjects – my sensitive nature", "I am only a thing swaddled in comfortable phrases", "Always look on the bright side" and "Not a cloud in the sky!" Opposed to him is the hard-minded, awe-inspiring Lady Janet who, in adapting her own

views after learning of her lover's fidelity proves his exact counter-
type. She is also the one who most regularly puts down other male
characters in the play as the last exchange in Act 2 nicely illustrates:

PAUL: (*very sorrowfully*) I did not know – I never thought –
LADY JANET: Men never do. (II. 247)

By adding a farcical world to the serious and melodramatic Barrie
probably did hope to universalise the idea of woman's superiority. In
the *Professor's Love Story*, the comic mode was constant, in *The
Wedding Guest* Barrie had introduced so many different moods and
modes that the stalls enjoyed Mr Fairbairn as a welcome relief but
only valued him in that way! The critics also called the draughts
match "quaint" but also wondered why it was there.

Seeing the Play

Ibsen's poetic and visual "limits on his realism" as described by
Northam offer a more promising alliance as they not only harmonise
with Barrie's artistic strengths but specifically coincide with his desire
to create by the same means a quintessentially poetic and theatrical
drama. Those aims had been formulated in the Scot's criticism before
"Ibsen's Ghost" but were given a new impetus by his early acquaintance with Ibsen's drama. Would *The Wedding Guest* successfully
mirror that debt?

    The Wedding Guest, appropriate to its place in Barrie's artistic
development, pushes a number of literary techniques to their limits.
Some of these run contrary to his natural strengths. But the most
obvious "extremes" he tests out are in an area where he has already
proved his talent. The idea that drama should tell a new story, but do
so by highlighting those visual and aural effects which are distinc-
tively theatrical may have been encouraged by Ibsen's example but
Barrie, following the "perceptive" arguments of Campbell Fraser had
accepted that critical position years before he studied the Norwegian's
art. In this area Ibsen's example had a more direct, practical influence.
Barrie's symbolic-poetic experiments did not accidentally begin with
Walker, London and continue in an unbroken line from there. It was at
that precise time, having effectively mocked Ibsen's ducks and dolls

in burlesque form, he introduced the same methods into the comic adventures of his "cuckoo" barber. *The Wedding Guest*, characteristically, combines both lines.

While Barrie shows skill in the miming sequences and the symbolic content of the play, a mere list of how many sequences and symbols are employed will explain why so many found technical virtuosity becoming its own justification and the power of symbols to suggest meaning struggling against the sheer number being introduced. Every act ends with a mime. Every act bar Act 2 ends with a mime and that is dominated by Mrs Ommaney's largely mimed madness sequence. There are as many symbols as mimes. As befits a drama concerned with natural creativity wedding dress and wedding ring as well the rice (fertility) and slippers (fairy-tale) thrown at the reception are symbolically presented. Against this, Mrs Ommaney has the baby, visually present on the stage with her. That these objects have significance is achieved in various ways. The ring, for example, is on view and a subject of discussion throughout the play but its significance within the drama changes from act to act. Given in love in Act 1, it is used as a weapon in Act 2, thrown away in Act 3 and recovered in Act 4.

The wedding dress is naturally the central visual focus of the opening wedding rehearsal. It status as another of the formal signs of Margaret's claim over Paul is achieved by keeping attention focussed on it throughout the act. When the curtain rises, Margaret is wearing it for the wedding rehearsal. After the rehearsal she takes off her train and throws it carelessly away. She then exits but the best man Armitage keeps attention on the now divided dress by folding the train away while criticising her carelessness at some length. When Margaret re-enters she is in ordinary clothing and engaged in showing off her presents to Lady Janet. Growing tired of this ("But never mind the presents, auntie") she turns and asks – "Do you like my wedding gown?" As she is gesturing to nothing, a tragic-comic effect is achieved, which leads naturally into a change of mood. In sadder, fearful spirit Margaret confides her darker thoughts about the union to her aunt by personifying it sentimentally.

MARGARET (*almost in a whisper*): Aunt Janet, last night I was so full of glee and I brought out my wedding gown and blew kisses to it, and I said, "O God make me a good (sic) wife to Paul," and suddenly, while I was so happy, a cold chill fell upon my heart. (I. 222)

After this she exits and returns triumphant in full wedding dress for the long marriage scene but not before her maid has recalled attention to its twofold form by entering in a panic, looking around for the train. In Act 2, the ceremony of the occasion and the formality of the dress meet with their mad equivalent. Mrs Ommaney, under the illusion that she is to be married to Paul, exits to find her dress. When she returns,

[She has flung a gay shawl over her shoulders and enters simpering over her appearance. She takes Paul's presence as a matter of course. JENNY stands at bedroom door.]
MRS. OMMANEY: Naughty man, where are the flowers? [Displaying herself in shawl] How do you like it? It is my wedding gown. Is the cab at the door?

In this way the difference between her status and Margaret's is visually realised.

While Margaret's marriage to Paul has been visually signed by the recovery of her entire dress and the placing of the ring on her finger, the same action has also seen Mrs Ommaney's collapse and Paul's recognition of his mistress. Barrie's skill in symbolically linking the themes of natural and artistic creativity in the opening act of this play have not been fully recognised. A closer look at the introduction of the "other woman" in the play will show how cleverly the two themes and the two women are introduced.

Mrs Ommaney's first stage entrance at once brings her face to face with her rival. It also offers the first of the good woman/bad woman dramas. Margaret's sympathy surprises Paul's mistress who had expected primness in cruelty from such a moral "child". But, strictly speaking, this is not the first time Mrs Ommaney has been seen on stage. Lady Janet has already "seen" her without knowing who she was. This revelation occurs when she also only partially recognises Paul:

LADY JANET: I seem to know your face, Mr Digby. Ever been in this part of the world before?
PAUL: Only once – before I knew Margaret – I was sketching, eighteen months ago.

And it is through his art that the identity of Mrs Ommaney first suggests itself to Margaret's aunt.

Recalling the occasion and the portrait, she also remembers something incongruent:

LADY JANET: I liked the boats, but the figure was wrong. You should have had a Boatman or a fisher-girl – instead of an elegantly dressed lady. Who was she bye the bye?
PAUL: She was – a lady who happened to be there – so I put her in. (I. 221)

Barrie's training in Campbell Fraser's classes meant that he was already sympathetic to the idea that all we have of reality is what we see or indeed record as seeing. The visual arts are Paul's forte and it is therefore appropriate that different accounts of a strange representation precede any actual evidence.

Another kind of pictorial representation strengthens the artistic side of the argument. This is the locket bearing Paul's picture which Mrs Ommaney wears as a sign of her loving sacrifice. For while she claims to have inspired Paul in his early years, a fear that she might inhibit his later work and deprive him of attaining the rank of genius led her to break up with him. In Act 2, Lady Janet opens it and learns the identity of her lover and the baby's natural father. In this way the two kinds of creativity interlink and the rules of the moral game are broken. In Act 3, Mrs Ommaney offers it empty to Margaret, encouraging her to put into it a picture of the same man whom she has just taken out of it. This apparently generous, actually vindictive, exchange relieves Barrie of the need to have her verbally challenge her rival. There is no need to have her explicitly say, "Create you own Paul and see if you can inspire him as well as I did". Another, *visual*, exchange has suggested those lines more subtly.

The fact that this is arguably Barrie's most relentlessly visual play means that, even more than usual, it has to be seen in order to be assessed. Lacking this opportunity, my own impression is that, while analysis of particular scenes may justly illustrate Barrie's developing skills in this area, other symbol-focussed exchanges do not ring true. When Margaret makes Mrs Ommaney's baby kiss her ring, the significance of the act in the female power battle may be clear but neither the psychology nor the language is convincing.

Mrs Ommaney is concealed and watching as Margaret plays with her son:

MARGARET: Are you laughing, baby? When your mother's tears fall on your face do you laugh on only? Oh, I see now why God gives the merriest babies to mothers who are the most sorrowful. It is because, when baby laughs, mother forgets to weep. (The hardness goes out of Mrs Ommaney's face – she is moved.)
MARGARET: This is my wedding ring, baby, kiss it!

(MRS. OMMANEY starts up, forming the word "No!" with her lips.)
Did you ever kiss your mother's wedding ring, baby?
(Mrs Ommaney looks bitterly at her left hand on which there is no ring.) (2.239)

The final scene also combines miming with symbolism to an extent where claims of "superabundance" seem almost an understatement. The locket as sign of artistic union and the ring as sign of natural union open the scene, secretly re-united round Margaret's neck:

PAUL: Margaret, I make no vows, but – trust me! You will wear my ring again?
(She inclines her head.) I will get it. *(Going).*
MARGARET: You will not find it there.
PAUL: She said you flung it –
MARGARET: (*in low voice*) You will not find it there.
PAUL: She said you flung it –
 MARGARET: I picked it up – when she had gone.
        (She slowly takes a thin gold chain from her neck. At the end of it is the ring which has been concealed in her bosom. She hands it to him. He takes ring off chain and puts it on her finger. Her face is averted, but she turns round and her arms go out to him.)
MARGARET: Paul!
PAUL: Margaret, what can I do to atone?
MARGARET: Help unhappy women.

One extremely unhappy woman, Mrs Ommaney, then enters. In the company of Lady Janet, she first of all refuses to wish the departing couple luck, then grudgingly throws two handfuls of a third symbol – the rice of fertility. Finally "she rest her weary head" on Janet's shoulder. With so many different symbols flying around, scant wonder that confusion rather than "questions, intelligently refined by the action" greeted the play!

To the Never Land and Beyond

This period saw Barrie experimenting at the extremes of his capacity. Only when that understanding replaces the idea of his retreating into simplicity can the progressive movement in his artistic development be understood. In a sense, it does not matter whether he succeeded in taking his audiences with him or not, he had learned how far he could go and would adapt accordingly. This is consistent with his declared intention of learning from the failure of a play whose excellence he had himself believed in. He had genuinely thought that he had met his own aims, hoped that everyone would see his skills also and conclude with Darlington, that it was, "a very important landmark in his career" (Darlington 1974: 867).

There would be other occasions on which Barrie's artistic theory would outpace his audience's ability to understand him. It was noted earlier that the fivefold allegory of *Little Mary* may have been understood by Shaw but practically everyone else was bemused by it. *The Adored One*, like *The Wedding Guest*, spoke the unspeakable in following the implications of woman's superiority in immorality. Barrie later revived it as a One Act play, a solution he also considered for *The Wedding Guest*. So how, if at all, does the play fit into his dramatic thinking at the end of the century? And how, if at all, does it look forward to the major dramatic successes which were to come?

The first answer is formal. I earlier argued that the three major dramatic successes of 1902–4 (*Quality Street*, *The Admirable Crichton* and *Peter Pan*) and the two major successes at the end of his career (*Dear Brutus* and *Mary Rose*) follow the circular structures of Shakespeare's pastoral and late romances. That is, they open in the real world, define the questions raised within it, then move into a "magic world" in which the issues are re-considered imaginatively. Finally, they return to the real world to reconsider rather than resolve. *The Wedding Guest* is the first of Barrie's dramas to follow this basic pattern since his University play *Bohemia*. The movement from the Old Keep to Mrs Ommaney's house in the Pans and back does not of course so clearly distinguish reality from fantasy and back but the circular pattern is the same and *The Wedding Guest* is planned at the same time as *Quality Street* in the Notebooks. The two worlds of Barrie's problem play are, rather, the "real" and "theatrical" worlds whose interplay would later be satirised in *Alice Sit By The Fire*.

The second answer is textual and involves thinking of the other works Barrie was planning at this time. The first result of so doing is to re-define most of the earlier evidence used to explain his "despairing" return to earlier models as intermediary links in a chain of development. The first Notebook entry for the play, "Scotch Wedding" does look back to *Auld Licht Idylls* but its re-appearance in *The Little Minister* re-contextualises it in terms of the gender battle set against a mythically focussed background. It is in that context, with the battle still biased in favour of women, that *The Wedding Guest* has its place. It too advances those new ideas which were crucial to Barrie.

The fact that the opening scene is dominated by Margaret in her wedding dress obviously looks forward to *Quality Street* and does so in the poetic-symbolic manner earlier employed for Margaret's story. In the 1902 play, the heroine is a bird (Phoebe), not a perfect pearl (Margaret). She alone flies away from the prison of the Street but in the final silent cameo she is shown, hair-down in her less successful sister's wedding dress. Susan, her hair still up in a spinster's bun, stands beside her as a reminder of how many *cannot* escape from the prison of patriarchal gentility. Barrie says he did learn lessons from the failure of *The Wedding Guest*. Toning down, without abandoning, the poetic-symbolic methods employed in it might well be one of those.

There is an early reference to the title of another play as well. When Margaret is suffering doubts about her capacity to be a good wife, Lady Janet calms her down by pointing out woman's superiority in unselfishness to man by saying "I know, my lamb, I know – *every woman knows*, and not a man among them, not a man" (I: 222). The child-mother, Jenny, also points forward, this time to Miss Thing in *A Kiss for Cinderella*:

JENNY: And if baby cries, will you call me?
MARGARET: You little mother! Jenny the best I can wish you is that when you are married you may have as many children as the old woman who lived in a shoe. (II: 236)

The presence of a Scottish butler two years before *The Admirable Crichton* might also be claimed as an anticipation of that play. Its hero, after all, had been named after a real Scottish hero. But that play was planned swiftly and had not entered the Notebooks when *The Wedding Guest* was at its planning stage. A parallel with *Peter Pan* is, however, literally enacted in the marriage rehearsal which opens the play. In "acting" a marriage they look forward to *Peter Pan* whose opening acts perform, in game fashion, the ultimate creative questions of birth, motherhood and death which are that play's central concern The Darling family act out birth in Act 1. In Act 2, the lost boys and Wendy play out copulation. Tootles' arrow pierces Wendy who falls, is placed in a womb house and later exits it from it as a mother. In Act 3 Peter melodramatically confronts a death which his weightlessness makes impossible to impress Wendy with his heroism at the end of Act 3. From *The Wedding Guest* this idea emerges.

It is not only *Peter Pan* which is echoed. More surprising is the anticipation of Barrie's last dramatic success. *Mary Rose* belongs to 1920 but material which will be revived from twenty years before and become part of her story is clearly evident in *The Wedding Guest*. In *Mary Rose* the curtain rises to reveal Mary's father, Mr Morland, and the minister, Mr Amy, childishly competing over the value of their respective art collections and their ability to detect old masters. They fall out and peace is only restored by Mrs Morland. They again open the final act – still puerile, still arguing over what is a Turner and what is not. Mrs Morland again maturely calms them down. Here, revived, is another father-minister conflict. Here again it takes a woman to demonstrate maturity when faced with male childishness. Substitute draughts for art, Mr Fairbairn and Lady Janet for Mr and Mrs Morland, Rev. Amy for Rev. Gibson and *The Wedding Guest's* comic illustration of female superiority crosses the years practically unaltered.

The question of why *Peter Pan* and *Mary Rose* are particularly anticipated in *The Wedding Guest* can be answered by looking at another part of the action. The effect of Mr Morland's optimism-in-passivity is explained as follows in the first Act:

LADY JANET: Ten. You were ten when your mother died, and your father has kept you like a stopped clock. (I. 221).

Like *Mary Rose* and *Peter Pan*, there is a sense that Margaret in this act is not only *called* a child but *is* one in the same time-defeating manner as Peter or Mary Rose. The forces which keep the others in that state are more mysterious and therefore more powerful. Margaret's fate by way of contrast is to undergo a crash course in adulthood which she passes with flying colours:

MR. FAIRBAIRN: This from my child, whom I brought up so innocently!
MARGARET: So innocently! But you don't deserve even praise for that, father. It was easier to keep me a child than make a woman of me. That is all you did. What I thought your fine philosophy, it was only an avoidance of disagreeable truths. (IV.267)

By going beyond time imaginatively, Barrie deals with the ultimate mysteries of life using an eternal boy in *Peter Pan* and a fairy girl in *Mary Rose*. The questions raised in the other mature romances before Pan are sociological or philosophical – the effects of a patriarchal society; the rival claims of hierarchy and democracy; the question of whether free will exists. The link which existed in Barrie's mind between these time-breaking plays is illustrated in the MS for *Mary Rose* where, as noted earlier, the Island is Peter's island and she crosses over to play games with him. The final stage directions describe another of the wordless scenes which characterised *The Wedding Guest*. The sounds of the sea lapping mingle with haunting, professionally composed, music as Joanna (the original name for Mary Rose) crosses beyond time: the stage darkens and only Tinker Bell's flashing light can be seen.

[Then there is a tremendous tearing sound, which is intended to make the audience scream. It represents the tearing of the veil that separates the known from the unknown, light from darkness, death from life…As the island clears we see part of the pine removed from inside so that it is like the trees of Peter Pan, which lead underground. Peter comes and sits on the trunk and plays his pipes. Joanna arrives (from a boat if this can be suggested) and the two meet. They do not kiss or shake hands – they double up with mirth at being together again…] (BVS M37/1)

As the last dramatic experiment of that period *The Wedding Guest's* allegorical range is understandable. The main problem is probably that "superabundance" noted by one critic. Barrie seems determined to impress by the range of his learning as well as the range of modes and voices he brings together in the play. He may, therefore, deserve the reaction he got. At the same time, there are signs in the same work that he is looking, perhaps over-ambitiously to his dramatic future rather than collapsing despairingly into the past.

    And there is a textual postscript to this evidence. In one sense, *The Wedding Guest* was not Barrie's last Victorian play. On 7th January 1901, a pantomime for children was put on at the Barries' house in Gloucester Road. Its title was *The Greedy Dwarf* and Barrie's aim in composing it, as he confided to Quiller Couch, was to convulse the four year olds. Sylvia Llewelyn Davies had the star role as Prince Robin, while the Barries played "The Good Girl" and "The Bad Boy". Sylvia's brother, Gerald made his first appearance in a Barrie play as Allahakbarrie. By all accounts the children were thrilled.

The pantomime idea in both its childish and adult aspects was now planted in Barrie's mind. Another set of planning ideas would soon emerge and on 27th December 1904, Gerald would first take to the boards as Hook in *Peter Pan*. Ironically, his "ashen face, those blood red lips, the long dank greasy curls, the sardonic laugh, the maniacal scream" initially had a less favourable effect on the children in the audience at the *Duke of York's* than Allahakbarrie achieved in the Barries' drawing (Du Maurier 1934: 110). After suitable accommodations had been made, however, the way forward was yet again open for Barrie. In the same way, not easily but determinedly his forward planning during his apprenticeship had brought him to that eminence and skilfulness which made *Peter Pan* possible.

Chapter Seven

To The Never Land and Beyond: A Novel Route

Hugh MacDiarmid's claim that he bring extremes together is not one which is usually extended to Barrie (MacDiarmid[1926] 1987: 87). But, especially when we reach the Tommy novels, a case can be made on his behalf. At this stage, he appears to be working some kind of literary magic for in one sense the novels seem to be the most overt confession of his sexual and artistic problems but also effective at concealing his identity. This is the point Jacqueline Rose makes when she notes "In point of fact it is too easy to give an Oedipal reading to Pan" before failing to find Barrie's identity anywhere within it (Rose 1984: 35).

The Tommy Sandys Novels

That is one extreme problem which faces the critic. Another concerns the form of the Tommy novels. While some to-day argue for structural complexity the claim that Barrie has returned to easy episodic narration was for a long time held by almost all biographers and commentators. Is a retreat from the interlinked plotting of *The Little Minister* and a return to linked short stories the whole story as Mackail argues?

Thirdly, the idea that *Tommy and Grizel* (Barrie 1900b) ends badly is still accepted by almost everyone. Whether this is fair or not depends on how you have understood what Barrie was trying to do. Those who see it as the end of a personal quest and those who attribute to it a wider metafictional and metaphysical range judge the ending from totally different perspectives. Both may of course find the demeaning farcically pathetic conclusion an unwise choice but the apposite criteria for making that judgment have to be determined first.

As my own approach seeks to test out the simpler, retrogressive account in order to discover whether it is justified or whether, as with *The Wedding Guest*, a counter case can be presented, I have headed each section with the basic assumptions made by those who see it as a despairing retreat to earlier and easier modes. My own basic premise can be explained by using Céline-Albin Faivre's account of Barrie's mimetic vision. Barrie, she observes, "wrote behind a glass, both a magnifying and frosted one" (Faivre 2010: 11). At once we see a story clearly written in capital letters but when we probe deeper it is frosted, in both mimetic *and* dehumanising terms. In those terms I shall begin with the magnifier and then probe the ways in which Barrie artfully freezes us out.

An Autobiographical Novel?

That the Tommy novels offer a general mirror of Barrie's life is obvious. That *Tommy and Grizel* shadows his sexual problems more closely than ever before is not at issue either. Similarly, the surface story does appear to revive earlier modes in a way which contradicts Barrie's own proclaimed desire to become less personal, more structured and to provide endings which his audiences would understand. But are we again in Hugh Walpole country? Are his "techniques" so subtle that "those who take him at his surface word" have been knowingly tricked by a man "who was his own murderer, murderee *and* detective in his own mystery story?" (Barrie 1938: x, vii).

First, there is every reason for Barrie wishing to work out his sexual and artistic problems at this time. Concerns regarding his status as a lover are never far from the bachelor novels. Indeed they begin to emerge under a different definition in his *Notebooks* as early as 1890. Notes for the adult period and, therefore, *Tommy and Grizel* actually precede those for *Sentimental Tommy* (Nash 1899c, Barrie 1896b; BVS A2/14–18). In the event, *Sentimental Tommy* was published first in 1896, the year which followed the tragic deaths of Jane Anne and Margaret Ogilvy. It is also the first prose-work to post-date his marriage in 1894 and was composed, therefore, at a time of crisis. More detailed accounts of his sexual problems had to wait four years for *Tommy and Grizel*. And there he presents them with astonishing directness. As Andrew Birkin observes, "it analyses the failure of the marriage even as it was failing" (Birkin 1980: 48).

Therefore, there is a sense in which these *are* personal novels. The account of their emergence on the other hand alters the way in which we have to see them. First of all the claim that they are the last novels Barrie wrote has to be reconsidered. Their planning, seen in the fuller context of the Notebooks, shows composition overlapping with the prose version of *The Little Minister* rather than neatly following it. Moreover, as a means of working out sexual and artistic problems at a time of particular stress they could claim to be ends in themselves. Once Barrie had survived this period of crisis his fictional account of it and the quest form could be abandoned.

With this material in front of him Geduld understandably finds the story line foreshadowing real people in an Oedipal context. A brief outline of the plot will make an assessment of his argument possible.[1]

Sentimental Tommy traces the early life of an imaginative Thrums boy from his earliest years in exile in London with his mother, Jean Myles. Jean has married a "magerful" husband (Tom Sandys) when her more affectionate suitor (Aaron Latta) shows cowardice. As a result she has been forced to leave Thrums. She now denies her poverty by writing letters claiming she and her son are living a life of luxury. Her husband has left her and Tommy shows himself to be just as imaginative in manipulating others in games and writing as his mother. After Jean's death, Aaron takes Tommy and his younger sister, Elizabeth back to Thrums. There he meets Grizel, the daughter of the disreputable "Painted Lady". A rivalry between this strong but vulnerable girl and Tommy the role-playing egoist emerges. Tommy meanwhile forces his less spirited friends to play the parts he assigns them in games based on Walter Scott's Jacobite novels. He also goes to the Hanky School run by Miss Ailie, the survivor of two spinster sisters. He begins to show signs of literary genius but fails to win a bursary to University because his essay stops short while he tries in vain to find the perfect word to convey his meaning.

The autobiographical line continues in *Tommy and Grizel*.

Taking up the story of Tommy when he is sixteen, Barrie's narrator returns his "hero" to London, where he finally gains a reputation as a writer. He returns to Thrums, full of his triumph. Soon he is engaged in the domestic lives of Elspeth and Corp while his love for Grizel also begins to develop. Eventually, although still in a spirit of doubt, he marries Grizel and takes her on honeymoon to Switzerland where he meets by Lady Pippinworth. Later Grizel, having undertaken a courageous journey to re-assure herself about Tommy's health stumbles on her husband being seduced by her rival. She become ill and for the first and only time Tommy unselfishly serves her. This kind of love, Tommy's employer, O.P. Pym had prophesied, he would never know and so would never write a work of genius. He does write another book at this time, inspired by Grizel, only to fall back into his old ways, once more he seeks out Lady Pippinworth who confesses she has burned the manuscript of an earlier work which Tommy believes is the only one of his prose pieces to proves his genius. Despite this he chases after his destroyer, tries to climb a wall but skewers his coat on a fence in

---

[1] For Geduld's own account see Geduld 1971: 45–51.

the process and dies. His failed life as man and writer is then contemplated in mark-edly different ways by Grizel, by his friends and family, by critics and biographers.

The major autobiographical elements in this story are easy to detect. One need only note that both Tommy and Barrie have a "Scotch wedding" in his home and then take their brides to Switzerland to see the situational parallels. That he could also impose a highborn female seducer on the honeymooners and then ask illustrators to base Grizel's face on Sylvia Llewelyn Davies's demonstrates either his naivety or cruelty in sexual matters.

Tommy's sexual immaturity is, indeed, a major leitmotiv of the novel. Both action and commentary confirm that "eternal boyhood" is, at the very least, a strong element in his character. The narrator, for example, is ever ready to explain his nature in this way: "He [Tommy] would have done it [made love] if he could. If we could love by trying no one would ever have been more loved than Grizel" (*TG*: 168). Like the literary "Superfluous Man" he is too busy analysing himself to act instinctively: "and having started he came back to kiss her again; he never forgot to have an impulse to do that" (414). Knowledgeable outsiders join the chorus of commentators. Pym for example wonders whether he has any sexual impulses at all (21). Tommy, as self-concerned sentimentalist also analyses his character in these terms: "Grizel, I seem to be different from all other men; there seems to be a curse upon me. I want to love you, dear one, you are the only woman I ever wanted to love, but apparently I can't" (179). And when he is silent, Grizel is ready to forge a link between his childish streak and his failure as an adult lover:

He did not love her. "Not as I love him," she said to herself. "Not as married people ought to love, but in another way he loves me dearly." By the other way she meant that he loved her as he loved Elspeth, and loved them both just as he had loved them when all three played in the den. He was a boy who could not grow up. (396)

And sometimes Grizel's:

"The most exquisite thing in human life is to be married to one who loves you as you do him." There could be no doubt about that. But she saw also that the next best thing was the kind of love this boy gave to her and she would always be grateful for the second best. (397)

For those who might miss the point, the narrator is again on hand to guide and interpret. This he does on both sides of the question, sometimes refining Tommy's thoughts:

Poor Tommy! He was still a boy, he was ever a boy, trying sometimes, as now, to be a man, and always when he looked round, he ran back to his boyhood as if he saw it holding out its arms to him and inviting him to come back and play. (117)

And sometimes Grizel's:

Poor Tommy! He was still a boy, he was ever a boy, trying sometimes, as now, to be a man, and always when he looked round, he ran back to his boyhood as if he saw it holding out its arms to him and inviting him to come back and play. (117).

Yet when Geduld tries to move on from that base in an attempt to match Barrie's family and friends with specific fictional characters in the story, he clearly struggles. Who, except a critic whose major goal is the discovery of Oedipal links would connect old Dr. McQueen dying in Grizel's arms with the death of young David Barrie in a lake or see the Elspeth-Gemmell romance as an "obvious" mirror of Margaret Barrie's marriage? The identification of Mary Ansell with Lady Pippinworth as "seductress" figure is at once anachronistic and unconvincing. Geduld has no doubt, "There is specific evidence pointing to an identification of the wife-seductress with Mary Ansell" (Geduld 1971: 50). But at this time Mary Ansell is a victim rather than a seducer. She has sacrificed her independence and her art to be part of an unsatisfactory manipulative alliance with an impotent, often cruel, celebrity. If Barrie is confessing through Tommy it is *this* bitter tale against himself he is foreshadowing. Geduld, does not in fact offer the promised evidence. Instead he repeats the central tenet of his faith – this is the story which has been "imposed upon the prototypic situation".

Other "certain" equations are also less than convincing. Is Elspeth really the young Margaret Ogilvy? Are McQueen and Gemmell really "projections" and replacements of "the two clergymen in Margaret Barrie's life?" Is Gemmell's marriage to Elspeth, the fictional "correspondence" to the union of James Winter and Elspeth. When dealing with Tommy's accidental death, an even more inventive case is argued. The coat which catches on the fence and contributes to his destruction once belonged to Dr. McQueen. In order to link it to

David and the trauma which explains all, that coat becomes a symbol "of the usurpation of his rival's identity" and then, by imaginative transfer, "recalls the child of the prototypic story dressing up as his dead brother" (51).

If this is the magnified Oedipal version of the plot, the first layer of artifice is already evident and its presence invites the question most often asked about these novels. If we are so clearly tempted to suggest "real" equivalents then why do the imagined characters and action fail to correspond easily with individuals in the author's life?

A return to *Margaret Ogilvy* will introduce the more complex situation with which we are concerned. That memoir was originally intended to be the preface to *Sentimental Tommy* and, as was argued earlier, it could be read in two ways. The first was Oedipal – as an account of repressed incestuous impulses. The second placed that line within a wider topical context. It proposed a rivalry between mother and son as two histrionic egoists, anxious to keep themselves at the centre of attention and using their powers of imagination and language to do so. As *The Wedding Guest* illustrated, this was a period when Barrie favoured hybrid forms and inclusive arguments. And it is with this view of Tommy as actor and power-seeker that his story opens.

He is first of all depicted as a young, vulnerable exile in London, boasting in highly imaginative terms, of the greatness of his home village to another boy. Next, he uses his story-telling abilities to gain power over a young girl. The narrator comments on the mixture of contempt and delight he feels at so easy a victory: "The ninny of a girl was completely hoodwinked; and see, there they go, each with a hand in the muff, the one leering, oh so triumphantly; the other trusting and gleeful" (*ST*: 9). His capacity for living in a fantasy land where acted parts become "real" is also exemplified in the Reddy incident, where he accepts the role of rescuer he doesn't deserve, then invents a story about two toffs to account for having the money to buy her a "guilty" present.

When we are introduced to his mother she is engaged in exactly the same kind of imaginative power-play. In the letters she sends home she recreates their miserable lot in London in fancifully positive terms. In that fantasy world she exchanges poverty for riches and turns her cruel, absent husband into a benevolent present one. She pretends, for example, to have bought a second black silk dress although the first one is "no none tashed yet [because] her gudeman fair insisted on buying a new one," saying "Rich folk like us can afford to be mislaid. And nothing's ower braw for my bonny Jean" (35).

Both Tommy and his mother play out these fantasies in order to survive. The part played by language in their power strategies is also emphasised from the start. Following the example of Babbie in *The Little Minister*, Tommy and his mother change from Scots to English as seems advantageous. Indeed, as the narrator informs us, "In the great world without" Jean "used few Thrums words; you would have known she was Scotch by her accent only" (*ST*: 17). This interest in the medium as well as the message will prove to be one of the ideas Barrie pursues more thoroughly than before in the Tommy novels. Even at narrative level therefore, characters and plot offer too complex a pattern to be fitted neatly into Geduld's prototype. Indeed he seems to become aware of this finally when he equates Tommy's sentimentality with "the masks he creates at the expense of his own character" (Geduld 1972: 51).

Any discussion of the Tommy novels even one which confines itself to the obvious story line has to face the balance between real and ideal which was central to Masson's literary theory. This is because fully developed, psychologically unconvincing passages mingle ostentatiously with character types and comic humours. Those who seek to justify this method usually return to Dickens as Barrie's model. Sir George Douglas is one who makes that claim, emphasising the highly imaginative and poetic nature of Barrie's work. He is even prepared to give Barrie credit for surpassing the "great man" in some ways:

It will perhaps be conceded that since Dickens, no kindlier humourist than Barrie has appeared. But after reading *Sentimental Tommy* one is prepared to maintain that the advantage in some of the highest points lies by no means with Dickens. (*Good Words* 1889: 200–3)

For J.B. Priestley it was a book which dealt primarily with "kinds" of people rather than individuals. At the centre stood Tommy as type, a "study of the sentimentalist being not unconscious of his own tendencies and not beneath doing penance in his art" (*London Mercury* 1924: 10: 627–28).

This does not mean that the Tommy novels forsook realism. Like Dickens, Barrie portrays realistically the sufferings of the Industrial Revolution as experienced by those who had been forced out of villages and hamlets. And notably, even in the midst of her rich fantasies, Jean Sandys does points out that the fate of other Thrums survivors in London was very different, "I have seen no Thrums faces here, the low part where they bide not being for the like of me to file my feet in" (*TS*: 73).

And when one asks what this outside world "really" is, the narrator confuses matters further. As a chapter heading illustrates, he himself prefers to distance the misery in literary terms as the "The End of an Idyll". He then tells us that he is not, anyway, trying to record accurate images of the real Thrums – "Ask not a dull historian, nor even go to Thrums" he advises "but to those rather who have been boy and girls there and now are exiles" (10). It is, in fact, as many non-historical visions as there are individuals. Alternatively, as Tommy himself sees it, Thrums is an imagined ideal – "I tell yer, everybody dreams of it, though not all call it Thrums" (26). We are even shown how Tommy's mind progresses from describing "the street exactly as he saw it" via associations with "the palace of Aladdin" to pure fancy when he imports "a square, a town-house, some outside stairs and an auld licht kirk" into it despite his mother's authoritative objection that the street in which he has set them doesn't exist (47). Then, having come to believe his own dreams the actual Thrums proves a huge disappointment – "Oh, Elspeth, it's – it's not the same what I thought it would be!" (147).

In personality terms, therefore, the confessions of Tommy as individual are concealed by Barrie's most thorough and sustained account to date of the histrionic sentimentalist. There are many references to that type in the novels, a number of them conveyed in long passages which explain the type explicitly. Here, for example is Mr. Mclean on the subject:

He is constantly playing some new part – playing is hardly the word though, for into each part he puts an earnestness that cheats even himself until he takes to another. I suppose you want me to give you some idea of his character, and I could tell you what it is at any particular moment; but it changes, sir, I do assure you, almost as quickly as the circus rider flings off his layers of waistcoats. A single puff of wind blows him from one character to another, and he may be noble and vicious and a tyrant and a slave, and as hard as granite and melting as butter in the sun, all in one forenoon, All you can be sure of is that whatever he is he will be in excess. (332)

Tommy himself is just as explicit: "'It's easy to you that has just one mind,' he retorted with spirit, 'but if you had as many minds as I have'" (380). In *Tommy and Grizel*, further confirmation is given.

Prior to rescuing a drowning boy, Tommy has turned into three differ-ent people and will add another when his "heroism" is complete:

> There were now no fewer than three men engaged, each in his own way, in the siege of Grizel nothing in common between them except insulted vanity. One was a broken man who took for granted that she had preferred to pass him by [...] number two [...] was a good-natured cynic [...] the third [...] was a haughty boy. (*TG*: 106)

Or again – "Tommy's new character was that of a monster. He always liked the big parts" (*TG*: 182). In this way, both the imagined and the ideal darken the reader's vision of the real.

Tommy's particular, sentimental "type" increases these difficul-ties. There are few more ambivalent guides than one who contains multitudes of personalities and assumes others. As a result, in Ormond's words, "The reader [...] is never very clear about the nature of the "real" Tommy. With no sense of a norm from which the fantasist, Tommy is deviating each of his roles is as valid for us as the others" (Ormond 1987: 79).

So far the discussion has focussed on the story line alone. To discover whether the narrative also has an exemplary function involves a different procedure as Barthes explains in his discussion of mythic narrative:

> To understand a narrative is not merely to follow the unfolding of the story, it is also recognise its construction in "stories", to project the horizontal concatenation of the narrative thread on to an implicitly vertical axis. (Barthes 1993: 259)

The presentation of Jean Sandys provides a good example of how this signing works. As maternal equivalent in the fiction to Margaret Barrie she has obviously some features in common with Barrie's mother. To discover if she also has an exemplary role to play involves asking not how far does she accurately mirror her supposed model but how far, if at all, does the fictional character *differ* from her supposed original?

The differences prove to be many and extreme. As argued earlier, Mrs Barrie never succumbed to a "magerful" man, never rejected a cowardly suitor. She was not hounded out of Thrums married to a man she hates. She never endured physical abuse nor gloried at her hus-band's death. She was never faced with the choice between gentle and "magerful" suitors.

Why is her part described in this way? To make her a perfect example of the power of natural selection. Once more we are reminded that we cannot naively treat all references to mothers *and* motherhood as a sign of authorial trauma. Had imitating a mother complex been Barrie's major aim, he would at story level have shown Tommy unnaturally continuing to think of his mother, after her death. Instead he soon enters into an adult relationship with Grizel and, as Hammerton comments leaves "the scenes of his mother's youth" behind him. (Hammerton 1929: 225). Had she not been meant to exemplify other ideas he need not have made her so obviously different as a sign that another logic was now in operation.

Leonee Ormond will make even more ambitious claims for the Tommy novels. But she begins by confirming the extremely clear Darwinian focus in both volumes. That begins at personal level with Barrie intending us to see Tommy and Grizel as both potentially dominant and locked in a battle for power (Ormond 1987: 78). She then goes on to explain how that romance is configured in such a way as to highlight the battle of the species. This we have seen in the presentation of Jean Sandys. It is repeated in the "history" of Miss Ailie in the Hanky School. A predecessor of Phoebe Throssel's spinster sister in *Quality Street*, she has lived a more adventurous life than Miss Susan in the play. Her role in the battle of the species occurred in her early years. We are introduced to her in middle age. When she remembers her "relationship to the magerful man [...] she shuddered to think of it herself for in middle age she retained the mind of a young girl" (*ST*: 153). Yet another Darwinian/childish example is introduced in the novel. In the play, which is also concerned with the battle of the species, her sister will live and be the heroine while Susan's one passionate encounter will be much less adventurous.

Ormond goes on from this scientific-philosophic base to prove that the overarching metaphysical questions behind the novels' central theme of origins and creativity are often addressed by the characters – "Time and the attempt to get outside it dominate the thoughts of the characters" (76). Even metafictional concerns, she suggests, are highlighted in novels which contain "an implicit commentary on the purposes and functions of fiction itself" (75). A case could be made for the relationship between Tommy and his mother anticipating these advances. While Tam is the source of the "magerful" element in Tommy, so Jean "creates" his imagination and verbal powers. But

Tommy is also brought face to face with the ultimate questions of life at a very early age. Reddy's death and Shovel's early schooling of the naïve Tommy at once bring birth and death together but leave him to make up his own conclusions – "'It's a kid or a coffin,' he said sharply, knowing that only birth or death brought a doctor here" (*TS*: 4). And throughout the opening chapters Tommy puzzles over birth as in the strange "case" of Elizabeth's annoying and inexplicable arrival in his home while death and desertion stalk the streets for all in London's slums.

That he gets completely out of his depth over the mystery of motherhood is, however, directly due to a much more serious fantasy imposed on him by his mother. Not only does Jean tell her children nothing about birth and death so that Tommy assumes the first baby he sees must be hers. She has largely replaced the truth about her own "origins" with lies. That she has split herself into Jean Sandys and Jean Myles, each with a son called Tommy he trustfully accepts as truth:

Unsuspicious Tommy soon had news of another letter from Jean Myles, which had sent Esther Auld to bed again. "Instead of being brought low," he answered, "Jean Myles is grander than ever. Her Tommy has a governess." "That would be a doush of water in Esther's face?" his mother said smiling. (72)

Characteristically, she only confesses the truth about her children's family origins when she herself is dying. Then she writes her first truthful letter to Thrums, asking Aaron to look after them: "There and then in the gaps when her pen falls from her hands, she at last told them that she was Jean Myles" (103).

A final example will demonstrate how subtly Barrie can suggest Oedipal links only to conceal them so deeply within his fiction that even the most determined prototypical scholar sees the insecurity of calling attention to them. The drowning boy incident in Chapter 9 of *Tommy and Grizel* is one such. Tommy and Corps see a boy drowning in the perilous waters of the Slugs of Kenny. Heroically, Tommy dives in and drags him to the side. He asks Corps to keep his heroism secret but the facts are later revealed by the boy's grandmother. Before the rescue, Tommy had been thinking of his youth and "seen his mother looking young again" (111). After it, the narrator comments, "He was still a boy, he was ever a boy" (117). There is more than enough here, surely, to revive and strengthen the idea that the David trauma was a major source of Barrie's problems.

How does the episode open, however? By subverting the idea that any single aspect of Tommy's character can define him. Before he sets out for the Slugs, he is already the three men in one referred to in the earlier discussion on his divided personality. By the time he joins Corps people may see two men advancing on the ravine, but four are actually present. The broken man, the good-natured cynic and the haughty boy all accompany Tommy's old friend to that "wild crevice through which the Drumly cuts its way" (*TG*: 111).

His histrionic nature having been established but still before his act of heroism Tommy creates a sentimental tale about the death of a lark which anticipates the bird myths of *The Little White Bird*. At this point the Narrator offers an intellectual reason for these fantasies – "Death was still his subject" (*TG*: 113).

And when Tommy looks into the pool it is not his brother but an unknown rejected lover he sees lying at its foot. This more obviously reflects the sexual problems he is currently facing as an adult with Grizel than any retained traumas from the past. And how does the episode close? First the narrator offers a thematic connection. Then Tommy decides to add "The modest hero" to his other three roles. He therefore asks Corps to keep quiet about the event. And when he is finally identified, Grizel refuses to accept even his actual heroism at face value. She develops her doubts philosophically in terms which would have pleased Berkeley and does so in the questioning manner favoured by his disciple Campbell Fraser. "Do we know the truth now?" she asks when all we have of it is our thoughts about it. She goes on to offer her version of Berkeley's central premise. If all we can claim to "know" is what we perceive in the present moment then our sense of things can offer very little "real" security indeed. Geduld, possibly because he sees the complicated context within which these echoes of the past are presented does not include this episode in his account of the book at all.

Of course, this increases the problems faced by those who emphasise only realism and the shadowing in art of real identities. That bias may, in part, have been caused by the power of the story line. Certainly, those critics who applaud the narrative pay little or no attention to the commentaries which frame *Sentimental Tommy* and overtly link the beginning of *Tommy and Grizel* with its predecessor.

Instead they assume that the organisation of the work is irrelevant and can be altered with impunity to favour their own prototypes. Thus Geduld, when he opens his account of the story, feels free to "start with the story of the hero's mother". That way, he explains, "the action begins in Thrums and moves to London" (Geduld 1971: 46). Even in naturalistic novels, this change of organisation would be a questionable tactic. When the text in question has opened with the narrator emphasising the importance of following *his* ordering it becomes untenable.

A Simple Form?

1. Form and *The Little Minister*

To explore the formal question further involves looking not only at the narrative voice but the dramatic and poetic as well. At this late stage in his apprenticeship, Barrie is seeking ways of controlling his loose narrative focus and so has turned to the tighter modes of the theatre. Are these techniques employed for Tommy's tale? Equally, do the poetic leitmotivs in the Tommy novels sign yet another new approach to the theme of creativity? And finally, does the promised biography of Tommy's artistic career mirror Barrie's own?

To address these questions, I shall begin with the expectations raised by the study of Barrie's apprenticeship so far. The closest parallel in time and range to the Tommy novels is *The Little Minister*. Here too an imaginative mythic approach had centred on the battle between the sexes but taken them mysteriously beyond time. In that instance Barrie used a number of interlinked plots, controlled by his narrator and the Thrums chorus to guide his readers in their understanding of the ideas he was presenting. He also employed a circular form to convey the ultimate questions his characters were addressing.

With the Tommy novels, critical reaction highlights a return to episodic construction but the analysis so far has suggested that, in fact, Barrie has used all the techniques of *The Little Minister* in them as well. Geographically the story of both books move in circular fashion from London to Thrums and back to London. This structuring mirrors, to darker ends, the central rustic moment in Shakespearean romance.

That form, which Barrie would later adopt in the *The Wedding Guest* and *Quality Street*, is here used to deny rather than promote the idyllic qualities of the simpler life. As the title to Chapter IV of *Sentimental Tommy* highlights, it is the *end* of the rural idyll, now destroyed by the industrial revolution, that the circular structure mirrors. Once more we are concerned with appropriate form originally re-translated.

The roles of the respective narrators are also similar. Like his predecessor, a learned man the Tommy narrator explains the organisation of his material from the outset. *Sentimental Tommy* will deal with the "hero's" youth from the age of five to sixteen. After picking up the major lines of argument at the start of *Tommy and Grizel*, the story will continue until his early death. As in *The Little Minister*, the end is implicit in the beginning.

Therefore, while the episodic line is strong we do have another hybrid form. Grafted on to the adventures of Tommy is almost exactly the same pattern as that discovered in *The Little Minister*. Here again is the biased narrator-commentator (see for example *ST*: 87; *TG*: 41, 413). Here again is the Thrums chorus of wise men, ever ready to give their critical assessment of Tommy's life and work (see *ST*: chapter 36). What is new but fitting for a novel concerned with the powers of language and literature, is the introduction, in *Tommy and Grizel* of an additional literary "master", who is ever ready to discuss a wide range of literary issues with his apprentice (see *TG*: 16–20). These conversations also offer a psychologically satisfying reason for detailed discussion of the two areas of creativity, natural and artistic, around which Tommy's quest will be centred. As both are writers themselves, they can conduct a virtual seminar on the kinds of art which are possible. These offer the reader clear parameters within which to assess not only Tommy's writings but the book in which he appears.

Tommy and Grizel opens with the narrator displaying his power – "Shall we begin with him [Pym] or with Tommy?" (1). This has the effect of making the reader an accomplice within what is self-evidently a fiction. The same power to organise is underlined by the next choice considered. He could follow the natural order and focus on either character. Instead, he decides to rush ahead, "hasten into Marlyebone before little Tommy arrives" and wait for them to be together. Another artificial arrangement of events soon follows. Tommy being the only focus of attention the narrator might simply show him as he is now. Instead, for the benefit of the reader, he will again defeat time, this time by going forward then backwards in epic manner. Chapter Two opens with yet another warning that we are under his power. "Six years afterwards Tommy was a famous man, as I hope you do not need to be told" (12). This time the fiction that he is recording actual events is used to bind reader and narrator more closely together. He will not need to play God with his material too often as his readers already know most of Tommy's tale already.

By introducing Tommy's new employer O.P. Pym as a fellow writer Barrie makes the lengthy discussions on literature which follow seem natural. And among those discussions the old clash between realism and idealism inevitably figures. Tommy, having admitted changing his employer's work, voices the realist case

"You re-wrote it!" roared Pym, "you dared to meddle with – " He was speechless with fury.
"I tried to keep my hand off," Tommy said, with dignity "but the thing had to be done and they are human now". (*TG*: 18)

It is, therefore, quite possible to argue that these novels, on their own evidence, are "in a subtle way [Tommy's] biography" (*TG*: 400) in art as well as life and, for that reason, that they confront their readers with an even more obvious account of the work's artifice than does *The Little Minister*. Barrie's openings as well as his conclusions are consistent with his modernist sympathies. *Tommy and Grizel* in particular opens in a way which Graham Greene will later neatly describe in *The End of the Affair* (1951) – "A story has no beginning and arbitrarily one chooses that moment of experience from which to look back or from which to look ahead" (7).

There is no doubt that the ideas of the Tommy novels are conveyed in this manner. It follows, however, that a failure to recognise that the framework of the story is the place where guidance is offered for the books' Darwinian, metaphysical and metafictional strands of thought is a major drawback. Yet, as we have seen, those critics who found only a simple structure and authorial desperation did concentrate on the action alone. Ormond adds a further crucial point which extends the distance between the two schools farther. The certainty of these critics implies not only silence on the frame evidence but also involves insensitivity to the syntax of the novels as a whole. Geduld may claim that characters "are" or "represent" their chosen models but Barrie consistently uses indefinite terms, appropriate to the profound, sometimes mysterious topics he is addressing. As Ormond points out "'Appear', 'might', 'set out to do', 'seemed', 'might do', 'was to' are all indications of a state of doubt or uncertainty" (Ormond 1987: 75).

Nor, it should be added, is this claim to metafiction at odds with the obvious realistic elements in the novel. Usually the two harmonise. As Patricia Waugh points out, "Very often realistic conventions supply the 'control' in metafictional texts as the norm or background against which the experimental strategies can foreground themselves" (Waugh 1984: 15, 18). The formal existence of the text indeed *must* be foregrounded in order that the fictional context of the story may be continually reflected against it. This is precisely what Barrie does.

2. Form and the Games of Life

Another controlling feature guides the reader through the complexities of *Tommy and Grizel*. Tommy from his earliest days has had great difficulty distinguishing between the real and the fanciful. While that theme is later extended into philosophical country in the discussions on "truth" he holds with Grizel, it begins realistically enough. His fantasising mother and his need to create a defensively triumphant vision of his home village while in the foreign slums of London combine to explain the situation. As the story line has also to convey *both* of these worlds merging into one another some controlling mechanisms are needed here too.

As noted in the study of *Sentimental Tommy* highlighting the Darwinian drama around the key word "magerful" was one of these tactics. In particular it helped to explain the rivalry-in-understanding of hero and heroine. But the broader power battles fought by them and their friends and companions are economically focussed in another manner. The interactive roles played in the Jacobite games of *Sentimental Tommy* are shown to change as the game of life replaces them in *Tommy and Grizel*. By allowing the characters to remember the first kind of power-play and using it as a continuing measure of their adult position, Barrie keeps this comparison alive in *Tommy and Grizel* as well.

This interrelationship between childhood games and the real business of life broadens the scope of the battle for power. Corp and Gavinia, David Gemmell and Elspeth begin as playthings of Tommy.

Corp's particularly confused passivity makes him Tommy's favourite actor precisely because he is so amenable: "Tommy took delight in his society, though he never treated him as an equal; Corp did not expect that, and was humbly grateful for what he got" (213). (*Littell's Living Age* 15 December 1900: 699). Grizel by way of contrast exerts her own will, from the days of childish play on. When Tommy, as Captain Stroke cum writer-director, orders her to play out the role he has assigned to her, she refuses:

"Now, then, Grizel, you kiss my hand."
"I tell you, I won't."
"Well, then, go on your knees to me."
"You needn't think it."
"Dagon you! Then ca' away standing." (258)

This reaction in part stems from her family inheritance as daughter of the Painted Lady – "If I had a whip like the one the slave-driver has, shouldn't I lash the boys who hoot my mamma!" (202). Recognition that hero and heroine share many characteristics, including retained childhood, continues in *Tommy and Grizel*.

"You child," said Tommy.
"Do you think me a child because I blow kisses to her?"
"Do you like me to think you one?" he replied.
"I like you to call me child," she said, "but not to think me one." (162; see also 207, 284).

And if at times each wants to be master, at others they are glad to submit:

Her gaiety! Her masterful airs when he wanted something that that was not good for him! The artfulness with which she sought to help him in various matters without his knowing; her satisfaction when he caught her as clever Tommy was constantly doing. (398)

As the balance of adult power swings away from those who were at the centre of the Jacobite games so they move to the sidelines in the games of life. The opposite process is also evident. The adult Corp who accompanies Tommy to the Slugs is no longer as dependent on Tommy as his name implies. In those days he *had* been the body and Tommy the brain. Now he is a father and so has become a bit of a creator himself. He may, in obedience to Tommy, deny his friend's role as hero but in explaining that fiction and creating his own substitute hero for Tommy "Captain Ure", he begins to embroider the script in his own right. As Tommy admits to Grizel when the truth has become known, "As for the name, Captain Ure, it was an invention of that humorous dog, Corp" (*TG*: 133).

The erstwhile "body" of the Jacobite games has developed a mind and now uses Tommy's skills. To make matters worse the "absent hero" he has created for the tea-party they now attend displaces that event's hero – Mr Tommy Sandys – from his intended position as guest of honour. Instead, all the conversation foreseeably centres on the Romantic absentee, Captain Ure. When the truth is known, the narrator makes Tommy's fury clear – "He was the guest of the evening, but they were talking admiringly of another man, and so he sulked" (124). On childish criteria, Tommy has sunk to a minor figure in Corp's play. On adult criteria, Corp is already on his way to leading a more fulfilling life than his erstwhile stage director.

The major reason for this revolution is enacted in the next chapter. Corp is not only freeing himself from dependency in the secondary creative world of games and the imagination, he and Gavinia have already won the primary battle of parenthood. "When Grizel opened the door of Corps's house she found husband and wife at home, the baby in his mother's arms" (141). The way in which the natural reversal of power is immediately succeeded by the game-playing triumph confirms that Barrie is using that motif as a continued focus for character comparison in the adult world. In *Tommy and Grizel* it will continue to guide.

The metafictional strand of the novel was highlighted in the early games motif as well. Naming, as a means of controlling or destroying the identity of others plays a part in *Sentimental Tommy*. The idea that one can posses the personality of another by naming him follows Sir James Frazer's study of primitive beliefs in *The Golden Bough* (Frazer 1900: 1: 403). A good example of the process is provided by Corp during the Jacobite games. Already defined as a non-intellectual via his own name (body) he receives so many fictional names and parts from Tommy that he loses all sense of identity:

For this voluntary service, Stroke clapped Corp of Corp on the shoulder with a naked sword and said, "Rise Sir Joseph!" which made Corps more confused than ever, for he was Corp of Corp, Him of Muckle Kenny, Red McNeil, Andrew Ferrara, and the Master of Inverquharity (Stroke's names), as well as Stab-in-the Dark Grind-them-to-Mullins and Warty Joe (his own), and which he was at any particular moment he never knew till Stroke told him, and even then he forgot and had to be put in irons. (*ST*: 251)

3. Form and Books

The strategic advantages of leaving the Pym-Tommy discussions on life and literature open in *Tommy and Grizel* has been noted in the two earlier discussions on form. When it comes to the third area of enquiry a different claim can be made for its importance. Apprentice and master carry their arguments on literary topics well beyond the realism-idealism debate to include other literary questions which concerned Barrie at this time. These included the author's need to conceal his personality, the nature of sentimental writing and the qualities of genius. That there is an intended relationship between Tommy's current position as a writer and Barrie's is therefore established at once.

But the Pym discussions do not suggest *parallel* quests. These are books in which the book-baby metaphor poetically proclaims interdependence as the new approach to creativity. In Tommy's case his status as lover and as literary genius have been viewed as interdependent from the outset. The psychological justification here is Pym's opinion that Tommy will never experience the higher forms of love and consequently will not prove himself a genius. Using the word sentiment in its higher, noble connotation he explains his position – "At your age the blood would have been coursing through my veins. Love! You are incapable of it...An artist without sentiment is a painter without colours. Young man I fear you are doomed" (21).

Only the narrator's artificial re-organisation of time gives the Pym discussions a place in the introductory chapters of the novel and anticipates the novel's metaphysical range "beyond time" as well. He has leaped six years to present these seminars and give the readers analysis before enactment. The same artificial ordering permits Tommy's first publication to be considered in Chapter II. Here the link with Barrie's own writing career is easy to detect. In *The Greenwood Hat*, the young Anon had found most satisfaction in writing imagined stories about what he knew least. *Letters to a Young Man about to be Married*, later known as "*Sandys on Women*" shows Tommy, the unloving, following suit by making a popular success out

of a book offering guidance on a passion of which he has no experience at all (28–30).

In this way, Barrie prepares his readers for a more wide-ranging
and interconnected study of the two kinds of creativity which have for
so long intrigued him. Defined questions have even been posed by
Pym on the reader's behalf. "Will Tommy find real love, defy Pym's
belief and fulfil his genius?" or "Will he become a genius anyway and
disprove the older man's opinion?" His situation at this stage has also
been analysed in those sentimental terms which define his character.
That quality's self-indulgent element he possesses in excess. Its nobler
qualities he lacks entirely.

A description of his next book follows and again the relationship
with Anon's early efforts is obvious. This volume is nothing but a
series of essays, which nonetheless attract the popular reading public
because they believe that in its pages "a human heart was laid bare"
(303). As this involves short stories posing as novels while adding the
pretence of noble ideas to that of the perfect lover, the autobiographical link with Barrie's practice is reinforced. There are also variations
on this old theme. Grizel's possible influence on Tommy's work is
suggested, when Tommy asks her to kiss the manuscript of the book
before sending it off. She concedes reluctantly:

But she kissed the manuscript. "Wish it luck," he had begged of her; "you were
always so fond of babies, and this is my baby." So Grizel kissed Tommy's baby, and
then she turned away her face. (295)

Whether so intended or not Tommy's request gives Grizel grounds for
believing that she had in part inspired the volume. When she later
reads it, she is horrified by its lies and pretensions and in writing a
furious letter to that effect opens up a theme which will return to the
centre of attention at the conclusion of the novel. Who, if anyone,
influences Tommy's work? It is a good thing that the premises of this
discussion are clearly established first, as that question will return in
much more difficult guise in Chapters XXXIII and XXXIV of the
novels' notorious ending. And just as the influence of *The Little
Minister* and the use of the games theme lacked "final" resolution so
the relationship between Barrie's books and Tommy's was unfinished.
It is therefore that supposedly "awful" conclusion which now warrants
attention.

Confusions and Conclusions?

1. Awaiting an Ending

The ending to *Tommy and Grizel* had been much awaited as a test of Barrie's ability to end his novels artistically. When it did appear many held it to be a complete failure made more disappointing by their having to wait for it so long. *Blackwood*'s review opens with that disappointment and judgement – "Barrie has been studiously conscientious [...] he has bided his time [...] And the result – the appalling, the damning result – is *Tommy and Grizel*" (*Blackwood's* 1900: 168: 738). Their correspondent's goes on to reveal his realistic credentials by condemning the presence within it of comic types. The potential of these types as used by Molière and Dickens he accepts in theory only. In Barrie's practice the habit only annoys him – "If we are told once that Grizel had a 'crooked smile' we are told a dozen times" (739). Ironically in the same year Bergson's explanation of the comic principle of "du mécanique plaqué sur du vivant" was being published in la Révue de Paris. There, he upheld the case that "humours" (and therefore classical comedy) were better adapted to thoughtful art than the passions of tragedy. The *Blackwood's* reviewer, unaware of this and probably unsympathetic to the thesis anyway, only forgives Barrie for the practice to demonstrate how far he is stretching his sympathies. That appeal to generosity (in what is actually a very damning review) is only assumed in order to prove that there *are* places which are beyond even this critical "mercy". Supreme among them is the book's awful ending:

But what we cannot forgive is his hero's intrigue with Lady Pippinworth. No more preposterous episode was ever fabricated by a writer of genius. (254)

Even those who regarded the novel as, overall, a sound work made an exception for the conclusion. Winfield Woolf begins by explaining the unusually intense interest directed at it. "No book in recent years has been awaited with such great expectation as Barrie's sequel to *Sentimental Tommy*" (*Sewanee Review* 1901: 9: 73). It is, for him, at once a new and profound study of a recognisable type and an artistic failure because Barrie fails to resolve the tension between the naturalistic and the artificial within it. This flaw, which has been detected over and over again in the criticism of these books, this time has a character focus. For Woolf, Grizel is more naturalistically presented and so we love her. Tommy is ambivalently described, making it "the great question of the book whether [he] is a consistent character or not" (76). Interestingly, he then decides that this weakness is a condition of the book's strengths, a reaction which is sympathetic to Barrie's new emphasis on the interrelationships between artistic and natural creation. The trouble in terms of characterisation he traces back to the original type being examined. Barrie's self-imposed task was to depict "the artistic nature carried to its farthest development, a portrayal of what a man is in whom the imagination makes the ideal more real than the actual" (76). And there the Catch 22 situation arises for, unfortunately, the nature of the artistic type being explored is defined not by consistency but changeability.

This account does also argues for attention to the "frame" of the novels, to the chorus of commentators and to the "sympathetic confidential narrator". It therefore harmonises with my own reading in many ways. That I disagree with Woolf when it comes to the ending of *Tommy and Grizel* is, therefore, of particular interest. He writes,

What will be the greatest disappointment to most readers is the fatal ending, and they will find it hard to get over. It is not that the book ends unhappily, for this is no valid objection, but that it seems not logical, not an artistic ending. (77)

But does it? I shall instead extend the Catch 22 argument to include the ending as well. A good deal of artistry is, I believe, evident in the ending but in themselves the overly ambitious aims Barrie set himself doom it to failure in practical communicative terms. In these terms and allowing for the fact that Barrie's open endings were still a matter of confusion and concern I shall revive discussion of that "awful ending".

The beginning of this enquiry involves returning to the comparisons made between the earlier and the later volume. Although *Sentimental Tommy* was regarded as superior to *Tommy and Grizel* and although many held it to be Barrie's final novel, it was by no means regarded as flawless. Among its weaknesses the different kinds of character employed once more loomed large. And indeed, when you have major characters who are presented sometimes really sometimes ideally; when many of your minor characters are never more than humours and when the slow romance of the Hanky School is conveyed more naturalistically than any of the other story lines it will be difficult to present a fictive world which people will understand. That view is nicely summed up in *The Fortnightly Review* – "In sooth, the story ought to be read as a pretty farce, and it is perhaps a fault of art that the author now and then seems to swerve from the point of view of farcical exaggeration and to take his hero seriously" (1897: 67: 227–28). How could Barrie convincingly join those worlds together when Tommy died?

But there were also weaknesses detected in *Tommy and Grizel* alone. Barrie's inability to write convincing adult sexual dialogue had not been an issue in *Sentimental Tommy* as it dealt with the early stages of Tommy's journey. This excuse could not be offered for *Tommy and Grizel* and the adult sexual discussions in it do sometimes substitute sickly sweetness for convincing dialogue. At other times passion is conveyed in the abstract language of anti-types in a Morality play. Examples abound but the discussion between Tommy and Grizel about her glove and "the sweetest drawer" (*TG*: 165) will serve as a good illustration of the first. The reduction of the climactic argument between Tommy and Lady Pippinworth into a Reason-Passion dialogue more appropriate for a Morality Play than a genuine exchange between lovers nicely encapsulates the other (*TG*: 338).

Ironically, too, in fulfilling one of his critics' hopes, Barrie made matters worse for himself. *Tommy and Grizel* does not lack humour. Indeed, a wide range of tones has already been detected in both Tommy novels. But overall it is a more serious narrative than its predecessor and humour is Barrie's greatest natural strength. Therefore, when he departs from a comic norm yet still lurches from time to time into farcical mode he could be (and was) said to be getting the worst of both worlds.

Against this background, all that was needed to maximise criticism was an ending which united all these perceived weaknesses. And that, in the opinion of many, was precisely what Barrie provided. Why subject his hero to an unconvincingly melodramatic confrontation with Lady Pippinworth followed by a farcically humiliating death? And why, when he had supposedly returned to a simpler form, did he still need to tie up loose ends in the final chapter?

Methodologically, some of the premises behind these questions have already been challenged. The sophistry of assuming that Barrie intended to present a wholly enclosed conclusion has been exposed. Structural logic would demand a neater ending than *The Wedding Guest* but the subversive spirit would continue to raise questions as well. Descriptively, the account also highlights the fact that there are two areas of "final" criticism. The more severe attack is centred on Tommy's last meetings with Grizel and Lady Pippinworth and his untimely death. These are described in Chapters 33 and 34. The second concerns are reserved for the summing up in Chapter 35. Its description of Tommy's future reputation and Grizel's later life was seen variously as unnecessary, anti-climactic and overcrowded.

It is worth recording that the view I am taking did receive some support in 1900. *The Critic*'s reviewer saw the serious questions the book had raised and praised Barrie's "power to make everything he tells tell many things beside". He also believed that the tale was mythically and microcosmically constructed in order to explore "the uncanny and the sense of infinite wonder that light his little world" (29 August 1896: 137). Moult also thought of the ending in technical terms as Barrie's response to a difficult theme. He, therefore, concluded, "Tommy's death is the most masterly *contrivance* of the story" (Moult 1928: 134 [my italics]). It may, therefore, be that some of the evidence already uncovered will help to resolve the problems presented by Tommy's death.

2. An "Ideal" Ending?

The most frequently voiced criticism of Chapters XXXIII and XXXIV is, yet again, based on the difficulty Barrie found in moving from individual to exemplary characterisation. The relative merits of real and ideal writing had, of course, been specifically raised in the debate between Pym and Tommy at the start of the book. There, it will be remembered, Tommy had voiced the realist case when admitting to changing his employer's work. Their clash had been violent and therefore memorable (16).

In returning to the beginning of the book at this stage, I am following the logic of having a dual structure marrying picaresque narrative to the "exemplary" form of *The Little Minister*. In the latter, guidelines were clearly established at the start and re-introduced at the end. And it is that structure which provides the artistic grounds for ending with types which represent the central ideas of the book in simpler form. That is why the rounded portrait of Grizel, the personified type of Tommy and the aristocratic humour of Lady Pippinworth as understood by Woolf must all be reduced to the lowest common denominator of the Bergsonian puppet. In more particularised terms this means that hero and heroine descend to the cameo definition of Lady Pippinworth. By reducing all three to that level in Chapters XXXIII and XXXIV Barrie also signs a change away from the logic and structure of the narrative to the logic and structure of ideas.

The end is the place for simplification and so the action is polarised. The two contrasted kinds of women currently performing onstage in *The Wedding Guest* are both shown to triumph over Tommy in the novel. Here too the basic Darwinian nature of their rivalry is most thoroughly and indeed poetically enforced on the reader's attention. Grizel's superiority over Tommy in Chapter XXXIII is established visually. During their honeymoon, "Her clear, searching eyes [...] were always asking for the truth," her "candid eyes would rest searchingly upon him" while he would derive inspiration by looking at her face (394–96). Lady Pippinworth's victories are also poetically translated in the clearest, most sustained Darwinian manner possible. Images drawn from boxing contests ("They began by shaking hands as is always the custom in the ring"), knightly jousts ("She had flung down the glove", "lift[ed] the gauntlet) and military conflicts ("it was as if she raised the siege") introduce her last victory over Tommy. Her triumph in vengefulness is also neatly set up in polarised contrast to Grizel's altruistic triumph in the preceding chapter. Meanwhile, Tommy's weaknesses in the battles of love are exhaustively re-stated. Lady Pippinworth's insistence on his physical weaknesses underline his most basic unfitness as a lover. That he is too small and too fat to be a Lothario offers light comedy in a highly serious situation.

The reduction of Tommy to a type grants her other comic advantages. As Bergson explains, the "type's" reactions are defined in advance and so he is easily manipulated by those who know where his obsessions lie. Appeal to M. Jourdain in terms of nobility or to Harpagon's avarice and they will dance to your tune. In the same way Lady Pippinworth "knows" Tommy's changeable type and uses that knowledge to destroy him. In addition it is his inability to hold any consistent position which disarms him for the Darwinian fight and makes him that failure in love which Pym had prophesied on his behalf initially.

3. A Novel Ending?

The second source of critical concern is less confidently expressed. The parallel between Tommy's writing and Barrie's has been established in the same general manner as his life had shadowed his creator's. When it comes to making specific links in this area the same difficulties encountered by those who seek to make Elspeth the young Mrs Barrie are encountered by those who want to identify the four Tommy publications with particular Barrie texts. As this remains an area of doubt in the final chapters, where it becomes a major focus for discussion, the artistic side of this "subtle biography" warrants discussion. Did Barrie simply fail to make the relationship between his own career and Tommy's self-evident? Or is there an obvious answer in narrative and Impish terms to this conundrum as well?

It is when one comes to the manuscript of "Tommy's Best Work" in Chapter XXXII that doubt and mystery replace the hitherto easily interpreted general parallels between Tommy's writing and Barrie's. Grizel's illness has had such an effect on Tommy that during it he becomes unselfish. Dedicated to her every need, he in fact does experience one kind of love, that whose ultimate model is the Christian virtue of charity. As she slowly recovers, the image of her sitting knitting while Tommy writes leads into the opening of Chapter XXXIII and her return to superiority as described in the previous, Darwinian, section. The book which results from this form of love is not the cherished manuscript which Lady Pippinworth mercilessly uses to raise his hopes only to destroy them when she burns it. Grizel instead inspires "The Wandering Child". This is judged by Tommy to be second-rate, an opinion shared by the narrator. That he expresses that opinion in terms of its failure to last is important as that, of course, was for Barrie the decisive dividing line between talent and genius:

The new book, of course, was "The Wandering Child." I wonder whether any of you read it now. Your fathers and mothers thought a lot of that slim volume, but it would make little stir in an age in which all the authors are trying to say Damn loudest. (399)

But it is another type of love which Tommy sees as inspiring his only work of genius. He returns to his changeable self and to Lady Pippinworth. And it is from that relationship as she dominates and mocks him that, he believes, his way to genius has opened up. Masochistic and guilty thoughts dominate, in a manner reminiscent of *The Little Minister*:

When his disgust with himself was at its height he suddenly felt like a little god. His new book had come into view. He flicked a finger at a reflection of himself in a mirror. "That for you," he said defiantly, "at last I can write, I can write at last." (340)

and

"For I did have the whip hand of you once, Madam." (408)

If one thought that Lady Pippinworth saw herself destroying her rival's "baby" this knowledge would add irony to her destroying a manuscript which was her own creation. the action does not make this clear but it seems more likely that she, like Grizel, has come to realise that Tommy's books will always be the love of his life and so reacts in the fiery way which defines her "kind" of woman.

Then, there is the nature of the "finest work" itself. Here too there is mystery. Only Tommy claims it as proof of genius and *he* was convinced of that the moment he felt real passion for Lady Pippinworth – that is, before he began to write it. Now it is destroyed. The other slim volume which everyone from the narrator via Grizel to the commentators after Tommy's death is dismissed as second rate. Well received yesterday, it proves too genteel for to-day's tastes. But when one is told that its central character is a woodland boy who thinks he cannot grow up a quite different perspective opens up. In the fiction this book is complete and condemned. For Barrie it is currently being prepared and will later actually emerge as *The Little White Bird* (114).

I have no problem with those who see the ending to *Tommy and Grizel* as unclear. Usually, however, that view is extended to include the premise that Barrie must also be unclear about what he is trying to do. But would a neat ending be appropriate? To mirror the end of an apprenticeship is to mirror work in progress and work in potential. These are open issues and therefore cannot be clearly foreshadowed in the fiction. Viewed in this way, Barrie does not seem to be confused at all. His own genuine belief that he had the potential for genius has been stated by Tommy but does not yet exist so the "great work" is described but burnt. The irony that *The Little White Bird*, dismissed by the editor, would actually lead to Barrie's ultimate proof of his genius in *Peter Pan* could not have been foreseen, What Barrie's ending permits is the possibility of that event. And this he does by having a *lost* manuscript, which *may or may not* have established Tommy's reputation stand at the centre of a darker, less reliably objective world of judgment than that implied by Cowley.

4. An Ibsenite Ending?

The third major area of critical discontent concerns Tommy's strange, anti-climactic death. It also raises problems when related to the issue of Barrie's literary development. Tommy's death is as pathetic as it is ugly. Despite being ignominiously treated by Lady Pippinworth he is chasing her when it happens. His skewering himself on the spikes of the fence, therefore, results from him his wilfully turning his back on Grizel's angelic influence and giving way to his own darker self – "the demon that burned [his] book" (*TG*: 418) .

That the model for this death comes from Ibsen's *Hedda Gabler* is obvious and recognised by modern critics. Substitute Eilert Løvborg for Tommy, Hedda for Lady Pippinworth and Thea Tesman for Grizel and an exact parallel is revealed. The reason for imitation is also evident. The idea of demonic possession in a battle for sexual power develops from Babbie's role as witch and gypsy in *The Little Minister*. But it does so more darkly in accordance with Ibsen's serious formulation of that metaphysical force in his Notes for *Hedda* – "The demonic thing about Hedda is that she wants to exert power over another person [...] The despairing thing about Løvborg is that he wants to control the world but cannot control himself" (cited in McFarlane 1994: xi).

Both Tommy on his fence and Løvborg in a prostitute's boudoir die morally reprehensible and aesthetically ugly deaths. Both in this way demonstrate how far some men can fall short of the ideals held by the two opposed "kinds of women" who are attracted to them. Lady Pippinworth is disturbed by Tommy's failure to match Bohemian ideals while Hedda laments Løvborg's inability to live up to her

Roman hopes of vine leaves and an aesthetically beautiful suicide (Binding 2006: 108). Grizel and Thea, for their part, are equally disappointed to discover that their own unselfish love is unlikely to be matched by even the most apparently talented of males.

Of course, Hedda received as mixed a reception initially as *Tommy and Grizel* and did so for essentially the same reason – that critics had not realised that new areas of attention were being addressed and so continued to apply old criteria inappropriately. Barrie had retreated to a more personal story line but used that to convey a wider referential range than any he had attempted before. Ibsen was also addressing personal rather than social conflicts in *Hedda*. Once these changes are recognised it is no coincidence that later critics when describing the tasks Ibsen set himself could just as well be writing about the Barrie of *Tommy and Grizel*. McFarlane in his introduction to *Hedda Gabler* points out that "studies of interlocked personalities" were now Ibsen's aim and that change in turn implied a complex balancing act so that the "manifold attractions and repulsions" of the battles they conduct could be held together "dynamically [...] in moment to moment equilibrium". This is subversively done with "the undertow of the unconscious mind and the persuasive force of dreams and visions" (McFarlane 1994: xi) never far from the surface.

Ibsen's higher aims and their extension into the realms of art are also practically identical to those traced for Barrie. Referring primarily to *The Master Builder*, but including *Hedda*, as parallel piece, McFarlane notes:

Potency, the capacity to exert some inherent power, is the theme to which the events of the dramas constantly relate. In a basic sexual sense in the first instance: the nature of the power of the male mind over the female and vice versa. And then by extension into the areas of artistic and professional potency (McFarlane 1994: xi–xii).

This is strong evidence but *Tommy and Grizel*'s metafictional bias as well as its claim to mirror Barrie's literary career make the echoing of Løvborg's humiliating death particularly effective. Here, in a novel which parades its sources as part of a study of literary origins, what could be more appropriate than returning at the end of your *prose* apprenticeship to the source which originated your *theatrical* career in "Ibsen's Ghost?"

This is also the justification for placing other sources at the fore-front of attention. Most obviously these include Walter Scott and the Jacobite games and Barrie's close imitation of Dickens' comically imaginative techniques. But it also accounts for the number of other echoes and influences detected by critics. From James to Thackeray, from Stevenson to Conrad they are recognized. But they are there because Barrie's latest Impish attempt at proving his uniqueness implies demonstrating how far he is not unique but relies on others.

The fact that the major Ibsen model co-exists with a particular folk-tale source could also be seen as an artistic, "influential" means of confessing debts to both the learned and the popular tradition in the manner of Burns and Ramsay. That influence is noted in Barrie's Notebooks for 1890 and recalled by Ormond, "Death might come to man as hawker hanged by his pack when the lad weary of his iniquity (or he might live on)" (BVS A2/12).

The reason for dwelling on the Ibsenite conclusion in a discus-sion on Barrie's literary development lies in the astonishing fact that none of the early commentators call attention to it. Given that *The Wedding Guest* was currently alerting theatregoers to Barrie's contin-ued interest in Ibsen and given that so many other sources had been detected for *Tommy and Grizel*, this seems very strange indeed. The fact remains that neither Chalmers nor Darlington nor Hammerton nor Moult nor Roy nor any of the commentators cited in Markgraf's extensive bibliography mention Ibsen in this connection.

One can think of extenuating reasons. The Barrie-Ibsen link had until then been confined to drama. Archer, who must surely have seen the Ibsenite ending had he concerned himself with the Tommy novels did not discuss them. For their part, those critics who were especially interested in Barrie's modal translations may have been put off by the fact that, unusually, he was this time translating material from theatre into prose rather than in the opposite direction. The farcical and melo-dramatic presentation of Tommy's death would also make reading the novel and seeing Ibsen such different experiences that the idea of their being linked might simply not occur. Add to this the misunderstanding of the new aims of both authors as discussed above and the silence becomes more understandable. Whatever the reasons may be, how-ever, the crucial fact remains that yet another obvious sign supporting the case for Barrie's forward-looking artistic aims went unrecognised.

5. One Ending Too Many?

Criticism of Chapter XXXV is less intense. Geduld ignores the final chapter as he had ignored the entirety of the surrounding structural framework in both books. Those not tied to prototypical argument and Freudian theory generally follow Mackail in his belief that Barrie has retreated to a simpler, episodic kind of composition which would seem to make the tying of loose ends unnecessary. And even those who accept that the end is explicable in topical and structural terms remain puzzled by the detailed updating which the chapter provides.

To resolve these problems one need only return to earlier ground and the basic rhetorical principles which were the foundation of Barrie's literary theory. The narrator's claims to organise his material as he sees fit and the topical-Darwinian presentation of the characters, including Jean Sandys, proved at an early stage that there are higher tiers to the Tommy tales. For a rhetorically trained reader, it is only a matter of following those signs. And what they reveal is a radically new configuration of Barrie's central theme, the battle of the sexes. This originality in turn recalls an even more basic rhetorical premise, recognised by Masson and essential to Barrie. Only if you have something original to say should you write.

The ways in which this latest version of Barrie's central creation theme *does* differ from his earlier explorations of it have also been identified and may helpfully be recalled. Essentially a more personal story line becomes the vehicle for a more ambitious range of reference than before. These extend to the mysteries of life and the inadequacies of language . They also link the natural and artistic kinds of creativity so closely that Tommy's idea of a poetic compliment to Grizel involves comparing her to a book – "'Ah, Grizel,' he declared by and by, 'what a delicious book you are, and how I wish I had written you'" (*TG*: 185).

The earlier account offered in the "Formal" section of the discussion has also lightened the task of explaining why Chapter XXXV has to round off both Tommy's artistic and Grizel's domestic tale. Not only are the worlds of sexuality and art drawn together, in many ways the characters of Tommy and Grizel are also seen to merge. The logic for this empathetic rather than polarised presentation of the gender battle can be found in Barrie's earliest Notes. Grizel's divided personality was due to her parents, her magerful father and prostitute mother

– "A beautiful girl, but this curse of passion in her blood" (*BVS* A2/12). The same genetic inheritance is described for Tommy with magerful Tam seducing Jean Sandys. The portrait of the Painted Lady, her sufferings and decline make Grizel's difficulties both practically and emotionally more serious than Tommy's but essentially they share the same heredity.

This is another sign of Ibsen's influence which exists but is not commented upon as Winfield Woolf's reaction illustrates nicely – "If there is a fault in Grizel it is that Barrie has insisted too much on the element of heredity" (*Sewanee Review* 1901: 9: 76). In fact Barrie's subsequent revisions lessened the strong genetic element implied by the Notes. Nonetheless, the similarity between "hero" and heroine detected earlier does remain founded in heredity and the fact that Ibsen's influence is not detected here either continues to protect the regressive view of Barrie's art at this time from the evidence he offers in his fictions.

Against this background, it is only necessary to carry the game motif into the later movements of the novel to see why Barrie concluded Chapter XXXV with a crowded cameo in which Grizel is surrounded by Corp's family and Elspeth's. What *Tommy and Grizel* traces in its later stages is the relegation of those who had been superior in the games of youth to the status of onlookers as their former lackeys win the primary battle of creativity, that of parenthood. That cameo is deeply moving because it shows Grizel already cutting an old maid's figure after Tommy's death among those who know the fulfilment of parenthood (430). In this way the happy domestic scene is at once proof of the superior power of natural creation *and* of Barrie's feminist interpretation of the gender battle.

At the start of Chapter XII, the signs of this revolution are already clear. But both Tommy and Grizel are slow to see the implications of Gavinia's child and Corp's newfound invention. They retain the old picture in which they remain the superior, favoured ones. Their handling of the other marriage between Elspeth and David Gemmell is similar. Tommy's condescending belief that he and not his sister should decide whom she marries is proudly voiced at the start of Chapter XIX:

To find ways of making David propose to Elspeth of making Elspeth willing to exchange her brother for David, they were heavy tasks, but Tommy yoked himself to them gallantly and tugged like an Arab steed in the plough. (217).

Grizel then in a spirit of benevolent condescension sets about arranging a marriage for Gemmell. She had rejected his suit as she still hoped to find, with Tommy, a fruitful union higher up the evolutionary scale of potential. As a result they later join forces to create a sort of reserve team-wedding for Gemmell and Elspeth.

I find the cameo deeply moving because it captures visually the full extent of Tommy's betrayal. Barrie leads into it by showing Grizel at her strongest. Bravely she confronts Lady Pippinworth and learns the facts about Tommy's death. Even more bravely, she decides to accept man's frailty and find comfort in the constancy of her own continued love for Tommy. Ultimate values are again appealed to as the first of these positions suggests the Christian doctrine of the Fall and her "higher love" mirrors charity, the highest of the theological virtues.

The last words of the book are as sentimentally pathetic as any of his popular readers could wish – "The little girl she had been comes stealing back into the book and rocks her arms joyfully, and we see Grizel's crooked smile for the last time" (431). But the reference is, once more, to books not life. More importantly, pathos finally disguises the "pitiless sarcasm and mordant irony" which has also been apparent and which Tommy's disastrous effect on Grizel truly warrants (*Littell's Living Age* 15 December 1900: 699). She has, after all, put her faith in a lover who cannot love and an artist who will never achieve fame; one who, at best, may be found "Haunting the portals of the Elysian Fields" hoping that "the great shades [may] come to the and talk with [him]" (424).

One should not be misled by the varied tones of the preceding chapters. Barrie is determined to show his "hero's" weaknesses in the darkest light possible. And certainly Chapter XXXV offers a clear tonal switch. Tommy's reputation is satirically analysed before the pathos and passion of Grizel's later life is covered.

But if pathos is the end, why is Grizel not alone? The technique Barrie employs, that of visual contrast is one which he will, more effectively, use in his later dramas. Later we will leave the theatre as now we close the book with a picture which reveals more than it obviously shows. In this case we "see" a childless, widowed, heroically tragic Grizel surrounded by happy fertile couples. She had stood out for a man who promised more but produced less. As a result she is reduced to the role of nursemaid to Corp's and Elspeth's offspring. That she likes to think back to the "best days" of the childhood games they used to play is one indictment of the powerless Captain Stroke's effect on her life. That she finds most adult comfort from Corp, the lowest of the low in that world, is another:

> It was sweet to Grizel to listen while Elspeth and David told her of the thousand things Tommy had done for her when she was ill, but she loved best to talk with Corp of the time when they were all children in the den. The days of childhood are the best. (431)

Appropriately for a book which sets out to consider the relationship between art and life, the earlier, satirical section of Chapter XXXV deals with Tommy's literary failings. The opening words fulfil structural expectations by offering a very clear judgment – "Tommy has not lasted, he is only 'a might have been'" (422–23). When one considers that Corps ends the chapter by lamenting Grizel's failure to have children "When you was a woman you would like terrible to hae bairns o' your ain" (431) the presence of what seems to be a neat, enclosed conclusion to both kinds of creative exploration is revealed. What the final cameo has done, however, is open up further questions. That principle of imaginatively subverting the obvious applies even more to the account of Tommy's reputation which follows the narrator's brief factual introduction.

He begins by expanding on his opening judgment. This involves focussing on the fickleness of public taste. Already his fans worship another idol and even the totally false legend that Tommy died climbing the wall for flowers to give to Grizel has failed to create enough interest to justify publication of even a slim selection of his works! In short, his quest for genius has failed when measured against Cowley's simple formula. Barrie had explored this question in much more detail both critically and creatively, however. Further, this a book in which the difficulties of accurate perception and the origins of fiction are also being discussed. And at once, literary comparisons enter the field. Tommy as a "might have been" is like Chatterton or, to be more precise, he is at once like and *unlike* Chatterton because he has "exploded that pernicious fallacy [...] that the consummate artist is able to love nothing but the creations of his fancy" (243). As Tommy's history has proved precisely the opposite of that, in the space of two paragraphs we have moved from apparently objective scales of judgment and "Tommy has not lasted" into an examination on false premises of the relationship between a real poet from the past and a fictional modern novelist according to the chaotic non-principles of *The House of Fame*.

According to the principles of springs and balances which governed Barrie's composition at this time, only one satiric technique is used throughout the Tommy section of the chapter. What has been enacted about Tommy's nature and writing is simply turned on it head. Biographers, literary critics and the Thrums chorus all re-translate Barrie's past in ludicrously misleading terms. For future ages the Tommy-Grizel relationship will show Tommy as "the purer spirit" and reduce her existence to the level of an advertisement for him – "she existed only that he might show how great he was" (423). The heredity question is similarly treated. To explain "how the twig was early bent so did the tree incline" Tommy's cruel and absent father is converted into "a retired military officer in easy circumstances". He is the source of Tommy's (non-existent!) "strong will" and "singleness of purpose" while his mother, "a canny Scotchwoman of lowly birth, conspicuous by her devoutness", is consigned to background irrelevance (424–25).

To The Never Land and Beyond: A Novel Route

Three immediate questions were posed in this chapter and this kind of virtuosity provides one way of answering the first. Barrie's unusually calm reception of those negative reviews which met *Tommy and Grizel* can be understood if one alters the assumptions made about his view of himself at this time. This was no longer the hesitant, financially insecure Barrie who allowed Toole to re-write "Ibsen's Ghost". After *The Little Minister* had established on secure foundations his popular reputation and his bank balance he felt able to speak out on his own behalf. As learned author he had the means and the appetite to answer the *literati* and would-be biographers on their own terms. This he did by mercilessly satirising the mercenary, simplistic and self-serving grounds on which their inaccurate judgments were based. That he did so in the last chapter of his first truly metafictional work as part of an exploration of art and perception adds poignancy to the challenge he offered. Lady Pippinworth may have thrown down the gauntlet to a helpless Tommy but Barrie also challenged the false custodians of future genius in his most subtle work so far. That they *did* fail was, for his perfectionist self anyway, sufficient vengeance.

This artistic sense of superiority was as much part of Barrie's outlook now as his fears of personal inadequacy. It had already established itself in that Napoleon complex commented upon earlier which led to both Moira Loney and Peter Pan visually representing the Little Corporal in 2003 and 2004. (Jack 1991: 140–41, 19–13; 2010: 137–39, 186–88). That heroic self-image and a different kind of revenge would later be wreaked on critics and public alike in *The Adored One*. In that case, boos greeted his most radical vision of the New Woman's potential for power. Barrie went home and at once composed the most sentimental ending possible, complete with thatched cottage and flowers (Jack 1993; 1995). It was met enthusiastically. What Barrie thought can only be imagined!

The second question posed was why he apparently gave up novel writing after publishing the two books in that mode over which he had toiled longest. Additional difficulties were highlighted. Most obviously another prose work *does* follow. Only if you deny to *The Little White Bird* the status of novel can the earlier conclusion be sustained. In addition, the fact that *Tommy and Grizel* drew *Sentimental Tommy* into its ambit of failure cannot totally erase the earlier book's fine reputation and the expectations of continued experimentation its quality implied.

If Barrie had thought about his art in discrete, generic terms these would be valid comments and the problems would remain. But he didn't think in this way and so they disappear. His Notebooks begin with *ideas* or *images* many of which are initially proposed for *either* prose *or* drama. Working with the interlinked vocal principles of rhetoric in mind, he also kept at the front of his attention the possibility of re-translating one mode into another. And he had by this stage firmly established himself as a mythical writer in the sense that a consistent metaphysical view of life informs all of his serious writing. Commentators now recognise a Barrie world distinct from this one but as immediately recognisable as Dickens'.

If one retrospectively re-examines the evidence from this point of view the neat chronological ordering presumed by Mackail is the first premise to lose its validity. In publication terms *The Little Minister* may clearly precede *Sentimental Tommy* but their planning overlaps. The dual assumption that the Tommy novels come later than *The*

Little Minister and constituted a retreat to an easier episodic form also falls. Having lost its chronological justification its structural claim falls as well. The multi-stranded form of *The Little Minister* is not after all rejected. Instead another overlapping pattern is revealed. By employing for Tommy a variation on the layered structure employed for Gavin Dishart, Barrie neither retreats nor simplifies.

Metaphysically too these novels offer variations on a similar theme – that of Barrie's feminist vision of the world according to Darwin. That vision will underlie Barrie's literary thinking and practice until the success of the Women's Movement and the advent of war combined to re-direct it. *A Kiss for Cinderella* in 1916 is the first of the major plays to change focus. But it is the world-view which alters not the mythically consistent patterning of Barrie's views on life within and beyond time.

The identification of this last overlapping principle re-introduces the third and most important question. Do the late Victorian novels like the late Victorian plays look forward in a new spirit of creative confidence or are they, as most critics and biographers assume, an exception to that movement. The belief that they do is, of course, crucial to the view that despair over his prose forced him to prove his genius in the theatre alone. The direct dramatic route to fame has been established in Chapter Six with *The Wedding Guest* in particular anticipating the later mature plays from *Peter Pan* in 1904 until *Mary Rose* in 1920. Can the equal influential power of the Tommy novels, claimed by a few of Barrie's contemporaries be similarly established and so destroy the "despairing" assumption as well?

The theme and variation principle which sustains Barrie's mythological universe at this time does suggest that there should be influence of this sort. Belonging to one genre rather than another is at best peripherally relevant when the different *kinds* of writing become the vehicles of variation in a literary world whose ultimate vision of life and afterlife remains substantially the same. And, of course, to trace the early evolution of the "wandering child" from *Tommy and Grizel* in 1900 via the *photograph album* of recording Barrie's actual games with the Llewelyn Davies boys at Black Lake Island in 1901, to the eternal boy's first named cameo role in an adult novel, *The Little White Bird*, is to encounter three different forms of the eternally youthful myth already.

It is probably fair to withhold from *The Little White Bird* the title novel. It *is* episodic and shapeless in part because Barrie had recourse to earlier material in assembling it. But as our first introduction to a character called Peter Pan in a work which develops the avian mythology of Tommy's dream sequence in the Slugs it has a crucial place in Barrie's canon. Hammerton in finding it, after *A Window in Thrums*, "his most important work [...] with respect to his development as a writer" (Hammerton 1929: 231) is probably overstating the case. But in seeing it as an important stage on the way to *A Kiss for Cinderella*, *Dear Brutus* and *Mary Rose* as well as *Peter Pan*, he shows his awareness that Barrie's prose does have an important role to play in establishing his genius (231). The fact that *The Little White Bird* places this new hero within the most overtly mythological part of a novel which returns the creation battle to its most basic form and does so in the most overtly analytic manner possible is also consistent with old ways being clearly re-established before being galvanised by a new idea and character. Geduld's comment that *The Little White Bird* is "not so much a love story as a conflict of shadow and substance" between "Creator-Artist and Creator-Mother" succinctly sums up this position (Geduld 1971: 55).

But we are still only at the earliest stage of one of the most sustained examples of modal variation in all literature. The next translation of the "eternal youth" myth into the full-length play *Peter Pan* is already the fourth such re-definition. In 1905 and 1906 "Pantaloon" and *Peter Pan in Kensington Gardens* not only add fifth and sixth re-definitions but are themselves interesting examples of different ways in which to extract and re-employ existing material. "Pantaloon" was originally a scene in *Peter Pan*, intended to trace the origins of drama as part of the metafictional line within that play (Jack 1990). When it had to be rejected on grounds of time, Barrie simply turned it into a one act play which went into production at the *Duke of York's* in April 1905. *Peter Pan in Kensington Gardens*, on the other hand, extracted and expanded Peter's avian origins from *The Little White Bird* myth so as to move him from part-player to hero in his own adult novel a year later. The children's novel, *Peter and Wendy*, next appeared in 1911 followed by the radical film scenario for *Peter Pan* which Barrie sent Hollywood in 1920. This was rejected, much to Barrie's fury especially when a conservative alternative was produced (Jack 2002). The short story, "The Blot on Peter Pan", in which he anticipated modern text-messaging (see Jack 1991 237–38; 2010: 232–33), and his speech, "Jas. Hook at Eton", saw the ending of the theme. If one adds to these the ballet, *The Origins of Harlequins*, on the grounds that it continues the metafictional study of literary origins within the Pan myth, a maximal number of eleven variations can be claimed.

This brings us to the most important area of all. The evidence provided by the Tommy novels support Moult's view that, at the turn of the century, Barrie is drawing together those themes and modes which will dominate his drama from *Quality Street* to *The Boy David*. That three of his first four major plays (*Quality Street, The Admirable Crichton, Peter Pan*) and two of his last (*Dear Brutus, Mary Rose*) are modernist re-workings of the Shakespearean Romance form advocated by Masson as the supreme test of genius confirms this new certainty of direction. That all five are mythic explorations of the human condition with the early ones concentrating on Darwinian heroism and the later offering a less hierarchical vision of the human condition also confirms Moult's view. That the only exceptions are two legends, the highest mode of all in the medieval and renaissance period is consistent with his adopting the highest forms as he makes his major assault on the London theatre. The legends in particular show Barrie's ability to range widely now that a narrower choice of modes has been decided upon. *Little Mary* is a quintuple allegorical riddle centred round a female "saint", *The Boy David* is a modernised Biblical tale surrounding the boy who will be king.

That the titles of all of these plays have survived as universal models for different kinds of life or personality underlines the mythic model. The dramas which belong to the period between *Pan* and *Dear Brutus* do not depart from these patterns entirely but their focus is more firmly fixed on the potential of women across the entire spec-trum of personality, from the absent mother and histrionic daughter in *Alice Sit By The Fire* via the practical intelligence of Maggie Shand in *What Every Woman Knows*, and the ruthless Leonora of *The Adored One* to her fairy-tale opposite Miss Thing in the war play, *A Kiss for Cinderella*.

I shall end this chapter by addressing one of the major difficulties implied by my choice of topic. As the title suggests, I have spent almost as long opposing the Oedipal-Kailyard myth as I have in advancing the counter-case. That bias was necessitated by the continued health of a vision which condescends to Barrie by dismissing, in terms of sub-conscious immaturity, one of the most intelligent and self-conscious of British writers. That he also explicitly asks to be judged for the imaginative powers of his plays but is condemned on the grounds that his earliest prose is bad realism means that the proponents of that myth have difficult questions to answer before the other psychological, canonical and biographical inconsistencies I have defined even come into the equation.

That Barrie had trouble in his relationship with his mother I accept. That this will continue to be of interest to biographers I do not doubt. But I cannot believe that two short, differently imagined accounts of his brother's death, neither of which appear in his major novels, justify the broad traumatic and Oedipal conclusions which originate from them. That these concerns in any way influence the careful planning of his plays seems particularly unlikely given his own explicit denials as offered in his Letters, the *Greenwood Hat* and his academic articles.

On these grounds, I shall address the last task proposed in the Introduction, that of linking the works of the apprenticeship period to the mature plays by using instead the very different critical principles which have emerged from this study of his educational training and the views of art which emerged from it. To do so economically, and in the exemplary comparative manner favoured by Barrie himself, I shall use as a fulcrum for that enquiry the links already established between the Tommy novels and *The Wedding Guest* and two of the early mature works in particular – *Quality Street* and *Peter Pan*.

Chapter Eight

Approaching the Later Plays

I began this analysis with Hollindale's definition of the massive critical divide between those who see Barrie as a light, sub-consciously limited author and those who see him as a self-conscious, learned writer, subversively balancing one level of his multi-layered texts against another. A return to those assessments, as re-defined, may also end it. After all, the critical account of the late apprentice-ship period discussed in the last two chapters has uncovered yet another radical opposition between the two schools, with the former seeing despair and a sudden turning to drama and the other arguing for continued mythic development.

The argument of the book has, however, produced a range of new evidence on the latter, Impish side of the argument. It has estab-lished a wide range of educational and journalistic influences on Barrie while questioning the literary and psychological assumptions on which his supposed entrapment in childhood are advanced. As the case for his genius rests firmly on his plays and as Barrie argues that the theatrical mode was especially inimical to autobiographical com-position, the grounds for treating him as a disturbed personality rather than a writer who uses comic methods to explore "heavy" themes are at their weakest there.

In a sense therefore this book is my own answer to the challenges Hollindale urged on future researchers following the publication of *The Road to the Never Land*. While accepting that it "establishes a new level and directs the way for future work" he correctly sees it as "over-ambitious" (Hollindale 1995: xxx). In the continued absence of such a work I have tried to offer a clearer critical basis on which the earlier claims may be examined, focussed on the apprenticeship period alone but granted to it the fuller canonical coverage necessary to trace Barrie's artistic progress reliably.

It is necessary to make these aims explicit at this point because my motivation for moving beyond the apprentice works to look at two of the mature plays is different and needs contextualisation. The stud-ies so far have not posed the question, "Does Barrie offer a progressively complex mythic vision of this world in his apprentice plays?" That question has already been answered positively by critics, from Jacqueline Rose on. Instead, the background evidence of Chapter Two and the broader canonical focus described above have allowed me to address the underlying problem behind all "layered" accounts of his work – "How can this sophisticated, erudite approach to art be reconciled with the dilettante student and subconsciously stunted Barrie of popular belief?" The nature of the new question and the strength of the new evidence has enabled me to return to those works which I have covered earlier in an inventive rather than imitative spirit.

In deciding to take the quest one stage further and look at representative mature plays, I was aware that the problem of repetition assumed a new dimension. On these plays, and on *Pan* especially, I had written at some length and in a manner which already proved in "innocence" that the complex mythic, allegorical and metanarrational patterns whose complexity was the source of critical disbelief did indeed exist. That these conclusions, shared by others, are now confirmed by the "experience" of Chapter Two is important but the need to re-consider the original argument might still mean that, potentially at least, imitation would outweigh invention. In short, if the question *"Is Barrie* a complex, multi-layered writer?" has already been replaced by *"How has Barrie become* a complex, multi-layered writer?" in the analysis of his apprentice works, a more practical formulation of the second question is posed for the mature plays. "Does a detailed understanding of Barrie's literary and critical development from *Bandalero the Bandit* to *The Wedding Guest*, from *A Child of Nature* to *Tommy and Grizel* help to reveal a more sympathetic way of entering the Imp's labyrinth?" is the question proposed now. The discussions of *Quality Street* and *Peter Pan* which follow are, therefore, primarily designed to show that there *are* clear lines of guidance which Barrie himself offered but these have been largely ignored because of the realistic, Oedipal assumptions of the past.

As the opening of this chapter links the end of the apprentice "way" to the new land of "authorised" drama in the *Collected Plays* edition, I shall pursue one version of origins – literary sources and influences – from the Tommy novels into Edwardian period. This approach is justified by the fact that already the imaginative world evoked in the late Victorian period highlighted artistic origins as well as natural ones. A wide range of sources, headed by Shakespeare,

Dickens and Ibsen, have already been detected in his works at that time. Indeed, special attention was paid in the last two chapters to outside influences and echoes from within his own canon. Intentionally, coverage of dramatic sources was completed in Chapter 6 but the Tommy novels left out of consideration. Given Barrie's interlinked planning methods, the prose as well as the drama has to be considered in this context.

If this confirms the interlinked methodology retrospectively, it also accounts for my choice of *Quality Street* and *Peter Pan* as the plays which, microcosmically, offer the most promising ground for looking influentially backward *and* forward. That is – among the early mature dramas, these are the ones which show Barrie's drama advancing qualitatively but they are also the ones which most clearly derive from the Victorian past.

Looking Back: Minor "Signs" in the Tommy Novels

There are strong a priori reasons for expecting the Tommy novels to look backwards and forwards canonically. We have seen that Barrie's Notebooks might remind him of earlier ideas making the existence, among his earliest notes, of the subject for his last play, *The Boy David*, a possible source across so many years. Further, at the turn of the century overt echoing of sources had become part of the emerging metafictional line in his work. Consideration of the minor sources also marks the end of one way and the beginning of another in terms of my own argument. It concludes the exhaustive coverage of the earlier material and anticipates the "exemplary" approach which will suggest ways in which that knowledge might be applied to the later plays.

On their own, none of the following examples constitutes a definite link in an obvious influential chain. Taken together as part of Barrie's current enthusiasm for overt imitation and invention, they can confirm in prose the same positive climate already established in the theatre.

Like *The Wedding Guest*, and probably for the same reasons, the Tommy novels anticipate the idea of the mother eternally seeking her lost child at the same time as they advertise Pan as eternal boy. Grizel's dream of a phantom child offers the clearest anticipation of *Mary Rose* so far and does so within a novel which thematically highlights the conflict between reality and fantasy. Sadly, she describes to Tommy the childless fate which will soon be hers: "'I remember vaguely,' she told him, 'a baby in white whom I seemed to chase, but I could never catch her'" (*TG*: 393). In her dream, like Mary Rose, she escapes into a world beyond time. She even enters the mist which will, twenty years later, become a crucial stage direction in the early versions of the play.– "She remembered everything up to her return to Thrums; then she walked into a mist" (392).

The satirical and linguistic focus of *Sentimental Tommy* also prepares us for *What Every Woman Knows*. When the narrator wants to underline the phonetic miracle achieved by Elspeth in saying "Auld Licht" correctly (when she has never been out of London) he chooses as the most extremely anglicised group of Scotsmen, those "gentlemen who sit for Scotch constituencies" (*TS*: 54). For them to speak like their constituents would be equally marvellous. Twelve years later James Shand would stride into parliament and upset that rule.

There are other contexts in which motifs and images, later to be developed on stage can first be detected in the Tommy novels. It is tempting for example to see the opening association between babies and coffins in *Sentimental Tommy* (4) as the source of Moira Loney's grocery box beds for the children in her care in *Little Mary* and for Miss Thing's box-beds for the children of foreign widowers in the wartime setting of *A Kiss for Cinderella*. The earlier connection is, perhaps, strengthened by the narrator attributing a particularly important function to the many coloured bottles in old-fashioned chemists' shops: "These bottles are the first poem known to the London child, and you chemists who are beginning to do without them in your windows should be told that it is a shame" (*TS:* 57). Far from banishing the bottles from *his* shop, Moira Loney's mysterious alchemist grandfather has them clearly visible in his stage laboratory of 1903 (Barrie 1942: s.d.423). *Little Mary* will also be the most aggressively difficult of all Barrie's plays at a time when the subversive Imp is playing a larger part than ever before. In it he challenges his audiences to match his cleverness, while knowing that the chances of matching Shaw in seeing the seriousness of this quintessential riddle was extremely unlikely. A similar attitude was detected at the time of the Tommy novels and I do not believe that it is a coincidence, that the most thorough fictional support offered for that position follows the chemical bottles reference. Almost immediately, the narrator anticipates Hugh Walpole's view of Barrie as proudly impenetrable: "To trick people so simply, however, is not agreeable to an artist" (*TG*: 63). In the same book, Tommy aspires to say the unsayable, to crack the unknowable joke and find the verbal perfection theoretically contemplated by the Universal Languages as proposed by Sir Thomas Urquhart (the original Admirable Crichton) and other Renaissance linguists (377, 440).

These individually inconclusive echoes may do no more than illustrate how economically Barrie uses and returns to a limited number of basic story lines. But he did himself believe that only a few of these existed and now that his own, fundamentally unchanging mythic world was emerging, so the need to effect variation within a limited range of story types increased as well. From that perspective practical evidence of these economies assumes greater importance.

Quality Street and the Tommy Novels

The classical principle of imitation and invention is fundamental to Barrie's view of art. It is unsurprising therefore that the transition from thorough analysis of the Victorian period to eclectic exploration of his later work can be seen as yet another variation on a theme. The interrelationship between the long, slow romance of Miss Ailie in the Tommy novels and its dramatic re-working in *Quality Street* provides a good example of this process. Soon, Barrie would free himself dramatically from his early prose but not yet.

Given the "mythic" conclusions of the earlier chapters and the critical focus of this discussion, a refinement on the obvious comparative duty to balance *varius sis* with *tamen idem* is justified. This does not do away with the need to identify similarities and differences. It does imply contextualising that methodology within the thematic expectations raised earlier. Beginning with the earlier text that means offering an answer to the following question: "What contribution, if any, does the extended story of Miss Kitty's death and Miss Ailie's romance in the Tommy novels make to either the prose battle of the sexes or the study of different kinds of women which were Barrie's governing concerns at this time?" When writing the précis for the Tommy novels I intentionally deleted that entire story line with this question in mind. For there is a sense in which it could be omitted and no one would be any the wiser. In *Sentimental Tommy* Ivie McLean and Ailie do enter Tommy's game world but as non-believing outsiders. In *Tommy and Grizel*, Ailie and Ivie comfort Grizel but remain outside the closer group of those affected by Tommy's death.

If it had been easy to add this material, Barrie's choice might have warranted only brief comment but it was, in fact, quite difficult. First of all the structure of *Sentimental Tommy* was complicated enough already. Secondly Ailie's romance, despite the poetic and symbolic elements within it, was generally told in a more naturalistic register than any of the other imaginative histories. Those who read the surface only had, therefore, some excuse for seeing it as a return to anecdotal autobiography.

But a stronger case for Barrie's choice emerges when referred to the broad mythic context which defines Barrie's world-view at this time. The Tommy novels' claim for uniqueness in that context was earlier defined in topical terms, as the closer interlinking of the twin themes of artistic and sexual creativity. In character terms it presented a new vision of the different kinds of women whose nature and gender conflicts were the major focus for his feminist version of the selection of the species. Referentially, its uniqueness was related to the new metaphysical and metafictional bias detected by Ormond.

The allegorical approach which re-defines the question on different levels and relates it to the overarching theme of creativity is the first way in which an understanding of Barrie's critical views helps to focus the critic and the playgoer. Relating the different layers of the text to the topical categories of allegory at once breaks down the problem and re-directs it.

Viewed in this way, Barrie's decision to return to his own early schooling and, therefore, the small Bank Street school run by the two Adams sisters, makes good sense. As the novel's account of the educational options available in Kirriemuir reminds us, Barrie was the first and last of his family to attend that school which also, of course, was the origin of his education. As original and interlinked point of origin, some acknowledgement of the Adams sisters would therefore seem logical. As part of a varied study of female types, Miss Ailie's "slow romance" offers the same kind of supportive double-plotting employed by Shakespeare and earlier exemplified in the Barrie canon by *The Professor's Love Story*. Miss Ailie (as Mrs Mclean) represents an older "kind" of woman to set beside Grizel, Elspeth and Lady

Pippinworth. She represents the unattractive heroine again in contrast to those three. In the crucial comparison with Grizel at the end of the second book, her appearance may be fleeting and outside the immediate group of friends but one could argue that it also constitutes the most damning condemnation on Tommy. Ailie may possess the lowest common denominator of "romance" – an ordinary husband in a childless marriage but Tommy has not even provided that comfort for Grizel. If the allegorical focus has re-directed the question, it has moved it towards another leitmotiv theme in his criticism – the definitions of real and ideal writing and the ways in which they interrelate lay at the base of Masson's entire literary "programme".

And once the introduction has been shown to follow known ground-rules, another principle is evoked. What, precisely, is the mode chosen? This is yet another "translation" from one mode to another, an area in which Barrie's favoured techniques and skills, strengths and weaknesses have been exhaustively established across the widest possible range of experimentation. In offering a comparative assessment of this latest example of staged prose in terms of themes and variations, the critic knows that Barrie follows the method of the makars and so pays attention to the ways in which the line is "translated" first. There, the most striking change is the resurrection of the novel's dead Miss Kitty as the play's heroine, Miss Phoebe. Miss Ailie, for her part, becomes Miss Susan and is reduced to the secondary role of guide and comforter.

If one relates these changes to the major trends in Barrie's literary development, they confirm the idea that his different experiments are coming together and doing so in the ambitious ways anticipated in the Tommy novels and *The Wedding Guest*. This, the earliest drama to gain entry into the *Collected Plays*, is also the first to harmonise Barrie's own critical criteria for excellence. In *Quality Street*, a layered plot based on the pattern of Shakespearean Romance focuses imaginatively on an aspect of the Darwinian gender battle which has both an immediate Edwardian application and universal relevance as well.

Of course, Barrie's views on the relationship between theme and form have been stated consistently in different critical and creative contexts from his University days on. His belief that the quintessential defining powers of the theatre should inform all of his plays is another reliable basis on which to base comparative analysis. I shall base my own approach to *Quality Street* (Barrie 1901b; HRC Hanley B; ADD 1902/27N) on these principles. At the centre of the discussion, I shall place three commonplaces of Barrie's art and vision: firstly, the Darwinian battles between the sexes; secondly, the relationship between form and meaning; and thirdly, the naturally histrionic power of the female which gives her (in both Barrie's politics and his metaphysics) creative superiority over the male.

This choice is made partly in the pre-emptive spirit of Barrie's decision to place the Darlings' home in Bloomsbury. There are, of course, many other ways in which the play can be interpreted some of which do not depend on awareness of Barrie's evidence on his own behalf. In the "exemplary" context proposed for this chapter I have simply opted to highlight how those views can provide one valuable critical perspective from which to see behind the blinds of *Quality Street*.

2. Dramatic Romance: Miss Phoebe as Histrionic Heroine

If the obvious character and story alterations raise these questions, the structure chosen to convey them goes a long way to solving them. At the end of Chapter Six, *The Wedding Guest* was seen to anticipate Barrie's first successful use of the Shakespearean Romance form as a vehicle for conveying those unique views on life and art which defined his imaginative world. But it is in *Quality Street* that this structure (so highly valued by Masson) is first successfully adapted to these wide-ranging themes. In terms of balance and counter-balance, it is the form's clarity which controls the allegorical complexity of that world. It allows a clear definition of the chosen themes in the opening acts, uses Act III to develop them imaginatively before returning finally to re-consider them. The validity of this claim can be established by following that thematic signing system through the play.

It is in Act II, that Phoebe sums up the difficulties faced by talented women in a paternalistic society:

PHOEBE: Susan, I am tired of being ladylike. I am a young woman still and to be ladylike is not enough. I wish to be thoughtless, bright and merry. It is every woman's birthright to be petted and admired! I wish to be petted and admired. Was I born to be confined within these four walls? Are they the world, Susan, or is there anything beyond them? I want to know (II: 299).

In the double fantasy world of Act III, where she "becomes" at once her niece and, fancifully, Cinderella at her ball, she finds the freedom to express all those ideas of woman's natural superiority over man which Barrie's earlier heroines have variously exemplified. In the part Phoebe has created for herself she can accuse the young males of triviality. She can for example castigate her ex-pupil, Ensign Blades, who now fancies himself in love with this old maid turned flirtatious vamp: "Tis such as you with your foolish flirting ways, that confuse the minds of women and make us try to be as silly as themselves" (317). Of the older if not wiser Valentine Brown, she sadly reports to her sister that in her guise as her own niece Livvy she exposed his triviality in no time at all:

PHOEBE: To weary of Phoebe – patient, ladylike Phoebe – the Phoebe whom I have lost – to turn from her with a "Bah, you make me old," and become in a night enamoured of such a thing as this. (III. 313)

Quality Street in its domestic and social context could be seen as a dramatic vehicle for all those warnings Barrie had delivered in the *Nottingham Journal* about the coming of a new age when women would at last escape from male imprisonment and realise their greater potential.

Here are all the reasons for having the younger, more dynamic sister revived for the play. Miss Ailie's "long thin romance" had little of the heroic within it. Indeed, its ordinariness largely defined it. Barrie wished now to return to the same themes from the heroic, Napoleonic point of view and for that, a resourceful, courageous heroine was needed. Miss Phoebe is clearly that woman. First of all, she sees herself in that light:

PHOEBE (*more firmly*). A woman must never tell. You went away to the great battles. I was left to fight a little one. Women have a flag to fly, Mr Brown as well as men, and old maids have a flag as well as women. I tried to keep mine flying. (IV:328)

Secondly, as the Act II quotation makes clear, she does so as a "histrionic sentimentalist". Quality Street prevents her inborn right to express *all* the personalities within her and so she effectively writes her own play, gives herself the starring role and achieves all her ends. Later Wendy will do the narrative equivalent when she "tells" her way into the Never Land and re-tells her way out of it. Miss Phoebe might, however claim superiority here. Wendy may tell the story of Cinderella to the lost boys, Miss Phoebe re-enacts it.

3. Dramatic Idealism: Miss Phoebe as Exemplary Heroine

If the romance form offers clear guidance as to why the heroine *has to be* heroic Miss Phoebe, rather than ordinary Miss Susan, those who read the play in the *drame du fauteuil* form of the Collected and Definitive editions are told that any of the other spinsters could just as well have been chosen. These are the kind of *versi strani* which obviously challenge the reader (specifically in this case) to find some way of reconciling the two positions.

In this opening explanation Barrie also stresses the anonymous nature of the street and the shared gentility of its inhabitants. The governing topic of the play will also be "general" – the fate of all "nice, genteel" woman condemned to live in a male society, which calls imprisonment, protection. As in *Sentimental Tommy* it is this claim which specifically ushers in the pre-emptive demonstration of authorial power, "There seems no sufficient reason why we should choose Miss Phoebe as our heroine rather than anyone of the others. But we gave her the name and so we must support our choice" (I: 275).[1]

The practical reason for this statement is obvious. Barrie is enacting those views on drama's impersonal bias which he had recently expressed to Violet Vanbrugh. The key variation here is his removal of the prose action from an imaginative re-creation of the real school he attended in Thrums to Quality Street as the dramatic type of any small town. The opening stage directions only define the street itself. The title defines the "type" of people within it and it is against this anonymous, humourised background, that Phoebe (and what Barrie will make of Phoebe) becomes an authorial *fiat*, preceding the play's "inky" birth.

---

[1] The association between naming and power was observed by Frazer in *The Golden Bough* and its consequences more fully enacted in Peter's power over Hook. The fact that Barrie has changed the original name is also "powerfully" significant.

The ultimate resolution to this problem of Phoebe as at once "necessary" and "accidental" choice has already been implicitly explained. Beyond time, the author has freedom of choice; within time he is constrained by the need to make her at once dramatically sympathetic and the best possible model for the ideas he seeks to represent. That Barrie meets this exemplary challenge can be illustrated in the final cameo. There we find the conventional happy ending in marriage – "Dear Phoebe Throssel. Will you be Phoebe Brown?" True, it has been presented as a pragmatic victory cum escape route for Phoebe rather than a passionate meeting of equally talented partners. Nonetheless the two are reconciled and Phoebe escapes from the street into the world outside to participate in those battles of life for which her courageous character is especially suited. That is her real success.

Barrie's great success lies in his showing Miss Susan about to depart at the end of the play but having Phoebe prevent her. Susan, too, must be part of their marriage, she tells Valentine, "Oh, sir, Susan also. [He kisses Susan also; and here we bid them goodbye]" (IV: 339). The "exemplary" logic behind this is clear. In giving renewed life to Miss Kitty as Miss Phoebe, Barrie does not reject Miss Ailie's qualities in the novel. Miss Susan comprehends them and in so doing becomes the voice of the silent, still imprisoned majority within that anonymously universal street. This is conveyed in a number of ways. Miss Susan, like Miss Ailie before her, has known romance. Indeed she might have been a subject for Tommy's book on unrequited love. Her experiences are not therefore totally different from her sister's. Inveterate spinsters such as Miss Willoughby are there to mirror *that* condition while younger girls such as Harriet and Charlotte flit in optimistically with the same hopes as the others once shared (III: 126). Whether they too will prove powerless within the grip of Quality Street depends in large measure on the heroism of those of their sex who have the will to escape. Miss Phoebe has shown that determination. But she and her "vehicle" (Valentine) are not the whole story and so should not take the curtain alone.

If the extremes of female potential come together in Phoebe, Miss Susan has shared her hopes and in that way some of the themes which Miss Ailie represented in the Tommy novels, are plausibly taken up again in the drama. One example of this is Grizel's discovery that women can only find fulfilment in the purity of their own love for inadequate manhood. One of the most powerful illustrations of this thesis in the novel was Miss Ailie's long romance for the untalented Ivie McLean. Translated on stage, this becomes a much clearer, more melodramatic situation. The name Valentine Brown announces the failed romantic man just as clearly as "Quality Street" announces the arena for battle. What Susan's history has already revealed about men, Phoebe's "play" ruthlessly enacts. Although they learn the same lesson, however, they interpret it differently. Grizel forgives and retreats to the margins of domestic life; Phoebe pragmatically accepts Brown's failings – "he has taken from me the one great glory that is a woman's life. Not a man's love – she can do without that – But her own sweet love for him" – remains the independent basis on which the New Woman founds her cause because it makes man ultimately irrelevant (III: 313).

4. Dramatic Warfare: Miss Phoebe as Warrior Heroine

Entry into this "new" world is not difficult so long as one remembers the central criteria behind the romance form as defined by both Masson and his student. The new world Barrie is examining is the world of 1902. But the Napoleonic setting of the play removes the action to the early 1800s and an enclosed small town environment. But this was precisely why the Romance form was so highly valued by Masson. It is also why one should not "ask a dull historian" about Barrie's methods. Like Shakespeare, he uses the distancing power of time to simplify the issues of to-day by imagining them happening yesterday. The economic strategies used to represent yet control that range have already been described. First, his histrionic heroine is one who can inhabit all of these worlds in her own imagination. Nor is it the historical Napoleon who defines the outside world. Rather one changeable vision is presented within another. For it is the already firmly established Napoleon of the Barrie myth, admired and deplored simultaneously, who offers another set of artificially controlled but varied perspectives for fanciful contemplation.

These techniques have been illustrated on the lower layers of the word-building. The relationship between structure and meaning, the chosen forms of characterisation and the theme of woman's subsidiary position in society have all been described in a way which highlights the author's control over his material. That he is, as promised, using the dramatic form to minimise the particular, the personal and the real has also been demonstrated. In this way he has been able to universalise even the social and political levels at which the drama primarily operates. The persuasive focus is on the plight of Victorian women but the earlier setting reveals that the war of the sexes is fought out in different ways from age to age.

But if he *is* following these methods one would expect him to meet two other challenges. The first of these is novelty. How does this dramatic world differ from his other explorations of the battle between the sexes? And how does he deal with the spiritual, metaphysical and even metanarrational areas of enquiry which have recently been annexed into his world?

The social foundation for this transition has been securely established and has itself entered a "new world" – that of warfare. Within that world Miss Phoebe's claims to be a martial heroine have been outlined. In her smaller world she has the same potential as Carlyle's Napoleon – that of the will to power which, single-handed, can lead to revolutionary change. That "story" ends happily. She may have to make accommodations. For instance she hast to sacrifice the passionate love she longs for:

PHOEBE: (To Valentine) I should love, sir, to inspire frenzy in the breast of the male. (II: 304).

Mr Brown, that "very average man" is, after all, no Valentine. On his own evidence, he offered her an "affection" which was "too placid to be love" (III: 321, 319). Escape from Quality Street is, however, the defined end of the social as well as the personal and political games and that she attains.

The novelty of *Quality Street* as a variation on Barrie's "creative" worlds is in fact both obvious and daring. All his earlier explorations of the theme have been "doubtful" in the sense that they evoke the differences between the will to power and the will to serve without specifically relating them to the doctrines whose different metaphysical accounts of the world are the source of that uncertainty. Even *The Little Minister* had approached the oppositions between Christianity and Nature/Paganism in broad and general terms. Phoebe Throssel, as modern Christian heroine, enters the doctrinal battle head on. Neither she nor the play itself will claim to resolve the Christian-Darwinian dilemma but she and her "niece" do refine the questions raised for those who believe both visions.

Barrie's rhetorical training had taught him to sign the "sentence" initially and so it is proper to look at that evidence first. Once Phoebe has been firmly established within *Quality Street*, she and the other spinsters come directly into contact with the outside world for the first time. The silent cameo which marks this has all of them on their knees trying to listen for the recruiting officer. That manly representative of the battles of life in their most obvious form sees them in that position, laughs and pretends to re-enter. Only Miss Phoebe is brave enough to face him and the first thing she does is make him conform to the clean, neat life of the street, by making him stand on a newspaper.

In the following dialogue, two strains intertwine. The first confirms the gap between the Christian codes of the street and the cruel world of conflict outside. Ignorance and, at times, a wilful retreat into comforting beliefs characterises Phoebe's role. As spokesperson for the street, she is the ignorant voice of protected, female gentility. As the only one who dares face the sergeant, however, her first question marks an intense desire to know what lies beyond:

PHOEBE: (*forgetting to be angry*) Sergeant, have you killed people?
SERGEANT: Dozens, ma'am, dozens. (I: 279).

It is this mixture between her lightly veiled desire to grind England's foes into the ground and the kind of unexamined, Christian fundamentalism which comes from living in a totally cut off world which provides the play with its first comic highlight but also vividly enacts the distance she has to travel to escape from her own intellectual and spiritual confusion:

PHOEBE: Oh, sir, I pray every night that the Lord in his loving-kindness will root the enemy up. Is it true that the Corsican Ogre eats babies?
SERGEANT: I have spoken with them as have seen him do it, ma'am.
PHOEBE: The Man of Sin. (I: 279)

This is Barrie at his best. Already he is anticipating the many-faceted mind of his "innocent" heroine by having it voice two extremes – Christian virtues and bloodthirsty imaginings – in a supposedly logical argument! That is, the comedy anticipates the new kind of heroine presented as well as the themes to be explored. Phoebe may hate Napoleon as the man of sin but she longs for the martial life which defines his genius. This is underlined by her immediate jump from Napoleon as shadow of the devil to Napoleon as military genius:

PHOEBE: The Man of Sin. Have you ever seen a vivandiere, sir? (*Wistfully*) I have sometimes wished there were vivandieres in the British Army. (*For a moment she sees herself as one*) Oh, Sergeant, a shudder goes through me when I see you in the streets enticing those poor young men.

The vivandieres were the women who accompanied the French army, selling provisions and liquors to the soldiers. Phoebe therefore lands herself in another unacknowledged piece of self-contradiction by showing her own desire to be in the battle and then criticising the sergeant for recruiting men to the same cause. He proves himself a better reader of personalities:

SERGEANT: If you were one of them, ma'am, and death or glory was the call, you would take the shilling. (I: 280)

What nearly stops Phoebe going through the Christian ceremony of marriage at the end of the play is also of importance. She has accepted Brown's inadequacies so that is not the problem. It is her extreme rejection, as "aunt", of all the self-determining values which made her "niece" so powerful a critic of men which threatens to prevent the union. Conscious that she has deceived people she laments, "We shall never be able to esteem ourselves again". It is, once more, Miss Susan who chides her for an exaggerated response, as futile as it is inappropriate – "Phoebe, if you have such remorse you will weep yourself to death" (IV: 145).

At this level of reference Miss Phoebe's demand that her sister be present in the final cameo signs the crucial role she has played as wise moral guide. Dramatically, it shows that some lessons have been learned in the imaginative world of Act Three. Development of the thoughtful Christian position rather than a return to old values is, in true Shakespearean fashion, the "end" of the play's spiritual as well as its social quest.

As sources (the origins of literature) have particular importance for Barrie's study of origins in life and art, it is appropriate to complete this section by suggesting that *Quality Street* may mark a new influence on Barrie's philosophical views at this time. In *The Road to the Never Land*, I noted that Barrie was writing *Quality Street* at the same time as Nietzsche's works were becoming known in Britain (see Jack 1991: 89–95; 2010: 85–97). As neither Barrie nor his critics mention the German philosopher when dealing with the play, one must be cautious in advancing the case for Barrie as Nietzschean. But it still seems unlikely that the Scottish dramatist, given his respected position among the *literati* not to mention his avid reading of journals, could have been unaware of the more radical attack on Christianity advanced by the German philosopher. Barrie's interest in and understanding of Darwin as revealed in this study could be said to strengthen that view as Nietzsche accepted so many of the opinions expressed in *The Origin of the Species* that some philosophers accused him of plagiarism.

What cannot be denied is that a more radical view of Christianity's subservience is mirrored in *Quality Street* and that the major new ideas within it conform with those lines of Nietzschean thought which caused controversy in Britain at the turn of the century. Initially in the kneeling scene, the doctrine's subservience is visually represented. Throughout the play, the opposition between the will to personal power and the passive values imposed by faith is dramatised with the spotlight moving searchingly from the personal implications of that tension to their social, moral and metaphysical equivalents. The last action of the play then focuses on conscience's power to make cowards of us all.

This is of course not the first time that an "obvious" source is practically ignored in Barrie criticism. Ibsen may not be an exact comparative analogy as he disappears from the critical consciousness only after "Ibsen's Ghost" had established that Barrie had read his work. But the key to *why* his later, more serious influence on *Tommy and Grizel* went unnoticed may well be the same which still keeps comparative consideration of even Nietzsche's most notorious views beyond the limits of Barrie criticism. If one starts from the assumption that *Quality Street* is a light, fantastic play "which is as far divorced from reality as this one", then the placing of it in the Napoleonic period will be welcomed on the same surface level – "The use of costumes, minuets, and furnishings of the period [become] a good show in themselves" (*Scholastic* 1937: 30: 21). This comment relates to the 1937 film version of the play which is, itself, a sentimentalised version of the original. As such it is the fulfilment of the "light" view, which denies all the signs of deeper meaning discussed above. That Ibsen or Nietzsche might have a role to play in a modernist reconstruction of *The Tempest* is an acceptable premise. That they are at all relevant to a pretty comedy set in a visually intriguing period is not. That the play may be both; attracting light minds comically and visually but challenging others to see behind the mirth to the tragic story which *Quality Street* obliquely tells is seldom contemplated. Yet that is the model Barrie advocated for himself. And according to it the major new ideas advanced in this – the earliest play he accepted for the *Collected Edition* – are in line with *The Gay Science* as well as *The Origin of Species*.

Yet this last scenario is the one Barrie has consistently painted for himself. It seems therefore safe to assume that he had at least a generally informed knowledge of the extremes to which Nietzsche had taken the ideas of Darwin (not to mention La Rochefoucauld and Paul Rée) and that they are absorbed into *Quality Street*.

5. Artistic Origins: The Sources of *Quality Street*

Barrie's achievement in *Quality Street* should not be underestimated. The basic techniques described above will soon be adopted and adapted in *The Admirable Crichton* and *Peter Pan*. There, further variations on the enduring themes of battle and creativity will be explored in the same economical way. For *Quality Street*, however, one final economy and one final level of reference remain open for consideration. Does the play use those quintessentially theatrical skills which Barrie had placed at the centre of critical vision and in this way call attention to the medium as well as the method in the manner anticipated in *The Wedding Guest*?

This development has been recently detected in one of the play's major sources, *Tommy and Grizel*. Its basic principle of emphasising the particular strengths of a given mode entered Barrie's thinking much earlier. The necessary link between human and verbal battles was regularly stressed by Darwin himself. Citing Max Müller in *The Descent of Man*, he makes the parallel in explicitly selective terms:

A struggle for life is constantly going on among the words and grammatical forms in each language, the better, the shorter, the easier forms are constantly gaining the upper hand, and they owe their success to their own inherent virtue. [...] The survival or preservation of certain favoured words in the struggle for existence in natural selection. (Darwin 1871: 91)

The biological organisation of Peter Roget's *Thesaurus* also encouraged this link as did Barrie's own mythological presentation of artistic as well as natural battles. In tracing the gradual advancement of that mythology a consideration of the sources of *Quality Street* is therefore called for.

There is one last justification for proceeding in this way. As George Shepperson points out both Roget and Darwin attended Edinburgh University. Roget continued his biological studies there and from these the human patterning of the *Thesaurus*. Darwin, for his part, entered a Scottish University at a time when the Scottish philosophical school was at the heights of its power. In describing its influence on Darwin's mode of thinking, Shepperson returns to John Millar's *Origin of the Distinction of Ranks* in 1711 and Lord Monboddo's *On the Origin and Progress of Language* (1773–92) to demonstrate the climate of thought which led to *The Origin of the Species* (Shepperson 1961: 23). It was that tradition which Barrie inherited as Shepperson's description of its distinctive features underlines. When he writes, that "The Scottish school's search for origins and its use of the comparative methodology" especially characterise it, he could be describing exactly the mythical methodology followed by Barrie. Here too the logic implies a return to sources and theatricality in a comparative context.

A beginning in certainties and the Definitive text can be established simply by "seeing" the stage directions as the curtain rises on Act One. Following Campbell Fraser's philosophical account of the primacy of sight among the means of perception, Barrie had always given that sense primacy among the defining qualities of the theatrical experience. In the extended stage directions offered in the *drame du fauteuil* texts of 1942, every possible aid is given to the reader who is anxious to understand the silent message of the opening. And what we see is the visual equivalent of the enclosed, protected, neatly unnatural world which subsequent events will dramatise. Only obliquely, through the bowed window at the back of the patterned blue and white room, can you see the outside world. Within it too the problems of the genteel, passive woman are already signed. Some of the spinsters, having lost hope of marriage, have their hair covered in a cap. The younger more optimistic ones (significantly a minority in the group revealed) still wear their hair loose, as a sign that hope is not yet dead.

Sounds then support sight. We hear the bell ring as the recruiting sergeant enters the street. We share their oblique view of him as he passes. That this is an imagined world, created by Barrie, is also voiced in the Stage Direction. The sergeant, we are told, passes before us for a purpose, "To remind us that we are in the period of the Napoleonic wars" (Barrie 1942: 275).

The connections between *The Wedding Guest* and *Quality Street* continue throughout the play and were widely recognised in Barrie's day. Visual symbolism was the major feature detected in both with the use of the "hair" motif and Susan's wedding dress accepted as signs of Barrie's theatrical prowess. This is entirely fair as the final cameo illustrates. That Phoebe as Miss Livvy wore her elder sister's wedding dress at the ball and had no time to change it in Act Four, is of crucial importance here, as it means that she takes her bow wearing the sign of Susan's failure to escape spinsterhood.

The importance of this cameo on all other levels of reference has already been examined (see Chapter 5). Phoebe has won her way out of Quality Street by embracing the will to power in all its singleminded selfishness. Only that imitation of the "ogre" Napoleon has allowed Christian marriage to be the sacramental end of her romance. Yet that romance in itself has not been particularly romantic. Indeed, as Phoebe's commanding of Valentine Brown to include Susan conveys, it has ironically highlighted the waste of potential implied in subjugating the sex with the greater power for Darwinian advance. And Susan's presence in its turn reminds us that the particular "happy" ending we are watching is not the message of the play. The fate of all women of quality in Victorian England is the topic and there, at the end as at the beginning, Miss Susan's bonnet remains the fate of most.

It is fitting, then, that the many different "endings" of this highly theatrical drama include one which has the heroine in her own Cinderella play act herself out of the doom awaiting the other spinsters in Barrie's version of the drama. It is here too that the wedding dress has a crucial part to play. It has fittingly been passed on by Margaret and Mrs Ommaney as a central symbol in their play so that Phoebe and Susan may give it the same significant attention within a different kind of conflict. For, as we watch Phoebe's "joy", it is not only Susan's presence, but the pathetic story of her failed romance of which we are reminded.

A fuller discussion of the theatricality of *Quality Street* is provided in *The Road to the Never Land* (see Jack 1991: 78–88; 2010: 75–85). In the present context, I am concerned with the need to "connect" at all times when studying Barrie's major plays and therefore my study of the play's origins will relate it comparatively to its most immediate sources, *The Wedding Guest* and the Tommy novels as well as tracing its own generative path from the earliest surviving texts to the Definitive Edition.

The first failure to link occurs in the most obvious comparative context of all. When relating *Quality Street* to its major dramatic predecessor the influence of Ibsen is accepted and used to account for those symbols and images which carry over from *The Wedding Guest*. What is not understood is why the poetic and mythic side to Ibsen attracted Barrie and differentiated his use of the Norwegian writer from Shaw's more obvious annexation of his sociological views.

The situation with *Sentimental Tommy* is different. Here, the presence of a plot line which obviously leads to *Quality Street* over-rides the normal, genre-specific approach so that even those, like Archer, who usually confine themselves to stage criticism have also to remind themselves of the "book" as well when assessing Phoebe Throssel's tale. From this prose perspective, no connections with Ibsen are made as none have been identified. There is also considerable hesitation in following Barrie's looser vocal approach and looking at the prose evidence theatrically.

This is particularly unfortunate as the earlier story of Miss Ailie and Miss Kitty is already full of those visual signs and poetic associations which equip it more fully for the stage than any of the other romances in the novel. Here already are the bonnet and the ringlets, the images of birds and gardens and the setting of the blue and white room, all of which invite theatrical development. Barrie has, therefore, made an intelligent choice when deciding to develop the potential of this sub-plot rather than dramatising the central romance as he had done for *The Little Minister*. And in its turn it is this "comparative" reluctance which permits the continuation of the simplified critical myth that *Quality Street* begins the neat, if despairing, change from prose to drama. In fact it presents another variation on the process of modal translation which has characterised Barrie's apprenticeship and will reach its zenith of ambitiousness in *Peter Pan*.

If one, then, returns to the earliest texts (HRC Hanley B; ADD 1902/27N) in order to discover how this latest prose dramatisation developed, one need go no further than the title and the names of the major characters to see that the implications of an essentially poetic and theatrical re-presentation have already been thought through. In Hanley B, the title is *Phoebe's Garden* and although this was dropped, that metaphor was consistently emphasised at subsequent revision stages. Indeed, it is fair to say that in a work, which has fewer revisions than usual, it attracts more attention than any other image or symbol. Its symbolic potential is obvious and develops as the plot unfolds. In Act One it associates her with innocence, constancy and modesty via daisy, hyacinth and violet. As sheltered garden, admired but unvisited, it nicely mirrors the sheltered gentility of Quality Street and its inhabitants. Latterly, when romantic tragedy seems inevitable it can be "destroyed". A comparison between the earlier and later texts in this context reveals Barrie's skill as reviser of his own work. In the Lord Chamberlain's text the garden vies poetically with another protective image:

VALENTINE: Never!
PHOEBE: That casket which contains all the admirable qualities that go to the making of a perfect female.
VALENTINE: It is what she is.
PHOEBE: That garden – (ADD 1902/27N)

In the Definitive text, the intruding casket has been removed and only the garden remains:

VALENTINE: Never!
PHOEBE: That garden –
VALENTINE: Miss Livvy, for shame.
PHOEBE: Your garden has been destroyed, sir; the weeds have entered it, and all the flowers are choked. (Barrie 1942: 323)

The value of looking at the evolution of Barrie's play texts has been discussed before. Essentially, the earlier texts offer a clearer statement of the ideas behind the work. The subsequent team-readings then move ever closer to indirect enactment. What distinguishes *Quality*

Street from most of its predecessors is the speed with which these corrections are made. Again this suggests a more than usually clear initial idea of the techniques required to convert an already theatrical prose story for the stage.

Barrie's confidence has been illustrated in the way in which he quickly chooses which symbols to highlight and which to abandon. The same selective principles can be detected in the number of overly explicit speeches he cuts. It may help the critic to learn from the characters themselves that Valentine is meant to be "a dull man", that the wedding gown and Miss Susan's sad history signs man's frailty in preferring pretty women and that religion in particular is being challenged (Hanley B: 12, ADD: 18, Hanley B Bright text III) but, as Phoebe reminds us in another deleted dialogue, "I fear we have already said more than is seemly" (Hanley B: 12).

This movement from the directness of the earlier texts to the poetic enactment of the later versions undoubtedly improves *Quality Street* as a work of art but this should not detract from the evidence these revisions provide for the critic. Even Barrie's toning down of his drama helps to confirm the all-important idea of Phoebe as a martial hero, whose will to power draws her as close to Napoleon as her Christian morality distances her from him. To delete the additional comparison between her and Julius Caesar in the later texts may be sensible but that parallel shows a desire to associate her bravery, within the Romance form, with the nine worthies of Romance specifically. The practical danger of incongruity leading to audience mirth was avoided but the idea behind Caesar's conclusion cannot entirely be erased.

The change of names is also significant. By re-naming the Kitty of *Sentimental Tommy* "Phoebe Throssel", Barrie provides his histrionic heroine with a surname associating her with the song thrush, a plain bird with an inspiring song. Her first name, however, has as wide a range of possible meanings as its bearer has potentialities towards heroism. Most pertinently this woman of change is named after the moon, the goddess of change. Mythologically, she bears the name of a number of goddesses and heroines. She is also identified with Artemis and with Helen of Troy's sister, the daughter of Leda. Even more significantly Phoebe is one of names given to the moon, the planet of change. Biblically, Phoebe also has a presence as a Christian warrior, being one of the Corinthian women mentioned by

Paul in First Corinthians, while in one of the play's formal models, *As You Like It*, Phoebe is the name of a shepherdess. Poetically the basic bird image permits development of the spinsters caught in the net of the world. Nominally, it provides as varied a range of models as Phoebe's different roles demand.

Introductions to *Peter Pan*

Peter Pan is the other Edwardian play most clearly anticipated by the plays and novels which mark the end of Barrie's Victorian apprenticeship. This comparative evidence offers one reason for considering it. Another comparative context further authorizes the choice. The myth of the little boy who will not grow up also recalls and develops upon the themes and forms of *Quality Street* and *The Admirable Crichton*. In accordance with Barrie's overlapping planning methods, therefore, both earlier and future contexts warrant consideration of the different literary manifestations of Pan and in particular the play which made him famous.

1. The Fairy Notes

To control the focus of analysis I shall confine myself to the different kinds of opening and introduction Barrie offers for this, his most extended examination of the mystery of the origins of creation. Clearly the most obvious of these Introductions in literary terms are Barrie's Notebooks

These are surprisingly seldom examined in detail in biographical accounts of *Peter Pan* (BVS P45). That surprise increases when one learns that there are more notes dedicated to it than any other work by Barrie. Indeed there is a separate manuscript entitled "Fairy Notes" whose 466 entries, all relate to the play. In those he is not the only pagan god to be considered. Cupids precede him:

2) Cupids teaching girl to fly away.
and remain his countertypes for some time:
51) Cupids shooting arrows into Prince.
204) Cupids bring back children (BVS P45.1903.)

In this plan the cupids represent the mischievous but "good" female face of life and love while the Peter Pan who emerges from Kensington Gardens is their malevolent male equivalent. In Notes 19 and 20, for example, Pan is thought of as a "sprite [...] enveigling children away from nanny [...] whom all mothers fear because of his drawing away of children". At this time, an even more serious moral opposition threatens to enter. In this, Pan's devilish nature is underlined. In Note 106 he is a demon, in Note 268 a usurper and as late as Note 347 he falls into pride the sin of the devil. Before this, another important change has occurred, however. This permits Pan to retain some of his sins, notably pride, but at once excludes the Cupids and gives the goat-god the right to be a more ambiguous personality, including virtues as well vices as elements in his ever changing personality.

The Pan of the early notes is specifically the god described by Sir Francis Bacon in his *Wisdom of the Ancients and New Atlantis*. That book, studied in an earlier edition at Edinburgh, had been reprinted in 1886 as part of a revived interest in the Renaissance philosopher caused by his anticipation of Darwinian ideas. In it, Pan moves from the dark side of love to become an embodiment of all natural forces:

Pan, as his name imports, represents and lays open the ALL of things, or Nature. Concerning his origin, there are only two opinions that go for current: either he came of Mercury, that is the word of God [...] or else from the confused seed of things [...] But as touching the third conceit of Pan's origins, it points to the state of the world not considered of Adam, exposed and made subject to death and corruption. (Bacon 1886: VI. 36)

And, as pointed out earlier, it is on this broad nominal base – Peter Pan, as eternal boy whose name associates the apostolic father of the church with a god of Nature – that this childish view of origins is centred.

Mythological concepts have, therefore, a major part to play in the earliest formulation of the play. The ultimate, ambiguous identity of Pan comes from a book Barrie studied by a Renaissance philosopher whose views on personality and Darwin had renewed his reputation in late Victorian England. To concentrate on imagined links between author and Pan without confronting this material is to do an injustice to both. After all, without awareness of Pan's mythic definition as a god of Nature who is going to see that the alliance with Peter, the apostolic founder of the Christian Church, is another of Barrie's nominal signs.

2. The Dedication

Another "sign" of the birth-creativity theme of Pan is the introduction to the play he wrote for the Collected Edition of 1928. It took the form of "A Dedication" to the lost boys and re-appeared fourteen years later in the Definitive Edition. I have cited the earlier text in this section because of the different organisations of the two editions. The 1942 edition adopts a chronological order and starts with *Walker, London.* By that time, Barrie was dead. The *Collected Edition*, over which he lavished so much time and effort makes an exception in the time line for *Peter Pan* and so the Dedication opens that volume as a specific guide to the artistry of Pan but also as a general introduction to all that follows.

The Dedication, then, represents Barrie at the age of 68 commentating on the play. His ostensible audience, as for *Peter Pan*, is a group of children. Throughout, he does exactly what he did in the play, maintain a consistent line of apparently naïve, confessional and jocular communication with the Llewelyn Davies boys. As so often happens, therefore, he is the one who provides biographers with the material on which their views of personality are based. But how does one read this account?

Not naively, that is clear. Those who remember *The Greenwood Hat*, written only two years later, will recall his confession there that facts remembered across the years are, by definition, already fanciful (Barrie 1930c: 5). Those who have looked at the photograph album of the boys playing with him on Black Lake Island will have further grounds for reaching out for a pinch of salt. That volume he will advance as major evidence for remembering the games accurately. Yet, clearly, he does not remember the text very well himself. Certainly his description of the different Chapters suggest that there is much more written material than does exist in the slim album. On the other hand, critics in the Oedipal school would do well to pay more attention to what he does remember factually of the photographs themselves. Blacked up as Captain Swarthy the oldest player would seem to become Jas. Hook in those games and not Pan.

Even the childishly confidential tone is suspect. The lost boys are
no longer children and so the medium of the Dedication is only imaginatively appropriate. Nor are children the economic group proposed
for an expensive anthology of his dramas. Yet, if anyone is adept at
suiting story to audience, it is Barrie. In his speeches for example, the
ideas for his best plays, the emergence of his most famous characters
or the true source of his modest greatness will change depending on
where he is and whom he is addressing. The Dedication translates this
movable principle into what might be called "An Address to the
Theatrically Knowledgeable as designed to make them buy this book".
What he gives the playing public is surface confirmation of the autobiographical story which now defines the play. The games with the
young boys which led to divorce and tragedy are imaginatively re-
instated by their author in a manner which would make any popular
journalist happy.

But the subversive techniques of the Imp also make an early
appearance and these can be revived by first of all re-instating the full
title:

TO THE FIVE

A DEDICATION

The relative size of the fonts suggest that the boys are the main people
to be honoured when in fact Barrie's skills as a playwright will be the
real focus for praise. The boys are also the main characters in the
opening paragraph. But already, and at the same time, Barrie is establishing the themes of the play. This is his usual practice following the
conventional rhetorical topoi for the opening. These principles have
been so thoroughly confirmed in the earlier study, that a critical
approach which starts with those expectations is now justified. On
these grounds, we would anticipate an opening which dealt with origins in a manner which included artistic as well as natural "birth".
More particularly, given Barrie's known views, the "birth" of a play
would involve teamwork.

And a discussion of authorship is precisely what does begin the
essay. Barrie's opening admission that he may not have written the
play at all allows successive attributions to be made. Perhaps one of
the lost boys wrote the play – "Any one of you five brothers wrote the
play […] I would not fight you for it" (Barrie 1928: 5). Perhaps the

man in overalls who watched it sadly and left without word was the disappointed author since "This hopelessness of his is what all dramatists are said to feel at such times" (6). Other, more tangential, possibilities are suggested. These including the "man in the pit" who so enjoyed the play that he had to be taken away in hysterics (5). The method is accretive. None of these proposed authors are rejected but Barrie does finally claim superiority on his own *primus inter pares* model for successful teamwork in the theatre – "Notwithstanding other possibilities, I think I wrote Peter and if so it must have been in the usual inky way" (6). In this way, the older Barrie confirms a fiction, which he had been keen to encourage when the play was first produced. Indeed the first night programmes offered an emblem of this inclusive, creative view of the birth of a play. At the head of the cast list he is named the author. But at the foot another bracketed attribution appears. There, Ela Q May, is also named, "the author of the play". In this way participants in the game, the audience and the actors are all given due recognition while the playwright only finally claims control for himself, "Notwithstanding other possibilities, I think I wrote Peter" (6).

Of course, origins on their own are not the subject of *Pan*. The romance structure of the play meant that the "games" of birth in Act I were necessarily followed by the copulation and death games of Act II and III. The reason advanced for this was that the question of human birth implied a mirroring of the entire process from birth to death. Barrie himself accounted for his many revisions of the ending in this fashion.

Again, expectations are exactly fulfilled. In the Dedication, he takes "the boys" forward in his life and theirs while philosophising on whether any amount of aging can change our personalities:

Some say that we are different people at different periods of our life, changing not through effort of will, which is a brave affair but in the easy course of nature every ten years or so. I suppose this theory might explain my present trouble, but I don't hold with it. I think one remains the same person throughout, merely passing, as it were, in these lapses of time from one room to another, but all in the same house. (6)

The fact that he is here re-opening the subject of one of his last plays (*Dear Brutus*) in order to explain one of his early dramatic Romances is in itself interesting. The way in which he does this is equally important as it confirms the themes and variations view of his life and

art. His own essential nature has not changed, only the rooms of life
he inhabits. Analogically, one might argue that, so far at least, he
looks out from one literary house (in terms of preferred forms, techniques and topics) on a world, whose major issues, though personally
defined, do not essentially alter. As different modal viewings permit
him to see through different windows, however, each new "room"
produces a unique vision and a unique work of art.

If one again works backwards from expectation to evidence, adequate proof in this area would demand explicit mirroring of Barrie's
own literary and especially dramatic "origins" to run parallel with the
account of his life and the development of *Peter Pan*. As this question
only emerges at the virtuosic edges of the model proposed for Barrie's
"world", confirmation that this evidence is clearly present would be
particularly significant.

And the signs *are* there. Not only does Barrie look backwards
from 1928 by referring to his latest full length plays at that date –
Dear Brutus and Mary Rose are both recalled (15) – he specifically
introduces a discussion on his first ever play, *Bandalero the Bandit* as
well as the first play to launch him on his London career, "Ibsen's
Ghost" (4–5). For good measure, his acting at Black Lake Island is
earlier contextualised in memories of Dumfries and Toole. And, as
The Era critic recognises, the play throughout overtly imitates the
style and character of its author's earliest reading, having "peopled his
newest fantasy with the choicest personages from the pages of
Marryat or Fenimore Cooper along with the heroes of our youth" (30
December 1904: 17).

But there does seem to be an important gap. At the defining
centre of Barrie's metaphysical vision stands the sexual battle. While
Pan has enough battles to please even the most bloodthirsty child or
the most enthusiastic Darwinian, the key to originality of vision is his
belief that woman with her "Russian Doll mind" is by nature more
adaptable than man and therefore will in future lead the evolutionary
ascent.

To argue this way is to leave out Wendy. As Barrie explains, this
would partly be his fault for he has literally held back the entry of the
girl whose "romantic mind was like the tiny boxes, one within the
other, that come from the puzzling east" (Barrie 1911: 1). "Wendy",
he tells us, "has not yet appeared", because although "she has been
trying to come in" he has resisted her power for as long as he could.

The images he uses to describe her entry are overtly male – "Perhaps she would have bored her way in" to the all-male games anyway (13). If her entry into this text – for of course she does not enter the games – is apologetically presented, her first victory in the wars of the play is heralded by a challenge to his readers. They will probably think that "Peter did not really bring her to the Never Land of his free will but merely pretended to do so because she would not stay away" (13). If one takes up this challenge and re-reads the departure scene at the end of Act One, it becomes clear that Peter is throughout manipulated. He would have been happy to return on his own having learned the end of the Cinderella story. It is Wendy, who first of all guarantees her own passage – "Don't go Peter. I know lots of stories. The stories I could tell the boys!" (I: 34). She then appeals to his male pride, praises his flying and so gains entry for her brothers as well.

In short, Barrie has admitted at once the masculine creative power of Wendy, "boring her way in", and turned his readers' attention to a passage in the play which enacts her darker manipulative powers. Already her natural superiority over the "men" in the scene has been narrated and dramatised. But that is not all. As part of an introduction to a specifically natural *and artistic* creativity myth, she has proved her superiority in specifically authorial terms. If she *had* bored her way into the games, we are told, she would have been the masculine force, the active catalyst, the "disturbing element" necessary to bring comfortable male role-playing dramatically alive. Significantly, she doesn't need to win that victory in real play, because the fictional play establishes these powers at the outset, as those who follow Barrie's advice and refresh their minds by re-checking at the flight scene will have *her* creative superiority confirmed. For if Barrie writes the story, Wendy is at once the story-teller within that story (she literally tells her way into and out of the Never Land) and she adds the dynamism needed to turn both tales into drama.

All of the essential principles of the Barrie myth have been anticipated. To suggest that even Wendy is outdone ultimately by Barrie might seem one step too far in the direction of critical ingenuity when discussing most authors. In Barrie's case, I think it is implied by the evidence. "Notwithstanding other possibilities" he created Wendy and has just "childishly" manipulated the play's theatrical history in order to defend the major principles behind his dramatic art. If the

Dedication is anything to go by this will be another play which will mean a good deal more than it says.

3. Formal Signs and Cowley's Low Road to Genius

Barrie's critical views have underlined the need for at least two levels of artistry to be addressed by the writer as well as his audiences. Biographically, it was Cowley's polarised account of the low and high ways to genius which initiated this kind of thinking. Masson's account of Greek rhetorical persuasion refined it, gave classical names to the divisions and taught how they might best be employed. As has been stated and tested for Barrie before the classical "rule" that *sensus* (sense) and s*ententia* (meaning) signed separate layers of the text was basic to his thinking. The pragmatic consequence that the orator should at once gain his audience's attention by using "sense" to anticipate "sentence" has also been followed by Barrie in both the novels and the plays of his apprenticeship. It is sensible, therefore, to begin a search for formal signs in this way.

Cowley begins at the audience reception "end" of the Aristotelian line when he says that the would-be genius must be able, simultaneously, to persuade popular and learned audiences. Topical and formal implications follow. Universal themes as well as transitory ones have to be addressed and a dual form is therefore called for.

That Barrie began from these principles and did so with his future reputation in mind has been exhaustively confirmed. Three questions follow. Firstly, what are the two, *formulated* logics which lie behind *Peter Pan*? Secondly, do they confirm the unchanging expectation for invention and therefore novelty in uniqueness? Thirdly, do they continue the referential and technical advances traced in his late Victorian works?

One only needs to describe the story line to give a positive answer to the second enquiry. Barrie has chosen a new mode and proposed a new audience. For the first time, he will write a pantomime and try to satisfy a primarily youthful audience. The route he has taken towards this decision has in part been traced already. In 1900, *The Greedy Dwarf* may have been a private production in the mode of the "immoral fable" but it ran parallel in time to the *Black Lake Island* games. But 1990 also saw him visit the Vaudeville where, every

Christmas, a children's play was performed. Seymour Hicks and Ellaline Terriss that year starred in a particularly attractive production. *Bluebell in Fairyland* was a musical play with a strong cast and authorial team. The book was written by Hicks himself , the lyrics were by Aubrey Hopwood and Charles H. Taylor and the music by the highly regarded Walter Slaughter. It tells of a little girl who is transported into fairyland where she goes on a search for the Sleeping King in order to restore him to his throne. Barrie was greatly impressed. At the same time this positive answer does not augur so well when its role as vehicle for those "heavy" themes outlined in question three is contemplated. To use the simple vision of the child as a means of conveying his, by now highly complex, artistic vision seems, even in a period when his radicalism is at its strongest, a strange choice.

Barrie does not always write Impishly of course and it might be, despite the subversive evidence of the Dedication, that *Peter Pan* was only intended as a pantomime in the spirit of its predecessors, the harlequinade and the *commedia dell arte*. Another description, this time of the draft he presented to London producers, is enough to provide the answer to at least one part of that hypothesis. For the script he produced was unconventional in the extreme. London managers were offered a cast list of fifty, twenty of whom had speaking parts. That outlay had to be justified by the success of a play which, contained:

A combination of circus and extravaganza; a play in which children flew in and out of rooms, crocodiles swallowed alarm-clocks, a man exchanged place with his dog in its kennel, and various other seemingly absurd and ridiculous things happened (Frohman 1916: 362).

This quotation comes from the biography of Charles Frohman, the man who *did* take a chance on the play, when at least one London impresario (Beerbohm Tree) thought the leading popular playwright had tipped over from eccentricity into madness (Jack 1991: 155–58; 2010: 151–54). At least four refused the strange hybrid despite the fact that it was being offered by the Andrew Lloyd Webber of the Edwardian West End.

There are a number of points raised by this evidence in the immediate formal context of the present argument. Those who have lamented Barrie's inability to sustain stories might see *Peter Pan* as an extreme example of this failing as it moves attention quickly from one unexpected spectacle to another. In the Never Land, one moment we are with the last boys, the next assaulted by pirates, the next waylaid by mermaids. Even the Darling household is defined by extraordinary and sudden changes of vision. In Act One, application of Shakespearean Romance conventions would lead one to expect a securely realistic setting, as in *Quality Street* or *The Admirable Crichton*. But when the curtain rises on this Bloomsbury nursery, this respectable room reveals a child-servant, a dog-nanny and a melodramatically eccentric father. Even its setting is artificial – Barrie places it there, according to the *drame du fauteuil* text because he uses Roget's Thesaurus and Roget lived there when studying at Edinburgh University. Already, the origins of communication are being related to what looks like being an unreal experience from start to finish.

Apply Barrie's own belief in the defining power of mode and it becomes clear that we are here concerned with a formal variation for a different primary audience. Critics correctly praised him for providing a form which catered to a child's short attention span. That realisation in turn strengthens the hypothesis that *Pan* might be an exception to the formal duality which elsewhere he adopts. It is not only the unusual mode which makes this idea persuasive. It is also the way in which he brings the childish spectacle of *Peter Pan* alive. The late apprenticeship period is a time when Barrie is pushing his artistic skills to the limit. One of the areas in which he has consistently tested out extremes has been that of theatrical effects. This tendency is itself based on and justified by his critical belief that quintessentially theatrical qualities do exist and should be especially highlighted. And that, following the extraordinary demands he had made on the stage crew in *The Admirable Crichton*, is what he provided in *Pan*.

His determination to pursue his own ends is well illustrated in the earlier play. The stage crew had protested and the carpenters actually went on strike before *The Admirable Crichton* opened (Jack 1991: 104–7; 2010: 102–5). One might, therefore, have expected an author who respected teamwork to shrink away from *this* extreme. Yet, in *Pan*, his demands are even greater. Characters must fly "invisibly", huge animals must strut the stage, Tinker Bell will be a creation of stage effects alone, sudden changes of costume will demand a stage double for Peter and covering action until he return – the list is so long that the properties script looks like a book in itself! No wonder a work which is now part of theatrical convention, in its own day, seemed too demanding to perform.

4. Formal Signs and Cowley's High Road to Genius

This argument could be applied to the next formal question. The possibility that *Pan* might be an exception to the "rule" that Barrie always works on two levels arose from an awareness of the vast gap between a drama designed to please children and the complexity, at this time, of the mythic world he sought to address. That contention can, of course, be turned on its head. What greater artistic challenge is there than to please children through the language of the senses while addressing the ultimate questions of life?

In fact, I believe, Barrie did even more than this. He brought together the pantomime mode and that of Shakespearean Romance in such a way that both the most naïve and the most sensitive levels of his audience would be satisfied each at its own level of "talented" appreciation. That is, in the manner advised by Scholastic humanism. That both audiences should be challenged in a troublesome way was also part of the original plan, with children scared witless by Hook and adults troubled by the dark world vision presented. So why and how did he hope to achieve this?

Barrie's approach to literature, following Masson's guidelines, usually begins with a clear choice of mode. In the case of *Pan*, the imitation of this method critically has helped to explain the nature of the children's story in itself *and* as a vehicle for exploring adult themes. An adaptation of the Shakespearean Romance form of *The Tempest* and *The Winter's Tale* has, on similar guidelines, been chosen to convey the "message" or "messages" of the Pan myth. The Dedication, in confirming the principles of development-in-complexity traced in the present study, has introduced problems as well. Put simply, both commentaries, suggest that *Pan* should continue to relate its author's basic Darwinian, feminist myth simultaneously to the question of origins naturally, artistically and metanarrationally. That this formulation of critical expectations is justified is signed in two ways. First, it has emerged in *Tommy and Grizel*, *The Wedding Guest* and *Little Mary* and so is part of a continuous line of development. Secondly, all versions of the play, from the Lilly Manuscript onwards define that question in the opening Act. (cf. Jack 1990; 1994).

Both enquiries begin with a re-consideration of the romance form. As the discussion of *Mary Rose* illustrated, Barrie took the basic logic of the Romance form and adapted it to the specific demands made by his chosen topic. One of the most obvious of these adaptations, noted in *Mary Rose* itself, applied to those dramatic enquiries which went beyond time into the mysteries surrounding human life. Thus, if all Barrie's dramatic romances, are based on the simple pattern

Enactment in domestic setting of question to be examined >
Fantastic setting and imaginative exploration of that question >
Open-ended re-consideration of that question

then these two plays alone need some form of structural extension to mark their mystic dimension. The study of the new woman in *Quality Street*, the debate between hierarchy and democracy in *The Admirable Crichton*, even the question of free will raised in *Dear Brutus* have their own unique formations but only *Peter Pan* and *Mary Rose* need to re-enter the never lands of doubt.

In *Mary Rose*, an additional time dimension opens the play. An ambiguous return to it marks the fall of the final curtain. The different texts of *Pan* offer an earlier variation on that pattern, in acknowledgement of the ultimate concerns about the human condition which they reflect. While the meetings of the ghostly Mary and her "lost son" son surround the basic pattern, in *Pan*, it is the dream extension to Act 5 and the different versions of Wendy's return to the Never Land which enact the mystery of its message.

The early invasion of the fantasy world into the Darling household, justified in comic terms and the children's division of the audience, can now be explained in adult, thematic terms as well. This has, confessedly, to be claimed in the face of widespread critical puzzlement. G.K. Chesterton's reaction may be taken as an example of this. He finds it – "to be inartistic, strictly speaking, that the domestic foreground should be almost as fantastic as the fairy background" (Chesterton 1920: 106).

Chesterton is an astute critic but surely he has forgotten the "first" childish audience for the play. It is this audience's attention which had to be gained quickly for the reasons discussed above. Having a fantastic reality greet them the moment the curtain rose served this purpose well. At the same time, the idea that fact and fantasy are always together in our perception of the world is consistent with another of Barrie's favoured beliefs. Derived from Campbell

Fraser's lectures, sustained in his own critical essays and later re-stressed in *The Greenwood Hat*, it is here enacted in a way which underlines the "perceptive" claims made by Berkeley. Moreover, the specific fantasies represented – the father-child and adult role-playing children under the control of a dog – are suitable vehicles for introducing those Darwinian ideas which have turned the adult world upside down in the same "disturbing" way.

There are therefore two major variations to the broad structural pattern of *Reality > Fantasy > Reality revisited* adopted for *Quality Street* and *The Admirable Crichton*. First, we are presented with different shades of fantasy, stronger in the central Never Land section (Barrie 1942: Acts 2 > 5.1) but present in the Nursery scenes which surround that country (Act 1; Act 5.2). Act 5.2, for its part, then merges into the timeless Never Land at a later, human date. These alterations are necessitated by the audience and the eternal themes of the play. They, therefore, appear at all stages of the play's evolution although in markedly varied forms from the Lilly MS until the Definitive edition.

The first of these helpful signs is provided by the extended presentation of the "Sententia" across three acts for the reason advanced in the Dedication. It is the whole process – birth, copulation and death – which has to be enacted. The first three acts mirror this, for what we actually *see*, act by act, are childhood (though not childish) visions of each:

ACT ONE: Birth (Barrie 1942: 506–7)
ACT TWO: Copulation (Barrie 1942: 530–36)
ACT THREE: Death (Barrie 1942: 544–45)

If the opening to Act 1 shows the Darling children giving birth to and withholding birth from each other, most of Act 2 follows the mythological promise of the *Fairy Notes* in mimicking love and reproduction. There, the Cupids are seen to shoot arrows at male as well as female characters ("Cupids shoot arrows into prince" n.51). The result is the blindness of sexual passion ("Cupids playing blind man's buff" n.134). In the revised version this becomes Wendy's flight over the Never Land and Tootles' shooting her down with an arrow under the false impression that she is a bird. The building of a womb-house around her follows. From this she exits, ready to play the mother's part:

OMNES: What we need is a just a nice motherly person.
WENDY: Oh dear, I feel that is just exactly what I am. (535)

This not only enacts the effect of Cupid's arrows in an innocent, de-sexualised manner, it also offers an extreme example of love's blindness. The lost boys are ignorant of their own identity as well as the facts of life. This form of impotence is nominally highlighted as in the Tommy novels. Thus Slightly is so called because he was found in a pinafore, labeled "Slightly Soiled" while the boy who most confidently claims to know his nominal identity – "It's [S]mee'!" is singled out by Peter as the one who actually knows least about himself.

The principle of overlapping is also particularly obvious here. The Act 2 "game of sex" derives from a discussion of birth and identity, which leads to Tootles shooting down the "White Bird" which brings babies (not mothers!) in the avian terms of Kensington Gardens. It also anticipates the "game of death" at the end of Act 3. This is done via the idea of sex as a "little death" popularised by Renaissance lyricists. Peter first announces that Wendy is dead and then changes his mind when Curly counters that only flowers die. From then on the game is to nurse her back to motherhood:

PETER: Great news, boys, I have brought at last a mother for you all. (531).

If the game of birth opens Act 1 and the games of sex begin and end Act 2, the game of death provides the final action for Act 3. Wendy and Peter are stranded on the lagoon. The waters rise up and will soon drown them. This is one of Barrie's most effective pre-curtain cameos. True to his belief that the aural and visual potential of the theatre should be fully realised, he provides detailed directions for the sound and lighting effects which will accompany this moment of crisis. These are developed in the extended, descriptively poetic manner chosen for the *readers* of the Collected and Definitive Editions:

(The waters are lapping over the rock now, and PETER knows that it will soon be submerged. Pale rays of light mingle with the moving clouds, and from the coral grottoes is to be heard a sound, at once the most musical and the most melancholy in the Never Land, the mermaids calling to the moon to rise. PETER is afraid at last. And a tremor runs through him, like a shudder passing over the lagoon; but on the lagoon one shudder follows another till there are hundreds of them, and he feels just the one.) (544)

That we are back in the playground of Tommy Sandys can easily be established. Sandys "wrote" his Jacobean scripts with one principle in mind. He had at all times to be the hero. Unlikely or even impossible changes of the story line were made when a new way of enacting his own wonderfulness occurred. So, it is no surprise to find Peter casting himself in the melodramatic, self-sacrificial role earlier inhabited by Dow in *The Little Minister*.

Wendy rather upsets things by wishing to match his courage:

WENDY: I won't go without you. Let us draw lots as to which of us is to be left behind
PETER: And you a lady, never! (III: 544)

After Wendy has used the one kite they possess to escape from death, Peter melodramatically proclaims that he will await death happily. In fact, having ended that self-glorification with a particularly good line – "To die will be an awfully big adventure" – he changes from stoic hero within a tale of death to intrepid adventurer within an escape drama! The change is marked visually as the blind, which has been used to give a misty appearance to the preceding action, now rises. The moon lightens the stage and hero-Peter, far from waiting, bravely saves himself by commandeering a bird's nest. He takes off his shirt and exits, "naked and victorious".

This is "playing" at death in a variety of ways and in a variety of roles. As inveterate child-actor, Peter has moved from the part of cavalier hero to stoic hero and adventurer hero in about five minutes of acting time. The subtler sense in which he is asking for participation in an essentially fraudulent play of death, has to be deduced by the audience. The readers of the anthology collections have, for once, the advantage. In an explanation masquerading as a stage direction, Barrie reminds them that Pan is weightless and so does not need a kite to escape. In making that knowledge Wendy's and placing it before the heroic death dramas begin, he makes her own, apparently courageous, utterance another example of that complicity in supporting Peter's exaggerated self-image which is the only real "law" on his Island.

5. The Manuscript

Another, usually obvious, point of origin is the earliest manuscript or printed text (Greene 1994; Jack 1990). As we have seen, for his most mysterious play, Barrie has himself clouded the issue both in the dedication and the programme. Interestingly, the obligatory copy for the Lord Chamberlain is also missing from British Library collection. Its disappearance must have post-dated R.L. Greene's consultation of it in 1954. While this is regrettable there is a compensatory sense that this *ought* to be, given Barrie's fanciful appeal that this is a play about origins whose own origins are in doubt.

As a result Jacqueline Rose believed the earliest texts were the draft typescripts held in BVS: P1904/5. But the Lilly Library in the University of Indiana, does hold the *Peter Pan* manuscript. It is dated 1903 on the first folio and 1904 on the last. The personal dedication given by the author is as follows – "To Maude Adams. This the MS of *Peter Pan* from her humble and affectionate friend. J.M. Barrie. Nov. 23. 1903."

In the study of Barrie's apprentice works, generative comparison has usually proved valuable as the original ideas behind play or novel are often more clearly expressed in the earlier evidence. Alternatively, changes in direction or emphasis may be reliably traced in this way. In fact, *Peter Pan*, will offer one important example of each. It will also reinforce the need for canonical thoroughness in the Edwardian, as in the Victorian, period.

The dramatic history of the play also makes it particularly difficult to avoid comparisons of this sort. Barrie significantly underestimated the acting time of his play. The extreme stress he had placed on visual cameos and stage effects were doubtless at the root of this error. The Lilly manuscript does not look longer than most of his playscripts. But most don't have flying scenes, a series of battles, seventy actors and a musical score. A number of scenes had to be cut after this was revealed. The nature of those cuts can best be assessed by introducing the original form of the play. In the manuscript there are seven scenes. Their titles and ordering are as follows:

1: The Night Nursery; 2–4: Adventures in the Never Land; 5: The Night Nursery; 6: Kensington Gardens and Harlequinade; 7: Night Nursery and Never Land.

Clearly, the most obvious difference from his earlier uses of the Shakespearean romance form lies in Scene Six where the title suggests a return to the world of *The Little White Bird*. Its action, some of which survived until the first performance or even later, has now been entirely excised. As that scene also provided the clearest evidence of Barrie's examining the medium of the play, it will be necessary to look at in detail. Before doing this, it is important to realise that even with those excisions his interest in these problems remains clear in all of the later texts.

That full canonical attention is needed is also illustrated here as the major dramatic grounds for believing these questions to be uppermost in his mind are to be discovered in both *The Admiral Crichton* (Jack 1991: 114–25; 2010: 111–21) and, more particularly, Pan's immediate predecessor *Little Mary*. In my own assessment of that "Riddle-Play", I concluded that "dramatic communication" was its major theme and Shakespeare's *Much Ado about Nothing* and *Measure for Measure* the major literary vehicles for adding this sixth line of enquiry to the quintessential form implied by its alchemist source and his triune resolution of the world's problems in a book, three in one (Jack 1991: 141–54; 2010: 138–50).

Deprived of these overtly metadramatic scenes how are the different kinds of communication enacted in later versions of the play? The range of primitive communication forms are the most obvious signs of this interest. Tom-toms, smoke signals, the crocodile clock, the fairy language as well as the songs of birds and mermaids are all shown to be part of a constant battle for power. By imitation or manipulation, the pirates can frighten or defeat the Indians. But in the same way Wendy can make Peter think a kiss is an acorn, or Peter draw Hook's essence from him by calling him a codfish.

In the battles which confirm Wendy's superiority over Peter and Peter's over Hook, each occupies a different "literary" position. It is as a story-teller but also as the catalyst of action, that Wendy deviously tells her way into the Never Land along with her brothers. It is as devious and egoistic storyteller that she tells her way out of it. Having at last decided that Peter is not a father figure she reminds the boys of her mother's misery at their absence. Moved, they agree to go. Yet Wendy has always known that her mother was suffering and arouses the boy's maternal memories when she is ready to go. Peter, whose failure as a father figure has produced her decision is the actor-director on the island, while Hook is only one of his creations. That is why the pirate throws himself into the mouth of the crocodile only when Peter has lost interest in him. Unimagined he does not exist. At the same time it is he, as orator and soliloquiser who reminds us of many of the literary sources for the play and of Shakespeare in particular.

The most refined code of all is language and this is the play whose domestic god is Roget. So, fittingly, language's vast powers in ultimate inadequacy are signed in the theatre before the curtain goes up. Indeed, the message *is* the curtain. It had the form of a giant sampler. At the top were the letters of the alphabet; at the centre the author's gratitude was expressed to Hans Christian Andersen, Charles Lamb, Robert Louis Stevenson and Lewis Carroll; at the foot there was a picture of children triumphantly carrying off pirates. The origins of writing, the sources of inspiration and the visual medium of the theatre literally faced the audience.

So what *was* excluded and why does it remain relevant when an introduction to language, to sources and theatrical potential is already up on the curtain and will be thoroughly presented in the play? The first answer is that the most extreme translations of the pantomime into its dramatic origins are contained in Scene 6. In the manuscript and earliest texts of Pan, Hook survives as a teacher, Mr. Pilkington. In that role, he seeks to draw Peter as spirit of light and youth into the "shades of the prison house". To escape, however, Peter turns into the clown figure of the harlequinade. Tinker Bell also helps him to outwit the pirates by making the lost boys and Darling children also look like clowns. When Hook-Pilkington (he is still "bearded and blackavised") seizes one of them and tears off the clown make-up only to reveal John or Tootles he knows defeat. Only then, without (or more precisely forgotten by) his creator, does Pan give himself despairingly to the crocodile and death.

The ideas of Pan as clown and harlequin were both anticipated in the Fairy Notes (e.g. "Note 198. Children having origins in Harlequin (Peter), clown, columbine, girl"). That they also appear in the earliest texts means that they were integral to Barrie's original plan for the play. Nor did he give these ideas up entirely when time and/or puzzled audience reaction dictated their excision. Both "Pantaloon" and the Harlequin ballet, the next modal translations to follow the full length play in 1905, re-instate the action of Scene Six. Revisions are needed but essentially the clown and the harlequin demit their part in the larger work only to seek public approval on their own merits.

This means that the earliest texts do have an important part to play in the interlinking pattern of development of the Pan idea from *Tommy and Grizel* on. Certainly, the first of these, the Lilly holograph, which still bears the title "*Anon*", has Michael called Alexander and alternates between Tippy and Tippytoe as names for Tinker Bell, gives the clearest possible evidence of the Darwinian battle between the sexes as originally conceived.

Those who see the play in a modern production are faced with Wendy's superiority over Pan as woman and as storyteller. That line, which analogically reduces both the poor father (Mr. Darling) and artistic pirate (*Jas.* Hook) to the lowest level of power is consistent with the "Swarthy" role played by Barrie on Black Lake Island *and* the earlier, devastatingly negative, view of that other failed father-artist, Tommy Sandys. If one starts from the supposition that Barrie's "perceived" role in life is as would-be author and failed father some of the questions surrounding the doubling of Hook with Mr Darling are solved. One of these concerns the nature of the sexual debate and the relative dramatic importance of pirate and father.

Its evolution begins with Scene Five of the manuscript. In the early versions of that Scene, Mr. Darling has a much larger part to play. Barrie had hired twenty actresses to welcome the lost boys and become their "mothers". This scene was still part of the opening performance. Barrie's determination to keep it may have something to do with his essays on the unfair treatment of female actors. But it was laughed off stage as many thought the women resembled a group of courtesans waiting for business. Mr Darling's failure to meet the key demands of storytelling were explicitly raised and enacted in that scene and disappeared along with these "mothers".

WENDY: Father, and why are you in the kennel?
DARLING: It's a long story, Wendy, but –
WENDY: If it's very long father, we'll excuse you telling it, but do come out. (Lilly MS Scene Five)

This is just one symptom of a dramatic reduction in his part. As this went along with an expansion of Hook's role, the balance now favoured the pirate. As this imbalance was later strengthened, critical attention to their shared identity diminished.

The other change of balance concerns the battle between the sexes. In this case, it is Wendy's role which is extended in later revisions. This time the effect is to reduce the original overtly sexual rivalry offered to the maternal Wendy by Tiger Lily and Tinker Bell as types of passion and flirtation respectively. Tiger Lily's speaking part is significantly cut in later versions. The scene in which she offers herself physically to Peter is excised entirely:

TIGER LILY: Suppose Tiger Lily runs into wood – Peter Paleface catch her – what then?
PETER: (bewildered) Paleface can never catch Indian girl, they run so fast.
TIGER LILY: If Peter Paleface chase Tiger Lily – she no run very fast – she tumble in a heap, what then? (Peter puzzled. She addresses Indians.) What then?
ALL INDIANS: She him's squaw. (Lilly MS: Scene Three)

Tinker Bell's use of the fairy language means that her part cannot be verbally diminished. Instead, other characters' references to her tempting appearance (e.g. her revealing negligée) disappear. This dilution of the sexual battle can in part be explained by the feeling, after the first performance, that the adult material was impinging too heavily on what was, primarily, a children's play. But in *all* versions, direct and indirect, the controlling idea that all three illustrate women's natural superiority to man is mirrored. Wendy and Tiger Lily leave him when his inability to make them mothers is revealed. Tinker Bell's needs being non-physical, she can continue to be his companion but one who can *and does* manipulate him.

Wendy's own part was also, originally, more physical. The idea that neither she nor Peter touch each other is a later addition. Indeed in Scene One of the MS, they sit together and Peter rubs her back. Wendy's histrionic identity is also more directly presented in the early texts. In Scene Three, for example, Robert Burns is added to the list of literary echoes which run through the play. In another sequence which is later deleted, she enters into a performance of "John Anderson, my Jo", the Ayrshire poet's sentimental celebration of love enduring into age. Giving herself the part of the aged wife, she asks Peter "I have now passed my best but you don't want to change me do you? We are an old couple now but am I still your jo?" They then sing the song together.

Once more, a study of Barrie's early planning has offered insights into the later development of one of his dramas. As the major changes in *Pan*'s case explored different kinds of medium and recon-figured the sexual conflict which they essentially conveyed in Barrie's mythic world, the value of generic analysis extends even to this, the never-ending play.

6. Actors, Rituals and Endings

The Era critic who recognised that *Peter Pan*'s reliance on the adventure stories which constituted the staple of children's early reading were part of a broader intention to imitate the origins of com-position nonetheless failed to see just how widely that imitation extended. This can be deduced from his puzzlement over one section of the opening production. Regretting the imposition on Gerald du Maurier to imitate the style of famous actors present and past, he admits that the strange interlude was well received on the night: "through all he did and said, he was accompanied by the instant appreciation, the quick perception and the constant laughter of the audience" (*The Era* 31 December 1904: 17). Nonetheless, he is at a loss to explain this eccentricity which he assumes would not have been tolerated, had it not been one of those Barrie *fiats* which occasio-nally transcended his other principle of teamwork. He is probably correct in this and in his insecure feeling about the exercise. Later audiences, less sophisticated than the prestigious group invited to the first night, did not have the compensation of knowing who were being mimicked. And indeed, that passage would soon be excised when it became clear that most adults and practically all children were entirely mystified by it.

The reason for Barrie's strong resistance in this apparently trivial context can be defined more exactly when one remembers two of his key dramatic principles. He sees his plays as specifically and defini-tively a theatrical experience. Given *Peter Pan*'s concentration on origins literary and linguistic, it follows that the origins of the dramatic tradition should be mirrored in performance terms as well as reflecting ancient modes such as the Harlequinade and Punch and Judy. Having Du Maurier imitate a variety of famous acting styles fulfils the need to explore the medium in another way. That would account for Barrie's defence of the mimicking exercise even if he were not still a follower of Berkeley. In that context, one's *perception* of theatrical reality becomes the key issue and that depends on actors' interpretation of their parts. As R. L. Greene illustrates in his full account of the play's production history over the year, the terrifying Hook of Du Maurier bears little resemblance to Alastair Sim's lovable, unthreatening pirate, although both speak the same words.

Barrie *did* have scenes which were authorially incontrovertible because they were so fundamental to his idea of the play. His insistence on Peter returning as Napoleon in Orchardson's painting will be remembered as one such. To have the figure who was a leitmotiv presence in his late Victorian and early Edwardian canon be seen "playing" at power fitted Pan's role perfectly. Orchardson's vision of Napoleon in Portsmouth, strutting the decks after his defeat fulfilled that symbolism exactly. All the staging difficulties this implied – doubling for Peter as he changed costumes and the introduction of additional gymnastic byplay – were necessary so that this exact image may be maintained. The mimicking of acting styles as the performance equivalent of written dramatic sources came into this ideological area and was only withdrawn when it became clear that it was not working at all.

The unique rituals which formed the actors' "Introduction to the Play" remain to be considered. This was a drama which fitted into no known theatrical category. Ostensibly written for children it also addressed final problems. Foreseeably, therefore, its radical form initially divided critics. Their basic question – "Is it genius or madness?" – did at first translate into mixed reviews and mixed audience reception. But after changes were made successive enthusiastic audiences resolved it favourably in the only place Barrie's plays are meant to be judged – the theatre itself. This suggests that the actors had met the unique challenges of the work successfully. And if they hadn't, it certainly wasn't the playwright's fault!

At rehearsals, actors are accustomed to having their own parts contextualised. For *Pan*, the stars of London theatre, including Nina Boucicault, Hilda Trevelyan and Gerald du Maurier were given neither the book of the play nor even those immediately surrounding cues which give some sense to your role in advance. This was because Barrie saw the play as a metaphor for human life. When we mix in company, we have no idea of what other people will say. That was the spirit in which the play had to be acted. Barrie taught it by making them "live" through it. Another associated conception was also explained at the outset. The play must be thought of as running in a constant time continuum, like life itself. When you buy a ticket you gain the right to drop in at a unique point to a unique production. When you leave, the curtain may fall but life in Bloomsbury and the Never Land continues behind it, ready to open itself to public contemplation when the gigantic sampler rises once more.

As a corollary, reflecting perhaps the Darwinian vision of nature red in tooth and claw, a third ritual preceded each year's cast selection. The child actors (including Noel Coward) were literally *measured* for their parts. As Pauline Chase describes it, "Every December a terrifying ceremony takes place before *Peter Pan* is produced, and this is the measuring of the children who play in it. They are measured to see whether they have grown too tall" (Chase 1909: v).

These rituals accurately mirror the range of the play's "message". *Pan* is conceived as the objective corollary in "play" for human life, for its origins, for its continuity in conflict and for those individual passages within it which end in death for everyone except its eponymous hero. That it will, in the parallel world of Ink and the Imp, establish Barrie's own immortality is the second part of that conception. The struggle for creative power between simple man and complex woman has consistently translated the will to power from world to page. Most recently it has moved from nature and page to question, simultaneously, the origins and ends of both worlds .

One last ritual mirrors all three lines of argument. It also returns attention to an important leitmotiv in Barrie criticism. The idea that he could not end his novels or his plays "properly " is repeated from *When A Man's Single* onwards. The criteria on which this judgment is based are, of course, false. Barrie is seeking to be Pirandello rather than Shaw and has to be assessed accordingly. His modernist tendencies have become noticeably stronger in the late Victorian period. The open endings of the first two Edwardian Romances – the ambiguous final cameo in *Quality Street* and Crichton's "waiting" on time as realised in the different accounts of his role he offers at each revival – vividly illustrate that experimentation in that area is particularly important.

The "final" variations within time suited to Crichton as waiter hero and the sociological context of its theme are extended beyond time in *Pan*. The practical outcome again derives from a nice matching of theme to techniques. Once the actors have been taught that the play mirrors life and so should think of every performance as unique, they (and we) ought to see that, strictly, Barrie should come up with seven different endings each week (including two on Saturday). Instead, he chose to sign the principle in pragmatic fashion by making a change for each yearly production. I have myself read twenty three "different" versions of the conclusion although, of course, if Barrie held to his original intention until his death, there must be more.

Barrie in *The House of Fame*

To end this book on questions rather than answers is appropriate. One major premise has been argued throughout – that Barrie at his best is a complex, subversive writer of the sort described in *The Greenwood Hat* and by Walpole in his Introduction to the speeches (Barrie 1930c: 1–9; 1938: vii). In recognition of that, even the sustained argument offered against the media's prevalent beliefs in Barrie's Oedipal personality and literary escapism has been presented in a series of counter-questions – biographical, literary and psychological. While I believe this list to be so long and the evidence so clear that there is practically no likelihood of Blake's criteria being fair nor Margaret Ogilvy being the Oedipal source of all he wrote, that same complexity warns one against absolute conclusions.

In the context of the critical myth, this can be exemplified in two ways. First, the histrionic personality as applied to Barrie comprehends rather than totally rejects those signs of mother love and family loyalty which lie at the roots of the myth. Second, the broadened canonical perspective does not always diminish the validity of elements within that myth. Sometimes, it may give them added importance albeit from a changed perspective. Margaret Ogilvy is a good example of this. From a literary point of view her high standing as Barrie's inspiration seems odd. In maternal terms, after all, it implies confining him to precisely the sentimental and introspective kind of writing which is then used to damn him. Viewed in histrionic terms, however, she retains her folk influence while becoming the positive character model for her son's role-playing personality, and the wide imaginative range it encompasses.

While the questions raised in re-assessing the critical myth were presented in a challenging spirit, those presented in the present chapter derive sympathetically from an understanding of the critical principles behind Barrie's own creative myth-making. Here, the number of interesting leads provided become the equivalent positive "proof" that a radical, modernist approach is the broad critical way forward for understanding Barrie's later drama as well. Narrowly focused lines of approach – "the heroine figure" in *Quality Street* and "Introductions" for *Peter Pan* – were chosen in order to make the test stricter while highlighting the "particularity" of the method. There are as many variations within this "general" route as there are endings to *Peter Pan*.

The last question returns attention to the opening concern with Barrie's critical "fortuna". How *would* a case for genius be mounted on his behalf before a (suitably reformed!) version of Chaucer's *House of Fame*?

The opening argument, following the critical method he had been taught, might define the modal context within which the appeal was being made. His dramas rather than his prose lie at the root of the case. His best prose, for example *Sentimental Tommy*, might offer peripheral support, but even it cannot escape the idiosyncrasies which caused him to abandon that route. Dramatically he makes no claim to be a tragedian. He comes as a comic and satiric writer but one who has the power to make people laugh in every way possible – frivolously, thoughtfully, even as a restraint against their own fear. As comedian and satirist he could also claim to have chosen laughter only after testing himself practically against all other modes, including tragedy

Was he a popular playwright? Statistics including the length of *Walker, London's* first run and the five plays which ran concurrently in the London West End would prove that point empirically. He could also fairly claim to be the most theatrical of playwrights, pushing the definitive resources of the stage to new limits. Thirdly, he merited the status of actors' playwright as accorded to him during his lifetime in recognition of his speedy acceptance that playwriting was different from novel writing. The solitude of the study might create the manuscript but actors, directors and even stage crew might argue proper cases for changing it. Teamwork without demitting overall control had soon became his byword after Toole's "appropriation" of his first play!

Was he a serious playwright? He could begin this contention with his boyhood and Cowley as proof that he knew from his earliest days that the attainment of lasting fame meant addressing *all* levels of intellect by adopting a medium which united the transient and the universal. Only those who read his work on realistic criteria alone could fail to see that it relies on different principles to achieve that end. The real and the ideal must unite imaginatively (as he had been taught) so that particular *and* universal topics may be re-considered potentially rather than actually. The same argument could be extended to counter the "Scottish" question. His muse was not escapist nor treacherous as his journalistic involvement with the problems of to-day and his choice of the Romance form indicate. To write politically against Masson's required background of "Scotch metaphysics" was his highest goal.

The apparent "lightness" of his work could be defended in these terms also. Here was a dramatist whose plays meant more than they appeared to say; might appear comic but feel tragic. Again he had argued for this practice intellectually. In his academic and journalist days he had insisted that a comic author can achieve indirectly the same serious ends as the tragedian. His additional plea, again derived from Masson, that artificial comic types are better vehicles for con-veying ideas and that comedy is therefore more philosophical than tragedy could be a supportive argument, if needed.

And finally, in more senses than one, what the apprenticeship evidence has illustrated is the gradual development in his work of an all-embracing mythic vision of the world. Appropriately centered in the Victorian period on Darwinian doubt it already has defined its own uniqueness as comic-satiric counterpart to that examination of the battle of the sexes being seriously addressed by Ibsen and Strindberg. Barrie's central belief that woman's greater powers of creativity, natural and intellectual were currently held in check by a patriarchal society alone is one of those tenets which is bound to alter as women's cause advances. The "Case is Altered" in *The Admirable Crichton* already bears witness to that. Similarly, while his interest in studying all kinds of heroine remains throughout his life so does his refusal to see them in neat categorical terms alone. As at once individuals dependent on time and as types beyond time they make a dual claim for attention. Thus Little Mary and Leonora in their respective "*Legends*" do represent an extreme contrast between altruistic and self-seeking types of women. But they do so in particular situations in individualised manner against the different social backgrounds of 1903 and 1913 respectively.

The chronological range of the present volume means that it can only authoritatively suggest the general way forward as, self-evidently, the plays on which Barrie's claim to genius rests post-date his apprenticeship. But the fact that Barrie opens his later career with three Romances (*Quality Street, The Admirable Crichton* and *Peter Pan*) and a legend (*Little Mary*) only to end it with another two Romances (*Dear Brutus, Mary Rose*) and a second legend (*The Boy David*) strongly suggests that the principle of themes and variations endured throughout his career. This gives mythic constancy to his world, a constancy which is methodologically mirrored in his retaining the basic tenets of his critical theory as revealed in the present study. It is in this sense that it may claim to have value beyond the Victorian period. Revising our vision of his art it may offer reliable guidance for approaching the major plays also.

Bibliography

1. J.M. Barrie

Major Collections

Printed Texts:
Novels: Unless otherwise stated, citations follow the Uniform Edition (Hodder and Stoughton 1916–37).
Plays: Unless otherwise stated citations follow the Definitive Edition (Hodder and Stoughton 1942).

Citations for MSS and Drafts:
ADD + ref. = Play texts in Lord Chamberlain's Papers, MSS Department British Library
ADV + ref. = Barrie's Notebooks in National Library of Scotland.
BVS + ref. = The Barrie Vault Shelves Collection in the Beinecke Research Library at Yale University
BVS A2 = Barrie's Notebooks
BVS A3 = Barrie's Letters
Earlier MSS and drafts from the Beinecke Vault Shelves collection are designated BVS.
HRC = Humanities Research Centre, University of Texas at Austin.

Other frequently employed references:
NJ + ref. = Barrie's contributions to *Nottingham Journal*
EUC + ref. = *Edinburgh University Calendar*
Letters, Reviews: These have been checked against original sources and are cited thus. For convenience, many may also be consulted in Meynell, V. (ed.) 1942. *The Letters of J.M. Barrie*. London: Peter Davies and in Markgraf, C. 1989. *J.M. Barrie: An Annotated Secondary Bibliography*. Greensboro NC: University of North Carolina Press.

Texts Cited

—. 1878. *Bandalero the Bandit*. Beinecke MS B34.
—. 1878–82. [Barrie's Lecture Notes]. NLS. ADV. MSS 6648–57.
—. 1878–83. EUC [*Edinburgh University Calendar*].
—. 1880. *Bohemia*. Beinecke MS A2/1.
—. 1882–83. EUC(W) [*Calendar of the Edinburgh Association for the University Education of Women*].
—. 1883–84. *NJ* [Contributions to *The Nottingham Journal*].

—. 1883a. *Vagabond Students. Nottingham Journal.*

—. [1883]b. "Tom Nash" [Cited as BVS T63].

—. 1883c. "Caught Napping". *Nottingham Journal* (Supplement). NLS Rb.s 2797.

—. [1884]. "The Rector of Diss" [Cited as BVS S354].

—. 1887a. "Women who Work". BVS W67.

—. 1887b. *Better Dead.* Swan, Sonnenschein and Lowrey.

—. 1888a. "Mr George Meredith: Novels" in *Contemporary Review* 54: 575–86.

—. 1888b. *Auld Licht Idylls.* London: Hodder and Stoughton.

—. 1888c. *When A Man's Single.* London: Hodder and Stoughton.

—. 1889a. *The Superfluous Man* in *The Young Man* 37.

—. 1889b. *An Edinburgh Eleven.* London: Hodder and Stoughton.

—. 1889c *A Window in Thrums.* London: Hodder and Stoughton.

—. 1889d. "Thomas Hardy: The Historian of Wessex" in *Contemporary Review* 56: 57–66.

—. 1890a. *Young Men I have Met* in *The Young Man* 38.

—. 1890b. *My Lady Nicotine.* London: Hodder and Stoughton.

—. 1890c. "Brought back from Elysium" in *Contemporary Review* 57: 206–14.

—. 1891a. with H. Marriott Watson. *Richard Savage.* Privately printed.

—. 1891b. *The Little Minister* [prose]. London: Hodder and Stoughton.

—. 1891c. "Ibsen's Ghost". BVS Ib6 and ADD 53475/L34.

—. 1892. *Walker, London.* London: Hodder and Stoughton

—.1893a. with Conan Doyle. *Jane Annie.* Savoy Script.

—. 1893b. "Becky Sharp". BVS B42, ADD 53528/D.

—. 1893c. "Jane Annie: An Introduction". Savoy Operas. <http://diamond.idbsu.edu/gas/other_savoy/jane_annie.txt> consulted 1997.

—. 1894. *The Professor's Love Story.* Comedy Theatre. London: Hodder and Stoughton.

—. 1895. "A School Revisited" in *The Youth's Companion.* Boston.

—. 1896a. *Margaret Ogilvy.* London: Hodder and Stoughton.

—. 1896b. *Sentimental Tommy.* London: Cassells.

—. 1897. *The Little Minister* [drama]. Haymarket. London: Hodder and Stoughton.

—. 1898. "A Platonic Friendship". ADD 53655/A.

—. 1900a. *The Wedding Guest.* Garrick. London: Hodder and Stoughton.

—. 1900b. *Tommy and Grizel.* London: Cassells.

—. 1901a. *The Boy Castaways of Black Lake Island.* Privately printed.

—. 1901b. *Quality Street.* Toledo, Ohio. London: Hodder and Stoughton.

—. 1901c. *The Greedy Dwarf.* Privately printed.

—. 1902a. *The Little White Bird.* London: Hodder and Stoughton.

—. 1902b. *The Admirable Crichton.* Duke of York's. London: Hodder and Stoughton.

—. 1903. *Little Mary.* Wyndham's. London: Hodder and Stoughton.

—. 1904. *Peter Pan.* Duke of York's. London: Hodder and Stoughton.

—. 1905a. "Pantaloon". Duke of York's. London: Hodder and Stoughton.

—. 1905b. *Alice Sit By The Fire.* Duke of York's. London: Hodder and Stoughton.

—. 1908. *What Every Woman Knows.* Duke of York's. London: Hodder and Stoughton.

—. 1910a. "Old Friends". Duke of York's. London: Hodder and Stoughton.

—. 1910b. "The Twelve Pound Look". Duke of York's. London: Hodder and Stoughton.

—. 1911. *Peter and Wendy*. London: Hodder and Stoughton.

—. 1912. "Rosalind". Duke of York's. London: Hodder and Stoughton.

—. 1913a. "The Will". Duke of York's. London: Hodder and Stoughton.

—. 1913b. *The Adored One (or The Legend of Leonora)*. BVS D913.

—. 1913c. "Half an Hour". London Hippodrome. London: Hodder and Stoughton.

—. 1915. "The New Word". Duke of York's. London: Hodder and Stoughton.

—. 1915a. Rosy Rapture: *The Pride of the Beauty Chorus*. London: French.

—. 1916. *A Kiss for Cinderella*. Wyndham's. London: Hodder and Stoughton.

—. 1917a. "The Old Lady Shows Her Medals". New Theatre. London: Hodder and Stoughton.

—. 1917b. "Seven Women". New Theatre. London: Hodder and Stoughton.

—. 1917c. *Dear Brutus*. Wyndham's London: Hodder and Stoughton.

—. 1920. *Mary Rose*. Haymarket. London: Hodder and Stoughton.

—. 1928. *The Collected Edition of the Plays of J.M. Barrie* London: Hodder and Stoughton.

—. 1930a. *The Entrancing Life*. London: Hodder and Stoughton.

—. 1930b. *The Prose Works of J.M. Barrie*. London: Hodder and Stoughton

—. 1930c. *The Greenwood Hat*. London. Peter Davies.

—. 1932. *Miss Julie Logan*. The London Times (Supplement). *New Theatre*. London: Hodder and Stoughton.

—. 1936. *The Boy David*. King's Theatre, Edinburgh. London: Hodder and Stoughton.

—. 1938. *McConnachie and J.M.B* (ed. Horace Walpole). Edinburgh: Constable.

—. 1942. *The Definitive Edition of the Plays of J.M. Barrie* (ed. A.E. Wilson). London: Hodder and Stoughton.

2. Other referenced work

Agate, James. 1976. *The Selective Ego*. London: Harrap.

Aristotle. 1984. *Complete Works of Aristotle* (ed. Jonathan Barnes). 2 vols. Princeton N.J.: Princeton University Press.

Archer, William. 1893. *The Theatrical World of 1893*. New York: Bloomington.

—. 1923. *The Old Drama and the New*. London: Heinemann.

Armstrong, Karen. 2005. *A Short History of Myth*. Edinburgh: Canongate.

Bakhtin, M.M. 1990. *Art and Answerability*. Austin, Texas: University of Texas Press.

Barker, Arthur. 1884. "Mumu and The Diary of a Superfluous Man" in *The Academy* 25: 453–54.

Barthes, Roland. 1964. *Essais critiques*. Paris: Seuil.

—. 1993. *Mythologies*. London: Vintage.

Binding, Paul. 2006. *With Vine Leaves in her Hair*. Norwich: Norvik.

Birkin, Andrew. 1978. *The Lost Boys Television Scripts*.

—. 1979. *J.M. Barrie and the Lost Boys*. London: Constable.

Beerbohm, Max. 1970. *Last Theatres: 1904–10*. London: Hart-Davis.

Bergson, Henri. 1900. *Le Rire*. La Révue de Paris, 1 février, 15 février, 1 mars.

Boyesen, Hjalmar Hjprth. [1894] 1973. *A Commentary on the Works of Ibsen.* London: Russell and Russell.

Blake, George. 1951. *Barrie and the Kailyard School.* London: Arthur Barker.

Bloomfield, Morton W. 1981. *Allegory, Myth and Symbol.* Boston Mass.: Harvard University Press.

Borger R. and F.C. Cioffi (eds). 1970. "Freud and the Idea of Pseudo-Science". Cambridge: Cambridge University Press.

Brandes, George. 1899. *Henrik Ibsen.* London: Macmillan.

Brown, Ian (ed.) 2006. *The Edinburgh History of Scottish Literature.* 3 vols. Edinburgh: Edinburgh University Press. 2: 331–37.

Caine, Barbara. 1977. *English Feminism 1780–1980.* Oxford: Oxford University Press.

Campbell, Ian. 1981. *Kailyard: A New Assessment.* Edinburgh: Ramsay Head Press.

—. (ed.) 2005. *J.M. Barrie, A Window in Thrums.* Edinburgh: Saltire Society, 2005.

Carlyle, Thomas. 1872. *Critical and Miscellaneous Essays.* 3rd edn. 7 vols. London: Chapman and Hall. II: 1–53.

Carpenter, Humphrey. 1985. *Secret Gardens.* London: Allen and Unwin.

Chalmers, Patrick. 1938. *The Barrie Inspiration* London: Peter Davies.

Chamberlain, John S. 1982: *The Open Vision.* London: Athlone.

Chaney, Lisa. 2005. *Hide and Seek with Angels.* London: Hutchinson.

Chase, Pauline. 1909. *Peter Pan's Postbag.* London: Heinemann.

Chesterton, G.K. 1920. "Barrie as Artist" in *Bookman* 59: 105–106.

Coren, Michael. 1995. *Conan Doyle.* London: Bloomsbury.

Csapa, Eric. 2005. *Theories of Mythology.* Oxford: Blackwell.

Colvin, Sidney (ed.) 2001. *The Letters of Robert Louis Stevenson.* 2vols. London: Methven.

Craig, Cairns. 1996. *Out of History.* Edinburgh: Polygon.

Crawford, Robert. 1992. *Devolving English Literature.* Oxford: Oxford University Press.

Du Maurier, Daphne. 1934. *Gerald.* London. Gollancz.

Daiches, David. 1960. "The Sexless Sentimentalist" in *The Listener* (12 May 1963). 841–43.

Darlington, W.A. 1938. *Barrie.* London: Merit.

Darton, F.J. Harvey. 1929. London: Nisbet and Co.

Darwin, Charles. 1859. *On the Origin of Species by Natural Selection.* London: John Murray.

—. 1871. *The Descent of Man.* London: John Murray.

Davie, George Elder. 1961. *The Democratic Intellect.* Edinburgh: Edinburgh University Press.

Dessaix, Robert. 1980. *Turgenev: The Quest for Truth.* Canberra: Australian National University Press.

Dukes, Ashley. 1923. *The Youngest Drama: Studies of Fifty Dramas.* London: Benn.

Dunbar, Janet. 1970. *J.M. Barrie: The Man Behind the Image.* Boston: Houghton Mifflin.

Egan, Michael. 1972. *Ibsen: The Critical Heritage.* London: Routledge and Kegan Paul.

Eliade, Mircea. 1964. *Myth and Reality.* London: Allen and Unwin.

Eysenck, H. J. 1985. *Decline and Fall of the Freudian Empire.* Harmondsworth: Penguin.

—. and G.D. Wilson. 1973. *The Experimental Study of Freudian Theories.* Methuen: London.

Faivre, Céline Albin. 2010 in *Barrie 2010: A Celebration of the Imagination.* Kirriemuir: Privately Printed.

Foulkes, D. 1982. *Children's Dreams: Longitudinal Studies.* New York: John Wiley.

Fowler, Alastair. 1987. *A History of English Literature.* Oxford: Blackwell.

Fraser, Alexander Campbell (ed.) 1878. *Selections from Berkeley.* 2nd edn. Oxford: Oxford University Press.

Fraser, Morris. 1976. *The Death of Narcissus.* London: Secker and Warburg.

Frazer, Sir James. 1900. *The Golden Bough.* London: Macmillan.

Frohman, Daniel and Isaac Frederick Marcosson. 1916. *Charles Frohman, Manager and Man.* London: The Bodley Head.

Geduld, Harry M. 1971. *James Barrie.* New York: Twayne.

Greene, R.L. 1954. *Fifty Years of Peter Pan.* London: Peter Davies.

Gregoire, Alan and John P. Pryor. 1993. *Impotence: an integrated approach to clinical practice.* Edinburgh: Churchill Livingstone.

Griffin, Penny. 1979. "The First Performance of Ibsen's Ghost" in *Theatre Notebook* 33: 30–37.

Gudgeon, Piers. 2008. *Captivated.* London: Chatto and Windus.

Hall, C.S. 1953. *The Meaning of Dreams.* New York: Harper.

Hamilton, F.S. 1920. *The Days before Yesterday.* New York: George Doran.

Hammerton, J.A. 1929. *Barrie: the Story of a Genius.* London: Sampson Low, Marston and Co.

Harker, Joseph. 1924. *Studio and Stage.* London: Ernest Benn.

Hartnell, Phyllis. 1968. *A Concise History of the Theatre.* London: Thames and Hudson.

Harvie, Christopher. 1990. "The Barrie who never grew up: An apology for *The Little Minister*" in *Studies in Scottish Fiction: Nineteenth Century* (ed. Drescher, Horst W. and Joachim Shwend). Peter Lang: Frankfurt am Main. 318–27.

Hekma, Gert. 1994. "A Female Soul in a Male Body: Sexual Inversion as Gender Inversion in Nineteenth-Century Sexology" in Herdt, Gilbert (ed.) *Third Sex, Third Gender: Beyond Sexual Dimorphism in Culture and History.* New York: Zone.

Hamilton, Frederick Spencer. 1920. *The Days before Yesterday.* New York: George Doarn.

Henderson, T.F. 1910. *Scottish Vernacular Literature: A Succinct History.* Edinburgh: J. Grant.

Hollindale, Peter (ed.) 1995. *J.M. Barrie: Peter Pan and other Plays.* Oxford: Oxford University Press.

Holtan, Orley I. 1974. *Mythic Patterns in Ibsen's Last Plays* Minneapolis: University of Minnesota Press

Howe, P.P. 1913. *Dramatic Portraits.* London. Martin Secker.

Hugh of St Victor. 1961. *Didascalicon.* trans. Jerome Taylor. New York: Columbia University Press.

Jack, Isla. L.1998. *Positioning the Author: Four Writers in the Field of Cultural Production.* Ph.D. Thesis: Edinburgh.

—. 1999. "J.M. Barrie, New Journalism and 'Ndintpile Pont'" in *Scottish Literary Journal* 26: 62–76.

Jack, R.D.S. 1985: "The Land of Myth and Faery: J.M. Barrie's dramatic version of The Little Minister" in *Scotia* 9: 1–16.

—. 1987a: "Barrie as Journeyman Dramatist: A Study of *Walker, London*" in *Studies in Scottish Literature* 12: 60–77.

—. 1987b: "From Novel to Drama: J.M. Barrie's *Quality Street*" in *Scottish Literary Journal* 14(2): 48–61.

—. 1990. "The First MS of *Peter Pan*" in *Children's Literature* 18: 101–13.

—. 1991. *The Road to the Never Land*. Aberdeen: Aberdeen University Press; reprinted 2010 Glasgow: Humming Earth.

—. 1992a. "The Hunt for Mrs Lapraik" in *Yale Gazette* 67(1–2): 47–57

—. 1992b. "Art, Nature and Thrums" in *Literatur im Kontext* (ed. Joachim Schwend). Peter Lang: Frankfurt. 155–64.

—. 1993. "James Barrie and the Napoleonic Heroine" in *Carlyle Annual* 13: 60–76.

—. 1994a. "Peter Pan as Darwinian Creation Myth" in *Literature and Theology*, 8(2): 155–73.

—. 1994b. "J.M. Barrie's 'The House of Fear'" in *Studies in Scottish Literature* 27: 1–46.

—. 1995. "Barrie and the Extreme Heroine" in *Gendering the Nation* (ed. Christopher Whyte). Edinburgh: Edinburgh University Press. 137–67.

—. 2002. "From Drama to Silent Film: The Case of Sir James Barrie" in *International Journal of Scottish Theatre* 2(2): 1–17.

—. 2003: "James Barrie as Academic: 'Tom Nash' and 'The Rector of Diss'" in *Swansea Review* 20: 1–22.

—. 2006: "J.M. Barrie" in *The Edinburgh History of Scottish Literature*. 3 vols. (ed. Ian Brown et al). Edinburgh: Edinburgh University Press. 2: 331–37.

Johnson, Brian. 1974. *The Ibsen Cycle*. Boston, Mass.: Twayne.

Jonson, Ben. 1985. *Ben Jonson* (ed. Ian Donaldson). Oxford: Oxford University Press.

Karpe, M. 1955. "The Origins of Pan" in *Psychoanalytic Review* 43: 104–10.

Kagan Kans, Eva. 1975. *Hamlet and Don Quixote: Turgenev's Ambivalent Vision*. Mouton: The Hague, Paris.

Kaye-Smith, Sheila. 1920. "J.M. Barrie, the tragedian" in *The Bookman* 59 (Christmas Supplement): 106–10.

Kline, P. 1973. *Fact and Fantasy in Freudian Theory*. London: Methuen.

Knowles, Thomas D. 1983. *Ideology, Art and* Commerce: *Aspects of Literary Sociology in the Late Victorian Scottish Kailyard*. Gothenberg: Gothenberg University Press.

Levin, Iu. D. 1995. "Turgenev, Shakespeare and Hamletism" in *Ivan Turgenev and Britain* (ed. Patrick Waddington). Oxford: Berg. 163–72.

Leneman, Leah 1991: *A Guid Cause: The Women's Suffrage Movement in Scotland*. Aberdeen: Aberdeen University Press.

Levine, Philippa. 1994. *Victorian Feminism 1850–1900*. Gainesville.: Florida University Press.

Lloyd, J.A.T. 1942. *Ivan Turgenev*. London: Robert Hale.

Love, Harold. 2002. *Attributing Authorship: An Introduction*. Cambridge: Cambridge University Press.

MacDiarmid, Hugh. 1943. *Lucky Poet*. London: Methuen.

—. [1926] 1987. *A Drunk Man Looks at the Thistle* (ed. Kenneth Buthlay). Harmondsworth: Penguin.

Mackail, Denis. 1941. *The Story of J.M.B.* London: Peter Davies.

McClure, J. Derrick. 1995. *Scots and its Literature.* Amsterdam: John Benjamins.

Markgraf, Carl. 1989. *J.M. Barrie: An Annotated Secondary Bibliography.* Greensboro, N.C.: University of North Carolina Press.

Masson, David. 1856. *Essays Biographical and Critical.* Cambridge: Macmillan.

—.1859. *British Novelists and their Style.* Cambridge: MacMillan.

—. 1865. *Recent British Philosophy.* London: MacMillan.

—. 1873. *Drummond of Hawthornden.* London. MacMillan.

—. 1914. *Shakespeare Personally* (ed. Rosemary Masson). London: Smith and Elder.

May, Keith. 1985. *Ibsen and Shaw.* London: Macmillan.

Masters, W.H. and V.E. Johnson. 1966. *Human Sexual Response.* Boston: Little Brown.

McFarlane, James (ed.) 1994. *Henrik Ibsen: The Major Plays.* Oxford: Oxford University Press.

Meisel, Frederick L. 1977. "The Myth of *Pan*" in *The Psychological Study of the Child*: 32: 545–64.

Meyer, Catherine (ed.) 2005. *Le livre noir de la psychanalyse.* Paris: Arenes.

Millar, J.H. 1903. *A Literary History of Scotland.* London: T. Fisher Unwin.

Minnis, A.J. and A.B. Scott (eds). 1988. *Medieval Literary Theory and Criticism.* Oxford: Clarendon.

Moult, Thomas. 1928. *Barrie.* London: Jonathan Cape.

Muir, Kenneth. 1979. *Shakespeare's Comic Sequence.* Liverpool: Liverpool University Press.

Munz, Peter. 1973. *When the Golden Bough Breaks.* London: Routledge and Kegan Paul.

Nash, Andrew. 1996. "'A phenomenally slow producer': J.M. Barrie, Scribner's, and the publication of *Sentimental Tommy*" in *Yale University Library Gazette* 71: 41–53.

—. 1998. "The Compilation of J.M. Barrie's *Auld Licht Idylls*" in *The Bibliotheck* 23: 85–96.

—. 1999a. "'Trying to be a Man': J.M. Barrie and Sentimental Masculinity" in *Forum for Modern Language Studies* 35: 113–25.

—. 1999b. "From Realism to Romance: Gender and Narrative in J.M. Barrie's *The Little Minister*" in *Scottish Literary Journal* 26: 77–92.

—. 2006 "The Kailyard: Problem or Illusion" in *The Edinburgh History of Scottish Literature*. 3 vols. (gen. ed. Ian Brown) 2: 317–23.

—. 2007a. *The Kailyard and Scottish Literature.* Amsterdam: Rodopi.

—. 2007b. "J.M. Barrie and the Third Sex" in Carpenter, Sarah and Sarah Dunnigan (eds). *Joyous Sweit Imaginacioun: Essays in Honour of R.D.S. Jack.* Amsterdam: Rodopi. 229–41.

Northam, John. 1952. *Ibsen's Dramatic Method.* London: Faber and Faber.

Olrik, Axel. 1965. "Epic Laws of Folk Narrative" in *The Study of Folklore* (ed. Alan Dundas). Englewood Cliff, N.J: Prentice- Hall. 129–41.

Ormond, Leonee. 1983 –. "J.M, Barrie's *Mary Rose"* in *Yale University Library Gazette* 58: 59 –63.

— 1987. *J.M. Barrie. Edinburgh: Scottish Academic Press.*

Osborne, Lucy. 2004. "Richard Savage: The Sorry Story of an early Georgian Poet" in *Colophon* 31(6): [unpaginated].

Paramount Studios. 2004. *Finding Never Land*.

Peters, Catherine. 1987. *Thackeray's Universe*. London: Faber.

Pick, J. B. 1993. *The Great Shadow House*. Edinburgh: Polygon.

Pittock, Murray. 1991. *The Invention of Scotland: The Stuart Myth and Scottish Identity*. London: Routledge,

Rose, Jacqueline. 1984. *The Case of Peter Pan: Or The Impossibility of Children's Fiction*. London: MacMillan.

Rowell, George. 1978. *The Victorian Theatre* 1792-1914. Cambridge: Cambridge University Press.

Salmon, P. "The Three Voices of Poetry in Mediaeval Literary Theory" in *Medium Aevum* 30(1): 1–18.

Salmon, V. (ed.) 1972. *The Works of Francis Lodwick*. London: Longman.

Sassi, Carla. 2005. *Why Scottish Literature Matters*. Edinburgh: Saltire.

Scholes, Robert. 1972. *Structuralism in Literature*. Yale University Press: New Haven, Conn.

Sedgwick, Eva. 1991. *Epistemology of the Closet*. Hemel Hempstead: Harvester Wheatsheaf.

Shaw, George Bernard. 1891. *The Quintessence of Ibsenism*. London: Walter Scott.

Shelton, George. 1928. *It's Smee*. London: Ernest Benn.

Shepperson, George. 1961. "The Intellectual Background of Darwin's Student Years at Edinburgh" *in Darwin and the Study of Society* (ed. M. Banton). London: Tavistock. 17–35.

Southern, R.W. 1995. *Scholastic Humanism and the Unification of Europe*.

Spencer, Herbert. 1996. *The Life and Letters of Herbert Spencer* (ed. D. Duncan). 2 vols. London: Routledge.

Stack, George J. 1970. *Berkeley's Analysis of Perception*. Paris. Mouton.

Storr, Anthony. 1989. *Freud*. Oxford: Oxford University Press.

Sussman, Herbert. 1995. *Victorian Masculinity: Manhood and Masculine Poetics in Early Victorian Literature* Cambridge: Cambridge University Press.

Taylor, Alan. 2010. "Where the Dream Came Alive" in *Scotland in Trust* 27(1): 20–26.

Taylor, Jerome (ed and tr). 1992. *The Didascalicon of Hugh of St Victor*. New York: Columbia University Press.

Templeton, Janet. 2001. *Ibsen's Women*. Cambridge: Cambridge University Press.

Thackeray, W.M. 1983. *Vanity Fair* (ed. John Sutherland). Oxford: Oxford University Press.

Tickner, Lisa. 1988. *The Spectacle of Women*. Chicago: Chicago University Press.

Tillyard, E.M.W. 1939. *The Personal Heresy: a Controversy*. Oxford: Oxford University Press.

Turgenev, I.S. 1884. *Mumu and The Diary of a Superfluous Man* (tr. Henry Gersoni). New York: Fink and Wagnall.

Vanbrugh, Irene. 1949. *To Tell my Story*. London: Hutchinson.

Waugh, Patricia. 1985. *Metafiction*. London. Routledge.

Walbrook, H.M. 1922. *Barrie and the Theatre*. London: Peter Davies.

Walizsewski, K. 1900. *A History of Russian Literature*. London: Heinemann.

Walker, Marshall. 1996. *Scottish Literature Since 1707*. London: Longman.

Whyte, Christopher. 2004. *Modern Scottish Poetry*. Edinburgh: Edinburgh University Press.

Winter, Alison. 1992. *Mesmerism*. Chicago: University of Chicago Press.

Wisenthal, J.L. (ed.) 1979. *Shaw and Ibsen*. Toronto: Toronto University Press.

Wright, Allen. 1976. *J.M. Barrie: The Glamour of Twilight*. Edinburgh: Ramsay Head Press.

Valentine, C.W. 1942. *The Psychology of Early Childhood*. London: Methuen.

Index

The Association for Scottish Literary Studies

Founded in 1970, the Association for Scottish Literary Studies promotes the study, teaching and writing of Scottish literature and the languages of Scotland. To these ends, ASLS publishes classic works of Scottish literature in our **Annual Volumes** series. Papers on literary criticism and cultural studies, along with in-depth reviews of Scottish books, are published biannually in our journal **Scottish Literary Review** (formerly Scottish Studies Review); scholarly studies of language in **Scottish Language**; and short articles, features and news in the ASLS newsletter **ScotLit**. **New Writing Scotland**, our annual anthology, contains new poetry, drama and short fiction in Scots, English and Gaelic. Our **Scotnotes** series of school- and college-level study guides provides invaluable background information to a range of major Scottish writers. We also produce collections of essays in our **Occasional Papers** series. Our website contains a substantial and growing body of downloadable essays, articles, papers and classroom notes. Other free online resources include the peer-reviewed **International Journal of Scottish Literature** and the ezine **The Bottle Imp**.

Each year, ASLS produces and distributes over 3,500 publications to its subscribers, and a further 2,800 to secondary schools and libraries. We hold annual conferences on Scottish writers in such diverse locations as Glasgow, Kirkwall, Edinburgh, Dumfries and Skye. We also take the **Scottish Writing Exhibition** to the **Modern Language Association** conventions in the USA and to **European Society for the Study of English** conferences in Europe.

Along with other Scottish literary organisations, and supported by Creative Scotland, ASLS campaigns for a greater appreciation, both at home and abroad, in schools, colleges and universities, of Scotland's literary culture.

www.asls.org.uk